HERBERT O'DRISCOLL

Prayers for the Breaking of Bread

*Meditations on the Collects
of the Church Year*

COWLEY PUBLICATIONS
Cambridge ✦ *Boston*
Massachusetts

Published in the United States of America by Cowley Publications, a division of the Society of St. John the Evangelist. No portion of this book may be reproduced, stored in or introduced into a retrieval system, or transmitted, in any form or by any means—including photocopying—without the prior written permission of Cowley Publications, except in the case of brief quotations embodied in critical articles and reviews.

International Standard Book Number: 1-56101-045-6
Library of Congress Number: 91-19446

Cover illustration by Bill Goffrier

Library of Congress Cataloging-in-Publication Data
O'Driscoll, Herbert.
Prayers for the breaking of bread : meditations on the collects of the church year / Herbert O'Driscoll.
p. cm.
Includes texts of the Sunday collects.
ISBN 1-56101-045-6 (alk. paper)
1. Episcopal Church. Book of common prayer (1979)—Meditations. 2. Church year meditations. 3. Collects—Meditations. 4. Anglican Communion—Prayer-books and devotions—English. I. Episcopal Church. Book of common prayer (1979). Collects. 1991. II. Title.
BX5145.A62037 1991
264'.036—dc20   91-19446

Third printing

This book is printed on acid-free paper and was produced in the United States of America.

Cowley Publications
28 Temple Place
Boston, Massachusetts 02111

For Kiera and Sarah
our new granddaughters

COWLEY PUBLICATIONS is a ministry of the
Society of St. John the Evangelist, a religious
community for men in the Episcopal Church.
Emerging from the Society's tradition of
prayer, theological reflection, and diversity of
mission, the press is centered in the rich
heritage of the Anglican Communion.

Cowley Publications seeks to provide
books, audio cassettes, and other resources
for the ongoing theological exploration and
spiritual development of the Episcopal
Church and others in the body of Christ. To
this end, it is dedicated to developing a new
generation of theological writers, encourag-
ing them to produce timely, creative, and
stimulating publications of excellence, and
making these publications available widely,
reaching both clergy and lay persons.

TABLE OF CONTENTS

PREFACE

IF IN the heavenly places there exist vast listening devices to pick up the innumerable prayers of mortals, there must surely be an immense surge of reception at regular seven-day intervals. For it is at such intervals that a single prayer is offered simultaneously by millions of people, and these prayers, sent on their way from the sanctuaries and pews of uncounted churches, are called "collects."

We can understand and appreciate the function of these brief and beautifully constructed prayers if we think of them in terms of a contemporary urban image. Imagine you are standing in front of the directory of a large shopping center. There are four stories, a dozen escalators, and three buildings—each, like the cherubim of old, having at least six wings! As you stand looking in vain for the location of the drycleaners, which you were certain was in the second building on the third floor just by the fourth pair of elevators, you see to your intense relief a small arrow pointing to a tiny colored circle that has beside it the three welcome words, "You are here." Immediately you know that all will be well. Now you can proceed with your quest. Like Dante, you have been given a guide.

What that little arrow and circle is to the shopping mall, so is the collect in Christian liturgy. In the liturgy we stand, not to mention sitting and kneeling, within a many-faceted structure. As with the shopping center, this structure also has its wings and stories and escalators; it is many-faceted and quite complex as well. What is being offered in this great structure is immensely valuable. The main items in stock are faith and hope and love, but they are offered by many and varied means. Here are hymns, psalms, anthems, doxologies, blessings, responses, confessions, absolutions, prayers, intercessions, in fact a whole cornucopia of things that are perfectly familiar and obvious and dear to seasoned churchgoers, but remain stubbornly incomprehensible to the unsuspecting who wander into this shopping center of the spirit. As we stand and sit and kneel amid all these marvelous if mystifying things, we may feel that we need desperately a little arrow and circle and the benediction of those words, "You are here."

Where is this provided? In the collect. There it sits, not far from the entrance, that is to say, not very long after the service starts. In a few lines this prayer sums up what it is all going to be about. Sometimes, if it is a really well planned shopping center or liturgy, we will be able to go back to the collect and realize with a kind of wonder that the Bible lections, the hymns, the anthem, the homily were also somehow hidden in miniature within those few lines. I am well aware that it is something of a counsel of perfection to say that all the elements of the liturgy will always be found in embryo in the collect, nevertheless it will almost always be possible to recognize the main theme that the liturgy is (or should be) expressing.

Within these prayers there is great wisdom, great beauty of language, and great insight about the human condition. I suspect it would not be an exaggeration to say that some of the most beautiful statements ever made in the English language are to be found among them. As a small boy in a parish schoolroom in the south of Ireland, and later in boarding school, I had to learn many of them by heart. To this day many of them remain in memory and have formed a personal golden treasury. The urge to open them for others has been too great to resist. Hence these pages. May they give as much pleasure to others as I have had in writing them.

Herbert O'Driscoll
Christ Church, Calgary

Advent
and
Christmas

A Clearing in the Forest   Advent 1

*Almighty God, give us grace to cast away the works of dark-
ness, and put on the armor of light, now in the time of this
mortal life in which your Son Jesus Christ came to visit us in
great humility; that in the last day, when he shall come again
in his glorious majesty to judge both the living and the dead,
we may rise to the life immortal, through him who lives and
reigns with the Holy Spirit, one God, now and for ever.*

THE PHRASE "works of darkness" sounds melodramatic,
even exotic. What can the works of darkness have to do with
my humdrum, ordinary life? The answer is—a great deal! A
human life is very like the floor of a forest. Light and darkness are dappled everywhere. Sometimes there are clearings
of brilliant light, sometimes great groves of deep shadow. My
darknesses are many—anger, hatred, betrayal, greed, lust,
envy, depression, anxiety, fear, and many more. Many things
that we "work" emerge from our inner shadows and darkness. They are our works of darkness.

Yet if we continue the image of the forest for a moment, it
is very important to realize that the forest, even with all its
mingling of light and darkness, is a single living form.
Mysteriously my light and my darkness is one. I am not two
beings, one wonderfully full of light, the other a rather hor-
rible pool of darkness! In fact my wholeness as a human
being depends on my bringing my whole self before God
and offering its light and its darkness. Then I find wonderful
things can begin to happen. Reconciliation can take place.
Creativity can begin to flow. I begin to discover the glorious,
liberating, and energizing truth that God can use both my
light and my darkness.

This very realization is itself a light to me. We need this
light so very much. Not flashes of light now and then, but a
constant source of steady light. In other words our reaching
out for grace cannot be merely at those times when we are
conscious of the fact that we need it. In our daily living there
are defences we rush behind whenever we feel attacked, but
there is also a means of defence we can *wear*. We can carry it

with us. It goes where we go. The grace of God can be like that. Worship, prayer, and praise cannot be practiced merely when we feel like it. Instead of reaching spasmodically for the light of grace, we have to wear it as we would armor.

My battle, my quest, always takes place in the ongoing events of my life. This task I may be doing now, this person I am with now, this joy or pain I am feeling now, this work of art I am experiencing now—each of these can become the context of the spiritual, each can become the meeting place with the eternally contemporary Christ. This is what the mystery we call the Incarnation means, that the Christ comes "in the time of this mortal life," in the seemingly ordinary fabric of today's events and tasks. This is the magnificent paradox of our Lord.

Voices have tried to express this throughout time. In this century Evelyn Underhill wrote, "I come in the little things, says God," and much spiritual writing gives expression to the God who comes by way of the ordinary. St. Francis looks in the eyes of a leper and sees the Christ. C. S. Lewis gets on a bus to go to the London Zoo and in the course of that most ordinary of journeys experiences the presence of God's Holy Spirit. Years later he said that when he got on that bus he was not a Christian, but on alighting from it he was! Both St. Francis and C. S. Lewis encounter the living Christ in the seemingly mundane. That word "seemingly" is so important. Why? Because to the eye of faith the mundane is anything but mundane! "The world," as Gerard Manley Hopkins once sang, "is charged with the glory of God." Christ is He who comes "in great humility."

Why is it so important to live in the "now" and to see Christ in the present event? Because there will for all of us be a last "now," a last present moment, a "last day." Our culture does its best to prevent us from acknowledging this fact. It has endless ways to keep our minds off such ultimate thoughts, mainly by keeping our minds incessantly occupied with busyness. In that "last day" all my pathetic and obsessive busyness will be swept aside and I shall be made aware of "glorious majesty," confronted with things over which I have no control. This majesty will judge me; it will be the measure of who I have become. This majesty will have a face, and that face will be the face of the Christ whom I have met countless times in the guise of humility.

The third reality is a paradox. My experience of the Christ encountered in majesty is also given to me daily if only my eyes are open to the majesty always hidden in Christ's daily humility. In that sense I am not asked to "rise to the life eternal" only in some future moment of crisis in my life, but daily invited to rise and to recognise ordinary life as possessing an eternal quality. I am also daily offered the grace to accept that invitation.

Merciful God, who sent your messengers the prophets to preach repentance and prepare the way for our salvation: Give us grace to heed their warnings and forsake our sins, that we may greet with joy the coming of Jesus Christ our Redeemer; who lives and reigns with you and the Holy Spirit, one God, now and for ever.

THERE ARE moments in life when you know you know you are in the presence of truth. Perhaps the most troubling and penetrating of such moments are those when you find it anything but pleasant to listen to what is being said, but you still know it is the truth. For me, such moments have been when I am in the presence of both widely known people, like Archbishop Desmond Tutu, and totally unknown people who are giving expression to the particular injustices under which they and others have to live.

For most of us, the prophets of the Bible have become distant and rather unreal figures. We tend to have vague ideas about when they lived and what exactly they did or said, and we know that some of them paid a high price for their outspokenness. We make sure to practice pronouncing their names if we are reading a lesson in the Eucharist! Beyond that, however, the prophets tend to remain marginal in our thinking.

What does it mean to say that someone comes to "preach repentance and prepare the way for our salvation"? It can involve many specific approaches, but all the men and women of the Bible who were prophets had one clear purpose in mind. They felt themselves to be possessed of a message from God to their time and their society. Their messages varied according to the time and the state of their culture, but its theme was always the same. The prophet demanded that individuals and the culture at large turn from pursuing its own willful path and begin to pursue the will of God. The prophet would often specify the signs of such willfulness and point out possible courses of action. That turning aside that the prophet always demanded is what we mean by the word "repentance."

Of all the biblical prophets, perhaps Amos is the one we find it easiest to meet. We certainly don't find him easy in terms of what he says or stands for, but he is the easiest for us to understand because he is talking about obvious injustices. In this sense the book of Amos is timeless.

Amos himself is a shepherd—straightforward, independent, and tough. He has no great education, but a deep sense of vocation. He arrives in the glamor and sophistication of a sanctuary like Bethel, a great center of worship. He looks at the worship and then at the surrounding society, disgusted at what he sees. Justice can be bought. Some people live in luxury, but most in abject poverty. Amos questions the validity of a religion that accepts this, dismissing its rites as meaningless piety.

"Woe to those who lie upon beds of ivory!" he calls out. His demand is stern and clear. "Let justice roll down like waters, and righteousness like an ever-flowing stream."

The response of the High Priest is interesting, ironic and contemporary. He and Amos meet on the steps of the king's palace, and their mutual contempt is almost palpable. The High Priest tells Amos he has no right to proclaim such things in "the king's sanctuary" and in "the temple of the kingdom." In other words, prophets had no right to question the policies and structures of their society.

They were often made the scapegoats for the fears and resentments their social criticism engendered. We have only to think of two modern groups of prophets, the mothers of Argentina and the women of the West Bank, both groups willing to challenge the highest and most powerful figures in their land. In Argentina they protest against the disappearance of many people into the torture chambers and death cars of the former military regime, while in Israel it is the Palestinians who are taken for interrogation and imprisonment without trial.

By their demonstrations these prophetic women convict the society around them of injustice and oppression. Often they say nothing, merely standing in public places. Their prophecy is their presence. They often receive the most vicious insults from passersby and some of them must dread doing this, but they go on doing it because they truly believe that certain things being done in their society must cease. They believe there must be a turning, a repentance, if the society is to experience salvation from itself. To carry out such a witness is to prophesy.

Our own society has had its prophets and still does today. Some feel they are called by God, others do not, but they all act as those who warn us about our attitudes, decisions, and actions. Christian prophets warn us of those things in our society that seem to contradict all we know of the God of the Bible and the Christ of the church. Why do we need to "heed their warnings and forsake our sins"? Because as individuals we are all finally accountable. We are accountable to ourselves and to others but we are also accountable to God. Societies are also accountable, not merely to something called history, but to the God of history.

This accountability is what we mean when we speak in this collect of "the coming of Jesus Christ." A Christian believes that our lives are lived under judgment, as are the lives of human societies. To say this is not to be "negative" or "judgmental"—favorite words these days—but merely to state a fact. Actually to say that human life is lived under the judgment of God as we understand God in Jesus Christ is to offer it real direction. To say that judgment exists is to inject a new joy into human existence, because it means that what we do and say actually matters! Without that element of judgment, life has no meaning. Is it not ironic that the fact that our lives are under judgment is what gives them meaning?

The God Who Cannot Stay Away   Advent 3

*Stir up your power, O Lord, and with great might come
among us; and, because we are sorely hindered by our sins,
let your bountiful grace and mercy speedily help and deliver
us; through Jesus Christ our Lord, to whom with you and the
Holy Spirit be honor and glory, now and for ever.*

AN OLD saying tells us that we should pray as if everything depended on God and act as if everything depended
on ourselves. As we say this Advent prayer near the end of
the twentieth century, it is wise to ponder the deep wisdom
of that saying. When we ask God, "Stir up your power...and
with great might come among us," what are we praying for?

Certainly we are acknowledging the power of God to be
a power beyond our own. We are acknowledging God's
might. We do not ask, however, that this power be exercised
in some magical way at our request and on behalf of our particular hopes and desires while we look on in approval and
appreciation! When mature Christian faith prays in this way,
it is fully aware of its own responsibility held in the freedom
to choose and to act. In such a moment of prayer we fully acknowledge our responsibility as free beings. We make
choices, we put those choices into action, and these actions
have consequences. In that sense, for better or for worse, we
are the channels of God's creative powers.

There is a problem, however, and this prayer expresses it
by saying that "we are sorely hindered by our sins." That is
our tragedy: between our creative powers and our carrying
out of God's will falls the shadow of our own wills. Our
human will is all too often pitted against God's, so that God's
ability to use us for the divine purpose is limited. Not only
are *we* hindered, but God's purposes for us and through us—
purposes sometimes affecting the whole of creation—are also
hindered.

What then are we praying for? In the fifth century Saint
Augustine in North Africa expressed one aspect of God's
grace and mercy in a magnificent short statement. He said,
"Without God, we cannot. Without us, God will not." We are

not asking God to detour around us, set us aside in the work of creation, and wield power without us. God is simply not that kind of God. It is both the "grace and mercy" of God that our humanity, in spite of being "sorely hindered by our sins," is still God's chosen instrument in the work of creation.

It would be difficult to find a more wonderful affirmation of our sorely hindered humanity than this prayer. God, source of all power and might, source of every conceivable element in creation, stoops to engage our cooperation. The prayer expresses either the most awe-inspiring of truths or the most pathetic of illusions. Yet even if it turned out to be an illusion, it would still be the grandest of all.

How do we know it is not? Because God, through Jesus Christ our Lord, has not only shown grace and mercy to our humanity, but has also entered creation. God does not engage our human powers in the forming of the world from some celestial vantage point far away, but stands among us in our "sorely hindered" condition. God in Christ has been "sorely hindered" on a cross. In resurrection this same Christ came, and comes daily, to "help and deliver" us.

The reason we find this difficult to believe is simple. It is difficult to accept the fact that the love of God is so great that God actually thinks we are worth it all! We so easily roll off our tongues the language of salvation, speaking of incarnation, of the cross, of resurrection, all with the ease born of familiarity. Too often the essential truth spelled out in this language escapes us, the simple truth that God loves us in spite of everything. Sorely hindered by our sins we most certainly are, yet God still refuses to dispense with us. We hear John the Evangelist telling us that God gave an only son to us, but we don't really hear why. Behind that "why" is an unbelievable fact—God could not help doing it! And the reason God could not help doing it is that God loves us so much.

Listen again to that great insight of Augustine, "Without God, we cannot. Without us, God will not." Think of the affirmation of our humanity the second half of that statement contains. If it is even half true what this God feels and thinks about us, there is every reason in the world to hope for "bountiful grace and mercy" from such a God. So let us say this prayer with confidence and let us expect much!

> *Purify our conscience, Almighty God, by your daily visitation, that your Son Jesus Christ, at his coming, may find in us a mansion prepared for himself; who lives and reigns with you, in the unity of the Holy Spirit, one God, now and for ever.*

OUR CULTURE talks much of having what it calls an "informed conscience." Implicit in this statement is the belief that conscience is largely or even entirely a product of information. One school of thought has always maintained that to make humanity more moral, we have only to offer it more education. If this is true, then if you have access to more and more information, you will become a person of better and better conscience.

The problem with this neat arrangement is that information itself can be tainted. The classic example in recent history is that of Nazi Germany, where a magnificently organized and financed educational system brought about for many the death of conscience. The fact is that conscience cannot of itself be good. By its very nature it is conditioned by so many factors of environment, upbringing, education, and personal character that it cannot be otherwise than limited and relative. Conscience needs grace, and that is what we are praying for when we begin this collect with the petition, "Purify our conscience, Almighty God." We are acknowledging that the formation of a good conscience needs a grace beyond ourselves.

Conscience and grace are related in much the same way as ancient biblical cities were related to their sources of water. Because the inhabitants of these cities knew that from time to time they would be besieged by enemy armies, they almost always took care to ensure a source of water outside their walls. They would then do two things. They would dig a tunnel from the city to the spring, and then they would disguise the entrance of the spring so that the enemy would not find it. Each of us is like such a city. Enemies, some from within ourselves and others from beyond us, besiege our conscience. We need to have a source of water beyond the inner citadel of the self if we are to withstand the siege of temptation.

This collect speaks of God's "daily visitation." Why? Because any worthwhile spirituality has to be a disciplined spirituality. It cannot be a matter of being "spiritual" when we feel like it. We can understand this better if we have ever had the experience of traveling in a hot desert area, where the golden rule is that you must drink lots of water. But there is a further hidden reality here. It is not enough to drink water only when we feel the need of it; if we do, we dehydrate. The traveler must drink far more than he or she wants, because in the desert our needs are far greater than our desires. So we must drink according to need and not according to desire.

That simple analogy points to the necessity for opening ourselves daily to God's presence. The fact is that in reality God does not "visit"—God is! Whether or not we are aware of the divine presence, God is present. What we have to do is intentionally open the self to that reality. As the old Celtic rune puts it, we have to "put bread in the eating place and drink in the drinking place" as our welcome to God. In that lovely old saying is the image of us not waiting passively on God, but reaching out to show our readiness and eagerness for relationship.

What does such a daily encounter do? Slowly and gently it builds a place for the soul to live in. It builds a mansion, as this prayer puts it. If we develop the idea of a mansion, we find ourselves thinking of our encounters with God as forming a roof for shelter, windows of insights and vision, walls of moral boundaries, rooms for eating and resting and cleansing and learning. But the prayer goes further. Who is the mansion for? Just the self? No, the mansion awaits another guest, and that guest is our Lord. There lies the difference between the human potential movement and the Christian spiritual quest. In the former the task is to build the house of the self for the self alone to live in; in the latter, our work is to prepare the house of the self for the presence of God.

This is the point at which we discover one of the delicious paradoxes of the kingdom of heaven. When we prepare to receive a guest, instead of building merely for our own sakes, we find that the mansion of the soul is a much more pleasant place for us to live in!

What Child Is This?   Christmas Day

O God, you make us glad by the yearly festival of the birth of your only Son Jesus Christ: Grant that we, who joyfully receive him as our Redeemer, may with sure confidence behold him when he comes to be our Judge; who lives and reigns with you and the Holy Spirit, one God, for ever and ever.

I HAVE DELIBERATELY left the writing of this reflection to the season itself, in fact, to the day itself. The Eucharist of Christmas is over, the smell of dinner is permeating the house. I am weary but exhilerated by the echoes of the worship of this large and varied congregation. In this particular moment I try to feel again the extraordinary welter of emotions that kept coming and going in me yesterday before the first service of Christmas Eve began, before the first candle was lit, the first eager children began to run through the pews searching for a seat.

Some reasons for my feelings were obvious. I knew at least a dozen people for whom this Christmas was the first one after some searing bereavement. A colleague of mine had shared his real fear that a young person he had just been with for two hours would commit suicide, and we had recently learned that an elderly and most wonderfully courageous parishioner had fallen in his nursing home and shattered some bones. But there were also present in me some shadows from deep within myself, above all a nagging fear that I would not be able to do justice to the preaching of this familiar yet almost inexpressible good news.

Why do I mention these things? Because there is something of all this in the experience of each one of us as we come to Christmas. For every adult the joy of this season is mingled with many other things. There may be, as I mentioned, a sense of deep loss. A child, perhaps now no longer a child, may be far away. Some relationship may be under stress. It may sound very obvious to say so, but the opening line of this prayer does not tell us that the Christmas season or Christmas carols or Christmas shopping or Christmas office parties or Christmas anything else make us glad! As we well know, these so-called Christmas things can sometimes actually make us very sad, so sad that millions of people enter a very shadowed world at this time of year, one that can bring anything from mild depression to suicide.

What makes a Christian glad is the ability to celebrate a single marvelous and glorious reality, the birth of God's only Son Jesus Christ. But even here we can forget something essential. Our becoming aware of the joy of this feast is certainly connected with the circumstances of our lives. Perhaps those circumstances are totally happy. Our family is gathered together. We possess health and well being. Gifts await opening. Dinner is in the very air we breathe. For all this let God be thanked and let our laughter and banter be heard without a twinge of guilt or imagined selfishness. These things too are the gifts of God to us at this particular moment of life, so let us enjoy them. But the further joy of this day, the mysterious joy within the heart that can somehow survive even the absence of all these wonderful human joys, is conditional on whether we decide this birth is of ultimate significance in the living of our lives.

This day is the Child's day. But there is a question about the Child which I must answer, a question that is being sung to me even as I write these words. It comes from downstairs in the pure dispassionate singing of some English choirboys, whose voices ask me, "What Child is this?" There is the heart of the matter for each of us.

There is in this prayer some insistence in the words, "your only Son Jesus Christ." Is there a hint that the name Jesus is not of itself sufficient for this day? I suspect so. The child's name was Jesus. We had nothing to do with that. That was for Gabriel to say and for Mary, and later Joseph, to repeat. But the title of the man into whom that child grew is "Christ." That has everything in the world to do with each one of us. Why? Because each one of us has in our possession the bestowing of that title. If I so choose, Jesus can be no more than a figure in history, a piece of information in my mind, a name to be remembered from Religion 101 in my college courses until something takes its place. Each of us decides if Jesus is to be the special one, the unique one, the one who makes all the difference, the one who provides the ground of deepest meaning in our lives. If this is true, then no wonder this yearly festival can make us glad. It can be what snatches that gladness from the grasping and demanding hands of sorrow or pain or loss. We will know that we are celebrating again the birthing of everything that holds meaning in life for us.

A Song of Birth and Dying   Christmas 1

Almighty God, you have poured upon us the new light of your incarnate word: Grant that this light, enkindled in our hearts, may shine forth in our lives; through Jesus Christ our Lord, who lives and reigns with you, in the unity of the Holy Spirit, one God, now and for ever.

MANY YEARS ago G. K. Chesterton spoke of this season in haunting words:

> To an open house in the evening
> Home shall men come,
> To an older place than Eden,
> And a taller town than Rome.

> To the end of the way of the wandering star,
> To the things that cannot be and that are,
> To the place where God was homeless
> And all men are at home.

I too want to take you to an older place and time. It is Saint Stephen's Day, December 26, 1936. I am eight years old and we are at my grandfather's farm in County Kilkenny. The fields are white—unusual in Ireland and therefore vivid in my childhood memory. Christmas Day is past, a wonderful day with food and gifts and friends and laughter and drinks of this and that. For me there was lemonade, the drink of childhood for special occasions in those days. It is very early in the morning, and up the driveway from the farm gate comes a small group of boys. One of them carries a pole with something like a small bush on top of it. They gather on the graveled driveway in front of the house and begin to sing loudly, raucously and insistently. Their words are as old as time, and for me they will always express the mood of the days that follow the feast of Christmas.

> The wren, the wren, the king of all birds,
> Saint Stephen's Day was caught in the firs.
> Up with the kettle and down with the pot,

Give us our answer for singing so well,
Give us our answer for singing so well.

At this point one of the boys runs forward and lifts the large black knocker on the door. The sound thunders through the house: "Give us our answer for singing so well!" This last line is repeated many times, accompanied by much lifting aloft of the crude bird's nest. I know from something overheard in adult conversation that sometimes the body of a bird is in the nest. I remember it all because I suspect that for a child there was something frightening, almost macabre about it. The door would open and my grandfather or someone else would give a gift, usually a small amount of money, and off down the driveway the group would go, their shouts and laughter fading away in the distance. The voices would gradually fall into silence, until one would hear the harsh cadences of their song coming from far away across the intervening fields as they hammered at the door of the neighboring farm.

Where did that scene and its song come from? Probably from an age before these fields were ever tilled and sown, before a church bell was ever heard sounding the call to Christ's Mass, before the voice of Patrick had ever been heard in these hills and valleys.

Why was it so frightening? I wonder if a child was being made to understand at a deep level the terrible contrast between the two days. First Christmas Day, a day of carols, and then the day of this chilling chant. What was the connection between the dead bird and the story I knew so well from school and Sunday School of the fearful death of Stephen? Why was I taken from light to darkness so quickly, from caroling to crying, from life to death?

As I read the single word "incarnate" in this post-Christmas prayer, I realize so much across the years. The prayer tells me that God has come at this season in light, but the image is not complete without an accompanying word. God may well come to me in light, but that light comes in a vessel of flesh. "Incarnate" is the word in this prayer.

The moment I am reminded that God has come to me in flesh I can identify. After all, that is the very reason why God has taken this fearful and costly way towards me. For light to encase itself in human flesh is unimaginably costly. This is what the long ago song was singing. The cost of life involves a dying. Mary's child comes eventually to the tomb, Stephen comes to the place of execution, the bird comes to the wild cold resting place of the nest.

I know from my own experience the costliness of bearing God's light. Even though I know that this same light is within myself—John the Evangelist tells me it is in every one of us—I know how my flesh makes it so difficult for this light to blaze as it should. My flesh, my humanity, my limitations reduce it to a flicker, a pathetic thing. My being a thing of flesh means that the light is forever dying, forever needing tending, needing grace, needing forgiveness for its own constant diminishment. So I know what it cost my Lord to lie in Mary's womb, to struggle from her body, to lie in the straw, to move through the years of childhood, to discover bit by bit his own humanity, to experience the little hurts that can loom so large in childhood and can therefore be so formative. All this he knew, as do I. All this is the cost of his coming. That is why I need to be reminded of the cost even as the light of Christmas still shines, the sound of carols still echoes, the debris of gift-giving still lies untidied, and the ashes of the fire still lie grey in the fireplace.

Jesus my Lord, now no longer the child of Christmas but the Lord of all seasons, is my Lord because he accepted not only birthing but dying. I think that is what was said in some embryonic mysterious way to a child in the Irish countryside years and years ago. The crude dark tumbling of twigs and moss on the gnarled pole, held high and shaken against the morning sky, is not only a resting place for the dead bird. It is also both a womb of incarnation and a garden of resurrection. Can it be also the Holy Spirit waiting to be released in me for new flight?

There is a further thought now that decades have passed. Is the dead bird actually within the nest? I was never allowed to look. And if it be true that the nest was empty, then that too is a truth, the many-splendored truth that the child lives and the flame blazes and the light shines and the song that comes across the years from that distant farmyard is at one and the same time both the shouting of little boys and the song of angels.

A Dignity Lost and Found   Christmas 2

O God, who wonderfully created, and yet more wonderfully restored the dignity of human nature: Grant that we may share the divine life of him who humbled himself to share our humanity, your Son Jesus Christ; who lives and reigns with you, in the unity of the Holy Spirit, one God, for ever and ever.

A FEW MONTHS ago I was visiting someone in a large nursing home. It was that part of the home where most people are able to look after themselves, and so it was usually a quiet and ordered scene of people coming and going about the ordinary little things of daily life. Suddenly in one of the rooms I happened to be passing there was a commotion and a voice calling for help—an elderly man had fallen in the bathroom and become jammed between the wash basin and the toilet. He was in considerable pain and even greater distress from shock, but as I saw him it struck me that the greatest pain of all for him must be the utter loss of dignity. Normally he is a precise and disciplined man who cherishes his dignity, and I knew instinctively that to lose it like this in front of others would be deeply distressing to him.

What is this thing we call our dignity? It is not vanity, although we could say there is a relationship between the two, since dignity includes my concern about how I look in front of others. We could also say pride is involved somewhere in dignity, pride of being in charge of our lives. Dignity is a very physical thing. A large part of it—though not all—involves the working of my body. Does it do what I will it to do, or does it in some sense reduce who I am and how I appear to others?

Dignity can be gained or lost in ways other than physical. You and I can both attain and lose dignity by our behavior. As we grow older we seek a certain air of maturity as if in compensation for the loss of our youthful effervescence. There is a sense in which dignity is less expected and less demanded of youth; in fact youthful dignity risks crossing over into pomposity. Yet it is interesting that youth can have the capacity to bestow dignity in its relationships with elders, and when we see that it is deeply moving. One thinks of small but vital things, such as the ways in which help can be offered by youth to an older person, the offer being made in such a way that the older person is not in any way patronized, but is treated with respect. Again, as the first really large generation of old people comes to terms with aging, there seems to be a kind of searching going on for those modes of behavior in senior years that can bring fun and celebration to life without loss of dignity.

We can see how much the sense of our own dignity is linked with the degree of physical freedom we possess. When we speak with anyone who has lost a measure of this freedom, perhaps by being confined to a wheel chair, we soon learn how easily a handicapped person can be robbed of dignity in small ways that usually never occur to those with them. The insensitive presumption that the handicapped person is totally helpless, or that a physical limitation means a mental limitation as well. Or the assumption that the handicapped person has no time constraints, but can always be expected to wait on the pleasure of others. These are among the ways we can all unknowingly rob another of dignity.

It is interesting to note that we can also lay aside our dignity by our own choice. Adults do this when they set out to play with a small child—they say and do silly things, place themselves in laughable positions and situations, shedding all pretence of dignity. Yet here is the paradox: when we willingly put aside our dignity, we do not lose it! In fact, to be unable to lay it aside is usually seen as a lack in our personality.

Such are the subtleties of this difficult to define but very real part of our human nature. It is interesting that this prayer tells us God created "the dignity of human nature." In what way? I suggest it is because God created us as free beings, able to choose for better or for worse. As soon as we say this, we realize the high cost of our human dignity. For God to give it to us in the form of our freedom means always to risk the whole enterprise of creation. We must assume that for God to take such a risk, it must mean that the gift of dignity is essential to our being fully human.

At the heart of Christian faith we see all these things embodied in Christ. In him we see God laying aside a dignity beyond our imagination. Having decided in love to do this, God in Christ then comes among us and assumes our human nature. In this act of immense self-sacrifice and self-impoverishment, God gives back to our human nature the dignity we lose by choosing a course of sinful self-will. As this prayer says in its magnificent opening sentence, God, having wonderfully created our human nature, now more wonderfully restores it.

Epiphany

The Road to Our Becoming   Epiphany 1

*Father in heaven, who at the baptism of Jesus in the River
Jordan proclaimed him your beloved Son and anointed him
with the Holy Spirit: Grant that all who are baptized into his
name may keep the covenant they have made, and boldly con-
fess him as Lord and Savior; who with you and the Holy
Spirit lives and reigns, one God, in glory everlasting.*

THE SCENE is familiar to anyone who is at all acquainted
with the gospel story. We are among crowds, an extraordinary mingling of rural and urban, as if something immensely
strong has crossed the barriers of class and life style and
welded them together in this barren river valley on the edge
of a desert. In front of the vast gathering that crowds down
to the river bank is the figure of John, half immersed in the
water, and all around him is a group assisting those who are
drawn fearfully to accept the preacher's fierce and compelling invitation to act out their own drowning. As we watch,
one figure moves forward in the crowd with quiet purpose.
As he and John catch each other's attention there is a change
in the demeanor of the preacher, a quieting, a watchfulness
for what happens next. It is out of character for John, almost
an acknowledgement that the decision for what happens
now has passed from him to the other.

The point of all Scripture, in the words of another prayer,
is that it is written for our *learning*. It is written so that we
may appropriate it to our own experience and our own
living. Likewise the point of liturgy is that the past event becomes somehow present within us. No place is this more true
than in our reading about the life of our Lord. If in this
prayer we are shown our Lord baptized, proclaimed as who
he is, and anointed with the Spirit, then these are the experiences we are being asked to incorporate into our lives. To
try to do this we move back from this moment at the river
bank to the decision that brings our Lord to this moment.
You are thirty and there are decisions you must make. There
is something calling, distant yet near, elusive yet strong.
Many times you have wrestled with this alone among the

hills. You have even named the voice that speaks within you. You have a secret whimsical name for the voice. You say "Abba" softly into the wind or to the night stars.

There is another voice that won't go away. It comes from the south where someone you know is talking about massive change and a new future. So radical is John's vision that he is asking men and women to know a moment of dying and resurrection in the water of the Jordan. You decide to go. It isn't an easy decision. Some question its wisdom. There are a hundred weird religious options these days. Why chase after one? Some say you have family responsibilities; others advise you to go. One day you do, leaving the town, heading down the river valley road, until a few days later you are moving through the crowd and you are looking into the eyes of the preacher.

He is strangely hesitant, but you insist. You throw away your outer robe and you move into the river. You breathe deeply and let yourself go. The water is everywhere, in your eyeballs, your eardrums, your nostrils. You are in prison yet being released, dying yet being born; there is darkness and light, fear and joy. Suddenly you are standing and the sun burns on your drenched skin. All around you is the crowd and yet you are strangely alone. There is a voice sounding in the deepest part of your being. It cries out yes to your own yes, response to your questioning, affirmation to your searching. You know with absolute certainty that it was right to come to this place at this moment. Because you know with certainty, because there are no more doubts, the heavens seem to open and a dove descends, bringing an indescribable sense of peace.

If this attempt to describe what our Lord might have experienced has any validity, we ought to try to express what such experiences might mean for us, too. Can there be for us a sense of being called beyond and out of what we are? Yes. Can there be a sense of being given a new identity as a servant, a follower, a disciple? Surely, yes. If we decide to respond to that sense of being called, risking what is for what can be, then is there not a sense of being anointed for further vocation and service? Most certainly, yes. To discover such things is to discover in a new and vital way the covenant made in our baptism. That event, received perhaps in childhood, becomes more than memory. There can be a clearing of our spiritual decks, a clarifying, a sharpening, a coming into focus of what Christian faithfulness and service can be. Strangely, what comes into focus for us is both our own face and that of Jesus, for in discovering him we also discover who we ourselves really are. When that happens, his life and ours fuse together. We have received the anointing of the Holy Spirit.

The Radiance of Glory   Epiphany 2

Almighty God, whose Son our Savior Jesus Christ is the light of the world: Grant that your people, illumined by your Word and Sacraments, may shine with the radiance of Christ's glory, that he may be known, worshiped, and obeyed to the ends of the earth; through Jesus Christ our Lord, who with you and the Holy Spirit lives and reigns, one God, now and for ever.

NOTHING IS brighter or more transforming than a flare sent aloft into the night sky over a pitch dark ocean. I can recall once being off the coast of Newfoundland in a destroyer, in the days when Canadian ships patrolled those waters to keep an eye on the giant Russian supply vessels that accompanied their fishing fleets. These Russian ships were equipped with the most elaborate electronic equipment, making it quite obvious that they were there to listen for more than schools of fish!

Sometime toward midnight, word came that we were approaching one of these ships. They had stopped all transmissions, and it soon became obvious that they had doused all lights, too. It was a calm night, unusual in the northwest Atlantic. Our engines stopped. Many of us went to the side to gaze into the darkness. Then the flare went up and the sky blazed, the surface of the ocean stretching away from us, dark and undulating. At the edge of the darkness the Russian ship stood out, massive and motionless. Light cascaded down the sky in waves. Each one of us became aware of the others around us, our faces lit by the white, searing illumination. Then the darkness came again. Our eyes held the light for a moment's memory, and then we were alone again in the darkness.

Light is the predominant symbol in the expression of the Christian faith. The New Testament is full of it, beginning with the gospels themselves. Light blazes in the heavens at our Lord's birth, and emanates from him at his transfiguration. Shining figures appear at his ascension. He himself says that he is the Light, that he has come that humanity may

have light. For John the Evangelist, light is constantly challenging darkness. Paul is confronted on the Damascus Road
by a blaze of light. On through the letters of the early church
and into the book of Revelation, light continues to be used as
the symbol of the presence of Christ. From there we leap into
the blazing vivid art of Byzantium, where light cascades
from mosaic, icon, and dome. So we come down through the
centuries to this prayer and its ancient opening statement
that "Jesus Christ is the light of the world."

Sometimes when we come to a statement like this, we
should pause and do a simple thing. We should quietly think
about the innumerable lips and voices who have said this.
Generations of men and women have gone on their spiritual
journeys as we do. Sometimes they have struggled in personal darkness as we do. Time and again they have said
these words to themselves, hanging on to this image of
Christ as light even as they felt themselves to be surrounded
by darkness and despair. Men and woman have prayed this
statement silently, sung it in praise, reflected on it in con-
templation. A statement such as this comes down to us as an
indescribably precious gift, a kind of heirloom from our vast
family who have now decided to entrust it to us for safe
keeping and faithful use.

We are praying here that people may shine with the
radiance of God's glory. It is a magnificent concept, but how
do we reach for it in reality? Putting it very mildly, most of
us for most of the time are not exactly radiant, and one can
hardly say we reflect the glory of God in our demeanor or in
our attitudes! But even as we say this, we also know something else for which we thank God. There is not one of us
who has not experienced at some moment or other a look
from someone, a gesture, an attitude, before which we almost
literally lower our eyes because of what we can only call its
radiance.

I can recall visiting a person who had long been a friend.
We had not met for some years. Hearing that she was very ill
in the city where I was visiting, I went to see her in the hospital. When I came towards her, she was turned away from me.
I had been warned that she had just had grueling radiation
therapy. She turned her eyes and I encountered such a mo-

ment of radiance as I looked into great pools of suffering in which there was unforgettable serenity. I recall the moment as one where I was privileged to encounter the radiance of God's glory.

By recalling this, I am reminded too of the way people involved in ministries of healing will suggest that as we lift someone in prayer for healing, we deliberately imagine them within a pool of shining light. This light is the outpouring love of God.

For some reason the phrase "illumined by your Word and Sacraments" causes me to imagine myself in the middle of a congregation. Perhaps that is because it is precisely when we are so surrounded that we find it most difficult to see the radiance of God's glory! When I myself am worshiping, if someone handed me a mirror, would I look radiant? Alas, not always!

In C. S. Lewis' *Screwtape Letters*, the experienced devil say to the young apprentice devil that he must not stop his newly Christian client from going to church; rather, the new Christian must be encouraged to go! Why? Because in church the wonderful new lens of faith through which the young man is seeing everything and everybody as radiant, will be ripped off! He will look around and see totally ordinary human beings, some of them not in the least attractive.

How wise Lewis is in that passage. Yet if, when I am worshiping, I really hear what the Word is saying, and if even for a moment I can come to realize the price my Lord had to pay for that small piece of bread in my hand and that bitter sweetness of wine in my throat—if for a moment I could know this, then in that same moment I might look with new eyes on everyone around me. I might see them in the way God obviously sees us all, radiant in a glory not our own, but reflected from the fires of God's creation and the even greater furnace of God's love.

A Way of Intimacy   Epiphany 3

Give us grace, O Lord, to answer readily the call of our Savior Jesus Christ and proclaim to all people the Good News of his salvation, that we and the whole world may perceive the glory of his marvelous works; who lives and reigns with you and the Holy Spirit, one God, for ever and ever.

FOR A few weeks recently our congregation has enjoyed the company of a very well known face and voice in our culture. Ann B. Davis, whose cheerful voice assures us on television that a certain rice will take only five minutes, and who delighted us for many years as the long-suffering nanny in "The Brady Bunch," was in Calgary while starring in a dinner theater play. Because she participated in many aspects of our life, she met many people and became a familiar figure to us. Before she left, we invited her to give the homily at the Sunday eucharist and share her journey of faith with us.

Those who heard her will not easily forget the experience. With simplicity and simcerity, spiced by humor and modesty, this immensely attractive human being spoke to us of Christian faith in a way that was deeply moving. She triggered both smiles and tears, the latter that most mysterious of things, tears of joy. Not for a single moment did she harangue or, in the bad sense of the word, preach. It was a magnificent telling of personal faith in God and in God's Son Jesus Christ. It also included something that such personal testimonies frequently omit. Ann spoke of her spiritual journey in the context of the life of the church. She made it quite clear that while she was not under the illusion that the church was perfect—to put it mildly—it was still the community for which Christ died. While I cannot recall her saying the church was "holy," that is what she communicated.

I want to take the substance of this prayer and move it from the vast canvas on which at first sight it seems to be painted. It tells us that our Savior's call to us is to proclaim the Good News to all people, that we and the whole world may perceive the glory of his works. The moment we read this we have images of vast throngs and far vistas. Now it is interesting that such images are also the very images in which the tempter in the wilderness wished our Lord to think of his own calling. The tempter shows Jesus "all the kingdoms of the world," but Jesus unhesitatingly refuses.

What does Jesus choose? He chooses a very different lens, a very different scale of designing and effecting his mission. He turns away from the vast panoramas offered by the tempter, leaves the wilderness, returns to the little world of the lakeside, walks down the beach and says to two people, "Follow me." In a word, Jesus opts for beginning in the immediate context of his own life and his own experience.

Surely this signals something to us. Mainline Christianity goes through agonies of guilt and good intentions when it struggles with the challenge of evangelism. Anglicans in particular, by tradition and temperament, are simply never going to be committed to mass evangelism. We need not think of this as a lack, as a kind of wound in our church's body. With rare exceptions, so rare as to prove the rule, such evangelism is not our gift. But there is nothing in the world to stop us from cultivating the ability to speak to other people simply, honestly, and naturally about their Christian faith and their church. Martin Marty has repeatedly said that survey after survey shows that eight out of ten people who have returned to the life of the church in the last decade report they have done so because someone significant in their lives asked them to!

Seen in this way, the call of our Lord is not necessarily that I or anyone else must speak to vast multitudes single-handedly, so that the whole world may respond. Such a prospect is immobilizing, as Jesus realized in the wilderness, a picture offered by the tempter to ensure that nothing ever happens!

The most productive image of evangelism for our tradition is much more like the one we are shown in the first chapter of the Gospel according to John. Andrew, a follower of the Baptist to this point, is drawn towards Jesus. The first thing he does is to go to his brother Peter. In verse 42 there are five utterly simple but deeply significant words: "He brought him to Jesus." The same thing happens when Philip discovers Jesus. Philip goes to a friend named Nathaniel. The first response he gets is not promising; Nathaniel grunts sarcastically about "nothing good coming out of Nazareth." But Philip keeps cool and says three little words with more effect than all the arguing and preaching we sometimes feel necessary. He said, "Come and see," and Nathaniel came. Such moments are the working of God through a human being. This prayer has a word for such moments, and the word is "marvelous." The simple truth is that every one of us can bring such a moment into being.

A Shared Governance   Epiphany 4

Almighty and everlasting God, you govern all things both in heaven and earth: Mercifully hear the supplications of your people, and in our time grant us your peace; through Jesus Christ our Lord, who lives and reigns with you and the Holy Spirit, one God, for ever and ever.

IT IS the Saturday evening of a winter weekend in the Divinity Hostel of Trinity College, Dublin. I am in first year theology. Each evening two students take their turn to sit on either side of the Warden of the Hostel at the long refectory table. It is a privilege, albeit not one that is sought out! The Warden is distant, taciturn, and formidable. I have grown up in the far south around Cork. As in any country where folk Catholicism is strong, many customs of pre-Christian days survive. At a certain moment in the meal I happen to spill the salt while passing it. Without thinking I pick some up and throw it over my shoulder to blind the devil to what I have done. Immediately there is an indignant response from the Warden. Am I or am I not a Christian training for Christian priesthood? If so, what do I mean by bringing pagan customs to this institution?

Why share this moment now? Because, you see, I was showing my true colors. I was acknowledging a rival to God, and I was propitiating that rival. I am not alone. That is the real faith of millions of people, whether or not they worship in Christian pews. That view of spiritual reality goes back to the dawn of time. At its simplest, it is straight dualism. If you want to see it in bronze you may look at the wall beside the main entrance to Coventry Cathedral, where Michael and Satan battle forever, neither fully vanquished and neither fully victorious.

The kinds of prayers we are thinking about, those we call collects, are very fond of the word "almighty" to describe the nature of God. More of these prayers begin with that word than with any other. Let's ask a question that may sound heretical. Is the word "almighty" really able to stand alone when we are talking about God? Does there need to be some small print attached to it if we are to use it honestly? I think so.

Is God really almighty? Does God really govern all things in heaven and in earth? When Christian liturgy claims this, does it mean what it says or is there such a special and technical meaning to this word that its use is almost dishonest? If God is almighty and governs all things, then why did my child die? Why has my dearest friend got cancer? Why did my husband return from Vietnam a physical and mental cripple? Why, if God is almighty?

We have now entered the deeps of religious faith. There are no simple answers here. When the Bible wants us to face these depths, it hands us the book of Job and the final chapters of each of the gospels, those chapters where we watch our Lord suffer and die. When we close both parts of the Bible and put the book down, we have not been given answers. We have had a great mystery named and we have seen human nature and the grace of God wrestling together with pain and evil and death.

Does God govern all things in heaven and in earth? If we are honest—yes and no. I think a way to begin wrestling with this question is to say that God has chosen not to govern all things. We have only to look at a certain part of God's creation, our own humanity, to realize that God has chosen not to govern creation completely in the sense of directing all its possibilities. The moment we recognize this truth, we begin to see the consequences of our own freedom. If I choose to drive at seventy through a school zone at lunch time precisely at the moment a child is dashing through a "No Walk" sign to get home, God does not govern that intersection of human lives and wills in the ways we may so desperately wish for.

Can God govern all things in the sense of finally giving meaning to everything that happens? That is a fair statement of Christian belief. A deep pastoral truth comes from this belief, that however devoid of meaning an event may be, God is able to give it meaning within the total purpose of God for humanity and for creation. To say this is not to claim that it is necessarily of wonderful comfort at the moment when our lives may be shattered by tragedy. We may be quite incapable of thinking in this way at that time; in fact we will probably be incapable of thinking at all. But life goes on and time goes by, and such an insight can eventually come to be deeply healing. In this prayer we should note that when we ask God to hear our supplications we acknowledge that the peace we are seeking will come "in our time." It is unlikely to come at the very moment of our prayer, but, as we say this, we must be careful. There are many who can witness to their receiving the peace of God even as they utter their prayer. Such things are mysterious but they are too well known and well proven to dismiss.

A Grace Beyond Therapy   Epiphany 5

Set us free, O God, from the bondage of our sins, and give us the liberty of that abundant life which you have made known to us in your Son our Savior Jesus Christ; who lives and reigns with you, in the unity of the Holy Spirit, one God, now and for ever.

PERHAPS THE most enigmatical statement our our Lord ever made was, "I came that they might have life and have it abundantly" (John 10:10). He says this in the context of a long reflection in which he sees his own role as that of a shepherd who is prepared to care for his sheep to the point of sacrificing his life for them, if need be.

The situation in which Jesus says this is a very public one. He is moving through the last stage of his ministry. This visit to Jerusalem has provoked the most intense conflict, a number of sharp confrontations that continue to take place after his reflection on the theme of the good shepherd. Tension is in the air, and Jesus, sensing that there cannot be very much time left before he endangers himself beyond recall, is becoming more and more direct in presenting himself and his claims to the crowds around him.

In any situation of limited time and real threat, we all tend to reveal our true selves. If there has been any holding back we now no longer do so. If this is true of Jesus, we can assume that this description of his own role comes from his deepest being. But the enigma remains for us. What does he mean by the life he offers us? We know by the Greek of this passage that Jesus is not referring primarily to physical life. If not that, then what kind of life? The prayer we are looking at speaks of "that abundant life" God has made known to us in Jesus Christ. It describes that life in terms of freedom from bondage and our gaining liberty. But suppose that as believing Christians we are asked what we think Jesus meant by these words, how will we reply? Religious language can become so familiar. It can slip off the tongue in liturgy so effortlessly it may startle us to be asked the meaning of what we say.

When we look back at something in the past, we can often see meanings that could not have been grasped at that time. It is clear to us as Christians that Jesus was well aware his mission could cost him his life. It is also clear that he believed the giving of his own life would somehow become the means of opening a new channel of spiritual energy, life, and grace into the human situation. Whether even Jesus himself knew how this would take place is a question we cannot answer. Whether this conviction and hope of our Lord became true is something every Christian must decide for him or herself. Every Christian must know whether or not the birth, life, death, and resurrection of Jesus Christ has affected the quality of their own living. But here is precisely where our Lord's statement becomes enigmatic. What do we mean by saying that his life has affected our own lives? Perhaps the only way to respond is by being utterly personal.

I am conscious of being alive, but I am conscious also of something almost impossible to put into words. I am conscious of limitations to my being, a shadow that can sometimes almost engulf me, a sense of incompleteness, of boundaries I cannot pass. Above all I am aware of an immense gulf between the ideal I can conceive and the actuality I can live. Of all biblical voices, Paul expresses this best in his great anguished cry of "Wretched man that I am! Who will deliver me from this body of death?" (Romans 7:24). What Paul is lashing out at, as all of us at some time do, is what the Bible calls sin. Our culture is very uncomfortable with this word, but it has not been able to avoid reaching for other language to describe what is an implacable reality.

I cannot escape from the prison of my humanity. I must live with my shadow. I must accept myself. I must take responsibility for my life. On and on go the admonishments of a score of admirable therapies. But Christian faith, while not rejecting the truth in these, demands that I go to a deeper level of truth. Christian faith says to me that it is indeed true that I cannot escape from the prison of my humanity, but the good news in Jesus Christ is that God in this Christ has entered my humanity. Christian faith says that it is indeed true that I must accept my shadow, but it also offers me the good news that before I even begin the painful process of doing so, my shadow has already been accepted by God through Jesus Christ. Christian faith agrees that I must take responsibility for my life and my human nature, but its good news to me is that, before I can take such responsibility, someone has already taken responsibility for my human nature at the cost of his own human life. That someone is my crucified and risen Lord.

A score of therapies advise me, and frequently can even help me begin the task of changing my self and, in that sense, saving myself. Christian faith begins all these processes by announcing to me what I can scarcely believe for the joy its news gives me. It announces to me that I am already changed, already free, already saved, for through my Lord this almost indescribably welcome news has come true. What I am being offered is life. What I have to do is to live it abundantly.

I have tried to put a mystery into words. The mystery remains a mystery. Thus it will always be. But the joy remains.

Fragile Trust   Epiphany 6

O God, the strength of all who put their trust in you: merci-
fully accept our prayers; and because in our weakness we can
do nothing good without you, give us the help of your grace,
that in keeping your commandments we may please you both
in will and deed; through Jesus Christ our Lord, who lives
and reigns with you and the Holy Spirit, one God, for ever
and ever.

I HAVE ALWAYS been intrigued by people who have a great capacity to trust God. To tell the truth, I have also envied them. I realized one day that my favorite reading was about solitary figures set against vast empty backgrounds. I would follow someone like Francis Chichester who would raise his small sail, wave farewell to friends in a quiet English harbor, and set off singlehandedly to sail around the world. I set off recently—in the safe pages of a book—to cross the Sahara alone from Dakar to Cairo. On and on go my journeys, not one mile of which I would commit myself to in reality!

There are at least two people who I am certain are my soul companions. One is the late film director David Lean, who always placed tiny human figures alone in vast panoramas. The second is the unknown writer of the Letter to the Hebrews. Chapter eleven of this letter is a magnificent evocation of men and women in different centuries of Jewish history, all of them making their way across tracts of desert or water or hill country. We begin at the dawn of time and we come up to our Lord himself. If you look at the list of names—Noah, Abraham, Sarah, Moses, Samson—to name a few, you realize that all of them have in common a tremendous capacity to trust God.

I read of all these familiar people. I read also of other men and women in my own century, Bonhoeffer in his wartime German cell, Janani Louwum in Idi Amin's Uganda, Martin Luther King, Jr. on the steps of the Lincoln Memorial, and I know so very clearly that compared to theirs, my capacity for trust in God is quite pathetic. So I come to the opening of this prayer with a very definite humility, if not guilt. If my strength depends on my capacity to trust God, then I am not very strong!

What do I mean when I speak of trust in God? I mean trusting life itself. Life is the creation of God, the domain of God. My life is the arena where I search for God and, at times, am aware of God's presence. But there are many times when I find my capacity to trust is very low. I sit in the doctor's waiting room, reading obsessively to assuage fear. I am tentative and careful in relationships, wary of rejection and betrayal. I wonder if I shall live longer than my father did. I have only to begin the sad litany to find it easily extendable. I also know that all of us have a litany that, if we are honest, is similar to mine.

But even as I recite that litany, I have only to read on for a phrase or two in this prayer to realize that the long centuries of Christian spirituality are already very aware of my pathetic capacity for trust. The very word "mercifully" sets the tone for the real quality of my relationship with God. The plain truth is that only God's mercy to me makes the relationship possible. To hope for a relationship with God based on the worthiness of my great trust and faithful service is to indulge in make-believe.

In this prayer there is a wonderful example of words becoming therapeutic simply by their coming together in close proximity. Place one after the other the words "mercifully accept...weakness...can do nothing...help...grace." You have a kind of chord, music that resonates deep down at the level of our sometimes desperate need. It tells us that our spirituality has no need to disguise its poverty, no need of wordy posturings, of nervously reiterated claims to sanctity. This prayer suggests quietly, calmly, gently, and lovingly that God is perfectly aware of the reality of every one of us. God has never for a moment been fooled. In fact God finds it a little amusing that I could ever for a single instant be under the illusion that I could dress up my trust and my faith in the fine clothes of fervent protestation and expect them to be seen for other than what they really are.

So much for the healing of this prayer, for the acceptance and the understanding it expresses. But now there comes a demand, a claim on me, a challenge. Having been grateful for the acceptance, I must now listen and respond to the challenge. The demand is that I *obey*. Once again we hear this ceaselessly repeated biblical refrain. The test of all our attempts at relationship with God is obedience. Do we claim to love God? Then obey God. Do we claim to trust God? Then obey God. Obedience is the litmus test of all our claims to be the servant of God. I please God to the extent that I will myself to do God's will. I shall certainly fail to do God's will perfectly. There will be ineradicable traces of self will in everything I do, but even if I will God's will in the teeth of my own so very obdurate will, that effort will please God. I will have at least sought God's will.

This is the heart of the human condition and God knows it well. We tie ourselves into knots trying to deny it. God implores us to see that this is the way things are. We cannot be freed of our humanity. But we can be freed of the guilt of our humanity by knowing one great truth. It is precisely because we cannot do God's will that there came among us one who, though fully human and exercising a human will, was able fully to will God's will. That is why we can offer this and every prayer "through Jesus Christ our Lord."

The Source   Epiphany 7

*O Lord, you have taught us that without love whatever we
do is worth nothing: send your Holy Spirit and pour into our
hearts your greatest gift, which is love, the true bond of peace
and of all virtue, without which whoever lives is accounted
dead before you. Grant this for the sake of your only Son
Jesus Christ, who lives and reigns with you and the Holy
Spirit, one God, now and for ever.*

THE INUIT people of Canada have at least twenty-four
words for snow. Each word refines the overall concept of
snow in some way. There will be a term for snow before a
storm, another for snow after a storm, another for snow lying
in a certain direction, another for snow at a certain season of
the year. The reason for this absolute precision of language
about snow is obvious: they live, eat, sleep, work, play, and
survive in snow. There is hardly ever a time when it is not
there. In the far north it is always there. Further south there is
the sudden burst of summer that reveals the strong stunted
grasses and the small wild flowers, both all the more lovely
for the shortness of the season.

Our thoughts in this prayer are not of snow, but they are
about something that is as much the context of human life as
snow is in that northern world. Our thoughts here are of
love. The prayer even points to something about love that is
also true of that northern snow and the people who live in it.
In the north, if you don't know a great deal about snow, it
could cost you your life! This prayer says in rather blunt language that if you and I do not know a great deal about love,
we too can die spiritually. Perhaps the prayer says something
even more chilling to us. It says that if our life is devoid of
love, then, even though we may be under the illusion that
our life is quite fulfilled and complete, the fact is that as far
as God is concerned we are dead!

Hardly a week goes by on the newsstands without some
magazine or newspaper reporting on a recent love and/or
sex survey. If an interplanetary visitor were to come among
us and try to discover our nature only through our use of

language, he or she would return to their distant world with the news that the universal preoccupation of the dominant species on the planet called Earth is the pursuit of—the practice of—the discussion of—the utter fascination with—believe it or not —love!

How wrong that report would be, because of the impossible burden our language and culture have put on the word "love." We can mean so many things when we use this tiny but immense word. We can mean obsession, desire, addiction, lust, affection. We may mean absolutely nothing at all, as in the moments when entertainers, microphone in hand, eyes misted as they gaze unseeing into the footlights, announce with utterly contrived and husky sincerity, "I love you all!"

The Greeks were wiser; they had several ways of expressing the English word "love." They spoke of *filia*, which perhaps translates best into English as "friendship." They also spoke of *eros*, that deeper and more demanding force in our nature that can include sexual desire. Then the Greeks added a word for which, interestingly, there seems to be no equivalent in English; they spoke of *agape*. By this they meant a quality of love that continues to give itself even when no love is returned. We are thinking here about an utterly self-sacrificing love. When from time to time we come across it we are humbled and silenced precisely because we instinctively know its rarity, and we also know that in its presence we come as near to the presence of God as we can get in this life.

A careful reading and savoring of this loveliest of prayers brings us to realize the immense claim that is being made for love. The claim is in the two phrases "without love whatever we do is worth nothing" and love is "the true bond of peace and of all virtue." Love, it is being claimed here, is not just another virtue. When Saint Paul writes his great hymn to love in the thirteenth chapter of his first letter to the Christians in Corinth, even though he names love in the same breath as faith and hope, he claims something fundamentally different for love. Paul is saying that love is the transformative element in all virtues. It is possible to have the capacity for great generosity. It is possible to have vast wisdom, to have fervent spirituality, to have an extraordinary degree of faith. All these he includes in the early part of his hymn. Paul has the insight to see that every one of these gifts, no matter how genuinely held and practiced, can be essentially sterile, cold, and lifeless, without the lifegiving element we call love.

Like the snow in the life of the Inuit, always and everywhere present, making its demand by its very presence, love insists that it be allowed to permeate every thought, every decision, every action. Like God, love is not merely a reality in itself, but it is also that to which all life looks for its transforming.

An Infectious Serenity   Epiphany 8

Most loving Father, whose will it is for us to give thanks for all things, to fear nothing but the loss of you, and to cast all our care on you who care for us: Preserve us from faithless fears and worldly anxieties, that no clouds of this mortal life may hide from us the light of that love which is immortal, and which you have manifested to us in your Son Jesus Christ our Lord; who lives and reigns with you, in the unity of the Holy Spirit, one God, now and for ever.

To STAND in the presence of spiritual greatness is always rather daunting. The person who embodies this greatness may be the most approachable of people. He or she may not be at all impressive in appearance, but if we know whose presence we are in and the kind of witness they have given, we cannot help but be aware of a certain awe towards them.

Dom Helder Camara, onetime Archbishop of Recife in Brazil, became the voice of that society's conscience when it was ruled by a brutal and repressive regime. He is physically tiny. His voice is quiet to the point that you need to concentrate very hard on what he is saying to hear him. But when you stand beside him and know who he is and what he has risked for others, things such as height become quite irrelevant.

When I read this prayer I have much the same inner response as when I encounter someone who is obviously a spiritual giant. I feel that this level of spirituality is beyond me. I read again what God wishes for us—that we give thanks for all things, fear nothing but the loss of God, and cast all our care on God. Presumably if we succeed in doing all these things we will be preserved from faithless fears and worldly anxieties, and nothing in life will hide God's love from us.

Would God that this could be so! That is my first reaction to the prayer. Then, as I try to deal with this reaction, I hear the voices of other people who in certain moments felt a sense of inadequacy in the presence of what seemed to be demanding a spiritual response they simply could not find in themselves. I hear Peter as he suddenly feels deeply disturbed about his friend beside him in the boat. "Depart from me, O Lord, for I am a sinful man," he says. This is the sense of unworthiness I feel when I read this prayer. Many of my fears may be faithless and my anxieties worldly, but I cannot prevent myself from feeling them! I am aware that there are some very dark clouds in this life only too capable of extinguishing in a great many people, including me, the light of faith.

My first response to the prayer, then, is to ask its demands to "depart from me for I am a sinful man." But as soon as I do so I am confronted with the fact that every condition of this prayer has been met by other great souls. I have met men and women whose lives seemed to me to be devoid of anything to give thanks for, lives racked by pain and loss, or limited by debilitating disease. Nevertheless they are eloquent in their thanks for the mercy and grace of God shown to them. I have met people who have an immense capacity for trusting themselves to the care of a loving God. Because of this they communicate an infectious serenity to others even in situations of great stress. What I find I cannot deny is that there exists a grace that is able to free certain people from "faithless fears and worldly anxieties."

It is at this particular point that I begin to come to terms with the spiritual qualities asked of me by this prayer. I can do so because I am coming to realize that God has no illusions whatsoever about my true nature. God's will for me is certainly in terms of what the prayer says—to give thanks, to fear only the loss of God, and to cast all care on God. But God is also totally aware, even more so than I am, of how far I am from such a state of grace. That is why the second half of the prayer changes to some very honest petitioning for ourselves. The three words "Preserve us from..." are the prelude to our confession of what we really are. We admit that our humanity is riddled with fears and anxieties. Far from our skies being unclouded, we constantly feel ourselves cut off from a sense of the love manifested in Jesus.

Because these unpleasant realities are the truth about us, we need now to look back to the first half of the prayer to realize that God is not doling out an impossible list of spiritual demands. God is showing an infinite capacity both to accept our human condition and at the same time to challenge that condition to become more than even we think it can be. After all, even on a human level it takes a particularly faithful quality of love to continue calling forth from someone what they themselves do not realize they possess. But, thank God, such is the love of God.

Lent

The Prisoner of Love   Ash Wednesday

Almighty and everlasting God, you hate nothing you have made and forgive the sins of all who are penitent: Create and make in us new and contrite hearts, that we, worthily lamenting our sins and acknowledging our wretchedness, may obtain of you, the God of all mercy, perfect remission and forgiveness; through Jesus Christ our Lord, who lives and reigns with you and the Holy Spirit, one God, for ever and ever.

I REMEMBER ONCE meeting Yehudi Menuhin. We were standing in the wings of a symphony hall where I had been asked to do the annual appeal for funds before this particular concert began with Menuhin as its star. Both of us were standing there waiting to begin our very different tasks. He showed me his violin, a Stradivarius, and I shared with him a memory gleaned from an old encyclopedia for children. There was a painting of Stradivarius at work and written underneath the painting was something he once said: "God could not make the fiddles of Stradivarius without the hands of Stradivarius."

Menuhin liked that. For all I know it may have been perfectly familiar to him, but he did not say so. He then told me something else about Stradivarius. It used to be said of the great man that he only made one violin, the one he was working on at any one time, and that when he finished it and it went from his hands to the waiting artist, Stradivarius would weep.

I suspect the relationship God has with us is not unlike that. The opening words of this prayer seem to imply that, almighty or not, there is something God cannot do. God cannot hate. Yes, I know the Old Testament tells us that God hates this or that. The prophet Amos is quite certain that God hates insincere worship, especially the kind that is utterly divorced from any concern for justice in the world. But nowhere does anyone try to tell us that God hates persons.

Thank God for the insight with which this prayer begins. It reassures us that God, for whom our minds cannot even find adequate language, does not despise our pathetic humanity. We ourselves very frequently do despise ourselves, sometimes with very good reason.

But there is an even deeper reason why this inability of God to hate is so important for us. The reason is that we ourselves hate—frequently, dangerously, and sometimes implacably. We hate more than we suspect because we are trained to hide it not only from others but, much more dangerously, from ourselves. Each of us has our list of things and people we hate, a list all the more lethal for its often being unconscious. This is why when people are challenged about a hatred that is very obvious to those around them, they can quite honestly deny its very existence. Individuals have their hatreds, as have societies, and these latter hatreds can marginalize minorities, destroy individuals, and, at certain terrible moments in history, bring into being such places as Auschwitz.

The prayer goes on drawing its portrait of God, a portrait that reveals a love that not only does not despise our human limitations, but actually affirms us in our humanity. A loving parent knows all too well the limitations of his or her children, yet will love them beyond measure. Even after we have broken our relationship with God times beyond number, God accepts us back. But there is something magnificent about this reacceptance that Jesus made particularly clear in his images of the kingdom, especially in the story of the prodigal son. Jesus was at pains to point out that the father does not welcome his son home out of pity or generosity or paternal duty. The full and open welcome we see the father giving his son is done for a much more wonderful reason. He does so because he simply cannot help it! He cannot do otherwise.

Jesus seems to be saying that it is the same with God. Out of a great love God longs to accept us back, and therefore, if we give God the slightest chance to do so, it is done. In some mysterious sense way we can say that God is the prisoner of love for us.

Perhaps the greatest brushstroke of all in this portrait of God is the revelation that God is not only what we long for, but also the source of that same longing. Like the Tin Man in

Oz, we ask for a new heart. We want it in order to realize who we really are in all our poverty and, as the collect says, our wretchedness. And why do we want to come to this realization? Because then and only then can we receive forgiveness from God and from ourselves. But to whom must we go for our new heart? The very same God from whom we hope to receive acceptance.

Even as I write this I have memories from very early childhood of getting my pocket money from my parents so that I could buy them a small present at Christmas. No wonder Jesus told us again and again that unless we can come to see our relationship with God in terms of the relationship between a child and a loving parent, we will have no real idea what the kingdom of God is all about.

A Time of Testing   Lent 1

Almighty God whose blessed Son was led by the spirit to be tempted by Satan: Come quickly to help us who are assaulted by many temptations; and, as you know the weaknesses of each of us, let each one find you mighty to save; through Jesus Christ your Son our Lord, who lives and reigns with you and the Holy Spirit, one God, for ever and ever.

IN THE early 1940s thousands of people left Ireland for the industrial areas of England. As a child who lived near one of the country's main railway stations, I became aware of the agony of that leaving. I would often lean across the low wall from which we could look down on the station area. The great engine, green and black and red, would be hissing and throbbing, sending its white clouds of steam along the dark crowded platforms where people were saying their frantic and tearful goodbyes. At the end of the platform was the dark entrance to a long tunnel. The engine would shriek its signal that it was time to go. This would be accompanied by a great instinctive wail from the crowds. Last embraces would be sought, some older folk would fall to their knees, and sometimes a distraught spouse or lover would pursue the train into the darkness of the tunnel until they were rescued, still struggling and weeping, by gentle but firm police.

For some reason that place and those scenes have always remained for me vivid images of the agony of leaving familiar places. I know that departing from the familiar also involves some level of excitement and anticipation, but their are times when the fear and the pain predominate.

I find myself wondering if it is thus and so for Jesus when he comes to the crisis point of his life that takes him from Nazareth. After all, Christian faith assures me of his utter humanity, so I must assume he experienced all the welter of emotion we attach to our many leavings in life. He must leave the gentle rolling hills of the southern Galilee. He will head southeast and down to the Jordan river valley. He will soon be in harsh unfamiliar terrain. He must eventually cross the river and face the dangerous and solitary world of the desert. Here he will come face to face with Satan, the shadow familiar to us all.

Jesus leaves the village for the wilderness. No two places in human experience are further apart. The village is the place of community, intimacy, security. The wilderness is solitude, unfamiliarity, threat. There does eventually come a time when we discover angels in the wilderness, but our first encounters tend to be with the demons of anxiety, fear, and loneliness, to name only a few. As we watch our Lord leave the village, we know that every one of us must do the same. It may be earlier or later in life. It may be for our different reasons and for very different destinations, but for each of us there must come a time of departure from the known and the familiar and a heading out for the unknown. As with our Lord, when we have made this choice we cannot avoid entering some form of wilderness and we cannot avoid encountering those things that test and tempt us.

There is an all-important insight in this prayer. We have it in the fact that Jesus is "led by the Spirit to be tempted." Why is this so important for us? Because it can have a transforming effect on our experience if, when we are going through a wilderness stage of life, we can see our situation as essentially a calling from God. Whether we like it or not, God does call us to be tested, sometimes terribly. It would be trite to pretend for a moment that it is easy to look on our times of testing as our calling; the fact is, however, that our Lord saw this to be true of his own experience.

How absolutely true this prayer is when it speaks of us as being "assaulted by many temptations." Life never comes to us in a neat, manageable order. We rarely have the luxury of facing the testing of life on one front only. If that were so, we could direct all our ability and energy to do battle in that particular part of the wall of our inner city that is under attack. But life is such that the attacks and the testing come at many parts of the walls simultaneously. At the same time we may have a minor physical illness, strain in an intimate relationship, stress in our professional affairs, temporary crisis in cash flow. On and on the list can go. Probably it is only in retrospect that our Lord was able to speak of his three temptations as coming in sequence. In actuality he may well have been presented with a kaleidoscope of possibilities as to how he would go about fulfilling his task.

How vulnerable we can feel in the face of such experiences, and how immensely heartening to know that we have the company of our Lord. A measure of our vulnerability is the note of near panic in this prayer: "Come quickly to help us"! Here this most pastoral and realistic of the collects is telling us two things. First, it tells us that life can be brutally and dangerously effective in its ability to pierce our personal defences. Second, it tells us that there is grace available to us. Our Lord, having himself experienced the testing we all undergo in some form or other, knows our human struggle, and offers us a grace that is "mighty to save."

The Quality of Mercy   Lent 2

*O God, whose glory it is always to have mercy: Be gracious
to all who have gone astray from your ways, and bring them
again with penitent hearts and steadfast faith to embrace and
hold fast the unchangeable truth of your Word, Jesus Christ
your Son; who with you and the Holy Spirit lives and reigns,
one God, for ever and ever.*

"GLORY" IS such a familiar word that it is easy to forget
how incredibly difficult it is to define it without using variations on itself! One has only to try defining it to discover this.
Already, before I write another word, I hear a great orchestra
playing Elgar's "Land of Hope and Glory." No sooner do I
hear that than I hear the equally vast sound of "Glory, glory,
hallelujah." Each is being played in a huge imaginary hall.
Already another image is forming, even grander and more
mysterious, as I look up with the shepherds and hear the
skies exploding with the chorus of heaven crying "Glory." I
must stop!

What do we mean by speaking of this thing we call
God's glory? What does it mean to be glorious? It is interesting to see how instinctively we reach for vast images, for
grandeur. We want to clothe God with trappings of power.
On the whole this was the instinct of John of Patmos, author
of the book of Revelation. For him God is enthroned in almost inexpressible glory. We have to try to pierce a blinding
effulgence of light surrounding God. We bow down in abject
humility, and, if the truth were told, in fear.

What do we mean when we use the word glorious in ordinary conversation? Very often we simply mean beauty. We
will speak of the glory of the sunset. Kipling writes that "the
glory of the garden shall never pass away." What do we
mean when we use the word glory as an exclamation, as in
"Glory, glory, hallelujah, our God is marching on"? Or we
will say of a certain act of worship that it was glorious. To
what end?

The common factor in all these uses seems to be a reaching out for something we can perhaps call magnificence, as

in the beginning of the song of our Lord's mother. She cries, "My soul proclaims the greatness of the Lord"—Magnificat! Very few of us could make a distinction between this affirmation of Mary's and our saying, "My soul glorifies the Lord." But when we examine what comes later in Mary's song, what terms she uses to describe the glory of God, we see also why this prayer begins as it does. The basis for Mary giving glory to God, and the basis for this prayer giving glory to God is one and the same: God shows mercy. With Mary there is a sense that mercy has been shown to her. She has been selected from all humanity to bear our Lord. She has been given this privilege without her having any apparent claim to it. Later Mary sings of God's mercy for those who fear God, and finally for God's mercy shown to Israel. For all of these mercies Mary gives God glory.

What is the common factor in all God's showing of mercy? It is that mercy is not accorded to our humanity because we earn or deserve it, but because it is the nature of God to do so. The glory of God is not in showing mighty power or authority or strength, but in the way such a God actually sets all power aside and acts in mercy.

To describe the elements within mercy we might seek language such as acceptance, forgiveness, or understanding. For us the essential glory of God showing us mercy is that God does not need to do so. There is, in fact, no reason for doing so given the reality of our humanity! One might almost risk saying that what our use of the word glory expresses is nothing less than our utter astonishment at God showing us mercy!

However, if there be any truth in that tongue-in-cheek suggestion, we very soon recover from our astonishment in this prayer in time to plead with God to continue showing mercy by being gracious to "all who have gone astray." We need to remember that this petition applies to every single one of us who says it. It is not a case of our coming to God as deserving and worthy citizens who importune the mercy of God for some shadowy minority other than ourselves! We hear again Isaiah grimly pointing out, "All we have gone astray."

But mercy is not merely offered; it pursues us even when we run from it. "Bring them again," we ask—once more, if we are wise, remembering that we are talking about ourselves. The implicit images are of the shepherd searching for the sheep, the father for the son, the woman for the coin. The depth of this love is hinted at in the word "embrace." There is a reason why those of us who are eventually found and brought home by a searching God should consider embracing and holding fast God's word. This prayer puts it very simply. The reason is that we ourselves have already been embraced by a Word made flesh, Jesus Christ our Lord.

Channels of Grace Lent 3

> *Almighty God, you know that we have no power in ourselves to help ourselves: Keep us both outwardly in our bodies and inwardly in our souls, that we may be defended from all adversities which may happen to the body, and from all evil thoughts which may assault and hurt the soul; through Jesus Christ our Lord, who lives and reigns with you and the Holy Spirit, one God, for ever and ever.*

THERE IS a very old story told of a golden-tongued Benedictine orator who was known far and wide for his gift during the Middle Ages. When he preached even the greatest cathedral was filled. But something out of the ordinary always happened on these great occasions. Just before the sermon, the figure of a humble monk would come and sit silently at the foot of the pulpit. The monk never said anything, never moved, until the sermon was over; then he would disappear again. When the great man received the praises and thanks of all who had heard him, this other figure was never seen, yet the next time, in whatever town or city there was to be a sermon, he would be there.

There came a day when the preacher was to speak before the king. The royal party arrived, the packed cathedral waited. At last the preacher entered, ascended the steps of the great pulpit, and began to preach. After a while the congregation became restive. What they were hearing was hesitant and dull. The preaching was lifeless and even boring. Then someone noticed that the familiar figure was not in his usual place. A whisper began and soon went through all the congregation. The person whose name none of them knew, to whom not one of them had ever spoken, had died. Hearing this, they forgave the great man, knowing that he mourned his friend. But days and weeks went by, months and years sped away, and never again was the preacher heard to speak with power and conviction. Then people realized that in some mysterious way the power of the preacher had resided in the presence of the humble voiceless man who had sat at the foot of the pulpit.

God knows that "we have no power in ourselves to help ourselves." So says our prayer. What does it mean? It cannot mean that we do not have gifts and abilities and strengths, because we have only to look at other people to see that they do, and we ourselves do, too. We know only too well that we have weaknesses, but not one of us would say that we have no gifts or strengths. After all, we constantly speak of offering these very abilities and strengths in God's service.

If this is true, the prayer can mean only one thing, that the source of our strengths and abilities and gifts is not within ourselves. This is the truth about ourselves the collect gives us, but it is not a denial of our gifts and abilities. The only denial is of any claim we might be tempted to make that we ourselves are the source. We possess these gifts, we exercise them, we can if we wish rejoice in them, but we must always remember that their source lies in God.

The eighth chapter of the book of Deuteronomy is a wonderful and eloquent passage where God gives the people of Israel a warning about this very thing. Through the voice of Moses the writer tells the people of Israel about the riches and loveliness of their land. The future is to be one of strength and prosperity. But God warns them that they will always be tempted to think they obtained all these wonderful things by their own power and their own hand. And Moses admonishes the people to forget at their peril that the source of Israel's creativity is outside itself—in God.

There is a moment in Christian liturgy that can easily remain unnoticed, a moment when in a different way we are reminded of what this prayer tells us about the real source of our human powers. It occurs in the marriage service. Near the beginning of that lovely liturgy, just after the bride and groom have taken their places before the altar, there is a short address to the couple and their families and friends. At one stage in this address the timeless reasons for the institution of marriage are stated: "The union of husband and wife in heart, body, and mind is intended by God for their mutual joy; for the help and comfort given one another...and, when it is God's will, for the procreation of children." Notice that unusual word "procreation." In ordinary conversation we often use the word "creation," but rarely do we use "procreation." What is it saying? Usually when the prefix "pro" occurs in front of a word, it means "in place of." What is being said here about a man and a woman is that they are not the creators of children. God is the creator of life. We men and women are the agents of God in the formation of life, but we are not ourselves its source.

At first sight this prayer seemed to say something negative about our humanity. It seemed to say that we are helpless creatures. We tried to see that the prayer is not saying anything remotely like that, although it certainly warns us that we must look beyond ourselves for our ultimate source of grace. To the extent that we do, we become channels of the grace of God. The moment this happens we have an immense contribution to make to life.

The Mystery That Is Bread   Lent 4

Gracious Father, whose blessed Son Jesus Christ came down from heaven to be the true bread which gives life to the world: Evermore give us this bread, that he may live in us, and we in him; who lives and reigns with you and the Holy Spirit, one God, for ever and ever.

....

IT IS within a day or two of our Lord's feeding a huge crowd. Longing for some peace and quiet, he has gone to the far side of the lake, but even there he is pursued. There are ceaseless questions. We are not told them all but we can surmise, human nature being what it is, that most of them were of the "Give me" or the "Give us" kind. Sometimes Jesus responds in an elusive way. "My father," he says, "gives you the true bread from heaven." Many take his statement in literal terms. This man has just fed thousands, and they want him to keep it up! They say, "Lord, give us this bread always." Jesus looks at them. Perhaps there was a long moment of silence while he decided whether or not he would painstakingly explain his meaning. Then he says with haunting and deceptive simplicity, "I am the bread of life."

John the Evangelist is fond of such moments in which Jesus says something on one level, but his listeners hear him on another. There is another such moment in Jesus' conversation with a Samaritan woman at the well in Sychar. Jesus is offering her spiritual grace, but he puts it in the immediate terms of their mutual situation. He says to her, "The water that I will give will become a spring of water welling up to eternal life." She responds as if he were referring to the actual water of the well they are standing beside, and with what is possibly sarcasm in her voice, she says, "Sir, give me this water, that I may not thirst, nor come here to draw."

What does it mean for us to speak in this collect of Christ as the true bread? We know that it means more than literal bread, if only because our Lord's language is constantly communicating on a number of levels. However, in our quest for spiritual meanings we had better not forget the words of Gandhi when he said, "To a hungry person, God can only come as bread." There are places on this planet where our Lord's words need to be spoken in their most literal sense. The availability of bread, if we are using bread as a symbol of justice in the allocation of resources in our world, is a paramount Christian issue.

Even as we speak of our Lord himself being bread for the life of the world, we must ask if this applies also to those of us who claim him as Lord. What about our own lifestyles? We could say that the lifestyle each one of us chooses, the way we use resources wastefully and selfishly, or sparingly and responsibly, can either nourish or rob the world we live in. By the way we live we can ourselves, if we choose, become bread for the world, or we can contribute towards its impoverishment. Perhaps the modern term "consumer" is exactly the opposite of what this prayer means by our being bread in the world.

Again, as we are thinking about spiritual bread, we might remember the instructions given to Israel for the gathering of manna in the wilderness. They could gather enough for only one day at a time. If they tried to hoard the manna, it would rot on them. This is why so much spiritual teaching is about the "dailyness " of life, of doing daily exercise for our bodies, of asking for daily bread, of having a daily quiet time, of setting out to encounter our Lord every day in some aspect of our experience, no matter how simple and ordinary.

In Christian experience, the one moment when all levels of meaning of the word "bread" come together is in the Eucharist. I can't help wondering if, when the disciples and Jesus were together on that last night, he thought again about that conversation about bread they had had on the lake. It was on this last night Jesus decided once and for all to bind himself to them and to us by the symbol of bread.

It was this bond he was forging at supper that night. For three years or so he had lived among them, and now Jesus had to get them to realize that he wished to live *within* and among them. He wishes us to realize the same truth. But there is something very important we need to be clear about. When as Christians we say that Christ is alive and that he lives in and through us, we are witnessing to a truth—but it is a paradoxical truth. Christ may indeed be alive in and among us, but it is because he also lives beyond and around us and apart from us. Christ's life may be in us, but it is not dependent upon us.

We do not give our Lord the gift of life by accepting and following him. Even our acceptance of him, when it happens, is a sign of his eternal life within us, nourishing, leading, attracting, and renewing us. Christ does not live by us. He lives within us by his own loving choice, so that we are enabled to live by him.

An Ultimate Commitment   Lent 5

*Almighty God, you alone can bring into order the unruly
wills and affections of sinners: Grant your people grace to
love what you command and desire what you promise; that,
among the swift and varied changes of the world, our hearts
may surely there be fixed where true joys are to found;
through Jesus Christ our Lord, who lives and reigns with
you and the Holy Spirit, one God, now and for ever.*

RECENTLY I saw two photographs juxtaposed to make a
point, one of a store in Moscow and the other a floor of an
American department store. In each photograph there was a
large group of people, each there for the same purpose—to
buy something. In the first store there was hardly anything to
buy. The faces of the people registered that fact. They looked
tired, angry, and frustrated. The second store was very different. Merchandise was everywhere, all the choice one could
wish for. But what was on the faces surrounded by all this?
Admittedly not anger, but in an extraordinary way the expressions on their faces were not significantly different from
their counterparts in Moscow. There was boredom, a look of
preoccupation. In no sense was there any sign of wonder, anticipation, or delight, all those expressions so beloved of ad-
vertisers in their commercials.

A recent cartoon in *The New Yorker* shows a middle-aged
man in front of a television set. Beside him is his channel
changer and program guide. The guide promises over a
hundred channels available to him. The man wears an expression of utter frustration and boredom, while his wife
says worriedly to a friend, "There's not a thing on that's interesting!"

Why introduce a reflection on this prayer in this way?
Because we are seeing a modern playing out of what the
prayer means by "the unruly wills and affections of sinners."
What we see in both these vignettes are the consequences of
endless stimulation, ceaseless novelty, and limitless choice.
Every one of these are elements of the dis-ease we call con-
sumerism, which is based on a lie. The lie is that the stimula-

tion of desire, constant novelty for the mind, and limitless choice of possessions brings happiness and contentment. The very opposite is true. What comes into millions of lives instead is unhappiness, discontent, and frustration. Perhaps even more distressing is the widespread sense of betrayal that what has been promised has not been fulfilled.

One of the refrains of the Bible is a deep questioning of whatever draws people away from that which truly satisfies. Again and again Israel is condemned for turning away from God to other gods. When Paul goes to Athens, Luke, who is writing the Acts of the Apostles, remarks bitingly of the Greeks that they are always seeking some new thing (Acts 17:21). Some years later, when Paul is writing a letter to the younger Timothy, he warns him of a future time when people will choose the kind of teaching that suits their own tastes and wishes (2 Timothy 4:3-4).

What is this prayer pointing to? The fact that our maturity can be measured by the degree to which we possess goals and loyalties that are clear cut and draw from us consistency, faithfulness, and singlemindedness. We have only to look around to see that this can be true for many people in ways other than Christian commitment. Some people may make loyalty to an institution or a cause the focus and bonding of their life—the military, for example, or care of the environment. It could also be the church or a political party. It is true that all such commitments can become obsessions, but there are many genuine and healthy commitments that give focus and unity to our lives.

This prayer goes beyond that level of commitment, as does the Christian faith itself. This prayer claims that it is necessary for a human being to possess a commitment that is ultimate. For a Christian there can be only one ultimate reality, and that is God as understood and experienced in Jesus Christ. To love what God commands and to desire what God promises is to possess in one's life a love and a desire that is ultimate. Unlike all lesser loyalties and commitments, its ability to call us further and deeper will never be exhausted. This does not mean that all other commitments or loyalties are dismissed or condemned, merely that they are less than ultimate.

To possess this ultimate focus for one's life is to put one in the very opposite state from those who constantly need choice, novelty, stimulation—what the prayer calls "the swift and varied changes of the world." One can still live in the world among such things. One can even enjoy these things, but the enjoyment is achieved by sitting lightly to them. We don't have to dismiss these novelties as evil. We simply refuse to be consumed by them. The great irony of the modern term "consumer" is that in many cases the so-called consumer is the one being consumed!

The Way of Suffering   Palm Sunday

*Almighty and everliving God, in your tender love for the
human race you sent your Son our Savior Jesus Christ to
take upon him our nature, and to suffer death upon the cross,
giving us the example of his great humility: Mercifully grant
that we may walk in the way of his suffering, and also share
in his resurrection; through Jesus Christ our Lord, who lives
and reigns with you and the Holy Spirit, one God, for ever
and ever.*

MANY WEEKS ago in the Christian year we thanked God
for wonderfully restoring our human nature by the coming
among us of our Lord Jesus Christ. We offered those thanks
when our hearts were still singing the joy of our Lord's birth,
between the night of his birth and the mysterious coming of
the Magi. Now, in the swift passing of the liturgical weeks,
thirty years have gone by in our Lord's life. For the last three
years he has carried out his public ministry. He has drawn
large crowds, formed a small band of apostles, and beyond
them a supportive community of friends. He has also made
enemies. The time has come when these enemies must be
faced, the price they demand paid. As we watch and worship
through the coming days of this week, we will see what it
takes for our human nature to be restored. We will be ap-
palled and humbled by what we see.

In this prayer we ask God for grace "that we may walk in
the way of his suffering." There is no better way to do this
than to try to walk with our Lord as he moves through this
terrible and glorious last week of earthly life.

It has been days since Galilee was left behind. You left it
unwillingly, perhaps fearfully and sadly, because you are
under no illusions about the chances of seeing these hills
again. Now they are far to the north. Here there is no
greenery, not since you left Jericho behind and began the
climb up the escarpment on the winding Roman army road.
The shouts of Bartimaeus are behind you. Fear and weariness
increase as you approach Bethany, relieved only by the

prospect of being with dear and valued friends. You sleep gratefully, probably fitfully.

In the morning you are ready to face the city. From Olivet you look at it across the valley. It crouches on its hills like a great golden beast waiting to devour you. You mount the animal you requested, the small crowd moves to follow you. Down the hillside, across the Kidron Valley, up toward the looming gate, and you are inside. There is no going back now. There are shouts, as some in the crowd tear at palm leaves and brandish them. They know what you are saying to them. You are claiming kingship. It is a political act designed to provoke a response.

You are in the great open area of the Temple. Everything about it is totally familiar, but this time something snaps inside you. The cynical financial machine spead out before you seems to deny everything you hold dear about this place. You throw yourself at it as if it were a single enemy. There is confusion and outrage all around you, and only because of the swift action of friends do you escape.

The next three days are a rhythm of resting in Bethany and facing a hostile public in the city. At times the confrontation is harsh and even dangerous. You know that you must stake everything on these few days. Deep inside you is the knowledge of what must be. On the Thursday you decide to gather the others for the meal. You arrange the room. Evening comes. For the next few hours you concentrate every remaining energy of mind and body on the task that must be done. There is so little time to ensure that the Father's work goes on. You reach for the cup and the dish. You try to tell them what it means, but you know they cannot understand the enormity of what is happening. The doing of it now is all important. Together you eat and drink.

Hours and events flow together in a deep overwhelming tide of weariness. You head for Gethsemane instinctively, throwing yourself into its shadows and letting everything go in a last desperate plea that there may be another way. But the torches and voices and the glinting of armour come through the trees. There are shouts, a struggle, and suddenly you are alone in the lights of Caiaphas' house.

The hours go by. Sometimes you are inside, dimly aware of sneers and questions and demands. Sometimes you are out under the night sky, hustled to this and that rendezvous with more endless questions and insults. You are aware of the governor's questioning. You sense his puzzlement and curiosity. You do not try to explain. It is too late for explanations. You are conscious of a great purpose lifting you.

The indescribable pain of that lifting. You are naked, utterly humiliated, the prisoner of iron and wood. In the hours of agony you are aware of every emotion. You sweep from being able to comfort the one who hangs beside you to the terrible sense of being utterly alone, betrayed even by the Father himself. You hear yourself screaming your desolation, and then, as long ago in the warm Jordan water, the dove comes. There is a sense of great peace. You offer yourself into the waiting arms.

We cannot walk further with our Lord. We will in time go beyond the threshold where we must now halt. But having walked in the way of his suffering, we will share in his resurrection.

Easter

The Victory of God   Easter Day

*O God, who for our redemption gave your only-begotten Son
to the death of the cross, and by his glorious resurrection
delivered us from the power of our enemy: Grant us so to die
daily to sin, that we may evermore live with him in the joy of
his resurrection; through Jesus Christ your Son our Lord,
who lives and reigns with you and the Holy Spirit, one God,
now and for ever.*

IT WAS only a few minutes before the beginning of the
eleven o'clock eucharist in Washington Cathedral. We were
standing near the great west doors. I was about to celebrate,
and she was on duty that Sunday welcoming visitors.

I have forgotten what triggered the conversation, and I
recall only the last of it. She had just returned from a medical
conference in Europe, where she had met a colleague, now
retired, and somehow the talk over dinner turned to the
Second World War. He had been a prisoner in the death
camps. One of his duties as a young person was to carry out
the bodies of those who had died during the night. He told
my friend that as he walked away from the mound of bodies,
he heard a voice coming from the skeletal form of a woman.
She stretched out her arm from among the bodies and said,
"I am not dead. I am alive."

On this day our Lord Jesus Christ addresses us from all
the dying and the warring and the suffering of our world,
and he says to us, "I am not dead. I am alive." When you and
I come truly to believe this, we too come alive. What does it
mean to say this?

The language of this prayer hides enormous meaning in
very few words. It is interesting that its key words tend to be
ones we no longer find frequently in common speech. This is
richly packed language; it has to be because it has a great
task to perform. It must express an event that, if it is true, is
without parallel in human experience.

With considerable trepidation, let me try to express what
a Christian believes about Easter Day. I believe that my being
human places me in a relationship with God that Greek

drama would call tragic. Created by God for God's purpose, I am incurably predisposed towards the fulfilment of my own purposes. This predisposition to carry out my own will rather than God's is what the Bible calls my sinfulness. It is an integral component of human nature. It is as if human nature has contracted a virus that runs all through human thought, human experience, human action. By being part of humanity, I am inescapably infected by this vast universal reality.

Such an infection demands healing. Since this healing cannot come from those of us who are infected, as all men and women are, healing can come only from beyond the human situation. This is why the opening chapters of Luke's gospel begin with angelic visitations. Initiative must come from beyond the human. If the seed of life is to be renewed and to be free of infection, it must come from outside. And so it does, mysteriously, silently, potently, into a human womb, and then a child comes among us. The child is in every way one of us, having assumed our human nature, but the child is also essentially unlike us. The child is not infected by the virus of sin.

So the child lives and grows and walks among us as a man, addressing us, drawing us into community, offering a new quality of life. Then conflict arises between the forces that wish to quench life and those that wish to nourish it. In this conflict the man who carries the new quality of life, who alone is able to offer his human will totally to the will of God, offers himself to the forces of death. In doing so, by a mystery for which all attempts at explanation eventually fail, he triumphs over death and returns transfigured from beyond it.

By this resurrection event, I am offered a quality of living which, to the degree I can embody it, is the same quality of living I see in Jesus Christ. This quality or Way, as it was once called, is his presence within me. That presence, if I wish to appropriate it in my living, is a grace, a resource, a strength, an energy, that enables me to rise from the many lesser deaths I must undergo, and that finally calls me to life beyond my physical death.

Such is the attempt of one Christian to state what Christian faith means in this particular human life. For me that is an attempt to express what I have heard from the many voices who have spoken to me about the mystery called Jesus Christ. Parents, Sunday School teachers, schoolmasters, friends, university lectures, colleagues, spouse. Most likely none of them would choose to express it as I have. They all wrestle with the mystery in their own ways. At the end of the day we would agree on one thing only, that the truth is hidden in a cloud of glory, and the name of the glory is Jesus Christ our Lord.

Almighty and everlasting God, who in the Paschal mystery established the new covenant of reconciliation: Grant that all who have been reborn into the fellowship of Christ's body may show forth in their lives what they profess by their faith; through Jesus Christ our Lord, who lives and reigns with you and the Holy Spirit, one God, for ever and ever.

THE FIRST two lines of this prayer are a good example of the power and the weakness of religious language. In one sense a vast and wonderful truth is encapsulated in a single brief statement. The weakness of it is that the language itself is as technical and specialized as any obscure equation in higher physics. Probably to a physicist the equation $E=MC^2$ looks as beautiful on the page as this opening sentence does to a theologian, but both the equation and the statement have to be unwrapped if their contents are to become useful in human experience.

In the coming among us of our Lord Jesus Christ, we encounter a great mystery. When our humanity encountered Jesus it was embodied in people like Peter the fisherman and Mary of Magdala. From what we can judge, they were very much aware that they were eating and walking and arguing and sailing and fishing with a human being like themselves. They knew his friendship, they witnessed his anger and his compassion, they witnessed his hurt and his pain, even his death.

But as they experienced this relationship, they also became aware that there was a mysterious and troubling otherness about their friend. More than anyone else it is Peter who gives expression to this one day when he and Jesus and others are in a boat on the lake. A sudden deep sense of awe sweeps over Peter. He backs away from Jesus and says, "Depart from me, O Lord, for I am a sinful man." Spoken in that culture and at that time, the words strongly hint that Peter felt himself in some mysterious sense to be in the presence of the divine. Peter gives voice to the same felt intuition later on at Caesarea Philippi when Jesus asks them

"Who do you say I am?" The silence is broken by Peter blurting out, "You are the Christ."

What Peter the fisherman and those others felt and groped to express, we as Christians believe. Peter himself, and Mary of Magdala, moved from intuition and wonder to belief and utter commitment when they experienced the presence of Jesus among them, not merely as a resuscitated corpse but as a person truly alive. In fact, he was so truly and utterly alive that they came to believe he had not only returned from death, but had somehow also moved triumphantly beyond it. It was obvious to them that he was now freed to express himself among them without being subject to the same limitations of time and space.

Such is the wonderful event this prayer calls "the Paschal mystery." The prayer also tells us what this event achieved. The words used in the prayer are "the new covenant of reconciliation." That statement has many levels of meaning. Perhaps the best way to wrestle with its meaning is to imagine the opposite of reconciliation in our own human experience. If I cannot be reconciled to you, then you and I remain alienated, separated from one another, and a very painful state it is if we care at all for one another and for the relationship we once had.

At all levels of our human experience we see an element of separation. We are constantly aware of being in a strange way separated from our own selves; we will even use language like "I can't stand myself." Again and again we feel separated from others, even those nearest and dearest to us. In fact, the more intimate the relationship, the more painful are those periods of alienation or separation from the other. There are times, and they can be terrible if they are intense and long-lasting, of being separated from any sense of the presence of God in our lives.

We could use yet another word, one that Paul uses in his letter to the Christian community in Rome. In Romans 8:18 and following, Paul points to a kind of built-in sense of frustration that permeates all of life. Our frustration, our sense of alienation, seems to arise from a deep longing for an ultimate quality of life we cannot realize. We grope for language to describe that quality of life, sometimes calling it eternal life. This quality of life is actually the life of God out of which our humanity is formed and by which we are always being called. We chose, and continually choose, something less, our own will or our own quality of life. The response of God to that choice we made is not to leave us alone either in the outer universe or in our own inner universe, but to come to us in utter humanity and in utter love.

This is the mysterious truth Peter the fisherman intuited in his bones, the truth that Mary of Magdala stretched to embrace when she met Jesus in the garden. This is the Paschal mystery. They encountered it as we do. For them it brought everything together, as it can do for us. That is what we mean by saying that the Paschal mystery establishes the new covenant of reconciliation. You and I will never understand this. But then we don't have to. All we have to do is live it and discover its truth.

The One Who Is No Stranger Easter 3

O God, whose blessed Son made himself known to his disciples in the breaking of bread: Open the eyes of our faith, that we may behold him in all his redeeming work; who lives and reigns with you, in the unity of the Holy Spirit, one God, for ever and ever.

THERE IS an old hymn that uses an image that sounds quaint to us today, but the image has great beauty and it teaches a great truth. The poet, as you might expect from the economy and vividness of the image, is one of the metaphysical poets, Henry Vaughan. The first verse says,

Lord when thou didst thyself undress.
Laying by thy robes of glory,
To make us more thou wouldst be less,
And becam'st a woeful story.

Vaughan is referring to our Lord's incarnation, that mysterious event when, as Christians believe, God took off the garments of Godhead and chose the garment, or the body, of humanity.

God undressed. What might that mean? Perhaps we might consider what it means for us to undress. We undress to sleep. We undress to dress again and be fresh and clean. We undress to prepare ourselves for special occasions. We will often use dress to communicate certain things to others. We will dress formally to express the seriousness of an occasion, or we will dress to reassure someone that we are like them and feel comfortable in their surroundings. We undress to make love.

Among all these, perhaps the last two apply especially and beautifully to God's relationship with us. This prayer says that our Lord wished to make himself known to us. Our belief as Christians is that God in this very Christ was making God's self known to us in a way we could comprehend and identify with. To effect this, God dresses in our human form, exchanging unimaginably fine clothing for the most pathetic coverings, exchanging glory for squalor.

But remember that we have spoken, too, of the undressing of lovers. Surely this is the true metaphor for the undressing of God in Christ. As we said, the prayer speaks of Christ wishing to make himself known. Lovers speak of knowing one another when they make love. We know too that God's coming to us in Jesus Christ was motivated by a great love for us.

We can follow the metaphor of our Lord as Lover even further. As a lover he hid nothing. All that is human we can see in him. Our fears, our angers, our anxieties, our vulnerability to hurts, our pain, our sense of loss, even our sense that God has gone from us, all this he showed us without any hiding. He even showed us his dead body, which for our humanity is our final vulnerability. As a lover he held nothing back. He gave utterly of the life that was in him.

Jesus also showed us other things. He showed us his intimacy with God. He showed us his power to heal. In the Transfiguration he showed us for a moment the inner majesty blazing within his humanity. He showed iron self-control and calm under intense pressure. He showed immense courage and resolution. He showed an awe-inspiring ability to forgive to the uttermost. Our Lord most certainly made himself known to us.

But this prayer selects one moment above all others. It reminds us that he made himself known "in the breaking of bread." He did so that evening in the upper room. He does it again in the nondescript village inn on the way to Emmaus, where he meets the two disciples on their frantic retreat from the city to the village. They walk with him and they converse, not knowing him. They are even slightly resentful that he does not seem to know of the events that for them have shattered their world.

Yet there is something about him that makes them want his company. Together they turn towards the inn and sit to eat. All is familiar and thoroughly ordinary until their guest performs the simplest of gestures: he breaks the bread. Suddenly familiarity takes on a different meaning. Suddenly they are back in the upper room. Yet this is not that room.

They are unnerved, confused, confronted by a possibility that cannot be and yet is. And in their confusion he is no longer with them. Hours later, breathless and almost inarticulate, they arrive back in the city to find that the impossible is a reality.

All of us tend to head for the village when things get rough. The village is the remembered innocence and simplicity of life, but the city is where we must struggle to survive, to believe, to discover an often tenuous community. In the city many dreams and hopes can be shattered, and when that happens we head out for our Emmaus, to begin again, to lick our wounds, to regather our forces. But on the way a stranger can meet us. The stranger can force us—help us?—to realize that the answer is not to be found in holing up. The answers are not in the past, in memory, in jealously guarded traditions. The answers are in eating with the stranger—who turns out to be no stranger—but one who shows us that what we thought dead is alive.

If we are fortunate enough to encounter the stranger as we flee the complexities and the ambiguities of these times, we will be given bread. His hands break it for us, day by day, week by week, if only we wish to eat with him. And when we eat this bread, watching it being broken, we are given the will to return to the city and to the community that awaits us there. There, among that community, we find the stranger who is no longer unknown to us, Jesus Christ our Lord.

The One Who Speaks Our Name   Easter 4

O God, whose Son Jesus Christ is the good shepherd of your people: Grant that when we hear his voice we may know him who calls us each by name, and follow where he leads; who, with you and the Holy Spirit, lives and reigns, one God, for ever and ever.

THROUGHOUT MY five years of boarding school we had a very stern, and, to tell the truth, frightening headmaster. He was very large, at least to a small boy, and he shouted a great deal. If circumstances warranted, he would use the cane. All in all he was a formidable person, although he could be the most generous of men, particularly where he saw genuine need or genuine potential in a boy.

There is one moment in his dealings with us I shall always remember. If you were trying to fudge an answer, trying to hide the fact that you did not really know it, he would suddenly stop your stammerings, look you straight in the eye—from very close range—and speaking very slowly and ominously, he would ask, "Yes or no, does the square on the hypotenuse equal the sum of the squares on the other two sides?" At this point you knew that no further postponement of confessing your ignorance was possible. You either said you didn't know, or you took a wild guess and accepted the consequences.

I share this memory with you because the liturgy is very like that headmaster in exercising a certain discipline over us, a discipline we very much need. The liturgy insists that you and I express the great truths of the faith without equivocation. Left to our own devices, we will frequently indulge in a great deal of equivocation both in public and in private. Who, in fact, was Jesus? What do we mean when we say the words "Son of God"? Was it not a common title for the great and the famous in that culture at that time? Did Jesus really rise from the dead? Do we believe that literally? What does "literally" mean, anyway? On and on we go, indulging our restless doubtings and wonderings. Too much learning makes us tentative believers.

Liturgy has the capacity to take us in hand like a firm but essentially loving teacher. Like a school teacher—at least the old kind, who taught us all day and often knew us better than our parents did—the liturgy knows well the mental games we like to play. From time to time, therefore, it takes us in hand and applies its firm corrections. It recognizes the real truth about us and about our faith. This truth is that we do not have minds great enough nor hearts large enough nor vision deep enough to say the truth in plain simple words of power and conviction. Knowing this, the liturgy offers us its disciplinary grace by forcing us to do what we seldom do ourselves.

The opening words of this prayer are such a moment. We say "O God, whose Son Jesus Christ…." For the moment we need go no farther. In one breath we have dealt with all that is tentative in our minds about Jesus. In fact the statement does more than link our Lord with God. By making the statement of this great Christian mystery merely the introduction to the further statement that Jesus is the good shepherd, the prayer suggests that the divinity of our Lord is so utterly and obviously true that it can be taken entirely for granted. One has no more to buttress its truth with elaboration or equivocation than one would to establish the existence of Mt. Everest. The faith in Jesus this prayer expresses is a quality of faith we possessed as a child, wish we possessed now, and, in rare moments of spiritual vision, do possess.

When in those moments we do achieve this level of faith in our Lord, we allow him to be our good shepherd. This is what Jesus wishes to be, what he always has been, and what he waits in unrelenting love and patience for us to recognize. This simplicity and sureness of faith in him as God in human flesh is what he waits for his church to recapture and rejoice in again. Whenever and wherever the church does recapture this conviction, it finds that our Lord becomes again its good shepherd. It then becomes possible for him to lead us where he wishes us to go, and to give us grace to follow him into places we sometimes do not wish to go or have the will to go.

This prayer reminds us of something else. It tells us that when we hear the voice of the good shepherd, what we hear is the most powerful of all sounds in our ears—our own name. All our lives we hear our name as we hear nothing else. We hear it called in every conceivable tone and setting, and for reasons and purposes too numerous to mention. Our name has been spoken by voices we will never forget and by voices we wish we could forget and cannot. Our name has been called lovingly, sternly, harshly, gently, angrily, seductively. We have heard it whispered passionately and shouted in exasperation.

To know that our name is on the lips of our Lord is to possess the richest intimacy with him. To know that he speaks our name gives us our ultimate sense of who we truly are. When we know truly who we are we can respond to his invitation to live fully and courageously. As this prayer calls us to do, we become capable of following where he leads.

To Follow Is to Know   Easter 5

Almighty God, whom truly to know is everlasting life: Grant us so perfectly to know your Son Jesus Christ to be the way, the truth, and the life, that we may stedfastly follow his steps in the way that leads to eternal life; through Jesus Christ your Son our Lord, who lives and reigns with you, in the unity of the Holy Spirit, one God, for ever and ever.

WHENEVER THE world of film tries to portray the scene with Jesus and his disciples in the upper room, the atmosphere is always one of utter serenity. Jesus moves among his disciples calmly, his gestures are quiet and restrained, his speech low and captivating. Usually the disciples are seated in rapt and attentive silence, their gaze fixed on their Master. I suspect the reality was very different. First of all, it is not in the nature of the culture to which Jesus and the disciples belonged to behave at a meal with the serenity that western artists tend to impose upon them! But there are other and grimmer reasons why we can be almost certain that the scene was very far from tranquil.

It is possible to make an educated guess that the air was electric with tension, that the sweaty smell of fear was obvious, and that fear was also betrayed by the heightening of the disciples' voices and the sharpening of their gestures. In fact, if we have any doubts about these things, we have only to listen to the voices John's gospel captures for us in the three readings associated with this prayer in the liturgical cycle. As we listen to those voices, it may occur to us that as an occasion to communicate ultimate insights regarding an embryonic faith about to be launched, this gathering left much to be desired!

Jesus is speaking to his followers quietly but intensely. He has left until this moment the great commandment he wishes to give them. "A new commandment I give unto you," he says, "that you love one another." Silence. Nobody knows quite what to say, or indeed if he wishes them to say anything. Then Peter speaks. He makes no reference to the new commandment; it is obvious he has not really heard it.

He will hear it and live it and sacrifice his life to it in years to come, but at this moment his mind is full of an agonizing suspicion that this night is the prelude to dreadful possibilities he cannot even specify. Rather like a lost frightened child speaking to a departing parent, Peter asks, "Lord, where are you going? Why cannot I follow you now?" There is quiet misery in every syllable. A moment later he is probably totally demoralized by Jesus saying, "The cock will not crow until you have denied me three times."

The evening stumbles along. Jesus is speaking of going before them, of preparing a place for them. This time it is Thomas who can stand the vagueness no longer. There is an edge of anger in his words as he bites out the question, "How can we know the way?" Jesus looks at him, perhaps for all we know even goes to him, and says, "I am the way, the truth, and the life." There is no reply from Thomas. I suspect that he shook his head in further bafflement at a response just as elusive and undefined as the statements that had triggered his question in the first place.

But Thomas is not alone. Only moments later, as Jesus mentions the Father, Philip expresses the same bewilderment as Thomas. His whole attitude is one of asking for clarification, for precise data, for something solid to cling to in the present ghastly situation where fear of the unknown is in the very air.

Peter and Thomas and Philip all wanted facts. They wanted things defined. Many of us do. The fact that we do gives many of us problems in relating to the faith, to Scripture, and to the church itself. We find it difficult to come to terms with the fact that the heart of Christian faith is essentially a mystery. That is not to say that Christian faith is not based on facts and specific events, but these facts and events are surrounded by what can never be fully and neatly defined. Archbishop Michael Ramsey of Canterbury used to say that in Christian faith there is what he called "the story and the glory." The former can be told to a child; the latter defeats the greatest human intellect.

As with the three disciples on that night long ago, we yearn for facts, for complete clarity and precision, for immediately understandable answers. But when this prayer speaks of "truly to know" and "perfectly to know," it is not referring to this kind of knowing. There is a paradox here we must admit into our lives. The prayer speaks of knowing Christ that we may follow in his steps. But the mysterious truth is that the following does not come after we know certain information and facts. The knowing comes in the following. I realize this reply may make some of us identify with the frustration of the three in the upper room, but the paradox is true. Knowing Jesus Christ comes in the following of his steps. That is why it does not take great intellect to know him. It merely takes faithfulness.

The Gift We Give to God   Easter 6

*O God, you have prepared for those who love you such good
things as surpass our understanding: Pour into our hearts
such love towards you, that we, loving you in all things and
above all things, may obtain your promises, which exceed all
that we can desire; through Jesus Christ our Lord, who lives
and reigns with you and the Holy Spirit, one God, for ever
and ever.*

THERE IS a well-known joke that is repeated from time
to time when questions of fundraising have to be dealt with.
Someone is trying to sell tickets for an benefit concert. They
approach a friend who says, "I'm so sorry I can't come, but
I'll be with you in spirit." Whereupon the person with the
tickets replies, "Good. Where would your spirit like to sit? In
a ten-dollar seat or a thirty-dollar one?"

We smile at this, but underneath it is a serious principle.
A theme running through the writing of John the Evangelist
is his idea of what it means to love God. Always there is steel
underneath the velvet, for the word "love" hardly appears
without words like "do" or "obey" following on its heels.
Again and again in his gospel, any claim we may make to
love God is immediately tested by John's insistence that
loving means doing. Loving God means doing the will of
God. If claims to love do not show themselves in action and
commitment, then they are invalid.

It is interesting to look at the scriptural context for this
prayer in all three years of the liturgy's cycle. Only if we do
this can we come to realize the "good things as surpass our
understanding." To enter these scriptures we must enter the
upper room. Jesus is gathered with his disciples and he is
giving them the great body of reflection and teaching that is
the particular gift of John the Evangelist.

At the point at which we join the desciples in the upper
room, Jesus is speaking about the nature of love. He is very
blunt and uncompromising. Any claim to love him or to love
God is quite invalid unless it issues in obedience to him
(John 14:23-24). Jesus then begins to speak of the gifts that

A Humanity Transformed

> *O God, the King of glory, you have exalted your only Son*
> *Jesus Christ with great triumph to your kingdom in heaven:*
> *Do not leave us comfortless, but send us your Holy Spirit to*
> *strengthen us, and exalt us to that place where our Savior*
> *Christ has gone before; who lives and reigns with you and*
> *the Holy Spirit, one God, in glory everlasting.*

SOMETIMES IN a movie theater the screen will widen as the program goes on. A fairly small screen will be used for such things as a notice about where one should place one's empty popcorn containers and drink cartons. Then the screen may widen to show previews of coming movies. These end, and then after a slight pause the curtains will begin to rustle back to the full width of the theater. There is within me a child who always thrills to this moment.

In recent years I have come to see the story of the first half of the first Christian century in the same way. Christian faith begins on a tiny screen. No wonder we can put it in miniature in a Christmas creche! There is the young couple with their donkey, the tiny swaddled child, around them the little town. Even later, when the child has become a man, the scene is not much larger. There is the lake surrounded by its busy little towns, its fishing boats. Higher up the slopes are the cornfields. Sometimes we see the small band of men and women focused on a single figure. Even at the end the screen is small—there is the ghastly hill, the three twisted bodies, the dwindling crowd.

Now there comes a pause, a waiting, a silence, and we are confronted by majesty. Earth opens in resurrection; the sky blazes in ascension. The band of men and women is welded as if by fire into community and creativity. A very few years go by and one of them named Paul, captured by the fire that blazed in his heart and literally blinded his eyes, wrestles to put words to the meaning of it all. As he does, he is writing to a community hundreds of miles away from him, at Colossae in Asia Minor. As he writes, Paul reaches for images that are cosmic in scope. His imagination begins to span the universe. The lake, the little town, the filthy place of execution, are all dwarfed by this explosion of imagination. For Paul, Jesus Christ has now become "the image of the invisible God, the firstborn of all creation." Paul says that Christ is now "before all things, and in him all things hold together.... In him all the fullness of God was pleased to dwell." In front of our eyes, in less than a quarter of a century, the Galilean carpenter has become the cosmic Savior.

In one vast, far-reaching sentence, the prayer we are looking at achieves the same thing. The language sweeps us from earth to heaven. Yes, it speaks of our Lord's being swept from earth to heaven, but one of the glorious insights of Christian faith, more richly preserved and developed in the eastern churches than in the western, is the realization that in our Lord's ascension our humanity also ascends. In the glorifying of Jesus, God glorifies Jesus' humanity.

But the moment I say this, I am suddenly aware that his humanity is my humanity. We share our humanity. Mine certainly does not have the beauty of his, the integrity, the perfection. The truth is that my humanity is a travesty of our Lord's, but mine is the humanity he took and shared and transformed. He took it from Mary's body when she gave him birth. He tasted this humanity in a thousand ways we know well, through heat and cold, hunger and feasting, joy and sorrow, desire and loathing. He carried it to the cross, brought it to the encounter with death, and then, in a mystery beyond words, he lifted it beyond death and swept it to a level of reality beyond description—except through the language of metaphor that forms this prayer.

To know this about our Lord's ascension, to realize that in his ascension we ascend, is to capture a great insight into the essential message of Christian faith about human nature. Our Lord's ascension affirms our humanity. It sends us the message that our humanity bears within itself the potential for transformation.

In the early 1950s a young Orthodox bishop used to visit Dublin a few times a year. His name, now widely known because of his writings, was Anthony Bloom. As Russian Patriarch in the British Isles he was visiting the small Orthodox community in Ireland. He used to stay as a guest in the Divinity Hostel, and he would sometimes preach the homily in the daily services. Years later I realize that in many ways he was trying to enrich our images of the supreme moment we call the Ascension. Bloom was trying to get us to see that the event was not about our Lord's "going away." Only when we realize this do we see that, far from being left comfortless, we are strengthened by the fact that our humanity has been exalted.

In plain language, at the very moment I scribble these words to you while flying thirty thousand feet above the Pacific, my half-drunk coffee precariously perched on the edge of my tiny plastic chair table—at this moment a part of my humanity stands in the unimaginable light of the presence of God. I stand there, and each one of us stands there. Why and how? Because Jesus stands there. When he ascended he took with him part of the humanity of each one of us. What more can one say?

The Opening of the Way   Day of Pentecost

Almighty God, on this day you opened the way of eternal life to every race and nation by the promised gift of your Holy Spirit: Shed abroad this gift throughout the world by the preaching of the Gospel, that it may reach to the ends of the earth; through Jesus Christ our Lord, who lives and reigns with you, in the unity of the Holy Spirit, one God, for ever and ever.

SOME THINGS can be told only as a story. Someone offers us the story, we listen, we receive it, and we know it is pointless to ask questions because there are really no answers. We know instinctively that we are not in the realm of questions and answers. The story is offered to us for one purpose, that we take it with us and wait for it to become true in our own experience.

A literary device that was once very popular was that of a story told to a group who for some reason—perhaps gathered before a roaring fire after a good dinner, or during a period of enforced isolation because of weather—are drawn into a story-telling mood. Sometimes the story will be told by a mysterious unknown guest who has come into the group, perhaps because of the storm. Often it is implied that the storyteller leaves the group after the story is ended. There can be no questions asked, only the felt response to the story inside each hearer.

The story of this day of Pentecost is such a story. What is there to ask questions about? The more we read Luke's account in the second chapter of the Acts of the Apostles, the more we realize that Luke knows nothing that we do not know. As he tries to tell of the event, he reaches again and again for metaphors, admitting he can do no more. He is sure of only one thing, that something of immense power and significance took place. But how it happened and what exactly it was that happened can only be expressed by metaphor. A wind? Yes, but something more, something "like" a wind. Fire? Yes, but something more, not just fire, something "as of fire." Even Peter, when he collects his wits and gets his breath back, stands shaken to the core and reaches desperately for the poetry of the prophet Joel, written centuries before. There is no neat explaining here, no slick analysis, because there cannot be. Whatever has happened is as far beyond analysis as a wild sexual encounter or a soul-shattering experience of some great music.

Peter has no sooner reached for the poetry of Joel (Acts 2:17-21) when he tries to order his thoughts into some coherent pattern (vv. 22-24). He lasts for just a few sentences and once again he lapses into the poetry he was taught as a boy in the synagogue (Psalm 16:8-11). Even if we want to agree with some scholars that Peter's speech is largely a recreation by Luke some years later, the fact still remains that Luke instinctively realized it was quite impossible to follow the shattering experience of the community by some neat piece of systematic theology!

What meaning is Luke determined to give to what happened in that room? Above all Luke sees it—and there is no doubt that the early Christians saw it—as an indication that whatever the birth, life, death, and resurrection of Jesus Christ means, it is above all a reality of universal significance. It is not merely for a particular culture or a particular race or nation. In the language of today, Luke was quite sure that the significance of Jesus Christ is planetary. Somehow his life, death, and resurrection had "opened a way"—and will always open a way—for a new quality of human living for those who choose to take his way. This is true until the end of time for men and women "of every race and nation."

That was the claim of Luke and the early Christians. It was the claim of generations of Christians as recently as the end of the nineteenth century. As this century runs its course, however, it has ceased to be the claim of millions of Christians. Many Christians in our time have great ambivalence about the consequences of this conviction. Is the reality in which Christians find themselves today so radically different that it precludes this claim?

As Christians all over the world begin a decade of evangelism, we may be coming to realize that the source of our ambivalence is not so much within the claim itself as within the attitudes and methods with which we have tended to make the claim. We can and should stop superimposing our Lord on the other great traditions, but we cannot and should not stop from offering him as the ultimate living out of human nature and as grace to those who choose to experience his spirit. The simple fact is that if we are not prepared to see this as our Christian duty, then we cannot in all conscience offer this prayer. We cannot go on praying what we do not believe. On the other hand, before we prepare to lay this prayer aside as meaningless for us in today's pluralistic world, we should also remember that the continual offering of this prayer is in itself "the preaching of the gospel" that reaches "to the ends of the earth."

The
Season
After
Pentecost

The Footprints of God   Trinity Sunday

> Almighty and everlasting God, you have given to us your
> servants grace, by the confession of a true faith, to acknow-
> ledge the glory of the eternal Trinity, and in the power of
> your divine Majesty to worship the Unity: Keep us steadfast
> in this faith and worship, and bring us at last to see you in
> your one and eternal glory, O Father; who with the Son and
> the Holy Spirit live and reign, one God, for ever and ever.

To GROW up in the south of Ireland was to be taught
above all else to remember. Up to the end of the Second
World War, the largely static, rural, conservative folk
Catholic world was seen essentially as a continuation of the
past, above all of a religious past. Standing at the far end of a
long corridor of time was the figure of Patrick, larger than
life, romanticized, part bishop, part king, part druid, even
part magician. To a small boy Patrick was very real. In him
myth and reality blended, inner and outer worlds met. Here
was a well sprung from the earth by Patrick's staff, still supplying the needs of the small town around it. And here too,
wrought in stained glass windows and statues up and down
the country, was the tiny trefoil with which Patrick taught
the mystery we call the Trinity. On the saint's own day the
small dark green clumps were on every suit lapel and every
dress. Smaller than the leaf of the clover, the shamrock spoke
of God as Father, Son, and Holy Spirit.

It was a primitive way of teaching, but it is open to question whether we have succeeded in improving upon it. If the
Trinity is our way of groping for an expression of the totality
of God, then what can be better than to stoop down to the
green earth and lift from it an image of God's truth placed
there by God's own hand?

There has never been an end to our search for images by
which to express the mystery of the Trinity. It is a long way
from Patrick and his shamrock to Dorothy L. Sayers and her
dismissal of the Athanasian Creed with an exasperated comment, "The Father incomprehensible, the Son incomprehensible, and the whole darned thing incomprehensible!" At

least in their very different way both of them acknowledge that they face a mystery, and while neither the symbol of one nor the exasperation of the other fully deals with it, both tell us that we must and will go on trying.

For myself the most helpful image for expressing the Trinity came one summer when the children were small and we were driving home from the Atlantic coast. We stopped for a while in the lovely old city of Frederickton. In the heart of the city is the Beaverbrook Art Gallery, and its particular pride is Salvador Dali's huge canvas of Saint James. I sat before it for a few minutes paying awed tribute. Then the first realization came. I felt I was confronting a reality that transcended my poor self to an overwhelming degree. The painting seemed utterly "other"—outside me, above me, beyond me.

Yet at the same moment I was aware of something else. I realized the painting was addressing me. It was telling me certain things, reminding me of other things, linking things together inside me that had not been previously linked, thoughts about discipleship, about our Lord, about the mysteriously open-ended nature of the gospel story, on the one hand so simple in its world of the small lake Dali loved to use, and on the other hand so unendingly rich in inspiration for great artists of every century and culture.

Later that day we left Frederickton. As we did I became aware that in spite of the reality of a station wagon packed with holiday gear, three small children, and two parents, the Dali canvas was still very much with me, as it has obviously stayed to this day, refreshed by two subsequent visits in the intervening years.

It was on that drive up the St. John River valley that I realized my images of the Trinity by means of that painting. First it had been utterly beyond and outside and above my being. It was not of my creation. It stood massively and serenely independent of my existence. My life would end. It would continue to be. I had been in the presence of transcendence, a source of creation other than my creatureliness.

I had also been addressed. The transcendent in the painting had spoken to me with some part of itself already immanent in my humanity. Something in the painting welcomed me as a child, as a son. A "thou" had reached out and taken flesh in my "I." Now, beside the dark flow of the river, shadowed and calmed by the evening light, amid the voices of children and the banality of traffic signs and interweaving highway lanes, I was aware of the presence within me. The great canvas was mine, not because I had dared to take it, but because it had chosen to enter me and to go where I would go. The spirit of the canvas had encountered, attracted, and entered my spirit.

Transcendence, relationship, presence. Such was Dali's painting for me. The metaphor could have come in another way. In fact it has come in other ways. Perhaps some of my ways of experiencing the tri-unity of God are your ways. A Beethoven symphony. An awesome encounter with nature. A moment of sexual ecstasy with someone who in that moment is both utterly other and yet one with you in total union, with otherness and oneness both present beyond all understanding. God has indeed given us "grace...to acknowledge the glory of the eternal Trinity, and...to worship the Unity."

We do not think about the Trinity so much as experience it. Only then do we understand. And here is the paradox, that we understand the Trinity most when we realize that we do not understand.

The God Who Works Within   Proper 1

*Remember, O Lord, what you have wrought in us and not
what we deserve; and, as you have called us to your service,
make us worthy of our calling; through Jesus Christ our
Lord, who lives and reigns with you and the Holy Spirit, one
God, now and for ever.*

THE PRAYER Book looks at human nature with much the
same balance and realism as we have a right to expect from
our family doctor. The analogy is also apt because the Prayer
Book is a doctor of the soul, speaking with both compassion
and realism. If we have had a reasonably good relationship
with our doctor over a fair number of years, then we accept
the fact that he or she has few illusions about us. We accept
this because we know, or at least we hope, that our physician
accepts us as we are. The other quality we desire in both our
doctor and our Prayer Book is a great deal of experience.
That is certainly present in the case of the Prayer Book.

All of this is a way of saying that the Prayer Book is very
wise, very compassionate, and very experienced. Since a
book cannot in itself be anything other than a book, what we
are really saying is that the Prayer Book expresses a spiritual
tradition that has acquired over the centuries wisdom, compassion, and experience.

Thank God the Prayer Book has these things, especially
in this prayer where we are thinking about what we deserve.
What we deserve is a very tender subject—few of us have
any illusions about what and how much we deserve! There
are voices in the Christian tradition, very stern ones, that are
only too ready to give us swift and crystal-clear answers to
the question of what we deserve. In such traditions we
deserve hell, burning and unending torment! We ourselves
would not wish to go quite this far, but even when we dismiss such theology with an indulgent smile we can never
quite ignore its voice. Why? Because we are well aware that
deep down we do deserve a lick or two of those salutary
flames. This is why this collect is very wise to send in its
quick sharp probe in the phrase "not what we deserve."

But because there is also experience and compassion in the prayer as well as realism, it immediately opens its other hand and displays something that quickens hope. By doing this the Prayer Book is once again like that physician, who having told us of a certain condition, and given us a stab of fear, immediately begins to balance the news by telling us steps we can take to deal with its effects.

We deserve the displeasure of God. We know this without any preacher or sage telling us. But we sometimes do need an outside voice to remind us that within us lie resources we can draw upon, resources placed there by a loving God who has worked within and around and upon us since our birth, a God who in fact has been forming our humanity since the beginning of time.

What has God "wrought" in each of us? The answer is that God has wrought so much that one despairs of making a list. Rich relationships entrusted to us. Gifts to be used and fostered. Dreams to be pursued. A faith to be our source of meaning and inspiration. Faces and voices who have and who do now touch our lives for good. Are not all these some of the things God has "wrought" in us? These are the elements wrought in our lifetime. But long long before, this God in Christ wrought so costly and so terrible and so beautiful a work for us. This God in Christ took our humanity, living it, accepting it, understanding it, testing its capacity for pain and fear and hatred, for celebration and hope and love. This too God has wrought, and our hope and prayer is that all this is greater and of more acount than the sadness of our deservings.

So our prayer is that God may "re-member" these things wrought in us. Notice how we use that word. We are not talking of God merely remembering what has been wrought in us. We are talking of God re-membering these things— putting all of them together again after we have damaged some of them. Our hope is that God may put these things back together within us. All of us need this being putting back together. Broken dreams, bruised relationships, soiled integrity, foolish choices, our fragile faithfulness in prayer, compassion, sacrament, scripture, praise—all these things need the carpentry of Christ for their re-membering.

To what purpose? So that having been called, we may be what the prayer defines as "worthy of our calling." Notice the glorious and easily missed implication. God has not waited for us to become worthy before calling us. Praise the Lord for this, because the call would never have come if it had depended on our being worthy of it. Once again, for good measure, praise the Lord!

The God Who Can Be Trusted   Proper 2

Almighty and most merciful God, in your goodness keep us,
we pray, from all things that may hurt us, that we, being
ready both in mind and body, may accomplish with free
hearts those things which belong to your purpose; through
Jesus Christ our Lord, who lives and reigns with you and the
Holy Spirit, one God, now and for ever.

IN EVERY Walt Disney movie there comes an episode
when the world darkens, the music changes, life becomes
dangerous and frightening and painful. Snow White actually
swallows the poisoned apple. Bambi's mother dies. Many
people used to protest to Disney that such things were not
suitable for children's movies. Disney would always refuse
to omit such moments even though they frightened many
children. He maintained that any presentation of life is incomplete without such times. Whether we like it or not life
can hurt, deeply and terribly.

This prayer begins, "Keep us, we pray, from all things
that may hurt us." At first sight the request seems to demand
the impossible from God. One might say that it makes a
demand that, even if it could be granted, would not be for
our spiritual well-being. Are we really beseeching God that
we never be hurt? Yes, we are. As creatures of a loving
Creator we have a right to make this petition. Of course, even
as we make it, we realize that our request cannot be granted,
not because God is not loving and caring towards us, but because we ourselves are free beings in whose hands much
potential harm lies. The painful paradox is that each of us is
potentially that "thing" from which someone else may be
praying to be kept unhurt! It is our human condition both to
be constantly wounded and to wound. Sometimes our hurting is conscious and calculated, perhaps in retaliation for
some real or imagined hurt received, and sometimes our
hurting of someone is quite unconscious and we never become aware that we have done it.

But if our request must be made in the face of a paradox,
why make it at all? Perhaps for two reasons, both hidden in

the opening sentence. The first reason is the goodness of God. We must believe this if we are to function as human beings. In saying this we are referring to something not limited to Christian faith. We are saying that trust is a necessary element in being human, and refusing to trust life or reality is to be crippled for the task of living.

Religion is not always accompanied by trust. Our early formation plays a great part in forming our capacity for trust. When Saint Paul says, "If God is for us, who is against us?" (Romans 8:31), he is revealing a deeply trustful attitude to life. When Einstein says "God does not play dice with the universe," he is doing the same. My Irish childhood makes me recall a remark frequently heard whenever we faced a mystery or a tragedy or any circumstance in which human action seemed powerless. Someone would say "Ah sure, God is good. God is good," and heads would nod. There, too, is deep trust. To say all this is not a for a moment to deny that such trust cannot be severely tested.

There is another easily forgotten reason why we pray to God to "keep us from all things that may hurt us." We do so because there is much within ourselves that can not only hurt us but even destroy us. We can be our own most dangerous enemy. We have only to look at the rest of the prayer to see the truth of this. What kind of hurtful thing are we praying to be kept from? We are praying to be kept from being unable to carry out God's purpose for our lives. In the words of this prayer we ask that we may be "ready both in mind and body [to] accomplish with free hearts those things which belong to [God's] purpose."

What are those things that prevent us from "being ready"? What is this quality of readiness that is so important to our spirituality and involves our whole being, physical and spiritual? Is it not the ability to give ourselves willingly, joyfully, eagerly to the living of life, knowing that this same life is the gift of God and is ours for the accomplishing of God's purpose? If there is truth in this, then what might hurt this readiness? What crushes it out of a person? The sad fact is that many things can do this, some with our own consent and by our own choices, but also much—and here is the mystery of existence—much that we cannot control, that comes at us from beyond ourselves. Our deepest and most valid prayer is that we do not become so hurt that we lose the capacity to remain ready for life and for the service of God.

Such readiness allows us to be "free." It allows us to possess, as the prayer puts it, "free hearts." And where does the greatest freedom come from? The answer is one of the great ironies of life. We are truly free only when we have given our allegiance readily to a purpose beyond our own purposes, to a will beyond our own wills. As the familiar hymn says,

> Breathe on me, Breath of God
> Until my heart is pure,
> Until with thee I will one will,
> To do or to endure.

The Community of Joy   Proper 3

Grant, O Lord, that the course of this world may be peaceab-
ly governed by your providence; and that your Church may
joyfully serve you in confidence and serenity; through Jesus
Christ our Lord, who lives and reigns with you and the Holy
Spirit, one God, for ever and ever.

In 1941 William Temple, then Archbishop of Canterbury, conducted a mission to the University of Oxford. During the course of the mission, Temple threw out a question without warning and asked for an immediate and unpremeditated response from each one in the circle. The question was, "Does God know anything about atomic fission?"

The result was very informative, because everyone without exception answered in the negative. Later, in chatting about the experience, the members of Temple's study group came to the conclusion that the reason they instinctively wanted to answer in the negative was the thought that atomic fission had come into being "after God's time"—that language like "atomic fission" seemed utterly outside the cultural context of the Bible.

Do we really believe that the world is governed by God's providence? It is so easy to let such language slide easily across the tongue, to hear it resound mellifluously in the religious compartments of our minds. But it is so much more difficult to come to terms with its real meaning in our contemporary situation. In recent decades there have been many voices to suggest that the stage of contemporary events is so vast compared to the Bible that the latter is no longer able to be an adequate framework for our questionings. It would seem that things have grown too large for the traditional God of the Bible.

This sounds reasonable until one realizes that the truth is exactly the opposite. Far from contemporary reality becoming too big for our being able to have faith in the providence of God, the truth is that it is our understanding of the Bible's revelation of God has grown too small. We do not need to spend much time with the kind of minds that gave us parts of the book of Isaiah, the first chapter of the letter to the Colossians, the eighth chapter of the letter to the Romans, and the twenty-first chapter of the Revelation of Saint John to realize the planetary, even universal scope of biblical thinking. We might add to this the fact that the dimensions and complexity of human events, from the microcosm to the macrocosm, have grown many times since that Oxford Bible study group sat down with William Temple. In spite of this, and maybe because of this, the overall result, far from being the diminishment of God, is instead richer than ever with the possibility and presence of God. Ironically there has perhaps never been a time in western culture where it has been more possible to speak of creation being "governed by providence."

Within that creation the church lives and serves. Notice that the collect begins by asking that the "Church may joyfully serve you," the "you" meaning God. The constant temptation of the church is to serve itself. Its other temptations are to serve in the wrong sense of subservience to what it should challenge and question. That, of course, is only another form of serving itself.

The collect continues with a prayer for the quality of the church's service to God, that it may be "in confidence and serenity." In the long story of the church it has put its confidence in unworthy sources. Sometimes, it has based its confidence on sheer power and it has seen that trust shattered when its power base is taken away. The church has at times also felt and shown the wrong kind of serenity, the kind that comes from an uncaring detachment from the pain and injustice of human affairs.

When this prayer asks for "confidence and serenity" for the church, it is asking for the grace that comes from confidence, not in itself, but in the Lord of the church. Likewise a serene church is not a church that stands apart from the ceaseless agitation of human affairs. After all, the heart of the Christian faith tells us that God did not stand apart from the world. God came into the world in Jesus Christ. That can mean only one thing for the church if it claims to be the body of our Lord in today's world. It means that the church is called by our Lord into engagement with the world, trusting the Holy Spirit will direct it. There simply is no other way.

Bane and Blessing   Proper 4

O God, your never-failing providence sets in order all things
both in heaven and in earth: Put away from us, we entreat
you, all hurtful things, and give us those things which are
profitable for us; through Jesus Christ our Lord, who lives
and reigns with you and the Holy Spirit, one God, for ever
and ever.

ONE OF the oldest and best-tried devices of comedians is
the delayed reaction. Something is said or done, the come-
dian makes no particular reaction to it, but a carefully calculated two seconds later he or she suddenly swings round,
eyes wide open, mouth agape, and we all laugh.

There are sentences in liturgy that also pull us up short—
not to laugh but to reflect and sometimes even to wonder. We
say or sing a phrase or a sentence, often thoughtlessly because of the utter familiarity of the words, and we pass on.
But sometimes we are suddenly arrested by what we have
just said or heard. Perhaps I should say that we are arrested
by what the liturgy has made us say, because the power of
such statements lies in the fact that, left to ourselves, we
would hesitate to say them. At the very least we might tend
to hedge them around with conditions and limitations.

The first sentence of this prayer is one of these statements. "God, your never-failing providence sets in order all
things." Do we really believe this as we look around the
familiar faces of the congregation among whom we worship?
Over there is a couple who have lost a daughter in the infer-
no of a ghastly traffic accident. Here is someone facing yet
another outbreak of a malignancy. Here is a person whose
business is in ruins. On and on we could go, noting endless
situations where, at least from a personal point of view,
human experience does not provide immediate evidence of a
"never-failing providence." To look at some human lives is to
know very well that, whatever one might say about all things
in heaven, some things on earth seem very far from being set
"in order."

We may wish to rush in with hasty theological corrections at this point. We may wish to say—and we would be
quite correct—that this opening of the prayer does not give
us iron-clad guarantees about our well-being in this life. But
the very fact that this is correct makes it all the more necessary that the meaning of such statements must be very carefully thought through. If they are not, we can so easily get
the impression that the liturgy is a context for making statements that do not have to reflect the reality of life outside the
places and times of the liturgy. As a means of discrediting the
liturgy, this could hardly be improved upon!

We ask God to "put away from us all hurtful things." At
first sight we know it is an unrealistic request. Life is not, nor
will it ever be, lived on those terms. Obviously if this were
the end of the matter, this request would not even be in the
prayer, because it would reduce our relationship with God to
an immature whining for total protection from all the consequences of human decisions and actions.

Look at the next request we make of God. We pray that
God may "give us those things which are profitable for us."
If we put this request beside the previous one—"put away
from us all hurtful things"—we can then see if these two
petitions taken together give us the reality of this prayer.

What are some of the hurtful things we can and must ask
to be kept from, and the profitable things we very much need
to pray for? Surely the most deeply hurtful things in life are
the consequences of an action or an event brought into being
because of the way we respond to life. I see before me the
face of someone whose spouse we buried more than a decade
ago. We stand at the grave on a bitterly cold winter's day. He
is understandably distraught. But now, ten years later, in
spite of family love, the support of friends and of more than
one worshipping community, there is still nothing but self-
consuming anger, bitterness, and self-pity. The same is true
in other lives after an experience of divorce, of searing illness, or of crisis in one's professional life.

The moment we look at this petition in this way, we
begin to see that "hurt" and "profitability" can be strangely
and wonderfully linked. For one person, an event may bring
personal disintegration; their sense of hurt never diminishes

and their inner journey comes to a grinding halt. Another person has much the same experience—someone deeply loved dies, a relationship fails, or an illness strikes. As we watch them we see a transformation. Hidden strengths appear. Aspects of their personality hitherto on the edge now begin to move to the center. New decisions are made, new plans form, new relationships are sought and developed. What certainly was a deep hurt has, in a mysterious way, become something to their profit. It has happened at tremendous cost and not for moment can the cost be denied. But it has happened. From this particular life, to use the language of the prayer, a hurtful thing has been put away and a profitable thing has been gained.

There may even come a time when this same person will look back on a searing and agonizing experience and actually regard it as providential. They may come to see it as an experience that "provided" them with unexpectedly rich things. What this prayer is really asking of God is for grace to seek, to expect, and to experience this transformation.

A Call to Thoughtful Action   Proper 5

*O God, from whom all good proceeds: Grant that by your in-
spiration we may think those things that are right, and by
your merciful guiding may do them; through Jesus Christ
our Lord, who lives and reigns with you and the Holy Spirit,
one God, for ever and ever.*

TO READ through the prayers that form the Sunday collects of the Christian year bring back a memory from my
childhood. In one of my very early English readers there was
the story, complete with an illustration, of the three blind
men who encountered an elephant. As I recapture this
memory I can see the actual picture in my lesson book. There
are the three earnest fellows, one pulling at the elephant's tail
and declaring that the beast is most certainly like a rope, the
other little figure on a ladder trying to climb up the
elephant's side and maintaining it is like a wall, while the
third valiantly tries to embrace a leg and declaring against all
other opinion that an elephant is most like a tree.

As these weekly prayers come to the task of describing
God, giving us this or that attribute of God in the opening
phrase of each prayer, they sound not unlike the three blind
men. Each says something about the nature of God. There are
some exceptions, but for the most part this is true. Each of
these images is helpful. All are incomplete. But even when
we assemble all of them together we know very well that we
are still infinitely far away from having a portrait of God.

Sometimes the sentence will sound self-evident because
of its familiar language. Consider the opening words of this
prayer: "O God, from whom all good proceeds." At first
glance, what could be more fitting to say about God? It is
only when we look again that we realize this opening phrase
may be far from obvious. It may in fact be making a claim
about God that is not at all clear in the harsh light of daily experience.

Are we saying that only good things proceed from God?
If we are, then what is good? How do we define it? Is all that
proceeds from God necessarily good for each one of us? If so,

we might like to have some reflection about this from a victim of a recent earthquake. Are we saying that God is able to
bring good, or what we might call final meaning, from everything that happens? If all things proceed from God, then
what of the evil, the pain, the suffering, the injustice within
human affairs and human experience? We find ourselves
confronted by the greatest and indeed the oldest mystery. All
we can do is to make tentative probes into this vast unknown.

Our Lord himself tells a story that may help us here. He
tells us about a landowner who sows good seed in his field.
This is really a portrait of God from whom all good proceeds.
The next night an enemy sows weeds. The landowner's ser-
vants wish to take out the weeds, but he forbids them to do
this, insisting that the field must remain both wheat and
weeds until the harvest. Notice that the good proceeds from
God and is willed by God. The evil seems to be allowed by
God, tolerated, as if within time and history both are forever
mysteriously linked.

What this prayer is quite clear about is that the action of
God on our lives is for good. God is the source of right thinking and right action. Here is where liturgy can deeply challenge the accepted attitudes of our culture. Today the human
brain is quite rightly seen as an immensely complex and subtle computer. All computer technology still falls far short of
what we can legitimately call the glory of the human brain.
But this prayer goes even further in its implied attitude to the
human brain. The prayer sees that same brain as an instrument of God's interaction with creation. To say that the spirit
of God inspires our thinking is to say that the spirit of God
inhabits the human mind to the extent that we are willing to
allow it. It is becoming essential to begin to think in this way.
Why? Because more and more voices in the new sciences are
beginning to speak of humanity as something the universe
has formed to reflect upon itself!

But the work of the spirit of God wishes to go further. If
we open our thinking to the inspiration of God's spirit, then
we open up the possibility of that same spirit energizing our
capacity for action. Always in biblical faith there is the conviction that thinking, even the most righteous and morally

impeccable thinking, is not enough in itself. When thought becomes an end in itself, it ceases to issue in action. More than any other voice in the Bible it is the apostle James who emphasizes this in his letter to the early Christians. In his blunt fashion the apostle declares, "Be doers of the word, and not hearers only" (James 1:22). James knows well the temptation all bureaucratic systems have, whether they be governmental, ecclesiastical, or any other kind, to substitute reflection for action. Here in this prayer we are asking to be given the grace to avoid this trap.

Two last thoughts. When we pray that we may guided in what we eventually do, there is always the necessity that we do not neglect thinking. In this prayer we ask that "we may think those things that are right." Relying on the inspiration of the Holy Spirit does not for a moment relieve us from the responsibility of thought, very careful and committed thought. Again, rushing off into action without reflection can be just as much a trap as remaining for ever in reflection. In just the same way, when the Bible says that we must be doers of the Word and not hearers only, it is not for a moment saying we should not do a great deal of listening!

The Household of God   Proper 6

*Keep, O Lord, your household the Church in your steadfast
faith and love, that through your grace we may proclaim
your truth with boldness, and minister your justice with
compassion; for the sake of our Savior Jesus Christ, who lives
and reigns with you and the Holy Spirit, one God, now and
for ever.*

THE IMAGE we choose to describe something can be all
important. This prayer wishes to talk about the church, and
to do so it chooses a beautiful image. It offers us the church
as a "household."

Paradoxically, the power of the image is in its setting
aside of power. The moment we say the word, "household,"
we think of our own household, past or present. Perhaps we
instinctively recall the familiar rooms, stairways, driveways,
or gardens of childhood. Perhaps we visualize immediately
our present household, the face of a spouse or child, a
favorite chair, the afternoon sunlight in a certain room. If we
are elderly, there will be the households we remember from
our past.

Think now of another common image of the church that
could have been chosen to open this prayer. If it compares
unfavorably with our first image of the household, the comparison may act as a warning, because it is an image we use
so often to refer to the church. Instead of the word
"household," substitute "organization." The petition would
now be "Keep, O Lord, your organization the Church." We
know immediately that this is absolutely unacceptable. We
simply could not pray these words. They would be like one
of those particularly ghastly chords on the organ when a
hymn book accidentally falls on the keys! Yet here is the
warning. In almost every other context, we do think and
speak of the church as an "organization," and we expect to
find "organizational" features about its life. We tend to act on
the assumption that it is an organization, and sometimes can
get quite alarmed and indignant at signs that the church's organization is slipping!

Can thinking about these different ways of referring to the church teach us something? Most certainly it can. It can teach us to be very aware of a real temptation springing from our culture, the temptation to think of "organization" as the be-all and end-all of the church. Of course organization must be a mark of the church's life, just as it is a mark of the life of even the smallest household, a sign of responsibility. But to make "organization" the ultimate value in church life is self-defeating. There is a simple reason for this. The church is not an organization, but an organism. Our Lord did not found an organization. He died and rose to bring a people into being. A people is an organism. That is exactly what we mean when we speak of the church as the Body of Christ. The loveliest, most precious, and most complex kind of organism is a human household. At its best it calls for mutual loyalties, mutual self-sacrifices, and endless acceptance. In a word, the human household demands love, relationship, nurture, discipline, and acceptance.

A Christian community demands all these things, too, even though different communities take different forms. It may be a community living out an ordered life around a mutually agreed upon rule of life. It may be a huge or small congregation worshiping and serving together with all sorts of differing degrees of intimacy among its members. It may be a small group focused on prayer or Bible study. All of these forms of the Christian household will have different demands made on them. The greatest demands will be where there is the greatest intimacy. The greatest intimacy will be where there is a mutual domicile, and it will make the greatest demands on people's capacity for mutual acceptance and mutual loyalty. But all the other kinds of community will be called to some degree of mutual acceptance and loyalty precisely because the church's truest nature is to be a "household."

The collect then asks that the household of the church boldly proclaim God's truth and compassionately minister God's justice. The interesting thing is that if the church knows itself to be truly a household, it will proclaim and minister by its very nature. Truth and justice will be not so much an aspect of its programming as the essential traits of its own life. Their living-out in the household of God will be their proclamation. It is not unknown for the church to expend great energies proclaiming those very things most glaringly absent from its own life! When truth and justice are seen to flow naturally from the church's life, then in a wonderful and mysterious sense this compassion shown within the household will itself become the church's power to witness beyond itself.

Maker of Our Humanity   Proper 7

*O Lord, make us have perpetual love and reverence for your
holy Name, for you never fail to help and govern those whom
you have set upon the sure foundation of your loving-kindness; through Jesus Christ our Lord, who lives and reigns
with you and the Holy Spirit, one God, for ever and ever.*

DESMOND TUTU of Capetown observed recently that
"God is continually breathing into our nostrils." It is a vivid
way of expressing the fact that not only is our life the creation of God, but that every moment of our life is also sustained by God. We are not only made. We continue to be
made. It is possible to say that we are not so much human
"beings" as human "becomings."

This prayer begins, "O Lord, make us...." It is so easy to
leave those four words behind, so easy to hurry on to the
seemingly more significant words that immediately follow.
But we would be wrong to do so. Instead, it is very much
worth our while to stop and reflect on the fact that God not
only has made us, but continually makes us.

Another reason why these four words are a valid prayer
in themselves is that all sorts of forces are brought to bear on
our lives, all of them trying to "make" and form us for their
purposes. A huge consumerist society sets out to make us
into consumers. Of course we cannot avoid consuming, but
that is very different from "being" consumers, whose lives
are defined by that purpose. Our professional life can also try
to "make" us. Unless we guard against it, our priorities and
commitments will eventually be formed in such a way that
our professional life becomes our whole life. It becomes who
we are. We are "made" by it.

In what sense does God make us? We are most aware of
being made physically. The Psalmist says, "I will thank you
because I am marvelously made." As each year goes by the
world of genetics and microbiology reveals more and more
clearly how right the author of Psalm 139 is. But we also realize more and more that we are not merely made physically.
As we learn to see life more in terms of the whole, we come

to perceive it as a great web of being. We realize we are being made in every way—physically, mentally, psychologically, spiritually.

The reason it is so important for us to realize this is that only then can we open all the elements of our lives to God. Western culture has so thoroughly divided up reality that we have lost a sense of the *whole* being through which God's grace is manifested. Our physical exercise, our eating habits, our sexuality, our thinking—all these can become as spiritual an activity as receiving the bread and wine of the Eucharist. Our reading, our use of television or movies, our education, and our job can all be channels for God. Our concern for self-development and the development of others around us, our fostering of relationships, all this energy in our lives can be understood as the process of God's making of us. Thus our spirituality does not float around on the margin of our lives, but every activity is the stuff of spirituality. To achieve this realization is to become a man or woman made by and for God, a truly whole human being.

The collect asks God to form us by giving us "a perpetual love and reverence for your holy Name." What might this mean?

First we link this with the next phrase: "You never fail to help and govern those whom you have set upon the sure foundation of your loving-kindness." When our lives are founded on God's attitude of loving-kindness towards our humanity, then we are most aware of God being constantly in our experience. This collect has us pray for perpetual awareness (that is, in every facet of our living) of God's name or nature. What is the essential mark of that nature? An attitude of loving-kindness. If we are open to the indwelling of such a God in the total spectrum of our living; if such an attitude permeates us personally and professionally; if we see it in our physical, mental, psychological, and spiritual lives, God will truly, wholly, and wonderfully become our maker. We in turn will constantly be aware of God's grace and guidance and discipline. Then, as the collect expresses it, will God be able "to help and govern us."

Compass and Cornerstone   Proper 8

> *Almighty God, you have built your Church upon the founda-*
> *tion of the apostles and prophets, Jesus Christ himself being*
> *the chief cornerstone: Grant us so to be joined together in*
> *unity of spirit by their teaching, that we may be made a holy*
> *temple acceptable to you; through Jesus Christ our Lord, who*
> *lives and reigns with you and the Holy Spirit, one God, for*
> *ever and ever.*

ONE OF the interesting things about the contents of most people's cars is that they almost always include maps. They are usually stuffed into the glove compartment and the side door pockets, very often out of date, and sometimes too crumpled and folded to be read. Why is this? I think it is because maps are comforting things. They may be of places you know like the back of your hand. Actually they usually are. It is not so much that we need them as we like to have them around.

C. S. Lewis once said that God does not give out maps for our spiritual journeying, God gives us a compass. Lewis was responding to our very human wish to have things spelled out, to have all the answers neatly presented for our journey. He maintained that instead we are given something much better, much more demanding and challenging, something that insists that we be adults. That "something" is our Lord Jesus Christ. Our Lord is not a neat predictable map for our lives—because there can be no such thing—but a compass, a reference point to which we must look again and again to get our bearings.

This prayer says much the same thing by giving us a central image as a kind of reference point. Jesus Christ, we are told, can be a cornerstone for us as we set out to build the structure of our faith. The cornerstone is by no means the only stone, but it is the essential stone if the building is to stand true and firm. The positioning of all other stones is measured from it. Like the compass, the cornerstone is a reference point that allows a process to go on. The compass allows the journey to go on, while the cornerstone allows the building to go on. Each allows freedom, initiative, and change to be brought to the process. So our Lord can be for our lives both compass and cornerstone.

"Almighty God," says this prayer, "you have built your Church...." We cannot be reminded too often that the ultimate architect of the church is God. We need to be told this again and again because there is much about the church that points to our own human work. Our money and our deepest commitments of time, energy, and thought have made the visible things of the church possible. Human intellect forms and expresses its theology. Human gifts of speech and song, of administration, of pastoral care and insight, of music, of planning, of artistic design—all go to the building of the church, and well may we thank God for all such gifts and for many others. But in that moment of thanksgiving comes the reminder that the true and only builder of the church is God's Holy Spirit.

On what does God build? The answer this prayer gives is that God builds "upon the foundation of the apostles and prophets." If we can see these apostles and prophets not just as a concept but as a living organism stretching across space and time, it will help us grasp the infinite richness and variety in the understanding and expression of Christian faith these men and women had. Why might this be helpful for us? Because it may help us deal with aspects of the church and the faith that deeply trouble many believers these days.

In biblical terms, we are being asked to live through a wilderness period, a time when change, with all its consequences, is not experienced merely in just one aspect of our experience, but all through it. There seems no respite from it. With such total change come all its daunting companions—the necessity for ceaseless consultation, the necessity for constant choices, and all the anxiety that comes with it; the impatience and anger that come with unrelieved tension and anxiety. Always there is the unrelenting pressure of many more questions than answers. Consequences are often unforeseen because there is no precedent either for the problem that must be faced or for the course of action decided upon.

At such a time we long for something established, fixed, predictable, dependable. Sometimes we want to find this foundation clearly defined in some particular time or place or voice. If only, we sometimes wish, the church could recapture the sanity and the certainty and the simplicity of this or that age, of this or that theological era, of this or that great leader, or this or that unity or purity! Angers would cool, fears be assuaged, hopes ignited and the ship of salvation would sail out into calm seas where the charts would all be clearly drawn! We think wistfully about how different it must have been for those well-founded, clear-thinking, sure-footed apostles and prophets!

The reality is very different. In the thinking, writing, preaching, and witnessing of the apostles and prophets throughout the ages—some of them alive today, let's not forget—there has always been a wide spectrum of opinion about issues and questions of the day. To think that once upon a time there was a wonderful consensus binding together all Christian thought and action, apart from periods and places where a transitory unity may have been imposed, is to deny reality. By the same token, it may well be that the very richness and variety of Christian life and thought is what allows the contemporary church to respond to the bewildering avalanche of experiences, questions, demands, risks, and mysteries we face today.

Realizing this, the really important petition of this prayer is that we may be given a "unity of spirit" to discern that, through all the many emphases of Christian life and teaching, "Jesus Christ himself [is] the chief cornerstone." This and this alone is what joins us together. The prayer speaks of us all as a holy temple. Within that temple there will be differing modes of worship, differing views of the function of the people of God in society, but all the elements of the temple will be measured against one particular stone, and that stone is our Lord. He is cornerstone, measuring rod, reference point.

Pure Affection   Proper 9

O God, you have taught us to keep all your commandments
by loving you and our neighbor: Grant us the grace of your
Holy Spirit, that we may be devoted to you with our whole
heart, and united to one another with pure affection; through
Jesus Christ our Lord, who lives and reigns with you and the
Holy Spirit, one God, for ever and ever.

In TODAY'S world of physics the phrase on many lips is
"unified theory." In his recent immensely popular book, *A
Short History of Time*, Stephen Hawking of Cambridge
University speaks of the renewed search for a single theory
or formula that will express in one equation all our insights
about the nature of reality. One of the great steps on the way
to this as yet elusive unified theory is Einstein's famous
equation—$E=MC^2$.

Millenia ago, and not in the sphere of physics but in a
sphere no less real and perhaps even more mysterious, men
and women searched for and found another kind of unified
theory. This search took place in the moral and spiritual
realm; its results used the language of that realm. It asked:
what is the single law or vision—notice that we are speaking
of an equation, but using other language—that expresses the
ultimate purpose for which human life is created? The
response to that search is in its own way a kind of equation, a
kind of $E=MC^2$ of spirituality. We express it in the opening
words of this prayer. We believe that God has taught us to
keep all of the commandments, that is, to unify all theories
about human activity, by loving God and our neighbor.

Now, while we certainly can speak of the laws of physics
and the laws of spirituality, there is one great difference between them. The laws of physics are observed by virtue of
what they are. In the world of spirituality, to state a law and
to have it observed are two very different things. Merely
knowing a spiritual law does not mean that we can or even
wish to observe it. To observe such a law in our lives we
need what the prayer has us ask for, the grace of the Holy
Spirit.

Every now and again in the collects we are given a shining jewel of language. As with any jewel one wants to lift it, to turn it and fondle it, to see its many facets. We ask for God's Holy Spirit "that we may be devoted to [God] with our whole heart, and united to one another with pure affection." What a magnificent description of our vocation as Christians! To say that it is a demanding vocation is an understatement. On our first reading this, the lovely parallelism of the petition can lull us into easy acceptance. What could be more reasonable than to ask that Christians be devoted to God and united with one another?

But then we look again, perhaps for no other reason than the fact that the loveliness of the phrasing holds us for a moment, and suddenly we discern the steel beneath the velvet. We are not being asked for a casual adherence to some vague principle called Christianity. Something of immense cost is being demanded, nothing less than "our whole heart." As "heart" is used in Scripture, this means our whole being. This is the demand the Risen Lord makes of Peter. It asks not merely "Do you love me?" but "Do you love me more than these?" and it allows no casual response.

"Grant...that we may be...united to one another with pure affection." Again the language is gentle and lovely. Again the demand being made is sobering. No wonder we pray for grace to respond to it. We might for a moment assess even our nearest and dearest relationships, measuring how much they are characterized by "pure affection." Affection is that form of human relationship that asks the least of the other, yet still can form deep and strong bonds.

We speak a great deal about the need for love in Christian community, but the word "love" has been so diminished and vulgarized in our culture that we might be wiser to use "affection" to describe the quality of relationships sought in congregational life. Such bonds of affection allow far more freedom than the bonds of human love. All but the most exalted of loves needs its love to be returned, while affection is far less threatened when it finds its object unresponsive. It is far more patient in waiting for response and far more understanding if it is not forthcoming. All in all, affection (as C. S. Lewis so brilliantly showed in *The Four Loves*) is the least ap-

preciated and the most undervalued of our loves. Our prayer
in this collect is that we realize its value among God's gifts to
us.

Knowing and Doing   Proper 10

*O Lord, mercifully receive the prayers of your people who
call upon you, and grant that they may know and understand what things they ought to do, and also may have grace
and power faithfully to accomplish them; through Jesus
Christ our Lord, who lives and reigns with you and the Holy
Spirit, one God, now and for ever.*

ON THE morning of August 6, 1923, a young French
priest stood in a rocky gorge somewhere in northern China.
He was traveling with a European archeological expedition
and on this particular day, the Feast of the Transfiguration,
he wished to say Mass here in this solitary silent place. When
he looked in his backpack, he found he had forgotten to pack
the bread and wine for his celebration. Annoyed with himself
he began to return to the camp. Changing his mind, he stood
still, thought for a moment, then lifted his arms and began to
reflect in words that have become a great statement of twen-
tieth-century spirituality. "Once again, Lord, here in the step-
pes of Asia I have neither bread, nor wine, nor altar. I will
raise myself beyond these symbols, up to the pure majesty of
the real itself. I, your priest, will make the whole earth my
altar and on it will offer you all the labors and sufferings of
the world." So began the great "Mass on the World" by Teilhard de Chardin.

The opening words of this collect—"O Lord mercifully
receive the prayers of your people"—make us realize that
our generation in the church has been given a great gift. As
with many gifts it is easy to take it for granted, easy to assume that it has always been ours. But it has not, at least not
in the form we now have it. The name of this gift is that part
of the Prayer Book we call the "prayers of the people," and
when we use this gift we find ourselves doing what Teilhard
de Chardin did on that Feast of the Transfiguration long ago.
We make the whole earth our altar and on it we offer the
whole world to God.

Every one of these six forms of prayer moves from a
panoramic beginning to the intimacy of personal life. We lift

to God "the peace of the world," and we pray "for all who govern and hold authority in the nations," or for "a reverence for the earth as your own creation." The other lens of these prayer looks at "all whose lives are closely linked with ours...the poor, the persecuted, the sick." The forms reach their ultimate intimacy and immediacy in a petition for "the special needs and concerns of this congregation," when everyone present who wishes to names those who are on their minds at that moment. We offer not only the totality of space, but also—in mentioning both the living and the dead—the totality of time. We lift up both the world and the minute particularities of life in the personal petitions. In all this the prayers of the people resemble the outline of Teilhard's famous Mass on the World. Both in turn resemble the much earlier song we know as Te Deum, from its first great universal burst of praise, "All creation worships you," to the quiet personal plea, "Come then, Lord, and help your people."

Why do we offer these or any other prayers? So that we "may know and understand what things [we] ought to do." The primary prayer of a Christian is to know the will of God in all things. The question of how we can know the will of God either for ourselves or for someone else is a very mysterious business. There is no question that there are occasions when people have received seemingly direct guidance, and will speak of hearing a voice inside themselves. But for the most part Christian experience speaks of a sense of overall rightness about a decision made, a course of action carried out. Even then, it is often not for some time that we may recognize the spiritual direction we have received.

What is also important is that we realize that the domain of prayer extends over all of life. When we pray to know the will of God so that we may do it, we need to realize that we are praying about every facet of our daily existence. This is what the prayers of the people help us do. We pray to discern the will of God in everything—in our personal lives, in our relationships with others, in our professional or public lives, in our participation in and understanding of social and political affairs. A Christian cannot be too aware that nothing less than all aspects of human activity involve knowing and doing the will of God. Our Lord would say to us that everything in our experience involves our participation in the kingdom of God. Anything less of a vision of God's will is to diminish God.

It is quite impossible to know the will of God in all the specifics of human experience. As we said, there will certainly be moments in life when we are aware of a strong sense of being guided. But Christian life is to be lived in the belief that the totality of life is never beyond God's loving purpose, though our living it from day to day will mean we encounter many things that are not in themselves the will of God. That is why the prayer wisely adds to our first request, that we may "know," a second—that we may also "understand." Often in life we know only too well what we ought to do. Perhaps after a dreadful bereavement we know very well we should gather our life together again. But knowing this will not be enough. Our agonized struggle will be to come to some understanding of what has happened to us.

But prayer is not a mere request for information or for knowledge or even for wisdom. We can have access to all possible information, we can have great knowledge and deep wisdom. But there is a trap, and this is the trap of much contemporary spirituality, particularly some New Age spirituality. We can come to regard knowledge or wisdom as the highest of spiritual gifts, without realizing that for Christians these gifts of knowing must be translated into doing. For a Christian, this is the ultimate challenge to all our claims to be spiritual beings. For a Christian, knowing and doing must be one.

Through a Glass Darkly   Proper 11

*Almighty God, the fountain of all wisdom, you know our
necessities before we ask and our ignorance in asking: Have
compassion on our weakness, and mercifully give us those
things which for our unworthiness we dare not, and for our
blindness we cannot ask; through the worthiness of your Son
Jesus Christ our Lord, who lives and reigns with you and the
Holy Spirit, one God, now and for ever.*

In David Lean's movie "Ryan's Daughter," there is a
moment when the elderly priest meets Rosie Ryan on the
coastline, on a windblown stretch of beach after a storm has
blown itself out. He comes upon her unexpectedly and the
two of them sit on the rocks looking out on the heaving
water. Very quietly the priest says to her, "Rosie, sometimes
if we're not careful God gives us what we want." This moment is as good an entry as any into this collect, a lovely,
graceful, and certainly ironic expression of prayer.

"Almighty God, the fountain of all wisdom, you know
our necessities before we ask...." Our efforts to escape from
the confines of our human ways of knowing and to capture
even the slightest understanding of the way in which God
knows are endless. All our efforts are fruitless, but something
in us will keep us trying until time ends. Then and only then
will we cease seeing all reality as "through a glass darkly," as
Saint Paul said to the Corinthians.

We can, however, express the ways in which God's wisdom and our human wisdom differ. All our knowledge is
partial and the knowledge of God is infinite. Our minds can
know only what has been and what is, while God knows all
that has been, all that is, and all that will be. Strictly speaking, we do not even know what has been and what is. We
know only our perception of these things. We give meanings
to what we know and all such meanings are subjective and
partial. God is beyond the bounds of such subjectivity. All
this was in Saint Paul's mind when he wrote that there
would come a time when "I shall know even as I am

known." He is in effect saying that our knowing and God's knowing are fundamentally different.

God knows "our necessities before we ask and our ignorance in asking." When we kneel before God, or indeed turn to God in any way, God already knows the totality of our being at that moment. God knows the totality of choices, chances, thoughts, actions, hopes, fears, and desires leading to this moment. God already knows what will emerge from all the as-yet-unfulfilled potentialities in this moment. It is essential for us to understand that God's knowing what will be does not mean that God has already fixed what will be. It is not that God makes us choose this or that, but that God knows which ones, among the infinite number of possibilities, will become actual for us. We might even say that in each moment of human decision, an infinite number of possible universes lie unborn. God knows the one that will be born. We do not know until it is actualized. Only then can we begin to deal with the consequences of our choice. The moment we do, we begin to bring into being yet another actuality from an infinite number of possibilities.

There are two spiritual insights we can derive from all of this. First, we can realize our total dependence on God, and at the same time see that because we are known through and through, we can be utterly honest before God. In the presence of God we can say with the poet who wrote Psalm 139, "There is not a word on my lips, but you, O Lord, know it altogether. You press upon me behind and before and lay your hand upon me."

The collect now gives us one of the most gentle and compassionate descriptions of our human condition, and once again it is an expression of our total dependence on God. We need the wisdom of the liturgy to remind us of this because we do not enjoy reminding ourselves. The prayer has us say, "Have compassion on our weakness, and mercifully give us those things which for our unworthiness we dare not, and for our blindness we cannot ask." Perhaps the word "weakness" here can be understood rather as "limitation." Two things limit us in our ability to pray. The first is our own sense of unworthiness, and the second is the fact that the total context of life is always hidden from us. In that sense we are blind. Because of these limitations that are part of our humanity, we simply don't know what we should pray for. The very thing we are passionately praying for may well be the very last thing for our ultimate good. Our not getting a prayer answered on our terms may well be the richest possible blessing to us.

The irony is that we will never know this. Meanwhile, we are quite capable of resenting for a long time what seems to us to be God's refusal to grant our prayer!

O God, the protector of all who trust in you, without whom nothing is strong, nothing is holy: Increase and multiply upon us your mercy; that, with you as our ruler and guide, we may so pass through things temporal, that we lose not the things eternal; through Jesus Christ our Lord, who lives and reigns with you and the Holy Spirit, one God, for ever and ever.

MANY GENERATIONS in the English-speaking world, my own among them, have been nourished by the reading, often aloud, of John Bunyan's *Pilgrim's Progress*. The story tells of a man named Christian who leaves the City of Destruction to journey in search of the Celestial City. On that journey the pilgrim moves through fascinating and sometimes terrible experiences. One feature of the story is the succession of companions who accompany Christian—companions with names like Greatheart, Standfast, Faithful—all of whom give help and encouragement to their friend. This collect has implicit images of the two main features of Bunyan's great work, for it speaks of life as a journey, and as a journey on which we need a guide and companion.

"O God, the protector of all who trust in you...." As we well know, God is not the kind of God who furnishes protection against the hard things that life can bring, especially against those misfortunes that by our own willful choosing we bring upon ourselves. When we say that trusting in God can bring protection, what are we saying? Are we not saying that if a man or woman has a deep and genuine trust in God, this very trust can be our protection as we struggle with those inner demons that assault us, such as depression, chronic unfocused anxiety, fear, and anger? We need to use the words "struggle with," because trust in God is not a magic talisman that removes us from this struggle in our lives. Our trust in God is a resource for the struggle, not a shield against its necessity.

"Without whom nothing is strong, nothing is holy...." The prayer does not say that someone cannot have strength or courage or integrity or resolution without acknowledging God as its source. We have only to look around us at certain people to know otherwise. But it does say that God, acknowledged or unacknowledged, is the source of all human strengths.

"Without whom...nothing is holy...." Even to think in terms of anything or anybody being holy or hallowed, we have to move beyond the existence of the things or persons themselves to their deeper meaning or significance. We must seek that of which the thing or person is a sign. Moses does not merely look at the burning bush. He looks through and beyond it, seeking what is communicated to him by and through the event. As he does this, and as we do it in our own experiences, we look beyond and through an event or moment to discern the face and voice of God hidden in the moment. We look through the created order to discern the Creator. To do so is to acknowledge that a particular event or time or object or person is holy.

"Increase and multiply upon us your mercy...." Again and again we are reminded that Christian spirituality is not so much a fixed state as a process. Here we are reminded that our relationship with God as the source of all grace is itself an ongoing process in our lives. Spiritually we either "increase and multiply" or we decrease. We either grow or diminish; we cannot remain the same. In an age of immense transition, this last is an illusion fondly clung to by many Christians and many congregations!

"With you as our ruler and guide, we may so pass through things temporal, that we lose not the things eternal." This image, magnificently expressed, sets us in the context of our journey. It first implies, simply and beautifully, that we do not go on our journey alone. God goes with us as companion. A companion does two things. We receive guidance; we are not forced to take it. Such is our human freedom and the generosity of God. But if we do accept God's guidance, we are also given a rule of life. We are given the capacity for spiritual discipline, the kind of discipline that is necessary if the demands of the journey are to be met.

This petition in this collect is offered in words that will forever be included in any anthology of the jewels of the

English language. We do not pray that we may avoid the temporal, escaping from life in the name of some misguided quest for safety or purity. We pray instead that we may live in such a way that we never lose sight of an eternal reality hidden in the heart of the temporal. The eternal is not something that exists apart; as human beings, our only entry point to the eternal is by way of the temporal. As Dag Hammerskold once said, "The road to holiness necessarily passes through the world of action." Our prayer is that with God's grace we may know and live this truth.

Let your continual mercy, O Lord, cleanse and defend your Church; and, because it cannot continue in safety without your help, protect and govern it always by your goodness; through Jesus Christ our Lord, who lives and reigns with you and the Holy Spirit, one God, for ever and ever.

IN GEORGE Bernard Shaw's *The Black Girl in Search of God* there is a moment when she meets Saint Peter. He comes towards her carrying on his back an enormous cathedral. She is worried about him because he is not exactly in the first blush of youth, and says to him, "Isn't that terribly heavy for you?" But Peter laughs and replies, "Oh dear, no, not at all." Then he gives her a sly grin. "You see, it's all made of paper." Then he goes lightly on his way.

It is a commonplace of our lives to criticize the church. Without this luxury, much Christian conversation would come to a grinding halt! But if we are wise, we will get up from our session of criticism and continue to offer our devotion to this same church. One very good precedent that all Christians have for this is no less than our Lord himself. Quite obviously he was under no illusions about the institutional religion of his time, but he did not use that as a reason to withdraw himself from participation in its life.

This realism about the church is implicit in the first sentence of the collect, which begins, "Let your continual mercy, O Lord, cleanse and defend your Church." It is a magnificently balanced petition, at once totally free from illusions and at the same time gentle and compassionate. We do not merely ask God for mercy for the church; we ask for continual mercy. In other words, we are squarely facing the fact that the church has been and always will be in need of that inexhaustible mercy!

So often Christians forget that we will always have the treasures of God in the very earthly vessel we call the church. So many Christians feel that they would become deeply involved if only some wonderful church of the future came into being, while many others claim they would become deeply involved if only some wonderful church of the past is restored! Meanwhile the real church, the only church we have, lives and struggles and witnesses, and God continues to give grace to those who commit themselves joyfully and determinedly to its service.

The prayer then reminds us that the church cannot continue in safety without God's help. Why? Because of our human nature. Our frequent disappointments and rages with the church are all the more distressing to us because at a deep level, we know that the humanity of the church is no more and no less than our own humanity. Furthermore, the church is the victim of our own inconsistencies. Let the Church adopt a social or political stance about some issue involving God's peace and justice, and we will tend to support or condemn according to our own particular political preferences. Rarely will it occur to us that the decision of the assembled Body might possess insights worth our serious consideration. Yet with another part of our minds we claim to believe that this same assembled people is the Body of Christ and that our Lord indwells the church.

To speak of the church's "safety" is not to imply that it should walk only in safe places pursuing safe policies and entrusting itself to safe people, even though some of the best-intentioned people would have it so. This prayer implies quite the opposite. It asks that the church may continue to witness courageously, sometimes even at considerable risk to itself and to those individuals who dare to speak and to act in its name, but that with God's help both it and they may do so in safety.

We are offering much the same petition when we ask that the church may be protected and governed by God's goodness. Again the implication of the term "protect" is surely the same as in the term "safety." Surely we are praying not so much for safety from various eventualities as safety for various possibilities, not so much for protection from life but protection for life.

Finally, we pray that God may govern the church. In past years those of us who rented cars on trips abroad would sometimes found to our annoyance that the rental firm had placed what it called a "governor" on the car, which allowed it to go only at a certain maximum speed. This is precisely the kind of "governor" some would like to see in the life of the church! Even as we may smile at this, we have to admit that there certainly have been times when the providence of God has prevented the church from careening into real danger. Some feel that it has already done so! Whatever our thoughts may be about these things, our prayer will remain the same, that God may be the "governor" of the church in ordering its life, its goals, and its standards, and challenge it always to become more than it is at any given time.

*Grant to us, Lord, we pray, the spirit to think and do always
those things that are right, that we, who cannot exist without
you, may by you be enabled to live according to your will;
through Jesus Christ our Lord, who lives and reigns with
you and the Holy Spirit, one God, for ever and ever.*

IN THE quietness of the Irish countryside the cathedral
stands amid the high grass and the mossy leaning
headstones. The small village is called Cloyne, the
cathedral's patron saint is Colman. Here George Berkeley,
bishop and philosopher, made his contribution to the world's
thought. Years later a nineteenth-century wag would whim-
sically express Berkeley's position about the nature of reality
in the following lines:

> A philosopher pondered that God
> Must find it exceedingly odd
> That a sycamore tree
> Still continues to be,
> When there's no one about in the quad.

To which a few days later this reply came:

> Dear Sir, your astonishment's odd.
> I am always about in the quad.
> And that's why the tree
> Still continues to be,
> Since observed by, yours faithfully, God.

The collect to some extent echoes this thought when it
has us pray to God as "we, who cannot exist without you."
In fact, one of the fascinating things about this statement is
that we no longer have to reach back to another century to
talk about it. Suddenly, as the twentieth century draws to a
close, we are seeing questions about the existence of the
universe once again inviting a response in language that is
becoming suspiciously like "God" language. We have come a
very long way since that moment in the nineteenth century
when one of Napoleon's scientists was explaining to the

Emperor the exciting new scientific probes that were in progress. The Emperor enquired, "Then where does God come into all this?" only to receive the famous reply, "Sire, God is not necessary to this hypothesis."

Much has happened since that conversation took place. Newtonian physics has passed into Einsteinian physics and both in turn are being superseded by quantum physics. In this particular pilgrim's progress of the western mind, our companions and guides have been the great physicists, Einstein himself, Nihls Bohr, and Eisenberg, to name a few. Some say the greatest of them all may be the comparatively young Stephen Hawking of Cambridge, England.

As we move more and more deeply into the mysterious realms of physics and microbiology, a strange and wonderful thing is happening. We can hear it expressed in a single sentence towards the end of Hawking's bestseller, *A Brief History of Time*. The scientist is talking about his search for a unified theory, and he writes, "Even if there is only one possible unified theory, it is just a set of rules and equations. What is it that breathes fire into the equations and makes a universe for them to describe?" We hear very clearly a question about transcendence. The question tentatively probes what the collect unequivocally states: Lord, "we...cannot exist without you."

The prayer itself is primarily concerned with God as the source of spiritual life. What we ask from God as the source of all spirituality is "the spirit to think and do always those things that are right." As always in Christian prayer, the request is not merely for guidance of our thinking but also for grace to act upon our thinking. If we look at the whole series of collects for the season after Pentecost, we discover an interesting thing. We come to realize that our praying for the grace of God is never complete if we ask only for grace in our thinking and believing. Every time we pray this, either for our own lives or for the life of the church, we also pray for grace to translate both thinking and believing into action. Quite obviously the link is essential to a healthy spirituality. Equally obvious is the fact that, since this insight is voiced so frequently in the Prayer Book, it must indicate there is a great need to emphasize it!

"The spirit to think and do always those things that are right." The phrase raises indulgent smiles in some. Is it not rather naive to think in terms of right and wrong in a universe of relativity? Christians must never bow to this attitude. Certainly the quest for what is right is infinitely more difficult and complex in our time and society, but to say this is a far cry from denying the existence of right and wrong. Our prayer for right thinking and right action is a categorical rejection of this denial.

Why must a Christian insist on the reality of right and wrong, however difficult it may be to define them? Because for a Christian there exists a source of reality other than our experienced reality. Without this ultimate source of reality, neither we nor anything else would exist. This ultimate reality whom we call God possesses a will. That will is a perfect will. Mysterious? Yes. Awe-inspiring? Yes. Inscrutable? Yes. The perfect will of God is all of these things. But for a Christian there is one thing more. This will has been revealed in Jesus Christ. Our prayer is to glimpse this ultimate reality and this perfect will so that we may see, not merely our way, but the way.

Almighty God, you have given your only Son to be for us a sacrifice for sin, and also an example of godly life: Give us grace thankfully to receive the fruits of his redeeming work, and to follow daily in the blessed steps of his most holy life; through Jesus Christ your Son our Lord, who lives and reigns with you and the Holy Spirit, one God, now and for ever.

FATHER BROWN was an elderly Anglo-Catholic priest of the old English school, charming when he wished to be, blunt and authoritarian when he deemed it necessary. Over the rood screen of the church he had placed a large representation of the crucifixion. One day a few of his more daring parishioners approached him with a problem. The problem was the large crucifix looming above their lives at Mass. Father Brown asked them gently why it was a problem. They hesitated, and then one of them said, "It offends me." Father Brown looked at them witheringly for a moment and said icily, "That is exactly what it is meant to do."

At the heart of Christian faith, at the heart of all liturgy, personal prayer, Scripture, and church life, there stands a single dominant image. It is the image of a human being impaled on a cross. Because we can become impervious to its power by overfamiliarity, we find it all too easy to forget that the central image of Christian faith symbolizes on the one hand brutality, betrayal, and hatred, and on the other integrity, faithfulness, goodness, and an almost unimaginable capacity for selflessness. The mystery is that both sets of polarities exist within our humanity.

It is important to note this mystery as we look at this prayer. Among all the collects of the season after Pentecost, this is the only one that has as its focus the moment of our Lord's sacrificial death. This particular prayer, coupled with that of Holy Cross Day a few weeks later, gives us all an opportunity to stand at the cross in a way we rarely do (at least in terms of liturgy) except on Good Friday.

So much powerful and salutary Christian reflection is neglected because we think it too obvious and familiar. The trap in this attitude is that it can prevent us reflecting on those things at the very heart of our faith. Take the phrase "to be for us a sacrifice for sin." It takes only a moment to say it or chant it in liturgy. However its depth of meaning is so awesome that if we were to call for a dead silence immediately after this phrase, we would not be giving it any more than its due. The reason this human being hangs here is nothing less than my life style, my moral choices, my ambiguous and shadowed humanity. Our Lord hangs here for us. As Mrs. Alexander puts it with such deceptive simplicity in her hymn,

> We do not know, we cannot tell
> What pains he had to bear,
> But we believe it was for us
> He hung and suffered there.

This prayer also speaks of our Lord "as an example of godly life." In contemplating his life we move now from darkness to light, from obscenity to magnificence. Instead of having to look upon something that revolts and appalls us—chiefly, let us remember, because it is of our own doing—we are now confronted by something that attracts and awes us. Again, just as we are revolted by the link between the dying figure and our own involvement in his death, we are attracted and awed by the life of our Lord, because in a mysterious way it too is linked with our lives. We look at him and we realize that we are looking at our own humanity transformed. He walks among us as the humanity we were created to be. Here is the ultimacy of which we are only the part. Here also is the ultimacy that never ceases to call us in our deepest being, inspiring us, motivating us, and, in our finest moments, transforming us.

Once again in the lovely rhythms of this prayer we return to the first image of the cross. "Give us grace," we pray, "to receive thankfully the fruits of his redeeming work." The fact is we can never find adequate language for the fruits of our Lord's work. What does he do for me? Above all he gives me back my deepest and most real self.

What that might mean I have tried to express above, but the very language I use is the language of a particular time and culture, as it always must be. Yet we must also speak of a great mystery in language that is timeless. By his dying, his rising, and his ascension, our Lord lifts my earthbound humanity to heaven. What does it mean to say this? We can try to explain it, but we will never fully unravel the mystery. Such things are mysteries, not in the sense that we can know nothing about them, but that we can never exhaust their meaning for our lives. One thing certain is that this insight of Christian faith, this glorious image of human nature lifted by our Lord to the highest level, returns to modern men and women that wonderful vision of the infinite value of human nature so diminished and impoverished in recent decades by the anonymity of mass living, the slaughter of repeated wars, the rise of urban violence, and the paradox of medical technologies that offer themselves for our healing, but at the same time threaten our humanity.

We pray that we may "follow daily in the blessed steps of his most holy life." Once again we hear the familiar rhythm of being and doing, receiving and responding, thinking and acting. We are called to respond to a life lived. Our response is to set out to live our lives on the terms we see in our Lord's living of his. Because we cannot do this completely, we also pray for grace to continue to follow daily. Once again we hear the wisdom of the word "daily." It is our Lord's legacy to us in his own prayer. Our Lord knows our human nature very well. He asks for no vast promises to follow forever. Our nature cannot give such promises. Instead, our Lord asks us for one day at a time. Given his grace, we can.

One Foundation   Proper 16

Grant, O merciful God, that your Church, being gathered together in unity by your Holy Spirit, may show forth your power among all peoples, to the glory of your Name; through Jesus Christ our Lord, who lives and reigns with you and the Holy Spirit, one God, for ever and ever.

ONE AFTERNOON in the emergency section of a large city hospital a single vivid image from the book of the prophet Isaiah came alive for me. A doctor was attending an elderly man who had come in with some injury. They spoke together for a while and then the doctor prepared to leave. As she did so, she hurriedly took a pen and scribbled something on her own hand. When asked later why she had done this, she revealed the fact that the patient happened to be one of her own in her general practice and therefore she wished to keep his name in her mind. In her hurry she scribbled the first few letters of his name on her hand rather than search for paper or risk forgetting it again.

This incident brought to mind a beautiful image that describes the love of God for Israel. It is in the book of Isaiah, a moment of magnificent insight about the nature of God. The prophet says that the name of Israel is written in the palm of God's hand. Surely this lovely statement can also be an apt and moving description of the relationship between God and the church.

"Grant, O merciful God, that your Church...." We should pause here before reading further. The important words are "your Church." They communicate to us the love of God. It is significant that in a number of the collects for this season, we hear again and again the possessive "your" to describe the relationship between God and the church. As well as the expression "your Church," we find ourselves praying for "your household" and "your people." Such language is even more important in an age when this same church can so easily become the focus of our anger and frustration. An unconscious hatred of the church can even develop especially among those of us most involved in its institutional life.

All too often our language for the church has about it the coldness of the organizational, the bureaucratic. We almost always speak of "the" church, "the institutional church," and other such phrases. These are valid terms, but we need to be aware of certain precious values and graces such language omits. From my Irish childhood I remember the frequency with which a farmer would refer to "the wife," so much so that one farmer, on being asked by a bank manager for his wife's Christian name, had to go out to the waiting horse and buggy to ask her! A simple old anecdote (and by the way, quite true) but one that points to the need for a language of affection and ownership of the church wherever possible.

In Samuel John Stone's great hymn "The Church's One Foundation", we hear the words

> Though with a scornful wonder
> Men see her sore oppressed.

As we read these lines we need to realize that one of the sad ironies of church life today is that "scornful" describes the attitude of many Christians towards the church that has nurtured and fostered them. That is another reason why we need to emphasize the significance of the lovely opening phrase of this prayer. To return for a moment to Stone's great hymn, perhaps the reason for its undying popularity is the very fact that it speaks tenderly and lovingly of the church, while at the same time fully acknowledging the struggle it always has to reflect God's glory while witnessing to it among the complexities of history and society.

"Grant...that your Church, being gathered together in unity by your Holy Spirit...." In an age of transition, full of both threat and promise, offering endless options for policies and decisions, it is inevitable that the unity of Christian communal life will be severely tested in every group, every congregation, every diocese, and every province of the church. Here we have yet another reason for choosing carefully the words and images we use for God's church.

A valuable insight we need to share with each other in the life of today's church is the fact that Christians, both clergy and lay, can so easily forget that every other structure in contemporary life is faced with the same challenges the church faces. All structures of institutional life—economic, educational, political, and medical—are facing the same high levels of frustration, complexity, and ambiguity that Christians experience in their church. We are all living in a contemporary wilderness. It is not the domain merely of Christians! In such a time, unity at every level of our church life is a blessing we should be prepared to seek very seriously. Frustration, anger, cynicism are the vicious enemies of unity. They are among those hostile spirits intent on destroying the work of the Holy Spirit. As the collect implies, without this Spirit the church of God is powerless to witness in society.

Source of Our Nurture   Proper 17

*Lord of all power and might, the author and giver of all good
things: Graft in our hearts the love of your name; increase in
us true religion; nourish us with all goodness; and bring
forth in us the fruit of good works; through Jesus Christ our
Lord, who lives and reigns with you and the Holy Spirit, one
God, for ever and ever.*

WITH EACH passing year, as the worlds of physics and
microbiology produce new wonders almost by the month,
there is a question that more and more voices in many dis-
ciplines are asking. One form in which we hear it asked is
"Why should the universe exist at all?"

This is a new question, at least new to the particular
scientific age that was born in the late seventeenth century
and has formed our world. It is of more than passing interest
that the formation of the Royal Society in London and the
composition of the 1662 Prayer Book are separated by less
than two decades. These few centuries have tended to ask
"How" questions rather than "Why" questions. The word for
such "Why" questions has almost been forgotten except by
theologians, but it is returning to western culture. The word
teleology comes from the Greek word *telos*, meaning "end" in
the sense of "purpose." We are beginning once again to ask
teleological questions, and Christians should get to know the
word because its return is good news for the strengthening of
the whole faith enterprise in western society.

The Bible is very much about teleological questions.
Among the themes of the New Testament that we have long
tended to neglect are those about the end or the purpose of
things. Very early on, great Christian minds, Paul and John
among them, began to realize that it was not enough to think
back to a remembered Jesus. They also had to probe the future, searching for the end or final purpose of the events that
had happened among them on so deceptively tiny a stage.
We see Paul doing this in the claims he makes for our Lord as
he writes to the community at Colossae. Jesus, he states, is
"the first born of all creation; for in him all things...were

created" (Colossians 1:15-16). Once again, as he writes to the community in Rome, Paul becomes universal in the scope of his thinking. "The whole creation," he writes, "has been groaning in travail together until now" (Romans 8:22). Creation may be in pain and conscious of great frustration, but this pain, Paul maintains, is the pain of birthing. In the book of Revelation, John paints the magnificent panorama of the Holy City "coming down out of heaven from God" (Revelation 21:2).

Such is the substance of the opening words of this prayer. God is named as "the author and giver." In God creation finds its source and its reason for being. About God two huge intuitions are shared. First, in God power and goodness coexist; second, God not only creates, or "authors," but also gives over what has been created. We are the recipients of this creation. This last is an insight Christians need to express again and again to an age searching for a spiritual basis for its new ecological awareness.

Now, having looked at the opening words of the prayer through a cosmic lens, we look at the creativity of the "Lord of all power" within our own spiritual experience. Such has always been the wonder of the God of the Bible, maker of galaxies but dweller in the human heart, cosmic and far flung but also intimate and near. When we look through this lens we see in terms of our own lives something that is known to be increasingly true of creation itself. We see that all is process. Just as God is not only Maker, but also Lover and Keeper of creation (to use the language of Julian of Norwich), so God is both the one who grafts in our hearts the love of His holy name and the one who increases and nourishes and brings forth the fruit of good works (to paraphrase the collect).

The moment of the conversion of a Christian is the moment of grafting. That grafting is God's. But that moment is the beginning of a process, if we are prepared to open ourselves to it. Our spiritual life is not a state of being, in the sense of something that is fixed, any more than our bodies can stay in a fixed state. Change is our normal experience physically, but this is no more than an outward and visible sign of an inward and spiritual reality. "True religion" is religion that increases. "To live is to change," wrote John Henry Newman, "and to be perfect is to have changed often." Without growing and maturing, religion diminishes and finally dies. Its death can be concealed as a sad remembrance of things past. To say this is not for a moment to belittle the power and even sacredness of memory and tradition. Memory, as with every human gift, can be healthy and creative, or neurotic and destructive. Memory is one of the spirits we need to test constantly in today's church.

As our religion increases, we need to be nourished. Our prayer is for that nourishment that comes from God. Finally, we pray that the new creation or "grafting" that God has worked in us, now that it has been given the nourishment to increase, may emerge into creative and faithful living. Once again we hear what is almost the chorus of the prayers for this season. Holiness achieves authenticity in holy living.

Root of Our Confidence   Proper 18

Grant us, O Lord, to trust in you with all our hearts; for, as you always resist the proud who confide in their own strength, so you never forsake those who make their boast of your mercy; through Jesus Christ our Lord, who lives and reigns with you and the Holy Spirit, one God, now and for ever.

ONE ANECDOTE always provokes some smiles. It is the story of a man who falls over the edge of a cliff and manages to grab a branch that stops his fall. Hanging in midair, he calls on God in desperation, "Is there anyone up there?" Eventually a voice says, "Let go of the branch." The man hangs there in dead silence for a few moments, looking up and then down at the yawning gulf beneath him. Finally he looks up and yells, "Is there anyone else up there?"

We always laugh at this point because we have just heard a perfect description of where we stand in this matter of being able to trust God.

The prayer has us ask, "Grant us, O Lord, to trust in you with all our hearts." Can we? Of course not. There are some great souls who rise to a tremendous level of trust in God, but for most of us our level of trust in God is limited. This is not said in the least bit harshly, but as a realistic and compassionate assessment of human trust.

The really extraordinary thing in our lives is the way in which we show trust in our everyday affairs. There are some people who have what can only be described as a deep trust in life itself. They trust that somehow it—whatever it is—will see them through. Consider the trust that we all have at some time or other placed in another human being. Admittedly this is frequently when we have no other choice, such as when we climb into a large machine and allow our bodies to be hurled across half the world at a height of five miles, all the time trusting in a group of people whom we usually know nothing about. Consider the trust a rock climber puts in a companion, or the trust both of them place in a piece of equipment.

What do we mean when we speak of trusting in God? Perhaps a good way of getting at this is to recall a moment as Jesus hung on the cross. At some point in those ghastly hours someone yelled out, "He trusted in God. Let God deliver him if he will have him." Actually that hateful and vindictive shout says a great deal about the idea of trust held by the person who yelled it. In that view, the result of trusting in God should be that God keeps one from all harm and failure. Presumably, if that does not happen, one is entitled to stop trusting.

Obviously this is not our Lord's view of trust. It is precisely because he trusted totally in God that he opened himself to the possibility of that very suffering. On what is such immense trust based? It is based on the belief that if one commits oneself and one's life to God, then whatever happens—and this is the point—*whatever* happens—it is not a reason for ceasing to trust. Instead, it calls forth an even deeper trust. Trust of this kind, the kind of trust we see all through our Lord's life, is the capacity to live life as something that is held in hands other than our own, and to be convinced that those hands will always bear us up and will never finally betray us.

The prayer says that God "always resist[s] the proud who confide in their own strength." This petition does not say that God resents human self-confidence and sets out to crush it, but that anyone who insists that he or she can of their own strength and ability always remain in control of life will surely discover otherwise. This is even more certain if someone is contemptuous of those who seek the help of God and others in living. This is what our Lord is telling us in the story of the Pharisee who boasts of his own moral achievements, while the publican behind him acknowledges his own spiritual poverty. In terms of this prayer, it is the Pharisee who confides in what he perceives to be his own strength.

God never forsakes those "who make their boast of [his] mercy." Simply stated, the prayer is telling us that self-confidence is without question a Christian virtue, but the important question is where that self-confidence is rooted. Belief in Jesus Christ does not involve eradication of the self. Our

Lord offers us a relationship with himself, not so that we become less ourselves but that we become so. His gift to us is the fulfilment of the self. What is significant for a Christian is that there is a descent past the self into a greater self. That greater self, which is the source of all selfhood, is God. Such self-confidence is unshakable; even if the human self itself is shaken and battered, it can draw from deeper wells than its own resilience. When Jesus said to his friends, "I have food to eat of which you do not know," this is what he was saying.

The End of All Our Striving   Proper 19

O God, because without you we are not able to please you,
mercifully grant that your Holy Spirit may in all things
direct and rule our hearts; through Jesus Christ our Lord,
who lives and reigns with you and the Holy Spirit, one God,
now and for ever.

RABINDRINATH TAGORE, the Indian poet who wrote
with great insight and beauty in the earlier decades of this
century, tells of a man who lived in a house on the edge of a
great forested valley. Very early one morning he looked
across the valley and saw a blazing golden door on the far
side. Greatly excited, he set off from his own small house,
made his way down the side of the valley, crossed the river
that flowed through it, and then climbed up the other side,
eagerly searching for the golden door. Eventually, late in the
day, he arrived at a small tumbledown shack rather like his
own dwelling. Its solitary window was dark and even cob-
webbed. Disappointed and very weary, he sat down to rest
before beginning the long journey home. He knew he had to
hurry to beat the darkness that would quickly fall after sunset. Then something caught his eye. There on the far side of
the valley from him, where he knew his own shack with its
solitary window to be, was a great golden door blazing and
beckoning and calling him home.

Most of us are rather like that seeker in the ways we understand or misunderstand the relationship that exists between ourselves and God. In the book *In His Spirit* Richard
Hauser, a Jesuit priest, provides a valuable insight. He maintains that in western spirituality there is a misunderstanding
that has cost us dear. It is the illusion that the self is outside
God, whereas, Hauser maintains, the biblical model is that of
the self *in* God. Because of this misunderstanding, he suggests, we tend to think of God and the grace of God and the
action of God's Holy Spirit as distant realities to be searched
for and relentlessly pursued. They are like the golden door, a
shimmering distant loveliness and power we constantly set
out for, not realizing that they are within.

Hauser says that the insight we need to recapture is that we already possess the Holy Spirit of God. Yes, it certainly is beyond and outside us, around us and through all creation, but it is also within us. As the seeker of the golden door came to realize that the golden door was set into the shabby walls of his own shack, so we need to discover that the glory of God is within our humanity. God is an "Emmanuel God," a God with us.

The collect has us pray, "O God, because without you we are not able to please you...." What might it mean to seek to please God? To serve God? To do God's will? To be God's steward? In all these ways I am searching, journeying, probing, and striving. How do I do the will of God in such and such a situation? How do I exercise stewardship of my gifts or possessions in such and such circumstances? Even as I search in this way for God's will, even as I open myself to become aware of the touch of God, I need to know also that everything I seek I have already found! All that I seek to possess I already possess! Because even as I set out to please God, it is from God's Holy Spirit that I receive the motivation to set out on my search!

Thousands of years ago a poet expressed this lovely and precious paradox. We call this poem Psalm 139. "Where can I go from your Spirit?" the poet asks. He then gives us images of journeying and searching through all space and time. Everywhere God is already there. Why? Because, as the poet says, God "knit me together in my mother's womb." I carry God within me even as I search for God. A paradox? Yes. A mystery? Yes. But a paradox and a mystery that is brimming over with good news.

"Mercifully grant that your Holy Spirit may in all things direct and rule our hearts." First, it is important to remember in this petition that in Scripture (and therefore in liturgy) the "heart" almost always means the totality of one's being, the very core of the self. We are not praying that God may direct and rule merely our feelings, but that God may direct feeling, thinking, and acting. The petiton goes further. God is a God who wishes to direct us "in all things." This means in all aspects of our living, professional as well as personal life, relationships, sexuality, finance, intellect, our use of time, everything. Is this an unreasonable demand of God? Surely it must be if our typically western understanding of religion is true. For many people Christian faith is an option to be taken up and dropped at whim. It is a completely private section of life. If this is true, then to pray that God may occupy all of life is unreasonable! But the good news is that once we have realized that God does indeed occupy the totality of creation and the totality of our human experience, then all thoughts of unreasonableness disappear. The indwelling of God in the world and the indwelling of God in our own being becomes the most reasonable thing in the world. As an added bonus, it becomes a joyful aspect of being alive.

The Lens of Heaven   Proper 20

Grant us, Lord, not to be anxious about earthly things, but to love things heavenly; and even now, while we are placed among things that are passing away, to hold fast to those that shall endure; through Jesus Christ our Lord, who lives and reigns with you and the Holy Spirit, one God, for ever and ever.

NOT VERY long before he died, Peter Sellers applied his great comic genius to making a movie called "Being There." Sellers played a classic English manservant who has lived all his life behind the wall of an estate. He knows nothing of life except what he has seen on television; for him, reality is what passes for life on the screen. So nothing in life is ever resolved for him; things just fade away, as they do on the screen. He is totally detached from reality. The irony of this vast ignorance of real life is that people begin to mistake it for a mysterious and enigmatic wisdom. He begins to be sought out as a guru, because his detachment from life is mistaken for involvement in life.

There are certain people one comes across who possess detachment even while they are very much in the midst of life. This may sound strange. Detachment obviously removes us from life. Yet in some people we can discern a peculiar ability to be totally involved in life yet somehow free of its many entanglements, and in that sense to be detached. Perhaps it is something of this we seek when we speak sometimes of longing for a simpler lifestyle, one that sees us less enslaved by the accumulation of things, less dependent on the endless flood of activities life offers us. In fact those who say they are in search of a simpler lifestyle are often very vibrant people, aware of everything going on in their world, thinking always about possibilities and consequences, and highly motivated to live their lives creatively. It is to capture this double gift, the gift of detachment from many things around us coupled with the gift of rich involvement in life, that we speak of someone as detached in the midst of life.

There is another way to be detached from the many entanglements of life. We can simply be incapable of handling them. We are detached because we are too frightened or too immature to accept responsibility for living. There is an element of this in Sellers' character in "Being There." Again, we can be detached from life because we hate it. It may have hurt us too much, or we may have come to think of life as in some way evil. None of these motivations are healthy and certainly none can be the basis of a healthy spirituality, which begins by learning to love life and the world and the whole creation. It grows through the realization that we receive every iota as a gift, and it fully matures by our developing the capacity to accept it all gratefully and, when life requires it, to let it all go gracefully.

Is this easy to accomplish? Far from it. That sequence of developing our relationship with the world around us is also our struggle to become a mature and balanced human being. Our struggle is to be involved with life, not to be consumed by it—to be capable of committing ourselves deeply to it, while also detaching ourselves from it. In other words, life can be wonderful and precious and worth our giving everything we have and are to it precisely because it is more than merely itself. Behind and beyond it, hidden within it and threaded through every part of it, is the source of life. That source is God. People who have stumbled on this single great truth about life and about everything around them, including themselves, are the people who know the meaning of this prayer. They have prayed it, tried to live it, and have had their prayer bring a response in their experience.

We ask that we may not be "anxious about earthly things, but...love things heavenly." Far from being an impossible invitation to an utterly unreal stance to life, this petition is potentially healing for our attitudes towards daily living. There is not a word about spurning earthly things. There are a multitude of things in God's creation we can enjoy and savor and delight in, but the mysterious truth is that our enjoying, our savoring, and our delighting are possible only if we can become free of the fear of losing them.

We ask that we may "love things heavenly." This phrase is so many-faceted that we can only look at one of the faces of the jewel. There is a way of looking at things and people so that we do not merely look *at* them but *through* them. This looking through something or someone has nothing cruel or judgmental about it. We are talking about the gift of looking through things and people so as to see an aspect of heaven in them. As we look at them we seek the God-ness within them.

Jesus walked down the beach one day and saw a perfectly familiar scene. Weather made it impossible for the fishing crews to take out their boats on the lake, so they were using the time to mend the tears that constantly appeared in the nets. Jesus may have passed many men. He may even have lingered and chatted before passing on. But when he came to a fisherman named Peter, Jesus looked and saw the glint of heaven in him that would become Peter the apostle.

So our petition in this prayer becomes a request to see the aspect of heaven that is hidden in a flower or a chalice of wine or the faces of a congregation. The best reason for cultivating this way of perceiving is that it is the way God perceives us. The real source of the great mercy shown towards us lies in God's seeing through us with the most terrifying clarity, yet looking upon that glimmer of heaven within us as of more worth than our all-too-obvious earthiness.

Treasures Old and New   Proper 21

IF AN image in one of the collects triggers a scene out of
our own childhood, we should think twice before hastily
deciding to put the idea aside. We should stifle the instinct to
begin immediately to search for some adult response, or even
for something reassuringly intellectual! So, without apology,
here is how this particular prayer speaks vividly to at least
one child of God.

It is midafternoon in summertime. The suburban streets
are quiet, and a bunch of children are playing around. Suddenly there is a distant sound. It filters through the houses
and gardens, through the trees and the driveways. It is as
seductive as the voices of the sirens calling to Ulysses and his
crew. It is the music of the ice cream man.

All play stops instantly. There follows a mad dash home
to ask for some money, then a mad dash back, just in time to
see the gaily colored wagon turn the corner and come down
the street. All of us are running to it, around it, behind it,
proferring coins, calling out our choices, grabbing the extended cone, tasting, savoring, devouring, until the wagon
passes slowly on its way, turning the corner again as the
music fades, only to be heard in other streets where there will
be more "running to obtain" the promises that the music
makes.

Running to obtain God's promises is indeed a vivid
image, and the child in us wants to go on calling up childlike
images. Imagine folk running to Bible study, running up the
aisles in their eagerness to receive bread and wine, running
to reach some small secret place to be alone with God! Silly?
Maybe so, for some, but I suspect not in the least silly in the
eyes of God. That is why it is here in the collect.

There is another word in this prayer that evokes childhood, and it is the word used to name what a Christian should run to obtain: "treasure." Is any word more thrilling for the child in oneself? In the dwindling world where Gaelic is still a living language, one of the most loving ways one can refer to another person is to call him or her *mo stor*, meaning "my treasure." Perhaps as Christians we would do well to look with new—or perhaps in reality very old—eyes at a number of things and realize the extent to which they can be treasures for us. Look at the Bible on the lectern, the community of faces in the stained glass, the cross or crucifix at the center of our vision, the face of someone beloved beside us, or someone we are remembering in prayer, the shining chalice on the altar or credence table, the soaring beauty of an anthem, the loveliness of a poem become a hymn, some beloved prayer. Look at them and see them as the treasures of God poured out in profligate generosity. So often all such things remain buried treasures, buried under over-familiarity, buried by disagreements, by boredom, by world-weariness, or, saddest of all, buried under an angry nostalgia for past things treasured jealously only because they are past.

Saint Paul would respond enthusiastically to the image of running in this prayer. He was fond of evoking the scene in the city arena where athletes ran to obtain a prize—perhaps we could say treasure. Paul offers the image to us as the pattern of a lively and eager spirituality that is never satisfied with a passive, merely receptive stance to the things of God. Such an attitude is not interested in waiting for the treasures of God to be presented to us in neat institutionalized packages and programs. Paul and all the other saints would have us listen eagerly for God's promises, hear them, and then run to obtain them.

"Grant us the fullness of your grace" that we may run to partake. Once again we are reminded of God being all in all to us and within us. We actually ask God for the grace to pursue God so that we may partake of God! God at the beginning, God throughout the journey, God the end of the journey. Again and again in the runes and the prayers of Celtic spirituality we hear this pattern:

God be in my head, and in my understanding.
God be in mine eyes, and in my looking.
God be in my mouth, and in my speaking.
God be in my heart, and in my thinking.
God be at mine end, and at my departing.

Something of the same mystery is seen and felt in the experiences of the disciples after our Lord's resurrection. There is a sense of his being behind them in Jerusalem, with them on the road, and before them in Galilee. Come to think of it, they did a lot of running! Mary ran. John ran. Peter ran. It's highly likely the two friends on their way back from Emmaus broke into a run from time to time. What would it mean for us to run to obtain God's promises?

Love Bids Us Sit and Eat   Proper 22

Almighty and everlasting God, you are always more ready to
hear than we to pray, and to give more than we either desire
or deserve: Pour upon us the abundance of your mercy, for-
giving those things of which our conscience is afraid, and
giving us those good things for which we are not worthy to
ask, except through the merits and the mediation of Jesus
Christ our Savior; who lives and reigns with you and the
Holy Spirit, one God for ever and ever.

ON THE 11th of September 1522 Sir Thomas More wrote
a short letter to his daughter Margaret. Obviously she had
asked him to send her some money, and in his reply More
wrote, "You ask for money, my dear Margaret, with too
much bashfulness and timidity, since you are asking from a
father who is eager to give....As it is, I send only what you
have asked, but would have added more....So the sooner you
spend this money well, and the sooner you ask for more, you
will be sure of pleasing your father."

We human beings are strange and complex. We claim
that we believe in and follow Jesus Christ as our Lord, but
when he tells us that to find his kingdom we must become as
a child, what do we do? We fight it tooth and nail.

Consider the statement about God with which this
prayer opens. "God," we are told, is "more ready to hear
than we to pray." I can't help suggesting that if the truth
were known, this statement should come as very good news
to most of us—considering the regularity and frequency of
our prayers! When we were children we may well have
asked a parent how it was possible for God to listen to the
prayers of everybody. If we were lucky, our father or mother
may have communicated to us the great truth that God can
hear the prayers of everyone at the same time. If we are wise
we will recall this insight now that we are adult, for when we
do, it gives us a portrait of the reality of God.

Yet another aspect of that portrait is shown to us in our
Lord's life and ministry. Again and again in his parables, and
most clearly in his own passion, our Lord holds up for us not

only the portrait of a loving God, but of a God who is loving in a way that risks vulnerability. The father of the prodigal son does not wait for his son to come home. Implicit in the story is the image of the father standing on the flat rooftop or on the nearby hillside or at the bend in the road, always more ready to wait than the son is to return, always more ready to give and give, even if the recipient has already taken everything that is his right and far more than he deserves!

All of this may seem very obvious and the stuff of Sunday school lessons, but it is remarkable how difficult it is for us in western culture to be joyfully aware that God is for us, that grace and love are not desirable things God grudgingly doles out in the smallest possible portions to those who have won grudging approval for their performance in life!

An episode from family life: a daughter and her husband come to her father and ask apologetically for the loan of a few thousand dollars. Knowing that it is not easy for them to do this, and also knowing that the reason for the loan is a sensible and reasonable one, the father takes his daughter aside in a private moment, puts his hand on her shoulders, and looks her in the eyes. He says, "Will you please try to understand that I want, I really want, to give this to you. It is a joy to be able to do it for you. In fact my only worry is whether I am giving you enough." In this moment in family life, as we saw in the letter of Thomas More to his daughter, lies the good news of this prayer.

Look again at the last thing the father says. "My only worry is whether I am giving you enough." This is exactly what we hear God saying to us in this prayer's next petition: forgive us "those things of which our conscience is afraid," and give us "those good things for which we are not worthy to ask." Unbelievable though it may be, the prayer is pointing us towards a God who says to us, "You are not asking enough. You haven't got the self-confidence, or you are too guilty, or you don't trust me enough to ask for what I want to give you. Why not dare to ask me and see?"

Again, if we look at the father of the prodigal son, we see this same overflowing generosity. The son doesn't ask for a robe. The father flings the best one available over his shoulder. The son doesn't dare ask for a meal; he is given a feast. He asks for no more than mere acceptance; he receives a celebration of his homecoming. Everything that guilt tries to silence, love utters. The prodigal, and we ourselves, are both quite correct. We deserve nothing. But we are not in the realm of deserving; we are in the realm of love. Why this generosity of God? Because before the prodigal comes home, and before we turn to God in our poor and unworthy prayers, something has happened. In both cases we have been preceded home. In the case of the prodigal son, love came home before him—if only in the sense that his father's love had never left home. That is the love that allowed the welcome to be given. In our case, when we unworthily and tardily return home, we have been preceded home by our Lord. He has already spoken for us in the most eloquent way of all by dying for us.

So when we arrive before God in our spiritual rags, full of profuse apologies and pathetic hopes, our apologies are silenced and the hope we did not even dare to hope is fulfilled. No one has ever put it more beautifully than George Herbert in his poem "Love":

> ...Let my shame
> Go where it doth deserve.
> And know you not, says Love, who bore the blame?
> My dear, then I will serve.
> You must sit down, says Love, and taste my meat:
> So I did sit and eat.

Called to Co-Creation   Proper 23

*Lord, we pray that your grace may always precede and follow
us, that we may continually be given to good works; through
Jesus Christ our Lord, who lives and reigns with you and the
Holy Spirit, one God, now and for ever.*

As ANYONE who has traveled in countries with long his-
tories knows, guides can sometimes overdo their historical
connections. There is an old story told of a group of tourists
being taken around the Vatican by an over-zealous guide.
When some hens were driven across the path of the group,
the guide halted the tourists, pointed dramatically at the
hens, and announced that these very hens were descended
from the cock that crowed at Saint Peter's betrayal of Christ!
There was dead silence among the weary travelers, and then
a rather exasperated voice from the group asked, "Do they
lay good eggs?"

It's a good question, and quite a reasonable one to ask.
It's the kind of question the writer of the letter to James
would appreciate. His criteria for things, especially about
faith, was whether or not it produced results. This is also
what our prayer is about. In the collects of the season after
Pentecost, no theme sounds more consistently or frequently
than the necessity not only of our believing in God, but also
of our serving God. Gradually the recurrence of this teaching
makes us realize that it would be better for us not to believe
in the first place if we are not going to move from belief to
some kind of service or action.

All through the Bible we hear a real concern about belief
that is devoid of action. The prophets reserve their deepest
contempt for those who meticulously observe the worship of
God but are quite content to live opulently amid poverty and
injustice. "Take away from me the noise of your songs,"
shouts Amos, "but let justice roll down like waters, and
righteousness like an everflowing stream" (Amos 5:23-24). In
the New Testament, the apostle James is a voice whose blunt,
crisp words sum things up very clearly: "Faith by itself, if it
has no works, is dead" (James 2:17). In the letters of John we

hear the same dismissing of people who profess to love God but quite obviously have no concern about the human need around them. When we have heard this theme again and again in the collects, we begin to become aware of a variation on this theme. Not only do we ourselves worry that we might fall into the trap of professing a faith that does not pass into action, but it is also implied, if we may speak of God this way, that God too is anxious. Why is it so important to God that "we may continually be given to good works?" We have only to think of the long record of God's dealings with us in the Bible to see why.

The God of the Bible, the creator of our humanity, has quite clearly got a most extraordinary agenda for us in spite of our all-too-flawed humanity. The God of the Bible is a God who, whenever anything needs to be done, searches for a man or woman through whom to do it. In other words, it would seem that God has a very big stake in our willingness not only to say that we trust and love God, but also to prove that same trust and love in daily service. God wishes to use human thought, human imagination, human commitment— all our human gifts—in carrying out the divine purpose. No one has put this more succinctly than Saint Augustine of Hippo: "Without God we cannot, but without us God will not."

There is a word being used more and more today that beautifully expresses what seems to be God's loving purpose for us, and the word is "co-creator." God is calling us to be co-creators, the agents or stewards of God. More and more God seems to be inviting our humanity into the task of forming the future. The evidence for this is all around us. In medicine the knowledge and techniques being revealed to us almost daily allow us to make increasingly significant decisions about our own lives. In our relationship with the rest of the created order around us, we know only too well that from now on it is our own human decisions that will decide if there is to be a human future. In both of these areas, to name only two, we see something happening to our creatureliness. It is not that we are encroaching on what was formerly thought to be the domain of God, but we realize that in areas like genetic engineering we are actually being invited by God to accept an increasing responsibility and involvement in the tasks of creation.

Someone has said that there is a single word implied throughout the Bible that is all-important for us. We hear it in the differences between the apocalyptic voice and the prophetic voice in Scripture. The apocalyptic voice says to us, "The world is ending!" The prophetic voice says exactly the same thing, but adds one all-important word. That word is "unless." By bringing in that single word, the prophetic voice issues an invitation to us from God. We are invited to join in the "good work" of cooperating with God in the task of creation.

To see ourselves engaged in nothing less than the work of God in creation is to become sure of who we are in a world where more and more people ask questions about human identity. If it is true that I can join with God in the work of forming God's creation, then it follows very logically that the grace of God will, as this prayer tells me, both precede and follow me. If my whole objective is to align my will and my actions with those of God, then presumably my activity is of concern to God, and I can expect that my claim on God's grace will receive a most generous response.

Christ of the Nations   Proper 24

> Almighty and everlasting God, in Christ you have revealed
> your glory among the nations: Preserve the works of your
> mercy, that your Church throughout the world may per-
> severe with steadfast faith in the confession of your Name;
> through Jesus Christ our Lord, who lives and reigns with
> you and the Holy Spirit, one God, for ever and ever.

SOMETIMES, FOR reasons that are hard to define, a particular fact will shatter traditional views of reality. Consider
the distribution of Christians around the world. We tend to
have a traditional mental image of Christianity as being
centered in the western and highly developed world, the
First World. The reality is utterly different. There are now, for
instance, more Presbyterians in Korea than in Scotland, far
more Ugandan Anglicans in church on Sunday morning than
in England, more Muslims in Britain than Methodists.

None of these facts is in itself world-shattering. They are
merely specific changes in a massively changing world. But
they do serve to introduce us to the first petition of this
prayer: "God, in Christ you have revealed your glory among
the nations."

What is of particular interest about this prayer is that we
have left the personal, which is the domain of most of the
collects, and we are suddenly very much out in the structures
and cultures of the world. Of all the biblical writers, I suspect
Isaiah would feel most at home with this prayer; for him,
God is very much the God of the nations. The prophet compares the nations to a mere drop from a bucket, mere dust on
the scales of God. No one could accuse him of having too
small a God!

If the earliest Christians could look across today's world
and see that Christian faith has spread to every continent,
they would be amazed at the actual extent of the world but
probably not at the distribution of Christians throughout the
globe. Instead, they would regard this as no more than
obedience to our Lord's command. From the very beginning
Christian faith has rebelled against being limited to a single

country or culture. Whether we like it or not, and the truth is that there is these days a certain ambivalence about this, Christianity's inclination is to reach out and to spread. In the course of evangelization many things have been said and done that we regret today, and many methods have been used that we are not prepared to use today. But the fact remains that, by the beginning of the third Christian millennium, the followers and worshipers of Jesus Christ are to be found everywhere on the planet. At least in this institutional sense, our Lord has certainly revealed his glory among the nations.

Any consideration of "nations" begins with our own. We have to decide what we mean by saying that God in Christ has revealed divine glory in this nation. That is not saying for a moment that America is in some way favored by God over other nations. That this nation is rich in Christian tradition, Christian social assumptions, Christian symbolism, Christian church life, and Christian organizations is merely to accept an even greater responsibility before God for our stewardship of these things. We may well have our questions about the extent to which much of this Christian practice is no more than nominal, but such things do constitute a judgment on us, in the sense of a test. We still have to prove ourselves worthy of them.

To live through the recent extraordinary changes in eastern Europe is to have witnessed an event probably unprecedented in the western world since the French Revolution. Before our astonished eyes a new political reality emerged in country after country, but it soon became clear that what we were seeing was more than political. It was also a spiritual event. Even more precisely, what unfolded was to no small degree a resurrection of Christian roots not visible for almost half a century, roots that had weathered the long winter of a system implacably hostile to Christian faith and thought and practice.

We should not easily forget the part played by the church in Poland. We need to note the fact that the East German crowds that spilled into the streets of Leipzig to begin the marching and the demonstrations that culminated in the toppling of the Berlin Wall came that evening from five large city churches, their candles lit at Christian altars. We need to hear again and again the great liturgies that were held to celebrate the emergence of both Hungary and Czeckoslovakia to their new freedom. In such ways the phrase in this prayer about God in Christ showing glory among the nations moves from the language of worship into the very center of contemporary political events.

However, the immensely difficult task for the churches lies in the future of eastern and central Europe. Already as I write there is resentment being expressed at the influence the Polish church is bringing to bear on the political scene in the newly free Poland. So often the same church that is used as the stepping stone to political revolution is immediately suspect as soon as that revolution is effected!

Perhaps this is precisely the reason why a petition for the church follows in this prayer. We pray that the "Church throughout the world may persevere with steadfast faith in the confession of your Name." That task will take great sensitivity and courage in the coming years. The cold facts are that the showing of Christ's glory among the nations does not necessarily mean the empowering of the institutional church in those nations, wherever they may be. We encounter a paradox here that forces us to ask certain questions to which there are no clear answers. Is the institutional church always unworthy of this display of Christ's glory? Or is it the inevitable role of the church not to be glorified through power, but purified through a servanthood that is often extremely costly?

The God of Duty, Love, and Joy   Proper 25

Almighty and everlasting God, increase in us the gifts of faith, hope, and charity; and, that we may obtain what you promise, make us love what you command; through Jesus Christ our Lord, who lives and reigns with you and the Holy Spirit, one God, for ever and ever.

ULYSSES IS old and the great voyages are over. He knows this, but something in him fights against it. Something tells him that the journeying is never over, must never be over, as long as there is life. In Tennyson's magnificent poem "Ulysses," the poet has his hero say,

> Come, my friends,
> 'Tis not too late to seek a newer world.
> ...my purpose holds
> To sail beyond the sunset, and the baths
> Of all the western stars, until I die.

Among the many timeless insights of spiritual experience that recent decades have returned to us is the realization that whatever the nature of our spiritual life, it is certainly not a fixed state. Nowadays we have got so used to the word "journey" to describe our spiritual experience that we can miss a great truth. If spiritual experience is indeed a journey, then change must be an integral part of it. Just as nothing in the outer world can remain the same—not our bodies, nor the town we grew up in, nor the church we love, nor the state of our world, nor the branches on the tree at the end of the garden—so must our spiritual journey move through its phases. Not only must we seek out our spiritual integrity in the face of implacable time, but we must also experience constant changing of the seasons of our spirit, knowing that the summertime of our joys can be swept away in a moment by the wintertime of our sorrow or hurt.

By its very nature our spirituality is always either decreasing or increasing. Because everything about us is in constant change, including our circumstances, our surroundings, our minds, our emotions, our very bodies, so our spirituality is in constant flux. Either our sense of the presence of God is becoming stronger or weaker; it is not by any means a stream that must always flow in the same direction. To know that our sense of the presence of God is now weaker is also to know that it can be made strong again.

That is what this prayer is about. The opening petition for an "increase" is itself a loving and compassionate acknowledgement that the human spirit is precisely that—human—and therefore we must inevitably know decrease of spirit, loss of faith, and a loss of our sense of the presence of God. Even as we say this, we should be very aware of the importance of the words "our sense of." We do not lose the presence of God. We can certainly have a sense of its loss, but the presence of God is there. God waits and wills for us to approach again, to break through into relationship again. God waits for and wills an increase to come again in us. In fact, as prayer after prayer expresses, God not only waits for us but makes that very waiting active by directing grace towards us even as we grope and probe and stumble towards God in our seeking.

We ask God to "increase in us the gifts of faith, hope, and charity." Why? First of all because if left to themselves, faith, hope, and charity will tend to decrease. Life can be very hard on all three of these gifts. There can be much in life that lessens our capacity to retain faith, to remain hopeful, and to continue to be loving. Also, because they are the three great medicines of the human spirit, faith, hope, and charity are like spiritual antibiotics which, if we are prepared to turn to the source who offers them and to accept them, can enter into us, permeate every part of us, and go to war against enemies both contemporary and timeless.

Faith, hope, and charity war against our inner darkness of meaninglessness, despair, and alienation. These three demons exercise free range in the modern world, and lie in wait for even the most gifted and confident and successful. In fact it is often the most gifted, confident, and successful who fall under their onslaught. In the face of these demons, faith, hope, and charity can be far more than pleasant religious words. They can be weapons offered to us by God to do battle with all that stalks us in the shadows of our lives.

They can help us move through the world while remaining whole and strong and, in the deepest and finest sense, human.

Then we pray, "Make us love what you command." "Make us" in the sense of "coerce us"? No, God is not that kind of God. Or "make us" in the sense of "form us, mold us"? Yes. The vivid images of Isaiah come to mind as he describes the potter forming the clay. But even then there is a hint of steel; we are brought up short with the word "command." We are not asked to love what God politely suggests, but what God *commands*. In our culture duty and love are often thought of as somehow being foreign to one another, so loving what we are commanded to do does not come easily to us. The great truth is that when duty and love meet, then great things happen in our lives. The Indian poet Rabindrinath Tagore has a lovely expression of this:

> I slept and dreamt that life was joy.
> I awoke and found that life was duty.
> I acted and found that duty was joy.

A Joy That None Can Move   Proper 26

Almighty and merciful God, it is only by your gift that your faithful people offer you true and laudable service: Grant that we may run without stumbling to obtain your heavenly promises; through Jesus Christ our Lord, who lives and reigns with you and the Holy Spirit, one God, now and for ever.

IN OUR relationships with our parents, one of the richest areas is in the matter of gifts. We all have certain memories of those times of year when we knew a gift was to be given to a parent. It may have been a birthday or Christmas. At the time we were very young and did not yet have access to money, at least not to any significant amount, so we began to conspire with our other parent to get the gift. At this very early stage we were entirely dependent on our parent to make the purchase possible; we might have had a tiny amount of our own money to throw in, but even this money was ours only because it had been given to us as allowance or pocket money.

Nevertheless we didn't even think about that, certainly not in any way that bothered us. Out we went to the shop to purchase the gift, and later we laboriously wrote the accompanying card. Shyly or confidently, according to our disposition, we presented our gift. In every sense it was *our* gift, the expression of our love, at a level we could express. So it was given and so it was received. There were hugs, joy, expressions of appreciation.

So, in exactly the same way, this prayer beautifully and gently describes our relationship of grace with God. We remind ourselves that it is only by the gift of God to us that we can offer back to God the gift of who we are in service. We can give only what we have been given in the first place. This collect is determined to make us understand clearly that our relationship with God is a relationship of grace.

Many of these weekly prayers of the church emphasize the same truth. "Without you we are not able to please you," says another prayer. "Lord," says yet another, "you are the author and giver of all good things." All through our lives we learn that every impulse to serve God is itself the working of the grace of God in us. Every act of service is itself energized by the work of the Holy Spirit. Yet as with those moments of childhood, there is no diminishment of our joy in God's service; we have great joy in offering who we are and what we have to God. There is a paradox at work here. Far from being diminished because what we give back is not our own, our joy is actually deepened by returning to God what God has given us in the first place. We have only to ask any one who takes seriously the stewardship of possessions. The joy of such men and women in their own generosity is usually in direct proportion to their realization that their giving to God is their returning of God's bounty to them.

Someone once said that if only people would realize the joy of giving, they would line up for the privilege! This prayer contains an image of people actually running to gain the privilege of serving God, running to get God's grace so they can in turn serve God. I can't help thinking of all the running around we see in the first incredible hours after our Lord's resurrection. Mary and the others hurry to the tomb, Mary herself runs from it to announce the incredible news, Peter and John race to the tomb, Peter dashes past the hesitant John. Later, as we learn of the two coming back from Emmaus with the great news, we can't help seeing them breaking into at least a trot at times on the way!

This image of people running toward the source of grace and life makes me want to ask a question. What would such eagerness mean for us today? Would it mean much more eagerness to worship, eagerness to receive the sacred bread and wine, eagerness to turn to share with someone else the reality of the peace of God we have glimpsed in this act of common worship? A hymn of George Herbert's resounds with this quality of eagerness:

> Come, my Joy, my Love, my Heart:
> such a joy as none can move;
> such a love as none can part;
> such a heart as joys in love.

But there is an unexpected image in the collect. We pray that we can run without stumbling. What can this mean?

Could one meaning be that eagerness and enthusiasm need to be mixed with some carefulness, some stewardship of time and energy and commitments? We all know the spiritual euphoria that can collapse in exhaustion, an exhaustion that can later turn to depression when we learn the hard way that realities have to be faced about our own ability to live on the heights all the time. Such endless "running" needs disciplining. We need to learn that spirituality can have its manic forms, which then need God's grace of calm, of balance, of the acceptance of self-limitations. Then we must learn that these things too are the gifts of a loving God who truly knows our human frailty, and is showing us our limitations only to make it possible for us to serve better.

The Hope of Glory   Proper 27

*O God, whose blessed Son came into the world that he might
destroy the works of the devil and make us children of God
and heirs of eternal life: Grant that, having this hope, we
may purify ourselves as he is pure; that, when he comes
again with power and great glory, we may be made like him
in his eternal and glorious kingdom; where he lives and
reigns with you and the Holy Spirit, one God, for ever and
ever.*

CHILDHOOD SUMMERS on the farm in County Kilkenny
in Ireland will always bring back for me John Brennan's face
and voice, the hired man on my grandfather's farm. John
was my friend. He would sit in the evening on a large flat
stone just beside the house and we would talk. He smoked
dark strong tobacco that he would cut with a large penknife
and stuff into a once-white clay pipe. The pipe would
protrude from a vast and thick mustache as he told me many
things, and I recall particularly that he had many memories
and a very simple hope. John went to Mass every Sunday
morning, as well as to weekly confession, and he was quite
sure that when he died he would go to heaven. In a word,
John knew where he was from and whither he was bound—
at least that is what he communicated to me—and I am
grateful to him.

Psychologists tell us that at least two things are necessary
for our self-identity. To know who and where we are, we
need to possess both memory and hope. Only if we have
some sense of where we have come from and where we are
going can we have a sense of selfhood. From such insights
comes a lot of our recent recapturing of the importance of
personal storytelling and of journaling.

For a Christian, much of this identifying of past and future is also expressed in the liturgy. A very powerful statement comes to us in three short phrases, so short as to be
almost mere exclamations. In fact so short and simple are
they that we tend to miss their tremendous importance. As
we move through the eucharistic prayer, we pause in our

telling of the salvation story. At this point we are with Jesus in the upper room. We have seen the bread and the chalice lifted. We have heard our Lord command us to continue to do this until the end of time. Then, just at this point, we are given an opportunity to join for a fleeting moment those guests around the table. We call out together who and what we are because of this bread and wine, because of this Jesus, because of who he is and what he did for us on the cross. Our shout and our song and our story is "Christ has died. Christ is risen. Christ will come again." In saying these ten words we express our memory, our present experience, and our hope as Christians.

The prayer speaks of us "having this hope." What hope? The hope that springs from who we are? Who are we? We are children of God and heirs of eternal life. We are the beggar in the fairy tale who finds out he is a prince. We are the orphan who finds out that she is the emperor's child. Suddenly doors of possibility are opened.

But there is more. The road to the shining castle that is our true home is not clear and free and open. It is patrolled by demons and crossed by shadows. We have no choice about traveling this road. But we travel it in the company of one who "came into the world that he might destroy the works of the devil." If as a Christian I truly possess this memory of one who came, if I experience his presence, and if I have the hope that we will journey together, then I must set about forming my response to his offer of company. If we set out on a journey of any kind with someone else, we must set about getting to know one another. Traveling together well is possible only if people in some sense align their behavior and their goals with others. Certain choices must be agreed upon, certain tastes and attitudes must blend together. Our response to the offer of the company of Jesus Christ must be to get to know him at least to some extent. However pathetic our efforts at purity may be, we must in some sense "purify ourselves as he is pure."

Why is this necessary? Because Jesus our companion, now familiar, intimate, understanding, accepting, will change. We will meet further down this road, or on another road, it matters not, and he will be changed. He will still be the Jesus I now know, but I will find it the most natural thing in the world to bow down before him. One day we may speak of our journeying together forever—who knows? But one thing I know, and this prayer reminds me of it again. Only if there has been a relationship with Jesus as the companion of my daily journeying will it be possible to have a relationship, albeit very different, with the shining being who will surely come to me "in power and great glory."

Highway to Hope   Proper 28

Blessed Lord, who caused all holy Scriptures to be written for our learning: Grant us so to hear them, read, mark, learn, and inwardly digest them, that we may embrace and ever hold fast the blessed hope of everlasting life, which you have given us in our Savior Jesus Christ; who lives and reigns with you and the Holy Spirit, one God, for ever and ever.

ANYONE WHO is involved in the life of the mainline churches, especially if the involvement includes teaching or preaching or spiritual formation of any kind, must come to terms with the grim reality of the loss of scriptural knowledge in contemporary Christian life. Nobody has expressed this with greater impact and greater sadness than George Lindbeck, in a recent essay entitled "The Church's Mission to a Postmodern Culture." He writes:

> The decline of biblical literacy has been abrupt and pervasive. Language, culture, and imagination have also been debiblicized at a remarkable rate, not least in this country. The decline affects intellectuals and nonintellectuals, the religious and the nonreligious, those inside the churches and those outside, clergy and laity, and, as I just hinted, Bible conservatives as well as purportedly less biblical liberals.

What we must realize about that loss is that it is the loss of a whole world and a way of seeing reality. For generations the world of the Bible was an inner country where we could walk and explore in a way that made it possible to walk more confidently and uprightly in the outer country where our lives were placed. Again and again we hear faint echoes of that lost inner world in literature, in vestigial phrases from the Bible in conversation, in geographical place-names on this continent. Places like Bethel, Gilead, Shiloh, Bethlehem, and Canaan, whatever their present reality as rural village or industrial city, were once named by those who settled there because something reminded them of another place, a place they had rarely if ever visited, but that existed as totally real in sacred imagination.

Until very recently, Jerusalem has existed for millions of people as a city more real in inner than in outer geography. Jordan was a river in which their spirits bathed far more regularly than their bodies were immersed in the local river! When one looks at the imaginary maps that accompany much fantasy writing these days, especially the Narnia books of C. S. Lewis and the lands of the Shire and Mordor in Tolkein's *Lord of the Rings*, it is hard not to suspect that these maps are an unconscious substitute for those largely ignored or forgotten maps so familiar to past generations and found at the end of their Bibles. These imaginary countries suggest that we are made to desire something more than those pedestrian atlases of countries we can look at through a video camera lens or through the plate-glass windows of air-conditioned busses! As the unknown writer of the letter to the Hebrews says of certain biblical figures, we "desire a better country."

In recent years the Episcopal Church has become a eucharistic community. Now that this rich sense of the Eucharist has been recaptured, it is even more necessary for us to realize that the scriptures are the other foundation on which our spiritual experience rests. If our eucharistic life is to be enriched, so must our biblical life. We have inherited these two great foundational gifts, the meal and the story. For nearly half a millenium we Christians have argued with one another over the importance of one over the other. In our time the argument has ended for millions of Christians; our vocation is to eat and drink the meal and tell the story.

To tell the story, we must know it. To know it we must go in search of it far more intentionally than most congregations are now doing. This need for a much greater sense of purpose about our scriptural life is implied in the intensity of the words in this collect, which tells us to "read, mark, learn, and inwardly digest" this God-given Word. Recovering this intensity is not going to be easy.

Consider why we choose to go to a certain country. We do so because we believe we have something to gain by going there. It may be Hawaii for rest, or Greece for history, or Yucatan for temples. The point is, we have a reason for going.

The reason this prayer gives us for going in search of the lost landscape of the Bible is expressed in one all-important word—hope. The gold to be found in this biblical country is Hope. It is one of the three most precious metals of the human spirit, the others being love and faith. Without hope the human spirit dies, human relationships falter, societies decay. We know this in ourselves, in the church, in our own society. Knowing this, the writer of this collect sends us a warning across time, that we should not forget that the Word of God is the highway into the country of hope.

To Restore All Things   Proper 29

> Almighty and everlasting God, whose will it is to restore all
> things in your well-beloved Son, the King of kings and Lord
> of lords: Mercifully grant that the peoples of the earth,
> divided and enslaved by sin, may be freed and brought
> together under his most gracious rule; who lives and reigns
> with you and the Holy Spirit, one God, now and for ever.

A WET WINTER'S evening in Dublin in the 1950s. I am
with my friend, the newly appointed curate in the old
Church of Saint Michan's. In the eighteenth century these
streets were the fashionable part of Dublin, but today things
are sadly different. My friend opens the side door into a dark
passageway. We grope our way along it to another door that
opens into a darkened place. "Up there," he says quietly, and
points to the gallery.

I can see the outline of the organ, the dark rows of the
gallery seats. Up there, about this time in the late evening of
April 13, 1742, Georg Friedrich Handel led the first performance of his new oratorio, "Messiah." As I looked up in the
shadows, the street lights shining beyond the windows, the
distant traffic a dull roar in the silence, I heard the thunder-
ing joy of the chorus that was to become a cultural icon for
the whole western world. "King of Kings, Lord of Lords,
Hallelujah, Hallelujah!" they sang. The words of the great
chorus thundered in my imagination until we turned and
locked the door behind us.

I thought of that moment long ago as I read this prayer.
Its backdrop is nothing less than the whole world and all of
humanity. In a single sentence, we see a planet enslaved and
then freed. We move from chaos to cosmos. At the center of
all this stands the figure of Jesus Christ.

What does this magnificent verbal flourish mean? To
Jewish and Islamic ears this prayer would be heard as the
worst kind of Christian imperialism. Phrases such as "King
of kings" and "brought together under his most gracious
rule" would mean only one thing to such listeners: the trium-
phalist language of power.

Is the prayer speaking the language of power? Certainly not in terms of political or military or even cultural conquest. There do exist some Christian traditions that would happily embrace the language of this collect as a sign of the spiritual superiority of Christian faith, and they would wish to set it over against other religious traditions. We can asssume that Catholic Christianity is not prepared to act in such terms.

But if this language is not an expression of power, or of the longing for power, what is this prayer saying amid the realities of today's world? We pray that God may restore all things in God's beloved Son. As we pray this, we are echoing across the centuries the words of an early Christian believer writing to the Christian community in Colossae: "Through Christ, God was pleased to reconcile to himself all things." The hope that all would be restored to its former glory was also in the minds of Old Testament prophets like Joel, who has God promise, "I will restore to you the years which the locust has eaten." Again and again Isaiah and Jeremiah express the hope of restoration, and even though they do so for a single people and a tiny country, you hear also in their voices a longing for a restored world.

But is not this our own longing? In the opening verses of the Bible we are shown creation in all its glorious perfection, balance, and peace. To use a word we hear more and more frequently, we are shown the creation in magnificent *symbiosis*. Life lives with life. Within the web of life, imaged for us as a garden, humanity takes its place. Adam and Eve name all other life forms, while at the same time, in company with the rest of creation, they acknowledge God as creator and source.

We then read that this perfect fabric is torn by human choice and act. We watch as the tear in that fabric in God's creation widens until, as the prayer says, "the peoples of the earth [are] divided and enslaved by sin." As the memory of that balance and unity of creation haunts us, we long for its return both in the world around us and in ourselves. Isaiah dreams of a holy mountain where opposites are reconciled, where balance, unity, and peace return, and where "the earth shall be full of the knowledge of the Lord as the waters cover the sea."

The power of this vision and the importance of recapturing it in our own time lies in the fact that we are given not just a nostalgia for a past *shalom*, but the deep hope of its return. We seek its return both in the present and in the future. We seek it in the present whenever we try to discern glimpses of God's restoring power in particular events in the world, and God's activity in our own lives. We seek it in the future whenever we try to envision God's will for our lives and for the life of the world. When we dream, it energizes us to work toward its fulfillment.

In all of this, our Lord is the focal point. In his total inner wholeness he embodies the *shalom* we seek. The balance, peace, and wholeness we long for personally and ecologically is seen in him. In him the torn fabric of our humanity is rewoven, its integrity restored. The degree to which we identify with him is the degree to which we ourselves are rewoven and restored.

This prayer is a vast dream. It may even be the greatest dream we are capable of. We are surrounded by evidence that our own lives and that of the earth itself may depend on our ability to bring at least some of that dream into time and reality.

The Anatomy of Inquiry

ISBN 0–915144–98–0
Previously published by
Bobbs-Merrill as ISBN 0–672–61251–8

THE
ANATOMY
OF
INQUIRY

*Philosophical Studies
in the Theory of Science*

ISRAEL SCHEFFLER
Harvard University

Hackett Publishing Company
Indianapolis / Cambridge

Cover design by Laszlo J. Balogh

For further information, please address
Hackett Publishing Company, Inc.
P.O. Box 55573
Indianapolis, Indiana 46205

Library of Congress catalog card number: 81-85415

ISBN 0–915144–98–0 (pbk)
0–915144–97–2 (cloth)

Printed in the United States of America

To Rosalind

Preface

Science explains particulars by bringing them within the scope of appropriate general principles. Principles are explanatory only if they are intelligible, and scientific only if they can be confronted with experience.

Assertions such as these are frequently made. It is, however, one thing to make them and quite another to interpret them in a precise and systematic manner. Indeed, to provide a clear and general account of scientific explanation, of the intelligibility of scientific principles, and of the confrontation between such principles and experience represents a basic task of the philosophy of science, entailing consideration of its most fundamental problems.

I have tried, in this book, to introduce the reader to such fundamental problems. My method has been to present and analyze central issues in the interpretation of *explanation, significance*, and *confirmation*, as these issues have taken shape in recent studies. I have attempted to engage the reader in current problems as quickly as possible, starting from an account of basic investigations and developing certain strands of the ensuing philosophical discussions. I have not limited myself to exposition, but have freely expressed my own ideas on many of the problems treated, in the hope that readers will want to share in the active exploration of unsafe, though fascinating, territory.

Some issues discussed in this book are considerably more difficult than others, but I have striven to explain necessary technicalities by statement and example along the way. Any section that still presents an initial obstacle may be left for a second reading; many readers will, for example, wish to treat Sections 6 and 8 of Part I in such fashion.

Much of this book grew out of my lectures and seminars in the philosophy of science over the past several years, though some of the leading ideas were developed earlier. Preliminary versions of some sections were presented as separate lectures at various universities, and certain portions incorporate, in revised or expanded form, material from the following articles of mine: "Prospects of a Modest Empiricism," *Review of Metaphysics,* X (1957); "Explanation, Prediction, and Abstraction," *British Journal for the Philosophy of Science,* VII (1957); "Thoughts on Teleology," *British Journal for the Philosophy of Science,* IX (1959); "Inductive Inference: A New Approach," *Science,* 127 (1958); "A Note on Confirmation," *Philosophical Studies,* XI (1960); and "A Rejoinder on Confirmation," *Philosophical Studies,* XII (1961). I am grateful to the publishers of these journals for their cooperation, and I wish to thank all those whose permission to reprint passages from various other publications is acknowledged in footnotes to the text.

As regards fundamental philosophical approach, I am especially indebted to Nelson Goodman. I am deeply grateful to him for philosophical criticism and encouragement, as well as for his formal teaching.

My thinking has also been considerably influenced by the work of W. V. Quine and C. G. Hempel, and I have profited greatly from discussions with them. Professor Hempel provided me with extensive comments on the text, and several of his suggestions have been incorporated in the final manuscript. I wish also to express my thanks to Ernest Nagel, from whom I first learned to appreciate the significance, as well as the subtlety, of issues in the philosophy of science.

To various friends and colleagues, I am much indebted for illuminating philosophical criticism; I cannot possibly enumerate them all. But I wish to thank, in particular, Noam Chomsky and Sidney Morgenbesser, with whom I have discussed nearly all of the problems treated in the text. As editor of the Borzoi Books in the Philosophy of Science, Professor Morgenbesser also made valuable comments on the present manuscript. And·to Henry D. Aiken, Herbert G. Bohnert, Burton S. Dreben, Dagfinn Føllesdal, Maurice Mandelbaum, Frederic Schick, Harold Weisberg, and Morton White, I am grateful for discussions relevant to special points. None of my teachers or colleagues is, of course, to be considered responsible for controversial positions I have taken; surely none is to blame for my mistakes or failures in insight.

Some of the preliminary work for sections of this book was accomplished during the period of a fellowship awarded me, for 1958-1959, by the John Simon Guggenheim Memorial Foundation. The National Science Foundation awarded me a grant for research assistance during the final stages of preparation of the manuscript. To both these Foundations I am grateful for support. And I wish to express my special appreciation to Francis Keppel who, as Dean of the Harvard Graduate School of Education, offered his constant and warm encouragement.

I thank Mr. Jack Reitzes for his help in the checking of bibliography and footnotes; and Mrs. Dorothy Spotts for her excellent typing of the manuscript and her assistance in various stages of its preparation. To Gerard McCauley I am grateful for his initial editorial interest, and I appreciate the considerable editorial helpfulness of Clifford M. Crist and Mrs. Leonore C. Hauck.

My son, Sam, and my daughter, Laurie, helped me in many, many ways.

The book is dedicated to my wife, whose unfailing trust, encouragement, and good judgment have meant more to me than I can conceivably express.

ISRAEL SCHEFFLER

Newton, Massachusetts
April, 1963

Contents

PART III: *Confirmation*

INTRODUCTION

*Philosophy and
the Theory of Science*

1. Approaches to the Philosophy of Science

The label "philosophy of science" is commonly applied to several diverse undertakings, all equally legitimate, all "philosophical" in seeking general knowledge—in this case, general knowledge about science or about the world revealed by science. A rough grouping of such undertakings may be effected under three main headings, "The Role of Science in Society," "The World Pictured by Science," and "The Foundations of Science."

Under the first of these headings falls the study of relationships between social factors and scientific ideas, for example, the influence of political constraints upon theorizing, the effects of scientific discoveries upon religious allegiances. Here also belongs the investigation of science as an institution, its social organization and procedures, the training and motivation of scientists, and the relationships of science with education, government, industry, commerce, and the military. Finally, we may here include fundamental considerations of policy with respect to the social role of science, the responsibilities of the scientist to society, and those of society to scientific endeavor.

Under the second heading, "The World Pictured by Science," belong attempts to describe the origin and structure of the universe as suggested by the best theories and the various relevant findings to date: cosmology. Also under the present rubric belong philosophers' interpretations of what they take to be the most pervasive or humanly significant features of the world revealed both by science and common experience: metaphysics.

The last heading, "The Foundations of Science," embraces investigations of the general methods, logical forms, modes of inference, and basic concepts of the sciences. The approach which is the concern of this book belongs here. We shall therefore attempt a more detailed description of several different enterprises within the present category. We hope thereby to bring out the distinctive features of the present approach and its interrelationships with other philosophical studies of scientific foundations.

To begin with, let us attend to those investigations in which the philosopher takes some particular branch of science as his domain, with the view of clarifying its foundations. He may conceive his task to consist in a *formal specification* of the branch in question, in such a way as to exhibit its logical skeleton, the systematic articulation of its basic ideas, definitions, assertions, and rules of inference. His goal is here not (in an important sense) to go outside the branch of science under consideration, but rather to formulate its manifest content in an explicitly systematic way.

By contrast, the theorist may approach a particular branch of science with external criteria of philosophical intelligibility in hand, and his objective may be to restate as much of its content as he can in terms intelligible by such criteria. To the extent that he is successful, he may be said to have offered a *reduction or translation* of a portion of science in terms that are philosophically acceptable to him. Most familiar, perhaps, are attempts to effect reductions to an observation vocabulary or to notions drawn from common experience with physical objects, but the idea of reduction to an independently intelligible conceptual basis is by no means restricted to such attempts.

The theorist concerned with a particular branch of science may, finally, "go outside" it, not by an attempted reduction of its content to some independently intelligible basis, but rather by an attempted *description,* in a separate discourse, of its epistemological features. His purpose is to show the status of its various elements in the grounding of knowledge claims within the branch in question. To this end, he may catalogue the fundamental theories and laws of the domain, showing how they explain the results formulated by accepted experimental reports, and how they, in turn, acquire their inductive warrant in the light of the evidence. He may classify certain ideas within the domain as observational and others as abstract, tracing the connections between them. He may describe the prevalent types of measurement, model, design, and inference, with a view toward explaining their functions in inquiry.

The terms in which this theorist couches his description (e.g., 'theory', 'law', 'experimental report', 'explains', 'inductive warrant', 'evidence', 'measurement', 'model', 'observational', 'abstract', etc.) do not normally figure in formulating the content of the scientific branch itself. They belong rather to another system of discourse, in terms of which the philosopher hopes to describe the epistemological structure of the branch in question. Let us hereafter refer to them as *structural terms*. To be sure, any scientific domain may be described in innumerable ways; the philosopher we are presently considering, however, is motivated by overriding epistemological concerns. He wants a description that is not only clear but illuminating as to the reasons which may serve to show certain statements within the domain to be acceptable and others not; moreover, he wants a description in terms that are applicable to other branches of science than the one under consideration.

The desire for a scheme of structural description that is generally applicable provides a natural link with descriptions of other branches. The attempt may thus be made to formulate descriptions of several scientific domains through the use of the same set of structural terms, thereby exhibiting the general applicability of the set. Each description of some branch becomes thus connected to descriptions of other branches, as well as to the further endeavor to determine a general descriptive scheme. The determination of such a scheme must square with what we independently know about the several branches, and serves further to shape the way in which we thereafter express what we know.

Having a descriptive scheme which he believes to be generally applicable, the philosopher may then use it not only to refine previous structural descriptions of particular branches or to apply it to the description of new branches, but also to provide an overall picture of science. He may, that is, use his scheme in giving an account of the epistemological structure of all scientific domains, by enumerating the elements belonging to each such domain and describing the characteristic relations among these elements. For example, he may wish to say that every branch of science has experimental or observational reports, law-statements and theories, systems of classification or measurement, and inductive as well as deductive arguments by which explanations and predictions are formulated.

Finally, the philosopher may undertake still a further task, but one clearly related to those we have been considering. He may address himself to the structural terms embedded in the prevalent descriptive scheme, and he may try to clarify these within some general theory. His problem is thus to provide a clear and systematic explanation of such terms as 'theory', 'law', 'explains', 'confirms', etc., which are themselves used both in describing the structure of particular scientific domains and in giving an overall structural picture of science. His task may thus be construed as directed toward a systematic and philosophically intelligible *theory of scientific structure,* or as we shall say (for the sake of brevity), a *theory of science.*

In undertaking this task, the theorist is guided by prior applications of the structural terms to particular branches of science as well as by prior indications as to their general applicability. Nevertheless, he reserves the theorist's right to revise such applications in the course of his own construction, for the sake of increased clarity and comprehensiveness. He hopes, further, to utilize his general theory in devising refined structural descriptions of the several sciences, as well as in giving an improved overall account of the epistemology of science.

What we shall consider in this book are various studies which may be interpreted as directed toward such a general theory, that is, various attempts to explain the structural terms commonly employed, in a systematic and philosophically intelligible fashion.

We shall address ourselves primarily to recent investigations centering on three key terms, 'explains', 'significant', and 'confirms', but we shall need to touch on several other topics and issues along the way. Before proceeding to our main problems, however, we shall attempt a further clarification of the notion of a theory of science, by considering several arguments urged against it.

2. Arguments over a Theory of Science

Various arguments have been offered purporting to show that the attempt to build a theory of science, in the sense of a theory of scientific structure, is misguided—that such a theory is unnecessary or impossible. A critical consideration of some of these arguments may make clearer the nature of the attempt and help in warding off prevalent misconceptions about it.

Let us begin with an analogy, suggested by N. Chomsky.[1] If we consider the field of linguistics, we find (1) various everyday spoken languages, e.g., French, German, English, (2) various grammars for each of these languages, each grammar purporting to give a structural description of some language, and (3) theories of linguistic structure, in which basic grammatical notions with cross-linguistic applicability, e.g., 'noun', 'morpheme', are analyzed in full generality. We may compare the everyday spoken languages to the particular branches of science, the grammars to the structural descriptions of these branches, and the theories of linguistic structure to theories of the structure of science, in the sense above discussed.

[1] Noam Chomsky, *The Logical Structure of Linguistic Theory* (Cambridge: Massachusetts Institute of Technology Library, microfilm, 1955), chap. iii, pp. 82-83. (See, too, Noam Chomsky, *Syntactic Structures* [The Hague: Mouton & Co., 1957], pp. 13, 14, 49, 50.)
I am indebted to Chomsky for discussions of structural descriptions and theories of structure, which have influenced my account in the latter paragraphs of the previous section. (The particular analogy in the text differs, however, from the one given in *The Logical Structure of Linguistic Theory* in that it compares the grammars of a language to the structural descriptions of a branch of science rather than to theories within the branch itself.)

Now, it is obvious that the need to specify a clear set of notions within the theory of linguistic structure is altogether independent of whether these notions occur in the everyday spoken languages themselves, e.g., French, German, or English. No one would think of arguing that, since the term 'is a morpheme in language *L*' does not occur in any of these languages, it is unnecessary for linguists to attempt to define it.

Yet it has sometimes been argued that, because such a term as 'is a (scientific) law', for example, does not appear in the vocabulary of any scientific domain, philosophers of science need not bother trying to define it. This argument seems no less a *non sequitur* in philosophy than in linguistics.

It is, furthermore, obvious that the linguist's attempt to define such general notions as 'is a noun in *L*' or 'is a morpheme in *L*' is independent of the practical goal of improving the handling or recognition of nouns or morphemes by speakers of any everyday language. His theory of these notions needs to be clear, needs to accord with acceptable grammars already available, and needs to meet other criteria which may be roughly grouped under the heading of 'simplicity'. But no theory satisfactory in these respects will be considered by the linguist defective or superfluous on the ground that it fails to improve the everyday use of everyday languages.

Nevertheless, the philosopher's attempt to define such a structural term as 'is a warranted inductive inference' has occasionally been described as naive or arrogant in presuming to improve the scientist's inductive habits. The scientist knows perfectly well, it is said, how to make and test inductive hypotheses, and he is perfectly competent to refine his own procedures in the course of inquiry. This charge is, however, clearly no more relevant to the philosopher than to the linguist, since the goal of each is a clear, simple, and true theory, not the reform of practice.

The argument just considered lays primary stress on the practical clarity of the notions to be explained in a theory of scientific structure, and concludes that such practical clarity makes the theory superfluous. Often, the opposite complaint is heard, to the effect that certain of the notions to be explained by such a theory are too unclear in practice to permit a theoretical reconstruction. The complaint is frequently supported by producing some striking example of practical indeterminacy in applying the notion in question.

It may be readily admitted that no theoretical account is properly presented as a valid reconstruction of any notion unless it is controlled by some body of clear usage within which the notion in question is initially embedded. Without such a body of clear usage, however, not only does the term fail to admit of theoretical reconstruction, but it also forfeits its eligibility for such reconstruction by the same token, being worthless as a structural term in the first instance. The argument thus constitutes an objection, not to a theory of scientific structure, but rather to taking certain terms as structural terms worthy of explanation within such a theory.

Such an objection is certainly legitimate in principle, but it cannot be adequately supported merely by producing a set of striking examples of indeterminacy. To illustrate, consider W. V. Quine's example of the indeterminacy of the counterfactual construction in ordinary speech.[2] As between the following two counterfactual statements, we find ourselves unable to decide:

1. If Bizet and Verdi had been compatriots, Bizet would have been Italian.
2. If Bizet and Verdi had been compatriots, Verdi would have been French.

The example establishes, however, merely the existence of *some* cases of indeterminate application, a condition that holds for every term without exception. It is thus insufficient to show that

---

[2] Willard Van Orman Quine, *Methods of Logic* (New York, copyright 1950, (c) 1959, Holt, Rinehart and Winston, Inc.), pp. 14-15. By permission. Quine writes, concerning the statements (1) and (2), "It may be wondered, indeed, whether any really coherent theory of the contrafactual conditional of ordinary usage is possible at all, particularly when we imagine trying to adjudicate between such examples . . ." Nonetheless, he allows that the problem of clarifying such conditionals, though it does not belong to pure logic, may well belong "to the theory of meaning or possibly the philosophy of science."

counterfactual statements, in particular, are peculiarly unclear, i.e., that there is no substantial body of determinate usage to control attempted theoretical reconstructions. In fact, alternative examples abound, in which our decision is immediately forthcoming:

3. If I had dropped my pencil on the desk five minutes ago, it would have split the desk in two and fallen to the floor beneath.
4. If I had dropped my pencil on the desk five minutes ago, it would not have split the desk in two and fallen to the floor beneath.

Finally, let us consider the argument that all theoretical definitions of structural terms are bound to be untrue to the prior meanings of such terms (1) because these meanings vary with context, or (2) because no general theory can represent the ways in which prior users of such terms would describe their understanding of them, if asked. We should, it is accordingly urged, not attempt to construct a general theory of such terms at all, but should rather (1') catalogue their varying uses in different contexts or (2') try to describe them in much the same ways that their prior users would describe them upon reflection. We should, for example, list the variety of uses to which the word 'evidence' is put, and we should try to find out how scientists or others who already use the term would be likely to explain it were they called upon to do so. Above all, we should not propose a general theory embodying a definition of the familiar term 'evidence'.

This argument, we may note, is clearly inapplicable to linguistic theory. No one supposes that the initial variability of grammatical notions constitutes an objection to their theoretical reconstruction in standardized ways. Nor does anyone imagine that the task of the theoretical linguist is to elicit grammatical pronouncements from informants concerning their native languages and then to summarize such pronouncements with the aid of statistical or other devices.

His job is rather to construct a general theory in which grammatical ideas receive systematic analysis. To this end, he may find it expedient to construe a given grammatical term largely in accord with some unambiguous body of usage belonging to the term within a selected prior context. He may then treat it theoretically as context-free, reconstructing in other ways those of its other previous uses that he deems important.

Further, his theoretical construction of any such term need accord with some prior use only with respect to the term's reference; the substance and manner of the construction need not in addition mirror the estimated interpretations of the term's prior users. Indeed, in the provision of a clear and systematic explanatory construction of the given term lies the linguist's opportunity of making a novel contribution to knowledge, over and beyond conventional interpretations.

What holds for linguistic theory, moreover, holds elsewhere as well. There is thus, for example, a world of difference between constructing a systematic theory of numbers and either cataloguing the variable everyday uses of numerical terms or asking those who employ such terms to explain them. There is, likewise, a world of difference between listing and describing the various everyday uses of length-concepts or asking the man in the street to explain them, and, on the other hand, providing a clear, systematic method for the measurement of lengths.[3]

Yet the philosopher aiming to provide a systematic analysis of the structural terms has often been declared misguided in seeking context-free constructions which are, moreover, indifferent to the interpretations of practicing scientists or other users of these terms. That his aim differs, indeed, from the cataloguing of variable prior uses and interpretations of the structural terms

---

[3] On the constructive tasks of philosophical analysis as against a "philological preoccupation with the unphilosophical use of words," see Willard Van Orman Quine, *From a Logical Point of View* (2d ed.; Cambridge, Mass.: Harvard University Press, 1961), p. 106. For the view that "explication must respect the presystematic application of terms" but not "the manner or order of their presystematic adoption," see Nelson Goodman, *Fact, Fiction, and Forecast* (Cambridge, Mass.: Harvard University Press, 1955), p. 49. By permission of the publisher and the author.

is clear. That he is therefore misguided is no more acceptable a conclusion than the analogous conclusion in the case of linguistic theory or the theory of numbers or length.

The arguments we have considered thus offer no serious objection to the attempt to formulate a theory of science. Let us now raise the question to what extent this attempt is compatible with the other approaches to the foundations of science, earlier discussed.

It is obvious, to begin with, that there are the closest of ties between the attempt to build a theory of scientific structure and the attempt to provide adequate structural descriptions of the several branches of science. Analogously to the case of linguistic theory with respect to grammatical terms, the theory explanatory of structural terms is controlled by the applications of such terms in descriptions of special domains, and in turn guides such further descriptions. There is surely no incompatibility here, but rather a division of labor between tasks that complement one another.

There is, further, no rivalry between efforts toward a structural theory and attempts at formalizing special branches of science. The relationship is here perhaps not as close as the one just considered; nevertheless, it is to some actual or supposed formal version of the several branches of science that the structural terms are typically applied. An understanding of the latter thus relates to the availability of formal versions, and to methods by which they are obtained, in much the same way that an understanding of grammatical terms relates to the availability of bodies of discourse in the spoken languages and to methods by which these are obtained.

Finally, there is no incompatibility but rather a parallel between the attempt to reformulate scientific domains in philosophically acceptable terms (whatever these may be), and the attempt to produce an explanatory theory of the structural notions. For each task may be seen as the problem of explaining a given set of notions on a clear base, and progress in the one may benefit from progress in the other. But, furthermore, a given view of the way in which the domains of science are to be restated in order to be philosophically acceptable may influence the content of formal versions to which the structural terms are to apply and so, indirectly, the general theory itself.

To engage in the attempt to build a general theory of scientific structure is thus not to commit oneself to an exclusive program for studying the foundations of science, but rather to investigate an area closely related to several others, with the success of which its own success is bound up. It is in this light that the various studies to be discussed may best be viewed.

One special point needs here to be noted, since it is often raised in criticism of the studies we shall treat. I refer to the fact that much of the discussion and analysis of these studies centers on examples which belong rather to everyday life or simple investigations than to full-blown theoretical science. The line between general epistemology and the philosophy of science seems to have disappeared.

There are, it may be suggested, two main reasons for this state of affairs. First, there is the general strategy of tackling simple or simplified problems first, a strategy which may be debatable but which has respectable scientific origins.

Secondly, the structural terms, e.g., 'theory', 'confirms', 'explains', 'evidence', have much wider applications than those in which they refer to elements of the developed sciences; for example, they all apply to situations of everyday life and to those depicted in detective stories. One might, of course, restrict one's attention, for example, to 'theory in physics' or 'evidence in quantum mechanics', and so cut out detective stories, but one would then be cutting out the social sciences as well. One would, further, be failing to draw upon obvious cross-disciplinary parallels, e.g., between theories in physics and theories elsewhere. One may then propose to focus on the *relative* expression 'theory in S', which is parallel to 'morpheme in L'. But whereas the variable 'L' clearly ranges over nothing but languages and segments of languages, the variable 'S' could only artificially be restricted so as to range over nothing but sciences and their parts.

To consider the structural terms in their natural generality is, thus, to face the fact that they apply not only to the highly developed sciences but to a much wider range of elements as well. This is perhaps one appropriate interpretation of the frequently encountered statement that science grows out of common sense and is continuous with it; a theory of scientific structure cannot help dealing with numerous common situations if it is to be a truly general and natural theory. Such a theory thus has a larger array of cases controlling it than just the ones provided by the sciences. Epistemology of science in this way does in fact merge with epistemology in general.[4]

The main point to note is that the job of a theory of scientific structure is to explain the structural terms, and that this job does not restrict the investigation to a consideration of the sciences alone, even though their structure *is* described by the terms in question. In this respect, our extended analogy with linguistic theory breaks down, and the very term 'theory of scientific structure' may mislead if taken to parallel 'theory of linguistic structure'. For, as we have seen, the general terms 'phoneme', 'morpheme', 'noun', etc., apply only to elements of languages, whereas the general terms 'theory', 'confirms', 'explains', etc., do not apply only to elements of the sciences. Nevertheless, there is no more paradox in the structural terms' applying to elements outside the sciences than there is in the fact that the term 'brick', which may be used to describe the structure of apartment houses, also applies to the constituents of some garden walls.

3. Approach to the Problems

We shall approach our subject through a consideration of recent studies that address themselves to the notions of explanation, significance, and confirmation. These problems are closely interconnected and they relate also to other widely discussed ques-

[4] It does not follow that all general issues in epistemology must be dealt with in a theory of scientific structure. See, in this connection, the argument for separating basic questions in the philosophy of science from the philosophy of perception, in Richard Bevan Braithwaite, *Scientific Explanation* (Cambridge, England: Cambridge University Press, 1953), pp. 2-9.

tions, e.g., the explanation of 'law', the thesis of empiricism, and the interpretation of theoretical concepts in science. An inkling of some of the connections may be gained from the following brief remarks: Explanation has appeared to many theorists to proceed by subsumption of events under general laws; it has, further, seemed to require formulation in terms that are cognitively significant. Both the notions of law and of cognitive significance have in turn seemed to rest on that of confirmation, a law being a statement confirmable by its positive instances, and a significant statement being one confirmable or disconfirmable by observational evidence. To complicate matters, the seemingly clear key notion of confirmation has turned out to present formidable problems of its own and to seem to presuppose rather than explain the notion of cognitive significance.

Any selection and ordering of these problems is to some degree arbitrary. Nothing is claimed for the mode of presentation to follow except that it is plausible, and presents some central themes of recent studies interpretable as directed toward a theory of scientific structure.

PART I

Explanation

1. The Humean Background

'Explanation' is an ambiguous word. We often apply it to the clarification of terms or statements. Alternatively, we use it to refer to the provision of reasons in support of a judgment. In yet another way, we frequently attach it to the weaving together of a theoretical fabric within which credible generalizations may occupy determinate places. Our present concern is with still a different employment of the word, according to which it applies to the causal diagnosis of particular events, occurrences, or facts. To ask for an explanation why a given patient has contracted a disease is, normally, to ask neither for clarification of the term 'disease' nor for a listing of the symptoms upon which the medical judgment of disease is based, nor yet for a theory of disease, but rather for an analysis of those antecedent factors in the situation responsible for the patient's falling ill.

Ever since Hume, such causal diagnosis has generally been taken to be a matter of connecting the event to be explained with other events by means of general principles gotten through experience, though not demonstrable on the basis of accumulated experiential knowledge. Hume denied necessary connections of matters of fact: between observed cases recorded in the evidence and predicted cases based on the evidence there is a fundamental logical gap unbridgeable by deductive inference. No event is thus explainable solely through specification of others from which it may be said necessarily to follow. For no event "necessarily follows" from any others. Rather, additional appeal must be made to principles which serve to connect events in general patterns, and which, though resting on past experience, far outstrip what can be demonstrated on the basis of such experience.[1]

That some such principles are required in order for us to connect cause and effect was argued by Hume to follow from the fact that cause and effect are not, in themselves, logically connected, that it is, therefore, always *consistent* to suppose a given cause to occur without a particular event alleged to be its effect. Thus, in his *Enquiry Concerning Human Understanding,* he says:

> When I see, for instance, a Billiard-ball moving in a straight line towards another; even suppose motion in the second ball should by accident be suggested to me, as the result of their contact or impulse; may I not conceive, that a hundred different events might as well follow from that cause? May not both these balls remain at absolute rest? May not the first ball return in a straight line, or leap off from the second in any line or direction? All these suppositions are consistent and conceivable. Why then should we give the preference to one, which is no more consistent or conceivable than the rest? All our reasonings *a priori* will never be able to show us any foundation for this preference. In a word, then, every effect is distinct from its cause. It could not, therefore, be discovered in the cause, and the first invention or conception of it, *a priori,* must be entirely arbitrary. . . . In vain, therefore, should we pretend to determine any single event, or infer any cause or effect, without the assistance of observation or experience.[2]

[1] David Hume, *A Treatise of Human Nature* (London: Printed for John Noon, at the White-Hart, near Mercer's-Chapel in Cheapside, 1739), Book I, Part III, section XIV, pp. 202-223, and David Hume, *An Enquiry Concerning Human Understanding,* in *Enquiries Concerning the Human Understanding and Concerning the Principles of Morals,* ed. L. A. Selby-Bigge. Reprinted from the posthumous edition of 1777 (Oxford: Clarendon Press, 1902), sections IV-V, pp. 25-55; section VII, pp. 60-79.

[2] Hume, *An Enquiry Concerning Human Understanding,* section IV, p. 29-30.

It is observation and experience that may reveal numerous instances without exception in the past, in which an event of a given kind is conjoined to an event of another kind. There is, to be sure, no way of *demonstrating,* on the basis of such instances, that events of these respective sorts will always be found to be conjoined. There is no guarantee that the course of nature is constant and uniform. Yet all our knowledge of matters of fact rests upon the principle of custom or habit by which such past conjunctions are generalized to future, unknown, and hypothetical cases.

Thus, Hume writes, "Having found, in many instances, that any two kinds of objects—flame and heat, snow and cold—have always been conjoined together; if flame or snow be presented anew to the senses, the mind is carried by custom to expect heat or cold, and to *believe* that such a quality does exist, and will discover itself upon a nearer approach."[3] If we are to say, in the spirit of this passage, that we have *accounted for* this heat by showing it to have been caused by this flame, we can do no more than show that the heat has in fact now been conjoined to the flame, and affirm our habitual or customary belief that heat and flame are always conjoined, having frequently and without exception been conjoined in the past.

Now, it often happens that we speak of one event as the cause of another, even where constant conjunction in the past has in fact failed. If, for example, the heat referred to above is taken as the sensation of heat, flame often has occurred without such conjoined sensation, e.g., when a discarded match has burned itself out at a considerable distance from the nearest living being. Yet, I do not hesitate to attribute the sensation in my finger, when I burn myself on a match, to the flame as cause.

Such an attribution is accommodated within the Humean tradition by treating it as an indication of some causal factor singled out from the total cause—which is in fact what is conjoined to the effect in question. In the present example, the total cause may be presumed to include not merely the flame, but the proximity of a sentient organism, the lack of insulating barriers, and still

[3] *Ibid.,* section V, p. 46.

other conditions, if the principle connecting it to the effect in question is to hold true of our past experience. The total cause may in some instances be unknown, or the additional conditions may be understood in context, or they may be relatively constant in duration by comparison with the factor singled out, or they may, finally, be less subject to our control. In any event, there is nothing *more* involved in causal explanation than the connecting of circumstances through principles of conjunction resting upon past experience.

The variability of ordinary causal attribution is elaborated in J. S. Mill's *A System of Logic*. "It is seldom, if ever," writes Mill,

> between a consequent and a single antecedent that this invariable sequence subsists. It is usually between a consequent and the sum of several antecedents, the concurrence of all of them being requisite to produce, that is, to be certain of being followed by, the consequent. In such cases it is very common to single out one only of the antecedents under the denomination of Cause, calling the others merely Conditions. Thus, if a person eats of a particular dish, and dies in consequence, that is, would not have died if he had not eaten of it, people would be apt to say that eating of that dish was the cause of his death. There needs not, however, be any invariable connection between eating of the dish and death; but there certainly is, among the circumstances which took place, some combination or other on which death is invariably consequent: as, for instance, the act of eating of the dish, combined with a particular bodily constitution, a particular state of present health, and perhaps even a certain state of the atmosphere; the whole of which circumstances perhaps constituted in this particular case the *conditions* of the phenomenon, or, in other words, the set of antecedents which determined it, and but for which it would not have happened . . . If we do not, when aiming at accuracy, enumerate all the conditions, it is only because some of them will in most cases be understood without being expressed, or because for the purpose

in view they may without detriment be overlooked. . . .
Nothing can better show the absence of any scientific ground
for the distinction between the cause of a phenomenon and
its conditions, than the capricious manner in which we select from among the conditions that which we choose to
denominate the cause. However numerous the conditions
may be, there is hardly any of them which may not, according to the purpose of our immediate discourse, obtain that
nominai pre-eminence. . . . The cause, then, philosophically
speaking, is the sum total of the conditions positive and
negative taken together; the whole of the contingencies of
every description, which being realised, the consequent
invariably follows.[4]

The view of the passage just quoted has been reinforced and
generalized by later writers. Thus, it has been widely remarked
that the notion of cause tends to disappear in advanced theoretical science in favor of the notion of functional association.[5]
The relative constancy of the former notion in everyday situations and in applied science has, further, been taken to under-
score its close connection with practical issues of control and
ascription of responsibility, in context.[6] Thus, given a set of

[4] John Stuart Mill, *A System of Logic, Ratiocinative and Inductive*
(1843), (8th ed.; New York: Harper & Brothers, 1887), Book III,
chap. v, section 3, pp. 237-241.

[5] See, for example, Herbert Feigl, "Notes on Causality," in Herbert
Feigl and May Brodbeck (eds.), *Readings in the Philosophy of Science,*
pp. 408-418. Copyright, 1953, by Appleton-Century-Crofts, Inc. By
permission of the publishers and the author. Feigl writes (pp. 410-411),
"On the whole, the ordinary cause-effect terminology fits best the qualitative macro-level; thus it is part and parcel of the language of common
sense and of those levels of science which deal with gross behavior and
have not as yet introduced quantitative (metrical) concepts. Once measurement is introduced, the gross cause-effect relation gives way to a
mathematical formulation in terms of a functional relationship."

[6] Thus, Toulmin writes, "The term 'cause' is at home in the diagnostic
and applied sciences, such as medicine and engineering, rather than in
the physical sciences . . . Problems of application and questions about
causes arise with reference to particular contexts, but physical theories
are formulated in a manner indifferent to particular contexts: it is when

conditions which, in Mill's sense, constitutes "the cause, philosophically speaking," of some effect, we may single out for causal status just that condition presumed subject to human control and thus capable of providing a basis for determining legal or moral responsibility.

In other cases discussed by recent writers, selection of some condition for causal status may hinge on the relative temporal constancy of other conditions belonging to "the cause, philosophically speaking," and in still other cases, the latter conditions are excluded by some pragmatic criterion: e.g., they are too well understood to mention, or they are as yet unknown. Causal status may, in an extreme case, be assigned to some particular event or object felt to be contributory, though we feel ignorant of any general condition it exemplifies which, properly speaking, itself belongs to the total cause.

It has further been remarked that control has two faces: we are sometimes interested in producing an effect, at other times concerned to prevent one from occurring. In the former case, we naturally attend, with Mill, to those contingencies "which being realised, the consequent invariably follows." In the latter case, we may attribute causal status rather to those contingencies which, being unrealized, the consequent invariably fails to follow. Thus, imagine a substance which invariably produces cancer when injected; the discovery of this substance does not constitute finding the cause of cancer, for our concern is to prevent this disease, and 'finding the cause of cancer' is accordingly interpreted, commonly, as 'finding some antecedent avoidable condition, failing the realization of which, cancer never occurs'. Here, as before, variable pragmatic criteria are involved: we may, for example, require the condition in question to be effectively avoidable within the limits of available technology and accepted moral principles.

---

we come to apply theories that we read off from them the causes of this and that, but there is no call for the term 'cause' to figure within the theories themselves." Stephen Edelston Toulmin, *The Philosophy of Science, An Introduction* (London: Hutchinson's House, 1953), pp. 121, 122. By permission.

While generally despairing of the term 'cause' as a precise theoretical notion, modern writers have largely upheld the doctrine that explanation of events proceeds by way of trying to connect these events with others through general principles based on, though not demonstrable by, experience. Instead of talking of "the cause, philosophically speaking," they have tried to reconstruct *causal explanation* as a pattern of deductive argument, in which the premises describe particular conditions and formulate general principles, and the conclusion describes the event or events to be explained.

2. The Deductive Pattern of Explanation

Three influential modern reconstructions of causal explanation as a form of deductive argument are those of K. R. Popper, C. G. Hempel, and Hempel and P. Oppenheim. We shall discuss these presentations with a view to bringing out their main common features as well as indicating divergent details of importance.

Popper writes, "To give a *causal explanation* of an event means to deduce a statement which describes it, using as premises of the deduction one or more *universal laws,* together with certain singular statements, the *initial conditions.*"[7] By way of example, he provides a causal explanation of the breaking of a thread, in terms of two laws and two initial condition statements. The laws he cites are (1) "For every thread of a given structure S (determined by its material, thickness, etc.), there is a characteristic weight w, such that the thread will break if any weight exceeding w is suspended from it," and (2) "For every thread of the structure $S1$, the characteristic weight $w1$ equals 1 lb." The statements describing initial conditions are (1) "This is a thread of structure $S1$," and (2) "The weight . . . put on this thread is equal to 2 lbs." From these four statements comprising the explanation (assuming also the principle that 2 pounds exceed 1 pound), the conclusion 'This thread breaks' may be

---

[7] Karl R. Popper, *The Logic of Scientific Discovery* [translation of *Logik der Forschung,* 1934] (London: Hutchinson & Co. Publishers Ltd., 1959), p. 59. By permission of the publisher and Basic Books, Inc.

deduced, and thus the event described by the latter statement causally explained.[8]

Popper considers both universal laws and initial condition statements to be "necessary ingredients of a complete causal explanation."[9] Hempel's account in "The Function of General Laws in History" is similar in this regard. The explanation of an event of a given kind E consists, as he here puts it, of

(1) a set of statements asserting the occurrence of certain events $C_1 \ldots C_n$ at certain times and places,

(2) a set of universal hypotheses, such that
   (a) the statements of both groups are reasonably well confirmed by empirical evidence,
   (b) from the two groups of statements the sentence asserting the occurrence of event E can be logically deduced.[1]

The later Hempel and Oppenheim paper generalizes the above account of explanation in no longer requiring non-lawlike initial condition statements to appear in the premises. The point of this generalization is to include as an explanation "the derivation of the general regularities governing the motion of double stars from the laws of celestial mechanics, even though all the statements in the explanans are general laws."[2] This change is of little concern to us here, since we are concerned with the explanation of events rather than regularities.

In another respect, however, the Hempel and Oppenheim paper differs even as regards the explanation of events: it requires the explanatory premises (the explanans) to be true rather than well confirmed. The reason here is that the require-

[8] *Ibid.*, p. 60, new footnote *1.

[9] *Ibid.*, p. 60.

[1] Carl G. Hempel, "The Function of General Laws in History," *Journal of Philosophy*, XXXIX (1942), 36. By permission. Reprinted in Herbert Feigl and Wilfrid Sellars (eds.), *Readings in Philosophical Analysis* (New York: Appleton-Century-Crofts, Inc., 1949), p. 460.

[2] Carl G. Hempel and Paul Oppenheim, "Studies in the Logic of Explanation," *Philosophy of Science*, XV (1948), 137. By permission of the publisher.

ment of well-confirmedness yields untoward consequences with respect to the way we commonly apply the notion of explanation: given a purported explanans initially well confirmed and now disconfirmed, this requirement would lead us to say that the explanans in question initially provided a genuine explanation but had now ceased to do so. It would seem rather more plausible to say that the earlier evidence had led us to suppose the purported explanans to be true and (fulfilling other relevant conditions) hence to provide a genuine explanation of the phenomenon in question, whereas the evidence now available leads us to suppose this same explanans to be false and hence not now or ever to provide an explanation of the phenomenon in question.[3]

However, in construing explanation of events as a matter of providing premises (inclusive of general laws) from which the descriptions of these events may be logically deduced, the Hempel and Oppenheim paper takes the familiar approach. It should be especially noted that what is said to be logically deduced in a given instance of explanation according to this approach is the description of the occurrence to be explained, and that what it is said to be deduced from are the explanatory premises, containing general laws. It must not be supposed that these general laws themselves are being declared to be demonstrable on the basis of available evidence; this would be a wholly different claim and one impossible to maintain, in view of the fact that available evidence embodies information about a limited number of cases whereas general laws affirm that certain properties hold for all cases. Popular opinion to the contrary, neither scientists nor detectives can strictly be said to reach their theories by a process of logical deduction from the specific clues available to them.

The deductive theory of explanation is thus thoroughly in accord with Hume in holding that the general principles included

---

[3] But see Carl G. Hempel, "Deductive-Nomological vs. Statistical Explanation," in Herbert Feigl and Grover Maxwell (eds.), *Minnesota Studies in the Philosophy of Science* (Minneapolis: University of Minnesota Press, 1962), III, 98-169, in which the truth requirement is again removed.

in our explanatory premises rest upon experience but cannot be logically deduced from experience. To say what is involved in "resting upon" experience is the problem of explaining confirmation, and we shall discuss this problem in Part III. At this point, it is, however, important to see that, despite the fact that explanatory premises are not themselves deducible from available evidence, explanation may consistently be held to be a matter of deducing *from* such premises descriptions of the events to be explained.

The thesis of emergence, for example, maintains that properties of wholes are not, in general, predictable on the basis of information concerning their parts. The thesis needs, of course, to be relativized to particular wholes and choices of properties, as well as to particular segmentations of their parts. So construed, the claim of unpredictability has been said to need further relativization to general principles: unpredictability (in the sense of non-derivability of the property descriptions concerned) varies with such principles and is not absolute. The lack of appropriate principles today may conceivably be remedied by the science of tomorrow. It has, however, been suggested that the latter criticism of the thesis of emergence is inconsistent with Hume, for, were all properties predictable in principle, logical deduction would rule in every case of empirical inference. Since Hume is right in denying necessary connections of matters of fact, therefore some properties must be forever unpredictable through eternal lack of appropriate general principles; hence the thesis of emergence is true.[4]

In the light of what was said in the previous paragraph, it may be seen how this argument breaks down. General principles may themselves outstrip the possibility of demonstration by available evidence, and yet they may help provide deductive grounds for inferring the occurrence of properties of any sort. It is a separate

---

[4] On these issues, see Hempel and Oppenheim, "Studies in the Logic of Explanation," Part II, pp. 146-152; David L. Miller, "Comments on 'Studies in the Logic of Explanation,'" *Philosophy of Science*, XV (1948), 348-349; and Carl G. Hempel and Paul Oppenheim, "Reply to David L. Miller's Comments," *Philosophy of Science*, XV (1948), 350-352.

question whether or not predictability is properly taken as a matter of logical deducibility, on an analogy with the deductive pattern of explanation. We shall raise this question at a later point. Meanwhile, let us return to the explicit account of explanation given in the Hempel and Oppenheim study.

This account construes every explanation as consisting of an explanandum, i.e., a statement describing the phenomenon to be explained, and an explanans, i.e., a set of statements explaining the phenomenon in question. Four conditions are stated which are held to be requirements for explanations:

    (R1)   The explanandum must be a logical consequence of the explanans.

    (R2)   The explanans must contain general laws required for the derivation of the explanandum.

    (R3)   The explanans must have empirical content.

    (R4)   The sentences constituting the explanans must be true.[5]

As noted earlier, the concept of explanation is here generalized, with respect to earlier treatments, in that the explanans is not required to contain non-laws. This is done so as to include under the rubric of 'explanation' not only explanations of particular occurrences, but also explanations of generalizations, i.e., laws and theories. Nevertheless, it is a simple matter to single out cases where the explanandum describes a particular event or particular events and, hence, where the explanans contains, in addition to general laws, also non-laws, i.e., what (following Hempel and Oppenheim) may be called "antecedent condition" statements. These cases, for which they suggest the name 'causal explanation', thus form a subclass of the class of explanations.

With regard to causal explanations so interpreted, the claim is made that they are formally or structurally identical with predictions, the difference being merely a pragmatic one, i.e., a matter of the time when the explanans is produced by the person, and of the assumptions he makes at that time. If, that is, we

[5] Hempel and Oppenheim, "Studies in the Logic of Explanation," pp. 137-138.

assume some event to have occurred and take its description as our explanandum, providing an explanans later on, we have causally explained the event. On the other hand, if we had assumed the same explanans to begin with, and performed the same logical deduction leading to the same explanandum prior to the occurrence of the event it describes, we should have been predicting rather than explaining this event. Causal explanation and prediction are thus said to be logically similar, and the same formal analysis, including the four conditions (R1)-(R4) is held to apply to prediction as well as explanation.

Accounts similar to the one just given are frequently supplemented with the claim that explanation and prediction are of basic importance in science. The paper by Hempel earlier discussed said that "the main function of general laws in the natural sciences is to connect events in patterns which are usually referred to as explanation and prediction."[6] The Hempel and Oppenheim study declares that explanation represents a "chief objective of science,"[7] and, further, that it is its "potential predictive force" that gives explanation its importance—"the major objective of scientific research" being to go beyond recording past experience toward prediction and control.[8]

The view we have been considering, exemplified in the Hempel and Oppenheim paper, thus provides a clear and comprehensive account of certain of the structural terms. This account makes room for both the explanation of generalizations and the causal explanation of events. It embraces both explanation and prediction, asserting their structural identity while distinguishing between them plausibly on pragmatic grounds. It assigns them both important roles as central objectives of scientific inquiry. Finally, it relates explanation and prediction to the notions of lawfulness and empirical content, notions which need in any event to be taken account of in a general theory of scientific structure. It is,

[6] Hempel, "The Function of General Laws in History," Section 2.1, p. 35.
[7] Hempel and Oppenheim, "Studies in the Logic of Explanation," p. 135.
[8] *Ibid.,* p. 138.

thus, not hard to see why this view has been the subject of much study, discussion, and criticism over the years. We turn now to selected strands of this critical discussion.

3. Statistical and Confirmational Generalization

Hempel and Oppenheim themselves suggest that the view we have been considering is ideal in requiring universal laws in the explanatory premises, and logical deduction from premises to conclusion. They propose that attention be paid to explanatory premises with statistical laws, "which assert that in the long run, an explicitly stated percentage of all cases satisfying a given set of conditions are accompanied by an event of a certain specified kind."[9] Presumably, what they have in mind is an explanation of the following type: Smith has had four cups of coffee just before retiring; a high percentage, say 90 percent, of those who take four cups of coffee just before retiring have difficulty in falling asleep; therefore Smith has had difficulty in falling asleep. The connection between premises and conclusion is not deductive in this case (the form of the transition from premises to conclusion is not uniformly truth-preserving) since the general premise is statistical rather than universal; yet something does seem to be accomplished in the way of explaining Smith's sleeplessness.

Furthermore, and "independently of the admission of statistical laws among the explanatory principles," the requirement of logical deducibility of the conclusion may be weakened to that of high confirmation of the conclusion relative to the premises.[1] A relevant example here is one suggested by Hempel in another context:[2]

Let '*P*' stand for 'is white phosphorus';
let '*G*' stand for 'has a garlic-like odor';

[9] *Ibid.*, p. 139.
[1] *Ibid.*, p. 164.
[2] Carl G. Hempel, "The Theoretician's Dilemma," in Herbert Feigl, Michael Scriven, and Grover Maxwell (eds.), *Minnesota Studies in the Philosophy of Science* (Minneapolis: University of Minnesota Press, 1958), II, 78-79. The example is here altered in certain respects.

let '*T*' stand for 'is soluble in turpentine';
let '*V*' stand for 'is soluble in vegetable oils';
let '*E*' stand for 'is soluble in ether'; and
let '*S*' stand for 'produces skin burns'.

Now, we shall further assume that the properties represented by '*G*', '*T*', '*V*', '*E*', and '*S*' are independent, that is, each occasionally occurs without one or more of the others. Finally, let us consider a theory which asserts that white phosphorus always exhibits every one of these properties, though it fails to assert the converse, namely, that exhibition of all these properties is always indicative of white phosphorus.

We may represent our theory symbolically as comprising the following five statements:

(1) $\qquad (x)\ (Px \supset Gx)$

(to be read: 'For every thing *x*, if *x* is white phosphorus, then *x* has a garlic-like odor'. The other statements are to be rendered analogously.)

(2) $\qquad (x)\ (Px \supset Tx)$
(3) $\qquad (x)\ (Px \supset Vx)$
(4) $\qquad (x)\ (Px \supset Ex)$
(5) $\qquad (x)\ (Px \supset Sx)$

We shall now add the following two laws to our assumptions:

(6) $\qquad (x)\ (Px \supset Ix)$
(7) $\qquad (x)\ (t)\ (Ix \cdot Cx, t \supset Fx, t)$

(6) tells us that white phosphorus has an ignition temperature of 30° C., and (7) tells us that every substance with such an ignition temperature bursts into flame at any time *t* when surrounding air rises above 30° C. in temperature. (The formula (7) is to be read: 'For every thing *x* and every time *t*, if *x* has an ignition temperature of 30° C. and *x* is surrounded by air above 30° C. at *t*, then *x* bursts into flame at *t*'.)

We want now to explain why a given object *a* bursts into flame at a given moment t_0, when the rising temperature of the surrounding air in fact crosses the 30° C. mark. We offer the information that *a* has exhibited the properties represented by '*G*', '*T*', '*V*', '*E*', and '*S*'.

We may elaborate the example by the addition of information sufficient to eliminate relevant alternatives to *a*'s being white phosphorus. Suppose, for example, that we know of two additional properties *W* and *Q*, such that:

(8)   Whatever possesses either one lacks both the other one and the property of being white phosphorus.

Suppose further that:

(9)   Whatever has *W* or *Q* always has *G*, *T*, *V*, *E*, and *S*.

Finally, suppose that:

(10)   Whatever has *W* always has also the property *J*,

while:

(11)   Whatever has *Q* always has the property *K*.

Finding that our object *a* lacks both *K* and *J*, we now know that *a* has neither the property *W* nor *Q*, either of which would be sufficient to preclude *a* from being white phosphorus.

Still, all the information given does not allow us to *deduce logically* that *a* is white phosphorus. At best, this information lends confirmatory force to such a conclusion, especially in view of the independence of *G*, *T*, *V*, *E*, and *S*, and the elimination of the reasonable alternatives *W* and *Q*. Accepting the credible assumption, then, that *a* is in fact *P*, and recalling that at t_0, *a* was surrounded by air above 30° C., we now logically deduce, with the help of (6) and (7), the conclusion that *a* bursts into flame at t_0, representing exactly the phenomenon to be explained.

Part of our chain of reasoning has indeed been deductive. However, the crucial link asserting that *a* is *P* has *not* been deduced from, but at best confirmed by (1)-(11) plus the information that *a* is *G*, *T*, *V*, *E*, and *S*, and neither *J* nor *K*. The total passage from explanatory premises to final conclusion has thus in fact not been deductive. At best, these premises may be said to have lent high confirmation to the conclusion of the argument, though every one of our general assumptions (1)-(11) is nonstatistical, unlike the previous example of Smith's sleeplessness.

A final illustration of a non-deductive relationship between explanatory premises and conclusion, again without statistical generalizations, is afforded by the following simple case; in this case, the crucial link allowing the final deduction is gotten without appeal to general lawlike assumptions such as (1)-(11).[3] A large sample of instances of P has been examined, and every one is also Q. We expect that a new instance c of P will also turn out to be Q, though we cannot, of course, demonstrate that it will be Q. This is offered as a case of expectation or prediction but supplementation with the universal premise '(x) $(Qx \supset Rx)$' provides an explanatory analogue. To explain why c is R, we may plausibly reply that c is P and that a large sample of other cases of P has been examined, which have all been found to be Q as well, thus leading us to accept the crucial supposition that c is Q and enabling us to deduce by our single universal premise that it is also R.

In the Hempel and Oppenheim paper, note is taken of the fact that definition of a statistically generalized notion of explanation requires the solution of certain technical problems, concerning the expression of statistical statements in the languages for which the definition is to hold. In addition, we may note that a non-deductive, confirmational generalization requires explicit attention to the notion of confirmation involved.[4] Apart from these relatively technical questions of statistical and confirmation theory, there remain certain general issues to which we shall here address ourselves.

Considering first the inclusion of statistical laws in the explanatory premises, we may remark that such inclusion renders explanation relatively incomplete, by comparison with its fully universal counterpart. Recall Smith's sleeplessness, and its explanation in terms of the effect coffee has on 90 percent of those taking four cups before retiring. That the explanation here is in

[3] *Ibid.*, p. 40, footnote 6.
[4] For a general discussion, see Hempel, "Deductive-Nomological vs. Statistical Explanation," *loc. cit.*

a relevant sense incomplete may be judged from the fact that the question persists as to why Smith should be counted among the 90 percent affected by the coffee and not among the 10 percent not so affected. We may, in fact, conjecture in such circumstances that there is some further constitutional difference that, coupled with the composition of the coffee, accounts for the statistical effect itself as well as for Smith's sleeplessness, according to the deductive pattern.

There are cases where, in fact, the statistical account seems less satisfying than here. To be told, for example, that Jones had a heart attack because in his age group 75 percent of men have heart attacks is, normally, to leave out of account just what we want to know, i.e., why *Jones* had an attack, how he was differentially constituted and how he differentially reacted. To say that there is a high incidence of cancer in Smith's age, occupational, and geographical group is compatible with saying we do not understand why Smith was afflicted with cancer.

There is, however, no incompatibility between the provision of a statistical explanation and the search for a deductive account of the phenomenon in question. We may, in fact, wish to construe statistical explanation as a special case of pragmatically incomplete deductive explanation, where needed elements are missing through ignorance. Such a construction seems obviously available everywhere except in the case of modern physical theory, which offers special arguments against it. To sum up, there seems no good reason to deny either that statistical explanations are less satisfying than their fully deductive counterparts, or that, as far as they go, they are genuinely explanatory in character. There does not seem to be any real objection to extending the concept of explanation in such a way as to include them.

The matter seems, however, different with respect to confirmational generalization, that is, independent weakening of the requirement of logical deducibility to that of high confirmation between explanatory premises and conclusion. To see where the difference lies, we shall need to examine our earlier examples in some detail. But one misunderstanding needs first to be removed.

It might be suspected that confirmational generalization reverts to Hempel's initial requirement of high confirmation for the explanatory premises, and that it thus leads to the same objectionable relativity of 'explanation' to avoid which the Hempel and Oppenheim paper adopted the requirement of truth. This suspicion is, however, unfounded. The earlier alteration of requirements which we have discussed concerned the status of the explanans *taken by itself*, whereas the present proposal to weaken the deducibility requirement concerns rather the *relationship* between explanans and explanandum.

Thus, in the white phosphorus example earlier discussed, the explanandum was:

$$Fa, t_0 \ (a \text{ bursts into flame at } t_0)$$

and the explanans consisted of statements (1)-(11), plus the singular statements:

(S1)	Ga
(S2)	Ta
(S3)	Va
(S4)	Ea
(S5)	Sa
(S6)	$\sim Ka$
(S7)	$\sim Ja$
(S8)	Ca, t_0

(That is, a has properties G, T, V, E, S, but not K and not J, and at t_0 is surrounded by air above 30° C.)

The explanans above still needs to be *true* under the proposal to weaken the deducibility requirement. This proposal simply rules that it need not *logically imply* what it explains; thus 'Fa, t_0' is ruled a genuine explanandum of the above explanans on the strength of its being highly confirmed (though not implied) by it.

The fact that the explanans still needs to be true enables the present proposal to avoid relativizing explanation to time by making it dependent on the changing fortunes of the explanatory premises themselves. We may, however, wonder if such relativization is not being introduced in another way. We have supposed

(1)-(11) and (S1)-(S8) to be true. Under the proposal of confirmational generalization, they will together comprise an explanans for '*Fa, t₀*' only if they provide high confirmation for it. Now, if this latter condition is here interpreted in such a way as itself to be relative to time, we shall have our objectionable consequence back again: our premises, true though they are, may constitute an explanans for the same statement '*Fa, t₀*' at one time but not at another.

To illustrate this possibility, recall that the confirmation given by (1)-(5) plus (S1)-(S5) to the crucial link '*Pa*' was strengthened by information asserting the independence of the five properties *G, T, V, E,* and *S*. If we are to take it that such independence needs to be *accepted* at a given time in order for the strengthened confirmation of '*Pa*' to accrue at that time, and if we allow that such acceptance may hold at one time but not another, we must allow that '*Pa*', and hence our explanandum '*Fa, t₀*' also, may be more strongly confirmed by our explanans at one time than at another. In principle, then, depending on the background assumptions that are in fact accepted, a given set of statements may, under this interpretation, be said to explain a given event at t_1 and fail to do so at t_2.

Such an interpretation is, however, not necessary. In the example before us, we may not require the actual *acceptance* of the independence assumption at all, in acknowledging its enhancement of the confirmatory strength of our premises. We may simply be saying that if this assumption is added to the purported explanans as an extra premise, the whole set of premises gains in the degree to which it confirms '*Fa, t₀*', irrespective of time. Now, if the whole set is, furthermore, true, it explains why *a* is *F* at *t₀*, independently of anyone's acceptance of any assumption at any given time. Explanation is thus again saved from relativization to time, though we are free to admit that our opinions may vary as to whether a given set of statements constitutes an explanans for a specified event.

The general point raised in the preceding discussion remains of interest, however, in the following way. Should further analysis of confirmation reintroduce some pragmatic factor rendering it time-dependent, explanation would again be relativized to time as a result of confirmational generalization. Nor is this a merely academic possibility, as we shall see in more detail later. Attempts to provide purely formal analyses of confirmation have, in fact, encountered serious difficulties, and appeal to pragmatic considerations has already been made explicitly in Goodman's theory of projection.[5] In the face of such developments, it might be argued that, in order to resist the temporal relativization of explanation, we ought to retain the strong requirement of logical deducibility between explanans· and explanandum, wherever we can.

That such retention is more widely possible than might be supposed and that it has the advantage of naturalness may be seen by a further look at the white phosphorus example. Our presentation of this example so far has given the explanans as (1)-(11) plus (S1)-(S8), and the whole example rests on the fact that this set of statements does not logically imply 'Fa, t_0'. An alternative account is, however, available, which involves splitting this set into two parts, and adding the statement 'Pa'. We now take the explanans as consisting just of:

	'Pa'
(S8)	'Ca, t_0'
(6)	$(x) (Px \supset Ix)$
(7)	$(x) (t) (Ix \cdot Cx, t \supset Fx, t),$

the whole set of four statements yielding as a logical consequence the explanandum:

$$'Fa, t_0'$$

The remainder of our *initial* explanans is now reinterpreted as falling outside the explanans but as providing grounds for judging 'Pa' to be true. That is, (1)-(5) plus (S1)-(S5) provide some ground for accepting 'Pa', and (8)-(11) plus (S6) and (S7) provide additional ground. They thus form part of the basis on which the explanans rests but they do not themselves belong to it. The explanans itself, meanwhile, fulfills the require-

[5] Nelson Goodman, *Fact, Fiction, and Forecast* (Cambridge, Mass.: Harvard University Press, 1955), chap. iv, pp. 87-126.

ments of the deductive pattern. Such an alternative account, preserving the requirement of logical deducibility, seems widely available in cases where a purported explanans is non-statistical but does not logically imply the explanandum.

This alternative account distinguishes between the explanans proper which may, in ordinary parlance, be said to give the *ground of the event,* and those assumptions which may be ordinarily said to formulate *grounds for acceptance* of the explanans as true. It is the preservation of this sort of distinction which makes the account a more natural way of putting things than its rival. For in fact it does seem wrong, ordinarily speaking, to say that a's bursting into flame at t_0 is explained by, or due to, a's having the properties of garlic-like odor, solubility in turpentine, vegetable oils, and ether, capability of producing skin burns and lack of J and K, as well as (1)-(11) and (S8). We should rather prefer to say, upon reflection, that what explains a's having burst into flame at t_0 is the fact that it was white phosphorus and surrounded by air above 30° C., given the principles (6) and (7) which formulate the relevant properties of this substance.

We might then wish to add that our *belief* in this explanation is based, in part, on the symptomatic behavior of a, that is, on its having a garlic-like odor, and so forth. We should thus be making the distinction between that which *explains a's bursting into flame* and that which *explains, or justifies, our belief* in this explanation, i.e., that which formulates the reasons we offer for such belief. We should, in effect, be separating the "ground," "reason," or "cause" of events from the "ground," "reason," or "cause" for acceptance of beliefs. This natural separation is blurred by the first construction according to which the explanans consists of (1)-(11) and (S1)-(S8), but it is preserved by the second, for which the explanans consists of Pa, (S8), (6), and (7).[6]

At the beginning of this Part, we distinguished causal explana-

[6] A related distinction is introduced for another purpose in Michael Scriven, "Explanations, Predictions, and Laws," in Feigl and Maxwell (eds.), *Minnesota Studies in the Philosophy of Science,* Vol. III, section 4.1, pp. 196-201.

tion of events from explanation of judgments or beliefs, in the sense of provision of justification for these judgments or beliefs. We have just seen how preservation of the logical deducibility requirement enables us to preserve such a distinction in a wide class of cases. Another illustration, with special reference to the related contrast between symptoms and causes, may be welcome at this point.

Dr. Jones, asked to explain his patient's high fever, replies by listing such symptoms as a particular blood count, certain pains, and a specific pulse rate. We shall suppose that these symptoms, B, N, and R, are always to be found where a patient has contracted a certain disease D, that is:

(12) $\qquad (x) (Dx \supset Bx)$
(13) $\qquad (x) (Dx \supset Nx)$
(14) $\qquad (x) (Dx \supset Rx)$

but not that B, N, and R are always, either alone or in combination, accompanied by D, though they are independent properties. We shall assume, further, that D is always followed by high fever:

(15) $\qquad (x) (Dx \supset Fx)$

In this situation, it seems clearly inappropriate to take the doctor's description of blood count, pain, and pulse as providing a causal account of the fever. The onset of the fever is not explained by the blood count nor any other symptom of D. We should rather take the doctor's statement as giving his grounds for suspecting the patient has disease D, and as suggesting that the presence of D would indeed account for the high fever. The symptoms listed are not ordinarily construed as explaining the fever; they at best support the diagnosis of D which, together with (15), explains the fever. Consideration of this example has not yielded a *criterion* for making the distinction between symptoms and causes. Rather, it has shown how confirmational generalization sometimes violates this practical distinction as commonly recognized.

We must, now, give consideration to the final example previously offered as illustrative of confirmational generalization. Though originally suggested as an exemplification of prediction, our earlier discussion provided the following explanatory analogue:

(16)	$(x) (Qx \supset Rx)$
(17)	$Pd \cdot Qd$
(18)	$Pe \cdot Qe$
(19)	$Pf \cdot Qf$
(20)	Pc
(21)	Rc

(21) is our explanandum, and (16)-(20) our explanans, on the assumption that $d, e,$ and f represent all the cases of P so far examined, with the single exception of c. So construed, the explanans does not logically imply (21), but at best confirms it, through confirming the assumption that c is Q, which yields (21) when account is taken of (16). We have, however, already seen how to resist confirmational generalization in such a case by providing an alternative construction: We add to (16) the confirmed assumption 'Qc' and logically derive the explanandum (21); asked to justify our confidence in 'Qc', we produce (17)-(20).

Moreover, an analogous course is available in case 'Qc' itself were to be suggested as explanandum, with (17)-(20) as explanans (despite the lack of a general law). We add to (20) the principle, '$(x) (Px \supset Qx)$' and logically derive 'Qc'; asked to justify our appeal to the principle, we call upon (17)-(19). Here too, this course has the decided advantage of naturalness in preserving common distinctions. For, while it *is* plausible to take (17)-(20) as the basis for a *prediction* of 'Qc' (in accordance with the original use of the present example), we should not, ordinarily, hold that c's having the property Q is due, even partly, to the fact that $d, e,$ and f have this property as well as P. We may well *predict* that the sample of copper before us will conduct electricity under test, on the ground that all previous samples have, but we do not *explain why* it does so by listing all these previous copper samples which have, in fact, conducted electricity.

The latter considerations indeed point to a serious divergence between explanation and prediction, in showing that not every predictive base for a given statement is an explanans for that statement (even when adjustment of the relevant pragmatic factors is made); the predictive base may justify our acceptance of the statement without explaining the event it describes. Confirmational generalization of the deductive pattern, though encountering the difficulties we have outlined with respect to explanation, is thus quite plausible for prediction. This is so, even though it may involve giving up not only (R1), the deducibility requirement, but also (R2), the requirement of general laws (as is clear from the example just considered where the predictive base lacked general laws).

This divergence between explanation and prediction shows up equally in the other examples we have considered. In each case, the set of statements we disparaged as a possible explanans seems to constitute a satisfactory *predictive* base. Thus (1)-(11) plus (S1)-(S8) seem to represent good grounds for predicting 'Fa, t_0', though failing to explain the event in question, in the usual sense of this phrase. Analogously, the doctor's listing of blood count, pains, and pulse rate seems a satisfactory predictive base for the onset of high fever, though it affords no explanation of it. Finally, the sentences (16)-(20) may not explain (21), but they constitute a genuine predictive base for it.

Indeed, corresponding to every fully deductive explanation, it may be suggested that there is some base which may be acknowledged as predictive though not as explanatory. Consider the derivation, previously discussed:

(16) $(x) (Qx \supset Rx)$
Qc

(21) Rc

and consider that (16) is itself presumably accepted on the basis of evidence embodied in a finite number of cases (e.g., '$Qm \cdot Rm$',

'$Qn \cdot Rn$', etc., though, of course, the evidence need not be restricted to this simple form). If this is so, then the explanans, in this instance, is itself correlated to the evidential base '$Qm \cdot Rm$', '$Qn \cdot Rn$', etc. . . . 'Qc'. The relation of the latter base to (21) is, obviously, non-deductive and exactly analogous to the prediction of 'Qc' on the basis of (17)-(20). It does not serve as an explanans for (21) but can hardly be ruled out as a predictive base for it. To sum up, the thesis of the structural identity of explanation and prediction seems untenable in the light of the differential relevance of confirmational generalization.

4. The Structural Divergence of Explanation and Prediction

We have found reason to distinguish explanation from prediction. The predictive base, we have seen, gives grounds for expecting some event to occur but need not constitute an explanans for it, even when repeated following the event's occurrence. Prediction can neither be wholly assimilated to explanation as given in the deductive pattern nor, conversely, can explanation be understood as merely the provision of a potentially predictive base, a matter of showing that the problematic event *was to be expected*—as suggested by several writers.[7] Explanation seems to require appeal to general principles, whether universal or statistical, serving to connect events in patterns.

These reflections constitute a denial of the doctrine that explanation and prediction differ only pragmatically, but not structurally. The argument hinged on showing that not every predictive base, which in fact gives grounds for the acceptance of some statement, is also an explanans for that statement. It is, of course, true that, in common parlance, the notion of prediction is not the same as that of predictive base. In particular, it does not imply the provision of reasons, but simply the assertion of something about the future. Given this familiar sense, however, it is perhaps even more obvious that structural identity fails, for not

[7] For example, Stephen Edelston Toulmin, *The Place of Reason in Ethics* (Cambridge, England: Cambridge University Press, 1950), p. 123.

even every true prediction in this sense becomes explanatory simply through restatement after the fact.

The restriction of the structural identity thesis to cases in science where grounds are offered for acceptance of beliefs concerning the future is unsuccessful in saving the thesis, for some such grounds are not explanatory, as we have argued, even when pragmatic adjustments are made, i.e., even when these grounds are restated after the time for which the event was predicted, and *even when this event has in fact occurred*. The failure of the thesis emerges even more strongly when we reflect that the event in question need not have occurred at a given time in order for the grounds to have predicted that it would occur at that time. If, however, the event has *in fact* failed to occur at the predicted time, restatement of the same (predictive) grounds can hardly be said to explain its occurrence, for there is nothing to explain. Such predictive failure may lead us (properly) to judge admittedly predictive grounds false, whereas we may never (properly) judge an admittedly genuine explanans to be false.

Looking back again at the four requirements of Hempel and Oppenheim, every set of statements comprising an explanation is (for them) true, consisting of an explanans required by (R4) to be true, and an explanandum which must also be true since a logical consequence of the latter. The truth of the explanandum is further, as intimated in the previous paragraph, an *independently* natural requirement in accord with common application of the notion of explanation and likely to be upheld irrespective of statistical or confirmational generalization. (That the occurrence of an event has been predicted does not imply its actual occurrence; that the occurrence of an event has been explained does imply its actual occurrence.) The contrast with scientific prediction is sharp. Such prediction may or may not be successful —and unsuccessful prediction, i.e., the grounding of a false conclusion on a genuinely predictive base, is an important circumstance for the testing of scientific theories. Such testing frequently involves the grounding of predictive conclusions upon such theories taken together with subsidiary assumptions; these conclusions are then independently examined for truth, a negative result constituting grounds for revision of the predictive base, and, most importantly, for an alteration of the theoretical part of that base. False predictions in science thus play an important part in procedures of testing. Indeed, to the degree that such testing is involved in confirming general laws, themselves required by (R2) for explanation, the possibility of false predictions is involved in the confirmation of explanations.

The structural identity thesis might perhaps be defended by reinterpretation as holding between (1) scientific predictions that are in fact gotten by deduction from general and particular assumptions, and (2) *proffered* explanations, which may, of course, be false in fact. Such a reinterpretation weakens the thesis considerably by limiting it to what is only a subclass of scientific predictions, as we have seen. In addition, moreover, the notion of proffered explanations is problematic, and will not serve the intended purpose without elaborate design.

For, in its usual sense, 'proffered explanation' refers not only to deductive grounds which may be false, thus violating (R4), but also to statements which may fail to constitute deductive grounds, as required by (R1), fail to contain general laws, as required by (R2), or lack the empirical content required by (R3). In order to parallel prediction in the desired manner, the notion of proffered explanation must, presumably, be interpreted so as to exclude these unwanted consequences; it must, in effect, be artificially restricted. Furthermore, in another respect it is perhaps too narrow, typically restricted to cases where the explanandum is true, whereas predictive conclusions may, on any account, be false.

To get a sense of 'proffered explanation' that will serve the purpose of the reinterpreted thesis, we should need, then, to specify that (R1), (R2), and (R3) are to hold, but not (R4), nor the truth of the explanandum. The prediction to which this notion is to correspond is to be not prediction in general, nor even scientific prediction in general, but just scientific prediction satisfying (R1), (R2), and (R3). We have admittedly gotten a structural identity in this manner finally, but at a cost which outweighs the achievement. For this identity is not only limited in scope but trivial, since it is no surprising congruence of two independent patterns, but a deliberate consequence of the way these patterns have been drawn.

In sum, aside from the case of statistical premises, we have seen reason to retain the deductive pattern as a model for explanation, while allowing that prediction may diverge radically. It may diverge not only in providing non-deductive grounds for acceptance of beliefs, but also in lacking appeal to general principles, and, finally, in failing to be true. Such divergence is surely structural, in any natural sense of the word.

5. The Centrality of Explanation and Prediction

The thesis of structural identity was associated with the claim that explanation and prediction represent the central purpose of scientific endeavor. To deny the thesis of structural identity, as we have done, is to render the claim of centrality, at the very least, ambiguous: are both explanation and prediction central, or is one more important than the other? Actually, if we look more closely at each, even independently of our criticism of structural identity, we find distinctive temporal restrictions which argue that neither is central to science.

We shall support this judgment by referring again to the deductive pattern as given by the Hempel and Oppenheim requirements (R1)-(R4). These requirements include no temporal conditions at all, whereas prediction and explanation are each temporally restricted in special ways. The pattern represented by (R1)-(R4) thus includes arguments other than those of predictive or explanatory character, and gives no ground for conferring primacy upon the latter sorts. We shall illustrate this contention by producing examples of scientific forms of argument satisfying the pattern but neither explanatory nor predictive. We shall then consider critically some general epistemological arguments in favor of the primacy of explanation and prediction.

It may be pertinent here to comment on the relationship between the present discussion and the issues of statistical and confirmational generalization. Our treatment will focus on the ungeneralized deductive pattern, and will try to show that it embraces arguments neither explanatory nor predictive in the common sense of these terms, i.e., that the pattern is too inclusive to represent just explanation and prediction. To generalize the pattern and so to render it still more inclusive will thus leave our present treatment unchanged. Furthermore, the modes of generalization envisaged are themselves neutral with respect to time, so that, even if generalization allows the admission of predictive and explanatory arguments hitherto excluded (e.g., statistical explanations, merely confirmatory predictive bases) it will also admit others which, for lack of the proper temporal restrictions, fail to be explanatory or predictive in the generalized sense. The main point to note, then, is the character of these temporal restrictions.

For convenience in the present phase of our discussion, we take *a* and *b* as distinct events, described by the statements *A* and *B,* respectively, and we take *L* as a law or conjunction of laws. We suppose also that *B* is a logical consequence of *A* and *L* but not of *A* alone. According to the structural identity claim we have criticized, if *B* is given, i.e., if we know that the phenomenon described by *B* has occurred, and *A* and *L* are provided afterward, we have an explanation, whereas if the latter are given, and *B* is derived prior to the occurrence of the phenomenon it describes, we speak of a prediction.

Note, now, that one inference allowed by the pattern but neither explanatory nor predictive is the following: If *A* and *L* are given, rather than *B,* thus precluding explanation, their logical consequence *B* may be derived not prior to, but simultaneous with or later than the occurrence of *b.* That is, *b* may have occurred not later than *B*'s derivation but (i) later than *a,* or (ii) prior to *a* itself.

For an example of the first case, (i), imagine an astronomer who, from statements describing the *beginning* of an ancient eclipse *a,* plus the appropriate laws, deduces a statement describing its *end b.* This end, *b,* is later than *a* but prior to *B*'s derivation, which is thus no prediction of it.

For an instance of the second case, (ii), imagine the same

astronomer who, from appropriate laws plus statements describing some relevant *configuration* of heavenly bodies at some time during his own lifetime *a,* deduces a statement describing some *eclipse* in former times *b.* Here, *b* antedates both the derivation of its description *B,* and the event *a.*

In neither example is *B* a prediction of the event *b,* yet both arguments fulfill the requirements of the deductive pattern. What is common to both examples and to the predictive arguments satisfying the pattern is not any given temporal relation between the production of statements and the events they describe, but rather the fact that *A* and *L* are first given and that *B* is derived from them. The latter sequence, however, bears no simple relationship to the sequence of described events.

The intended interpretation of the pattern for prediction may be diagramed as follows, with the left-to-right direction symbolizing the order of temporal succession:

(1)   *a, A, B, b*

Here, *a* has occurred, its description *A* is then combined with *L* to yield *B,* which is produced prior to the predicted event *b.* Case (i) offered above, however, receives the diagram:

(2)   *a, b, A, B*

Here, *a* and *b* have occurred long before *A* is combined with *L* to generate *B.* Case (ii), finally, may be diagramed as follows:

(3)   *b, a, A, B*

Here, the order of *b* and *a* is reversed, with *b* still preceding *B.* Still other variations are possible, e.g., *a* may follow *A,* and still *A* may be asserted with confidence (and, moreover, be true) as a basis for derivation of *B.* What (1)-(3) have in common is the order of *A* and *B.* Only (1) is predictive, though in each case *A* is given (with *L*). To refer to all such arguments in a temporally neutral way, so as to suggest the full potentialities of the pattern, we may employ the term 'positing'. From assumed laws and information about certain events, we posit other events in any spatial or temporal relations to our assumed events or to our own utterances. Some positing happens also to be predicting, but prediction has no more primacy for the pattern in question than positing events to the left of us in space.

Consider now the situation in which *B* is given and *A* and *L* are provided afterward. Again, we find arguments fitting this description, which, besides being non-predictive, are also non-explanatory. An illustration of such an argument is afforded by any case where the event *b* precedes the event *a*. Imagine, for example, that we are given a description *B* of some *eclipse* in former times *b*, and that we now provide appropriate laws *L* and statements describing some present *configuration* of heavenly bodies *a*, from which *B* is deducible. We have conformed to the pattern but we have not explained the earlier eclipse *b*. For explanation, we require that *a* must not temporally follow *b*. But to say we need to provide some *A* (and *L*) from which *B* follows logically still allows *a* to follow *b* temporally, as in our example.

The intended interpretation of the pattern for explanation may be diagramed as follows:

(4)   *a, b, B, A*

That is, *B* is given, *b* having already occurred earlier. *A* is then provided, describing some event *a* prior to *b*, and such that it logically yields *B* when combined with *L*. Our example of the preceding paragraph, however, receives the diagram:

(5)   *b, a, B, A*

Here, again, *B* is given, *b* having occurred long before. The later provision of *A*, however, gives a description of some event *a* which occurred after rather than before *b*. (Again, other variations are possible where, e.g., *a* follows *A*.) (4) and (5) give different temporal orders to *a* and *b*, but what they have in common is the order: *B* followed by *A*. Only (4) is explanatory, though in both cases *B* is given (with *L*). To refer to all such arguments in such a way as to suggest the full potentialities of the pattern, we may employ the term 'substantiating' for the class of arguments of which explaining is one sub-type.

Sometimes the notion of explanation is treated as if it had

some special connection with the ordinary use of "why?" in framing questions. It is, however, worth noting that the difference between (4) and (5) cannot be readily made out by reference to this use. For, whereas explanations, represented by (4), often answer the question "Why did b happen?" interpreted as "In accordance with what laws and because of what antecedent conditions did b occur?" the example represented by (5) answers the question "Why must b have happened?" interpreted as "By reference to what laws and conditions can b's occurrence be substantiated?" Substantiation provides excellent grounds for accepting B, but does not in every case also provide an explanation of b. Again, we find it important to distinguish between the ground of an event and the grounds of belief.

It is perhaps the failure to make such a distinction that beclouds the analysis of certain so-called "teleological" or "functional" explanations. For, as frequently analyzed, functional "explanations" share the form of (5) rather than (4), and may hence be construed as types of substantiation, but not readily as explanations.

We shall here consider one example.[8] Nagel considers the statement:

(a)   The function of chlorophyll in plants is to enable plants to perform photosynthesis.

as equivalent to:

(b)   A necessary condition for the occurrence of photosynthesis in plants is the presence of chlorophyll.

Given the common interpretation of 'necessary condition' as referring to the consequents of conditionals with respect to their antecedents, the statement (b) above is itself presumably equivalent to:

(c) $(x) \ (Px \cdot Phx \supset Cx)$

---

[8] Ernest Nagel, "Teleological Explanation and Teleological Systems," in S. Ratner (ed.), *Vision and Action* (New Brunswick: Rutgers University Press, 1953); reprinted in Feigl and Brodbeck (eds.), *Readings in the Philosophy of Science*, p. 541. By permission of Rutgers University Press.

where '*P*' stands for 'is a plant', '*Ph*' stands for 'performs photosynthesis', and '*C*' stands for 'contains chlorophyll'.

Nagel suggests that the distinctive "teleological" content of (a), hinging on the use of the term 'function', results from (a)'s picturing photosynthesis as a consequence of the presence of chlorophyll. That such "teleological" content is, however, inessential he believes to be shown by the allegedly equivalent restatement (b), lacking the term 'function' altogether, and picturing chlorophyll as a condition of photosynthesis. In Nagel's words, "A teleological explanation states the *consequences* for a given biological system of one of the latter's constituent parts or processes; the equivalent non-teleological explanation states some of the *conditions* . . . under which the system persists in its characteristic organization and activities."[9]

Now, if it is correct to interpret (b) as itself equivalent to (c), it is obvious that it does not provide a correct analysis of the 'function' statement (a), since some statements of the same form as (c) yield intolerable results when translated into presumably equivalent functional form. Consider the true statement:

(d) (x) (Organism $x \cdot$ Breathes $x \supset$ Dies x)

This shares the form of (c), and gives death as a necessary condition of breathing in organisms. Translation of (d) into functional form, however, yields the falsehood:

(e)   The function of death in organisms is to enable organisms to breathe.

Presumably some temporal restriction is intended here, to rule out such an awkward consequence, though it is doubtful that temporal restriction alone is sufficient to establish the general adequacy of the analysis. Waiving the latter point, however, let us then deny that (c) is sufficient to give the intended sense of (b). 'Necessary condition', we shall say, is to be taken as 'necessary non-subsequent condition'; since death *is* subsequent to breathing, the function of death cannot be to facilitate breathing.

So understood, Nagel's suggestion seems thus to be that to explain *b* functionally is to refer to a suitable *non-antecedent a,*

[9] *Ibid.*

such that A and L together imply B. Taking (c) above as representing simply L, we now reformulate it so as to make it clearly satisfy the time restriction mentioned:

(f) $(x)\ (t)\ (Px \cdot Phx,t \supset (\exists s)\ (Cx,s \cdot \text{Earlier } s,t))$

where 't' and 's' are variables for times, where 'Phx,t' means 'x performs photosynthesis at t', and 'Cx,s' means 'x contains chlorophyll at s'.

Note that (f) alone is simply L, and does not itself provide grounds for deducing the presence of chlorophyll and hence for explaining it; it is itself hardly an explanation. Let us now add a suitable A, for example:

(g) $Pa \cdot Pha$, 2 P.M., November 4, 1959

We may now infer:

(h) $(\exists s)\ (Ca,s \cdot \text{Earlier } s$, 2 P.M., November 4, 1959)

that is, a contains chlorophyll at some time earlier than 2 P.M., November 4, 1959.

The argument here accords with the deductive pattern, yet fails to explain why chlorophyll was present earlier than the time mentioned in (h). What it does rather is to substantiate such occurrence, to state grounds for believing such occurrence to have taken place. The premises here, in short, answer the question "Why must chlorophyll have been present?" rather than "Why did this plant contain chlorophyll?" The appropriate diagram here is (5) rather than (4), and it is thus inaccurate to speak of (b) as providing a non-teleological *explanation* equivalent to the functional explanation (a).[1]

---

[1] It is, of course, still open to us to suggest that *functional explanation* is not a sub-type of *explanation-why*, generally. We may, that is, construe the functional explanation of a given process as (roughly) showing its contribution to the welfare of the organism in which it takes place. To have provided a *functional explanation* of some process would then *not* be to have *explained why* the process has occurred, but rather to have given an *account of* its characteristic functioning, or working, from the perspective of the organism's welfare. Such an account would not, in particular, represent a "non-teleological explanation" of the process. In-

To summarize our preceding discussion, if we take into account the full potentialities of the deductive pattern as expressed in Hempel and Oppenheim's four requirements, and if we decide to separate those of its instances where the premises are initially given from those where the conclusion is initially given, we shall be separating two types of argument (what we earlier called 'positing' and 'substantiating'), distinct from prediction and explanation. From the standpoint of the deductive pattern itself, prediction and explanation thus lose their scientific primacy. Is there, however, some independent epistemological basis for such primacy?

We may begin by noting that the peculiar temporal asymmetry of explanation is parallel to that of cause and effect in ordinary use; effects do not precede their causes. We may also remark, in passing, that the lack of attention given to other forms of substantiation is perhaps due to the ambiguity of '*initial* or *antecedent* conditions', as between a logical and a temporal interpretation. Such ambiguity lends itself to an interpretation of the deductive pattern according to which not only must A represent initial conditions, in the sense of premises for the derivation of B, but the event described by A, namely a, must precede b, after the pattern diagramed in (4). This interpretation is further reinforced by the presumption that the search for causes is primary in science and that the provision of an explanans, describing an event prior to the problematic event, is therefore, likewise primary.

If, then, we have independent reasons for supposing the search for causes to be scientifically primary, we have independent justification for taking explanation as primary, that is, for upholding the interpretation of the deductive pattern after the manner of (4) rather than (5). It has, however, frequently been remarked that the notions of cause and effect recede progressively into the

---

deed, the mischievous consequence to be *avoided* above all is the suggestion that an account of the characteristic beneficial effects of a process provides some occult explanation of why the process occurs, in which the future works back upon the past.

background with the advance of science, though they remain of relatively constant importance in everyday practical affairs and in applied science. It has, further, been suggested that this difference stems from the special relation of causal notions to such pragmatic questions as control and intervention by action. R. B. Braithwaite, for example, writes:

> If an earlier event's occurring is a nomically sufficient condition for a later event to occur, we can (in suitable cases) ensure that the later event should occur by taking steps to see that the earlier event does occur. For this purpose it is irrelevant whether or not the later event's occurring is a nomically sufficient condition for the earlier event to occur . . . if a later event's occurring is a nomically sufficient condition for the earlier event to occur, we cannot indirectly produce the earlier event by producing the later event, since by the time that we should be producing the later event, the earlier event would irrevocably either have occurred or not have occurred. This difference between the case of regular sequence and that of regular precedence is, I think, the reason why we are prepared to call a nomically sufficient condition for an event a cause of that event if it precedes the event but are not prepared to call it a cause if it succeeds the event.[2]

Whatever particular account is given of the reason, it seems true that in science, as distinct from practical affairs, neither the search for causes, nor causal explanation, is *primary* in any likely sense that may be assigned to this vague term. Unlike our concern with control in practical affairs, our concern in science is not directed particularly toward the future, but frequently involves employment of general principles in the effort to substantiate past events on the basis of later events, as, for example, in history, cosmology, archaeology, paleontology, and geology. Non-explanatory substantiation may be illustrated by the use

[2] Richard Bevan Braithwaite, *Scientific Explanation* (Cambridge, England: Cambridge University Press, 1953), p. 313. By permission of the publishers.

of various methods of dating historical remains, or the analysis of rocks in connection with principles of radioactivity to determine the age of the earth. On the basis of dating methods applied to remaining scrolls, for example, we do not explain why the scrolls were produced at the estimated time; we establish, at best, that they must have been produced then. The positing of past events is illustrated by the use of all available current information to paint a picture of earlier times, say, the life of medieval people; the historian is often concerned just with the painting of such pictures, rather than with explanation proper, and the same holds true for investigators in other realms.

If these considerations are relevant, then the view of science as directed primarily toward explanation is too narrow. A more comprehensive view would indeed stress the scientist's effort to construct a simple network of true general principles relating events to one another. But such a view would allow for the use of the network currently available, together with other information, in constructing a wide variety of arguments, of which explanation and prediction might be seen as special sorts. Such a view is suggested by S. Toulmin's analogy to a route-neutral map, quite abstract in avoiding preference for any direction, but (therefore) capable of guiding travelers with various itineraries.[3] Like the map, the network sought by science helps not only to guide itineraries but also to give a "picture" of the territory.

So far, we have spoken of explanation. Prediction, too, is clearly analogous in having a more intimate relation to control than non-predictive positing, and much of what we have earlier argued holds here too. Sometimes, however, the primacy of the predictive component in science is defended by epistemological arguments (in the vein of the philosophy of pragmatism) relating to the acceptance of statements.

It may, for example, be conceded that we posit events both past and future to our present posit-utterances, but it is argued that an independent reason exists for holding these utterances peculiarly contingent on the future: given any present posit-utterance, there is a possibility that it will be reasonably rejected

[3] Toulmin, *The Philosophy of Science, An Introduction,* pp. 121-123.

later, owing to future rejection of some derived confirmatory statement asserting some future occurrence. But, in the first place, such future rejection may be due to rejection of some derived confirmatory statement asserting an occurrence in the past, i.e., prior to the posit-utterance in question. Secondly, it is equally true for any posit-utterance that there is a possibility that it may have been reasonably rejected earlier. That some statement is represented by a posit-utterance at t implies neither its acceptance at all times following t, nor its acceptance at all times preceding t.

It is sometimes suggested that the contingency on the future, of any given posit-utterance, is not a matter of its own future acceptance, but relates rather to the fact that it is false (or at least subject to reasonable rejection) if any derived confirmatory statement asserting a future occurrence is determined to be false. Clearly, however, it is also false (or at least subject to reasonable rejection) if any derived confirmatory statement asserting a prior occurrence is determined to be false. It may, perhaps, be further suggested that a posit-utterance, all of whose confirmatory statements asserting prior occurrences are true, is false if and only if some confirmatory statement asserting a present or future occurrence is false. But (if this suggestion is accepted) then, by the same token, a posit, all of whose confirmatory statements asserting present or future occurrences are true, should be judged false if and only if some confirmatory statement asserting a past occurrence is false.

It may, finally, be argued that we cannot now choose to carry through any past test, while we can now decide to carry through some future tests of given posits. This is, however, a general point: we cannot now choose to do anything in the past; *a fortiori* we cannot now choose to test a scientific proposition yesterday. There is no specific relevance to science in this general fact.

Pragmatist and positivist philosophers have championed the general doctrine that the content or meaning of a physical object statement is determined by its future verifiability. On this view, for example, the posit-utterance 'Caesar crosses the Rubicon', produced by a historian in 1960, is really concerned with future possible confirmations or disconfirmations in experience. This general doctrine is, however, ambiguous. Are the future confirmations in this example future to 1960 or future to Caesar's crossing the Rubicon? Only if they are future to 1960 is it possible to construe the meaning of our historian's assertion as given by its testing future to the assertion, but the consequences of such an interpretation are awkward. For example, a replica of our historian's utterance in 1955 has a different meaning.

On the other hand, if the future confirmations in question are future to Caesar's crossing the Rubicon, then replicas of our historian's utterance (in the same language and with ambiguities eliminated) will have the same meaning, but this utterance now refers to confirmations prior to itself, and its *predictive* content is no longer primary. (We may as well allow its content to include possible confirmations prior to the historical event itself.) [4] The general difficulties encountered by doctrines of meaning of this sort are, moreover, weightier than the ambiguity just discussed, as we shall have occasion to note in the next Part. Meanwhile, it is already clear that such doctrines give no firm support for the primacy of prediction in science.

6. The Problem of Ontological Interpretation

Throughout our discussions of explanation and prediction, we have used what must have seemed to be robustly materialistic language, in conformity with the bulk of the recent literature.

---

[4] For a discussion of related points, in reference to C. I. Lewis' analysis of historical statements, see Israel Scheffler, "Verifiability in History: A Reply to Miss Masi," *Journal of Philosophy*, XLVII (1950), 164 ff. See also Goodman, *Fact, Fiction, and Forecast*, pp. 121-122, footnote 3: "The pragmatist may perhaps be insisting . . . that all we can learn even about past cases is by means of future experience; but this . . . is correct only if it amounts to saying, quite needlessly, that all we can learn in the future even about past cases, is what we can learn in the future . . . I am suggesting . . . that pragmatism . . . must be careful to distinguish its theses from wrong pronouncements to the effect that truth for future cases is sufficient for the truth of a hypothesis, and also from empty pronouncements to the effect that true hypotheses are true and that future tests are future."

That is to say, we spoke of *events in the natural world* as explained or predicted by statements of certain sorts, namely, those related in given ways to *descriptions* of the events in question. With reference to the deductive pattern of explanation, in particular, we talked of *explaining* the *event b* by providing appropriate statements *A* and *L*, having *b*'s description, *B*, as a logical consequence. We seemed in this way to be giving a straightforward account of explanation as a relation between sentences and concrete occurrences in the natural world, construable as spatio-temporal regions, or chunks, of certain kinds.

This impression is, however, illusory. Such an account is far from straightforward, for it leads directly to trouble. Imagine a particular spatio-temporal chunk, *k,* which is described as being blue, by the statement:

(1) $\qquad\qquad\qquad\qquad Bk$

and as being hot, by the statement:

(2) $\qquad\qquad\qquad\qquad Hk$

Now suppose we have the following set of premises:

(3) $\qquad\qquad\qquad (x)(y)\ (Wx \cdot Rxy \supset Hy)$
(4) $\qquad\qquad\qquad Wj$
(5) $\qquad\qquad\qquad Rjk$

where (3) is assumed to be lawlike, *j* is a spatio-temporal chunk, '*W*' stands for a predicate applicable to certain such chunks, and '*R*' stands for a relational predicate applicable to certain pairs of them. Assume also that (3), (4), and (5) are true. In this case, the deductive pattern may be seen to apply with respect to (2). That is, (3), (4), and (5) together are true, contain a general law required for the derivation of (2), which is indeed forthcoming as a logical consequence of the set, interpreted as having empirical content. So far as the deductive pattern goes, then (and assuming all relevant pragmatic criteria to have been met), we should be able to say that (3)-(5) constitutes an explanation of *k,* or:

(6)   E(3)-(5), k

But (3)-(5) does not yield (1) as a logical consequence, and so cannot be said to explain the event described by it. That is:

(7) $\sim$E(3)-(5), k

We have, in short, ended up with a contradiction as between (6) and (7).

The trouble seems to be that spatio-temporal regions, chunks, and objects generally, are each describable in alternative, logically independent ways, and that it is thus false to say of any given description of such an individual thing that it is its *unique* description. Since the same concrete individual has multiple, logically independent descriptions, one of these may well be implied by a given set of explanatory premises while others may not. Clearly, then, we cannot construe explanation as a relationship between explanatory premises and concrete events. We seem to have, rather, a relationship between such premises and events-as-qualified-in-certain-ways, or, alternatively, a relationship between such premises and *facts that* events are so qualified.

The upshot is that we cannot represent any given fulfillment of the deductive pattern as having explained some concrete spatio-temporal entity *e*, but, at best, as having explained *e*-as-described-by-*P*, or the fact that *e* is truly described by *P*. In the above example, we should have to say, *not* that (3)-(5) explains *k*, but rather that it explains *k*-as-described-by-(2), or the fact that *k* is hot. But see how far we have come from robust materialism. The object of explanation is now no longer the spatio-temporal individual chunk, but something of another sort associated with it, of which there are as many as there are logically independent descriptions of the chunk. These new entities (let us call them hereafter 'facts') are not themselves spatio-temporal entities: they are neither dated nor bounded. Nor are they identified with the descriptions themselves. They are abstract ("logically intensional")[5] entities, intermediate between

---

[5] I owe the use of this term to a suggestion of W. V. Quine.

chunk and descriptions, each such entity corresponding to some class of logically equivalent (true) descriptions uniquely.

The utility of this picture is that it avoids the sort of contradiction noted above, for in place of the one entity, k, it now embraces two entities associated with it, i.e., *facts*. In implying (2), (3)-(5) is now said to explain, not k itself, but rather *the fact that k is hot*. In failing to imply (1), (3)-(5) is now said to fail to explain, not k, but rather *the fact that k is blue*. There is surely no contradiction between:

(8) $\qquad\qquad\qquad E(3)\text{-}(5), f(Hk)$

and

(9) $\qquad\qquad\qquad \sim E(3)\text{-}(5), f(Bk)$

Our problem is apparently solved by the introduction of *facts*. However, since, according to this general idea, the *same fact* may still be associated with different descriptions, i.e., logically equivalent ones, may not a contradiction be expected to arise on a new level, since our previous trouble resulted from the *same event's* being associated with multiple descriptions of it? The answer is no, for if a given set of premises implies some description D, it implies also every description D' which is logically equivalent to it. Thus, unlike the case we earlier discussed, in which the same entity k was associated with (1) *and* (2), and where (3)-(5) implied (2) but not (1), the case with respect to facts is such that, for every pair of descriptions associated with a given fact, whatever implies one implies the other.

For example, (2) is equivalent to:

(10) $\qquad\qquad\qquad \sim\sim Hk$

and we may thus conclude:

$$f(Hk) = f(\sim\sim Hk)$$

and hence associate:

$$f(Hk)$$

both with:

(2) Hk

and:

(10) $\sim\sim Hk$

But this can cause no problem analogous to the earlier one, since nothing which implies either (2) or (10) can fail to imply the other also. It thus cannot happen, for any set of explanatory premises, in line with the deductive pattern, that it implies one but not the other and so both explains and does not explain $f(Hk)$.

We have thus succeeded in avoiding contradictions such as that between (6) and (7), but the price we pay is that the explanatory relation is no longer construable as applying between sentences and concrete events. The price is seen clearly if we consider the existential generalization of (6), namely:

(11) $(\exists x)\ (E(3)\text{-}(5), x)$

which says 'There is something x which is explained by (3)-(5)'. What is the reference of the variable 'x' here? What is it that is explained by (3)-(5)? Surely it cannot be the concrete event k, for (7) is true. So, to assert the existence of *something* explained by (3)-(5) is, generally, *not* to assert the existence of something concrete. or any set of sentences, s, to say:

(12) $(\exists x)\ (Es,x)$

is to assert the existence of something, but something which is not concrete. The something asserted to exist, according to our prior discussion, is rather a fact. Thus, we can make sense of (11) by reconstruing the reference of its variable, making it refer, not to k, but to $f(Hk)$. (We are, that is, to treat (11) as if it were an existential generalization of (8) rather than (6).) We need to construe the range of 'x' in (11) and (12), generally, as consisting of facts.

But, surely, it might be argued, we can avoid this abstract ontology. We need not be driven to conclude that all talk of statements explaining things must presuppose the abstractness of these things. Let us, instead of using sentences such as (12), which employ the term 'explains' as a relational predicate applying to pairs of entities, rather attempt an altogether different mode of analysis.

We take as our basic and indivisible term '. . . explains-the-fact-that ————' (or '. . . explains why ————'), which is *not* a predicate at all, for its second blank is not fillable by a name of any entity, but only by a sentence. It is, thus, *not* a relational predicate applying to pairs of things. Instead, it is an operator of a special kind, namely, such that a sentence results if its first blank is filled by a name and its second blank by a sentence. We symbolize this operator by '. . . EF (————)'. Now, given the fulfillment of the deductive pattern by (3)-(5), we can describe the situation by the sentence:

(13)   (3)-(5) EF (Hk)

which reads, '(3)-(5) explains-the-fact-that k is hot', (or '(3)-(5) explains-why k is hot').

We are now precluded from asking what sort of *thing* it is which is explained by (3)-(5), for we do not any longer have the notion of explanation as a relation between sentences and things. In short, we have given up existential generalizations such as (11) and (12), which assert the existence of things explained, since we have renounced use of the relative predicate 'E'. We are still able to generalize (13) existentially with respect to '(3)-(5)', however, as follows:

(14) $(\exists x) (x \, EF \, (Hk))$

for '(3)-(5)' *is* a name of something, unlike 'Hk' which is *not* a name but a sentence, and (13) as a whole is naturally taken as describing the something named by '(3)-(5)'. Furthermore, this something, which is explicitly asserted by (14) to exist, is a string of sentences, so that the assertion is ostensibly innocuous and, in any event, common to previous analyses considered. In particular, (12) is also subject to existential generalization with respect to 's', which names a string of sentences. The appeal of (14) over (12) is that, unlike (12), it bars the added existential affirmation of entities such as facts, to serve as *objects of explanation*.

Moreover, now that the latter sort of ontologizing is blocked, we can, it would seem, reintroduce reference to the concrete event, k. Sentence (13), after all, tells us that (3)-(5) explains the fact that k (in particular) is hot. It should thus be possible to take (13) as implying that *something* exists (namely, k), such that (3)-(5) explains the fact that *it* is hot:

(15) $(\exists x) \ ((3)\text{-}(5) \ EF \ (Hx))$

We can now combine the existential generalizations in (14) and (15), so as to make clear at once the total existential affirmation of (13), representing our new mode of analysis. We thus have:

(16) $(\exists x) \ (\exists y) \ (x \ EF \ (Hy))$

to be read 'There is something x, and something y, such that x explains-the-fact-that y is hot'. It seems we have clearly succeeded after all, in interpreting explanation talk as presupposing the existence of sentences and of concrete events, and of nothing else.

We must, however, look more closely at the reasons for this apparent success. It is already clear how we have managed to avoid reference to facts. For the motivation of our new mode of analysis was just to preclude such reference by renouncing 'explains' (symbolically, 'E') as a relational predicate with two argument places (i.e., two blanks fillable by names to form sentences). We chose, instead, to employ the operator 'explains-the-fact-that' (symbolically '. . . EF (————————)'), which functions in such a way as to connect names with sentences so as to form new sentences; its second blank is fillable neither by names nor variables referring to entities of any sort. This operator is construed as *indivisible,* its component words all welded together, so that 'explains' is *not* a genuine constituent of it, and 'the fact that' can emphatically *not* be split off from it and assigned referential import. (The latter temptation is perhaps more naturally resisted by the alternative spelling of the operator, as 'explains-why'.)

Though we have, in this manner, avoided the presupposition of facts, how has our analysis managed to affirm the existence of concrete things or events, in addition to sentence strings, without leading to contradictions of the sort which motivated our talk of *facts* in the first place? The answer lies in the embedding of the event-name or variable within a *sentential context* reflecting the explanandum in question. Recall that (6) and (7) contradict each other in saying, of the same event, k, that it is explained and not explained by (3)-(5), the ground for (6) being that (3)-(5) yields 'Hk' and the ground for (7) being that it fails to yield 'Bk'. According to our present analysis, however, such a contradiction does not arise, for, rather than saying simply that (3)-(5) explains k, since it implies the explanandum 'Hk', we now have our earlier sentence:

(13)   (3)-(5) EF (Hk)

And rather than asserting, simply, that (3)-(5) does *not* explain k since it fails to imply the explanandum 'Bk', we now assert:

(17) $\sim$(3)-(5) EF (Bk)

There is clearly no contradiction between (13) and (17) parallel to that between (6) and (7). Obviously, too, the reason is that the sentence which (17) negates differs from (13) in having 'B' where (13) has 'H'. Whereas (6) and (7) jointly affirm and deny "the same thing" of k, (13) and (17) do not. Thus it is that the existential generalization of (6) considered earlier, namely:

(11) $(\exists x)$ $(E(3)$-$(5), x)$

could *not* be sensibly interpreted as referring to k, for such interpretation was blocked by (7)'s direct denial, whereas the present situation is quite otherwise. We *can* sensibly interpret as referring to k the parallel existential generalization of (13) earlier discussed, i.e.:

(15) $(\exists x)$ $((3)$-(5) EF $(Hx))$

for (17) does not here constitute a direct denial. To interpret the variable 'x' of (15) as referring to k is to say that (3)-(5) explains-the-fact-that k is hot. Clearly, this assertion is compatible with (17), which says merely that (3)-(5) does not explain-the-fact-that k is blue.

We thus see how it is that the present analysis fares better than the earlier one referring to concrete events. In particular, we see the advantage of treating 'k' not as an argument (i.e., blank-filler) of the relative predicate 'explains', but rather as initially embedded within a sentence, representing the explanandum, which is operated on *as a whole* by the operator 'explains-the-fact-that'.

We may now, if we like, further interpret the latter operator as follows: it is a *predicate-forming* operator, for when any predicate is attached to the operator within the scope of its 'that' (or inside the parentheses of its symbolic representation), it turns into a predicate itself. When the operator is thus supplemented with the one-place predicate 'is hot', for example, we get:

(18)   . . . explains-the-fact-that _____ is hot

or, symbolically:

(19)   . . . EF (H———)

which functions as a two-place predicate relating sentence strings and concrete events. Supplementation with 'is blue' yields another such two-place predicate, symbolized as:

(20)   . . . EF (B———)

Predicates of higher degree may also be formed in this way, e.g.:

(21)   . . . EF (_____ burns more quickly than - - -)

is a three-place predicate resulting from supplementation with a two-place predicate. On such an interpretation, it is clear why (13) and (17) do not contradict each other: (13) applies one predicate to the pair $((3)\text{-}(5),k)$ while (17) withholds quite a different predicate from the same pair. By contrast, (6) applies the predicate 'E' to $((3)\text{-}(5), k)$, and (7) withholds the very same predicate from the identical pair. The advantage of the analysis we have been discussing thus may be put summarily in the following way: Instead of retaining the general predicate 'explains' and appealing to a new ontological realm of *facts* as argument-values of this general predicate, the analysis retains a concrete ontology but rejects the general predicate, splitting it up into a multiplicity of specific explanation-predicates associated with the multiplicity of predicates appearing in relevant explananda. It thus seems able to avoid both contradiction and ontological extravagance, while offering a plausible interpretation of explanation talk.

Unfortunately, however, the analysis fails for another, though related, reason. Despite the fragmentation of the general notion of explanation, to accommodate the multiplicity of predicates appearing in explananda associated with each concrete event, the analysis breaks down in the face of the variety of specifications which uniquely determine any such event. To illustrate the difficulty, we take our old sentence:

(1) Bk

as explanandum, and suppose a set of premises g, which fulfills the deductive (as well as pragmatic) criteria of explanation, with reference to (1). According to the analysis we have been discussing, we then may assert:

(22) $g \, \mathrm{EF} \, (Bk)$

to be read, 'g explains-the-fact-that k is blue'.

We have supposed 'k' to name a specific spatio-temporal entity. We may take 'k' as a proper name, or as abbreviating some individual specification or description of the entity by reference to its spatio-temporal area (e.g., 'the thing occupying such and such a region over such and such time').

The point that now concerns us hinges on the availability of totally disparate ways of singling out the same concrete entities. Thus, suppose k to have been, in fact, a flame resulting from certain experimental operations in the chemistry laboratory of University X on January 8, 1907; suppose further that it was the only flame in this laboratory that day, representing the happy climax of Dr. Frankenstein's long unsuccessful efforts to perfect a certain new process. Imagine, finally, that it was the very first flame ever to have been produced by a procedure later much refined but still referred to as 'Frankenstein's Method'. Then, it will be the case that the following identities are true:

(23) $k =$ the flame in the chemistry laboratory of University X on January 8, 1907

(24) $k =$ the first flame produced by application of Frankenstein's Method

Yet, we cannot *logically infer* from:

k is blue

either:

(25)   the flame in the chemistry laboratory of University X on January 8, 1907, was blue

or:

(26)   the first flame produced by application of Frankenstein's Method was blue

Thus, granted that g logically implies (1), we cannot suppose it therefore implies also (25) or (26). The premise-set g may, for example, provide a purely chemical explanation, making reference only to laws of chemistry as well as the constituent substances and chemically relevant circumstances of the reaction culminating in k. In such a case, it will surely not yield any conclusion as to k's being the (one and only) flame in the chemistry laboratory of University X on January 8, 1907, nor will it imply k's being the first in a long line of flames produced by application of Frankenstein's Method. Despite the truth of (23) and (24), an explanans for either (1), (25), or (26) cannot generally be expected to be an explanans for any of the others.

Taking g, in particular, as we have above described it, it implies (1) but neither (25) nor (26). This means that if we replace 'k' by 'the flame in the chemistry laboratory of University X on January 8, 1907', or by 'the first flame produced by application of Frankenstein's Method', in the sentence:

g explains-the-fact-that k is blue

symbolized as:

(22)   g EF (Bk)

we turn its truth into falsehood. The truth of the above sentence thus depends not merely on the mentioned *event k,* but also on the *way* in which this event is specified in the sentence.

Using W. V. Quine's terms, we may say that the occurrence of 'k' in (22) is *not purely referential.*[6] The symbolic representation (22) does not, in effect, simply express a truth about k, for if it did, this truth should remain invariant no matter how k is described.

Note, for example, how different is the case of (22)'s subsentence:

(1)   *Bk*

Here, if we make the same replacements as before (i.e., if we substitute for 'k' the right side of the identities (23) or (24)) we fail to alter the truth of (1). If k is in fact blue, the flame in the chemistry laboratory of University X on January 8, 1907, is blue and the first flame produced by application of Frankenstein's Method is blue, for the entity referred to is one and the same in each case. 'k's occurrence in (1) is, then, *referential.*

When the subsentence is embedded in (22), the very same replacements do alter the truth of (22) as a whole. We call (22) *referentially opaque,*[7] to signify that it may change referential occurrences into non-purely-referential occurrences, in the manner just noted. The model of a referentially opaque context is that of direct quotation, for though it is true that:

(27)   Massachusetts = the Bay State

and that the interchange of 'Massachusetts' and 'the Bay State' therefore leaves invariant the truth of:

[6] Willard Van Orman Quine, *From a Logical Point of View* (2d ed.; Cambridge, Mass.: Harvard University Press, 1961), p. 140.

[7] *Ibid.,* p. 142.

(28)   Massachusetts is in New England

the very same interchange alters the truth of:

(29)   The words on the poster read, "Massachusetts is in New England"

Quine has not only described referential opacity and associated phenomena; he has warned against quantifying into opaque contexts from without, that is, against prefixing an opaque sentence with a quantifier governing a variable inside the subsentence. The disaster resulting from such quantification may be illustrated by the following existential generalization of (29):

(30)   ($\exists x$) (The words on the poster read,
              "x is in New England")

(Or, perhaps: 'Something is such that the words on the poster read, "it is in New England." ') Here, rather than having a quantifier binding a variable in an open sentence, we have a genuine, and false, sentence (since the poster really reads "Massachusetts is in New England") prefixed by a quantifier that is totally irrelevant.

Consider, now, what happens if we attempt an existential generalization of (22) with respect to 'k':

(31)   ($\exists x$) (g EF (Bx))

or:

(32)   Something is such that g explains-the-fact-that it is blue.

The something here in question is purportedly k, namely, the flame in the chemistry laboratory of University X on January 8, 1907, and also the first flame produced by application of Frankenstein's Method. But this cannot be, for we have already seen that the following statements are false:

(33) g EF (B the flame in the chemistry laboratory of University X on January 8, 1907)

(34) g EF (B the first flame produced by application of Frankenstein's Method)

The fact that the occurrence of 'k' is not purely referential in (22) thus blocks the existential generalization (31). The far-reaching consequence is that our old:

(20)   ... EF (B———)

cannot, after all, be construed as a two-place predicate relating sentence-strings and concrete events, nor can (15) be tolerated as an existential generalization of the referentially opaque (13). We cannot, in short, construe sentences such as (13) or (22) as about concrete events, directly and simply. We cannot generalize such sentences existentially so that the resulting bound variables take such events (mentioned in the relevant explananda) as values. Our hopeful attempt at a consistent construal of explanation talk, without logically intensional ontology, has broken down decisively.

We thus appear driven back to the conclusion that consistency in analyzing statements such as:

(35)   . . . explains-the-fact-that _____
(36)   . . . explains-why _____

requires an abstract, logically intensional ontology, e.g., some reference to *facts,* of the sort previously discussed. Under all the apparently concrete language of the theory of scientific explanation, there lies an abstract, and logically intensional, base. Explanation is, then, to be taken as a relation after all, but one holding between sentences, on the one hand, and facts explained, on the other. The theory of explanation, it would seem, is not ontologically neutral.

The natural conclusion just cited is, however, too quick. The troubles besetting the analysis last considered result not simply from a concrete ontology but also from quantification into opaque contexts after the manner of (15) and (31), coordinate with construal of:

... EF (B———)

as a relative predicate, and of:

EF

as a predicate-forming operator, in the fashion described above.

Such construal may, however, be renounced, together with the troublesome quantification it invites: We give up the interpretation of explanation talk as referring to concrete events mentioned in explananda. We further renounce 'E' as a relative predicate applying between sentences and facts. Our new course is the following: We acknowledge '. . . EF ————' simply as an *operator,* forming sentences by connecting names and other sentences. Avoiding quantification into the subsentences from outside, we avoid the previous difficulties. Our "explanation" ontology includes sentences (whose names are linked to sentences by '. . . EF ————') but nothing else.

We may, if we like, still construe '. . . EF ————' as a predicate-forming operator, but of a critically different sort from that earlier discussed. Instead of forming predicates of two or more places, it always forms one-place predicates applying to sentences. And instead of forming the latter by insertion of *predicates* into its second blank, it requires the insertion of whole sentences. Thus, for example,

$$g \, \mathrm{EF} \, (Bk)$$

is to be taken as consisting of the name '*g*' and the one-place predicate 'EF (*Bk*)', formed by inserting '*Bk*' into the second blank of '. . . EF ————'. The whole statement thus applies a one-place predicate to the sentence-string *g*. It does not relate *g* to anything else. But, of course, the statement is true if and only if *g* fulfills the criteria of explanation with reference to '*Bk*'. Since, moreover, the two predicates:

$$. . . \mathrm{EF} \, (Bk)$$

and:

$$. . . \mathrm{EF} \, (B \text{ the first flame produced by application of Frank-} \\ \text{enstein's Method})$$

are clearly not identical (nor subject to dissection, with interchange of equivalent parts) there is no difficulty in supposing *g* to satisfy one but not the other.

Finally, another strategy may be suggested, one which retains consistency and avoids an ontology of facts, but yet, unlike the last course, construes explanation in *relational* manner. Instead of relating sentences to *events* or *facts,* however, explanation is now taken as relating sentences to *other sentences.* The underlying idea here is that fulfillment of the deductive explanation-pattern involves connecting two sorts of sentence-strings, i.e., explanantia and explananda. When we first saw the difficulties in taking explanation as relating certain premises and concrete events, we postulated facts as objects of explanation, each fact associated with a class of logically equivalent event-descriptions, representing explananda. Now, we achieve the advantages of the latter analysis by going directly to these event-descriptions themselves, skipping over the intervening facts.

To avoid the merest whisper of reference to facts, let us give up the expression 'explains-the-fact-that', and use the alternative 'explains-why', symbolically, 'EW'. As a whole, 'EW' forms sentences through connecting names with other sentences. We do not however, rest content with noting the operation of 'EW', as a whole. Nor do we, as in the course just previously discussed, take 'EW' as forming one-place predicates upon insertion of sentences in its second blank. Rather, we now *split* the 'E' from the 'W', and treat 'W' itself as a predicate-forming operator, producing a *one-place predicate of sentences* when its blank is filled by a sentence. The analogy here is to our earlier splitting of 'E' from 'F' and taking the latter as an operator forming the *name* of a fact when its blank is filled by a sentence. Now, instead of splitting 'E' from 'F' and saying:

(37) $x \mathrel{E} f(Bk)$

where '$f(Bk)$' is a singular term denoting the fact that k is blue, we split 'E' from 'W' and say:

(38) $x \mathrel{E} y \cdot W(Bk) y$

where '$W(Bk)$' is a one-place predicate of sentences, the whole to be read, 'x explains some why-k-is-blue sentence y'.

The difference is ontologically crucial. In (37), '$f(Bk)$' stands in a place construed as accessible to variables, and allows for:

$$(39) \qquad (\exists z)\ (x\ E\ z)$$

with 'z' ranging over facts. In (38), on the other hand, 'W (Bk)' does not stand in a place taken as accessible to variables and so precludes existential generalization with respect to itself. Of course, 'x' and 'y' in the latter sentence do allow themselves to be bound by quantifiers, but range solely over sentences.

We return, for illustration, to the case where g explains why k is blue. 'Why k is blue' is now to be treated as a single, indivisible predicate applicable to sentences of a certain sort. The situation is now analyzed as follows:

$$(40) \qquad (\exists x)\ (g\ E\ x\ \cdot\ W\ (Bk)\ x)$$

namely, 'something is a why-k-is-blue sentence and it is explained by g', or perhaps, 'stands to g as explanandum to associated explanans'.

Where the latter relationship is presumed specifiable further, 'E' may, of course, be supplanted by the result of its analysis. For example, if the deductive model were to be taken as a complete analysis of explanation criteria, we might replace (40) by:

(41) $(\exists x)$ (g implies x · g contains general laws · g has empirical content · g is true · W $(Bk)x$)

The important point is that 'E' is now treated as relating sentences to sentences. At the same time, since 'W (Bk)' and 'W (Hk)' are different predicates, there is no difficulty in supposing some given x to satisfy one but not the other, even where the 'k' in 'Bk' and that in 'Hk' denote the same event. Which is merely to say that the analysis allows us to express consistently that different explananda are associated with k, and that what serves as explanans for one may fail to serve for another. Analogous remarks hold for the different predicates 'W (Bk)' and 'W (B the first flame produced by application of Frankenstein's Method)'.

We still need to say, however, what sentences are to be taken as denoted by 'W (*Bk*)'. Recall that *facts,* introduced in our earlier analysis, were well taken as determined by classes of logically equivalent sentences, for if something implies one of the members of such a class, it implies each of the others as well. We gain the same effect here if we construe 'W (*Bk*)' as a predicate applying to every logical equivalent of the sentence within the parentheses, inclusive of this sentence itself.[8]

We might here, as in the case of facts, attempt to broaden this idea so as to include also translations into other languages, but, in view of the difficulties involved in clarifying the notion of translation, such broadening is perhaps best resisted. Instead, we might here suppose all analyses restricted to one particular language, construed as formulating all explanations (or all those of a certain type) in which we are interested. If this restriction is held artificial, there is always the alternative of broadening the scope of 'W(————)', and swallowing the obscurities of 'translation'.

We shall here take any predicate of the form 'W(————)' as denoting every logical equivalent of the sentence inserted within its parentheses. It is now possible to render the whole analysis explicitly concrete, by construing sentences themselves, generally, as *inscriptions* (physical objects of certain shapes), rather than as *abstract shapes*. Every 'W(————)'-predicate-inscription will, in this interpretation, denote every sentence-inscription which is a logical equivalent of the sentence-inscription within its own parentheses. We need, moreover, not worry that there might perhaps be no appropriate inscription in existence to warrant an analysis such as (40). For merely to formulate the question what explains why *k* is blue, for example, is to produce an inscription of the right sort, namely, the '*k* is blue'-inscription used in putting the question. And to produce the explanatory argument itself is, of course, to produce another appropriate inscription. We need, of course, to assume the questions and arguments written, for present purposes. But there seems, in prin-

---

[8] A related interpretation was originally proposed for indirect quotation generally in Israel Scheffler, "An Inscriptional Approach to Indirect Quotation," *Analysis,* XIV (1954), 83-90.

ciple, nothing to prevent the broadening of the present conception to include not merely inscriptions (physical surfaces of certain shapes), but also utterances (physical sound waves of certain patterns).

One result of the last analysis just presented is to assimilate event-explanation to the explanation of laws (or generalizations), in a certain sense. For the explanation of laws is readily construed as taking *sentences* as objects, even by those taking facts as objects of event-explanation. Now the analysis just given of event-explanation provides *sentences* as objects here too. This assimilation of event-explanation to the explanation of laws serves to underline the fact that *abstractiveness,* which is so important a feature of science, is distinct from, and need not involve, *admission of abstract entities* in the theory of science. For a mode of inquiry to be said to abstract from raw experience or from the world, it need not be thought to take abstract entities as its objects.

Clearly, the explanation of laws is no less abstractive relative to experience than event-explanation, though conceivable in straightforward fashion as taking law-sentences for its objects, and concerned with showing appropriate relationships among certain of these objects. Its abstractiveness relative to entities referred to by its explananda might be said to consist just in the multiplicity of explananda with the same reference (i.e., correlated with the same domain of entities), and the consequent need of *selection* in any given case of explanation. If all laws, that is, share the same ontology of entities as values of their universal quantifiers, each law-explanation abstracts from everything within this universe in selecting as explanandum only one out of many sentences, all linked to the same domain. Such selection in no way depends on these initially choosable sentences' being abstract.

Analogously, though event-explanation be taken as not requiring abstract entities for its objects, it is yet thoroughly abstractive relative to the events mentioned in its explananda. For each event thus mentioned is correlated with many sentences, i.e., all those expressing true descriptions of it. In the selection of one of these as explanandum on a particular occasion lies the abstractiveness of event-explanation. As before, the crux of the matter might be seen as the correlation of a multiplicity of choosable units with the same entities rather than the abstractness of these units. We may, then, conclude that the theory of explanation does not require us to adopt an abstract ontology, but offers the possibility of a concrete interpretation. Moreover, such concrete interpretation may allow us to affirm the abstractiveness, i.e., the selectivity, of scientific inquiry.

7. Explanation of Psychological and Historical Events

We have emphasized the importance of general principles in explanation. To this extent we have concurred with earlier writers, in viewing explanation as a matter of subsuming particulars under laws. Actual attempts at explanation, however, often fall short, and we earlier noted Mill's allowance of variation and incompleteness in causal accounts, which he connected with pragmatic circumstances, e.g., variability of purpose. Hempel, in "The Function of General Laws in History," and Hempel and Oppenheim in their later study also deal with purported explanations lacking general laws.

For such cases, the earlier paper develops the notion of an 'explanation sketch'. This term is intended to refer to purported explanations that are testable but incomplete by reference to the deductive pattern, either because missing assumptions are taken for granted as too obvious to require statement, or because they cannot yet be formulated with sufficient confidence. The explanation sketch serves, in effect, as a hypothesis directing the search for its own supposed missing links. The notion of an explanation sketch is also presented as a tool of criticism: to pinpoint the places at which a purported explanation falls short of completeness is to raise the question whether it is presently reasonable to take its various missing assumptions for granted.

It is clear from the foregoing that proponents of the deductive pattern of explanation do not wish to deny the *existence* of *pur-*

ported explanations which do not conform to its requirements. Their point seems rather to be that such purported explanations should be given a separate status rather than grouped with the explanations proper. Such a division allows the latter to be seen as sharing a common form, and shows the former heterogeneous specimens to be alike at least in that each is subject to filling out by reference to the deductive ideal, and incurs reasonable criticism so long as such such filling out has not been carried through.

To separate explanations from explanation sketches is thus part of an attempt to give a significant account of the structure of science. It enables the isolation of the class of explanations proper, which may profitably be studied alone. It further enables the characterization of much of scientific work as involving criticism of sketch by reference to full explanation, or as movement from sketch to fuller explanation, a movement directed by hypotheses incorporated in the sketch itself. To classify sketches together with complete deductive explanations would be to give up an opportunity for characterizing important aspects of science. It would be like classifying complete with incomplete syllogisms as alike forms of argument. Such a classification would be disastrous for logic, despite the fact that common usage lends it greater support than it gives a strict separation.

It is apparent, if these remarks are correct, that much of the criticism of the deductive pattern has been quite wide of the mark. It has frequently consisted in producing cases, notably drawn from commonsense and social science contexts, in which deductively incomplete arguments are yet acknowledged to be explanations. The mere existence of such cases is, however, not denied by proponents of the deductive pattern, as we have urged above. The proposal in question is rather to separate such arguments under the rubric of 'explanation sketch' and to describe their functions by relating them to explanations proper. This proposal cannot be disposed of simply by showing that explanation sketches *exist* and may ordinarily be *called* 'explanations'. As well say that the theory of the syllogism is defective because it omits the inference from 'Socrates is a man' to 'Socrates is mortal', which is commonly considered a good argument.

Another form of criticism is likewise wide of the mark in suggesting that the deductive pattern is applicable only to non-unique, or recurrent events, such as are thought to fall within the scope of the physical sciences; psychological or historical events are, on this account, unique and cannot be grouped together under laws. It follows that explanation of such events is not covered by the deductive pattern, in principle.

The trouble here is that the required distinction cannot be maintained; the illusion that it can is a product of the ambiguous notion 'event'. Recall the example cited earlier (Popper's paradigm) of the breaking of a thread when a given weight is suspended from it. Strictly, the example needs to be elaborated so as to refer to the breaking of the thread at a specific time. Suppose, then, that we have provided such an elaboration and explained why a particular thread broke at exactly 2:45 P.M., November 15, 1960. Which is the event explained in this case? According to the "normal" interpretation we have given of the deductive pattern, it is the particular thread's breaking at 2:45 P.M., November 15, 1960, since this latter event is what is signified by the explanandum. But surely this event is unique. Unlike the event consisting in mere *breaking,* it is not itself attributable to a time nor to an object; it cannot, *a fortiori,* recur. Though it falls within the scope of the physical sciences, in the sense required by the argument, it is no more repeatable than any psychological or historical event—for example, the passage of a twinge of remorse through a particular person at a precise moment in the past.

Suppose, then, it is argued that we must take the event in some such abstract way as to permit recurrence—for example, as consisting simply in *breaking,* without restriction to a particular thread and without date. So specified, the event is truly not unique: many threads break, and breaking occurs at various times. But analogous specification yields recurrence in the psychological and historical cases also. Many people experience remorse, and twinges of remorse occur at various times. Greed, ambition, conflicts over power, inflation, rivalry—all these occur in various situations at various times. The desired distinction on the basis of repeatability cannot be carried through.

Sometimes it is argued that historical or psychological explanations obviously do not conform to the deductive pattern for patent lack of the appropriate lawlike premises. Consider the explanation:

(1)   The Conservatives won the recent election in Britain because Labour stressed nationalization.

Here, the deductive pattern is appropriate (it is said) only if we have the general law:

(2)   Whenever Labour stresses nationalization, the Conservatives win.

But (2) is not available, since it is obviously false; therefore the historical explanation (1) does not conform to the deductive pattern.

This argument falsely assumes, however, that only if we have (2) can the deductive pattern apply. But consider this (nonpsychological) parallel:

(3)   The match ignited because it was scratched.

Here, the general lawlike statement:

(4)   Whenever matches are scratched, they ignite.

is, likewise, patently false. It is clear, however, that some other generalization, involving additional conditions, may hold where (4) fails. The deductive pattern is *not* restricted to cases where the lawlike premise is a generalized conditional formed of explicit antecedent condition statements and explanandum. (So much was evident from our discussion of Hume and Mill in Section 1.) Nor is the deductive pattern restricted to generalizations, of whatever degree of complexity, formulated in the initially available, familiar language of the explanandum: there is no stipulation that a generalization which has broken down may be repaired only through addition of qualifying conditions, which continually shrink the "antecedent class." Invention of wholly new language for description and generalization is always possible theoretically. Hence there is no point to the worry that we will run out of historical generalizations through whittling down their scopes to the single case.[9]

Accordingly the failure of (2) carries no force with respect to the alleged *distinctiveness* of historical explanation. Nor will it help to argue, from the *de facto* difficulty of establishing so-called historical generalizations, that there *are* none—that every such generalization must be only speciously general in order to stick, and hence no law at all. How could one ever hope to show this, short of a detailed theoretical argument such as is based on quantum theory, favoring a statistical rather than a "deterministic" model of explanation? Indeed, the present argument attempts to go further on much less. Without such a *theoretical* reason, it has the force of denying statistical historical laws as well, for these too are difficult to find. Difficulty, however, proves nothing about nature, as the example of pre-modern science shows.

A more interesting argument is that psychological or historical explanation is often concerned with the provision of reasons rather than causes, with stating the goals which have, in fact, motivated the action of historical figures. We try, for example, to explain Khrushchev's behavior by giving an account of what he is after, by stating the factors he takes into consideration in making his decisions, by discovering the rules by which he evaluates his own and others' conduct. In this way, we picture his action as it appears to him, "from within"; we identify with him and take the agent's role with respect to his conduct.

It cannot be denied that we often do offer accounts of a man's goals, reasons, and rules in explanation of his conduct. There seems no objection to treating such accounts as we did statistical explanations; i.e., recognizing their explanatory force and extending the general notion of explanation to include them, while recognizing their deductive incompleteness.

[9] Such a worry is suggested, for example, by William Dray, *Laws and Explanation in History* (London: Oxford University Press, 1957), chap. ii; see especially p. 39.

Such a course is, however, compatible with the views of proponents of the deductive pattern, who are, as we have seen, not denying the existence of incomplete explanations but only giving them separate status as explanation sketches. The present course, in particular, isolates a special group of such explanation sketches, characteristic of psychology and history, acknowledging their partial explanatory force, as well as their incompleteness. Sometimes, however, it seems to be argued that explanation by reference to reasons, goals, or rules *does* represent a decisive counterexample to proponents of the deductive pattern. The claim here appears to be that such explanation should not be treated simply as a special sort of incomplete deductive explanation. For it is unlike the case where, for example, a needed premise is unstated through lack of knowledge, though we believe some such premise to be both true and discoverable. Explanation in terms of reasons, goals, or rules (it is suggested) does not provide simply a temporary, hypothetical framework to be filled in with the progress of investigation; it gives us rather a stable resting point for social, psychological, and historical research, a *complete* explanation of another sort, deserving separate status as an explanatory pattern, on a par with the deductive pattern.

This suggestion does not, however, appear to be sufficiently well grounded. It may be granted that knowledge of a man's goals, reasons, and rules of evaluation frequently helps us to achieve a sense of identification with him, and a measure of confidence in gauging the sort of actions appropriate to his situation. It may also be conceded that we often give and receive such purported knowledge as if it were completely explanatory, i.e., without thought of supplementary hypotheses required by the deductive pattern. Nonetheless, such complacency may well be due to the fact that, in familiar cases, *we take such supplementary hypotheses for granted.* That they are theoretically required may be seen from the fact that, with increasing unfamiliarity, they come increasingly into the foreground as critical assumptions.

Consider a purported explanation of a man's action by reference to his goals, reasons, and weighing of considerations relevant to his decision. The further removed such a man is from the norms of our own reference culture and our own environment, the more we realize that certain other sorts of information are relevant to assessment of the explanation. What are the man's beliefs about the environment within which he is acting? If they differ radically from ours, the action we take to be reasonably oriented toward the goals in question may in fact not have this reasonable orientation at all. To what extent is he capable of pursuing his goals within the relevant environment, given his abilities; to what degree is the action in question crucially shaped by environmental factors, perhaps unforeseen or unknown by the agent? How rational is he, i.e., to what extent, even within the range of his abilities in given environments, does he tend to act most efficiently in line with his own beliefs and rules, in pursuit of his own goals? Where we have reason to suppose a man's beliefs to be bizarre, from *our* standpoint, or his abilities unequal to his goals, or his conduct irrational, we do not, upon reflection, take an account of his goals, motives, and rules of judgment to provide an adequate explanation of his action.

Thus, students of Soviet policy are not, in point of fact, satisfied with accounts of Khrushchev's behavior referring exclusively to his goals, motivations, and strategic considerations. They seek also reliable estimates of his beliefs concerning the state of the world, estimates of his actual power within the environment of his action, and a determination of the rationality with which he normally acts. It is a generally acknowledged pitfall of research on political policy to proceed simply from goals, reasons, and strategy to explanation of deeds. Accounts of goals, reasons, and rules of strategy are accordingly best construed as incomplete explanations, directing research into supplementary assumptions, and focusing critical attention on these assumptions.

There is no need to deny that reference to relevant goals and rules may (as already suggested) be profitably singled out for special consideration, as representing a peculiarly convenient and frequent sort of explanation sketch for the social sciences. K. R. Popper, in this vein, has discussed what he calls "the zero method." According to him, this is "the method of constructing a model on the assumption of complete rationality (and perhaps also on the assumption of the possession of complete information) on the part of all the individuals concerned, and of estimating the deviation of the actual behavior of people from the model behavior, using the latter as a kind of zero-coordinate. An example of this method is the comparison between actual behavior (under the influence of, say, traditional prejudice, etc.) and model behavior to be expected on the basis of the 'pure logic of choice', as described by the equations of economics."[1] It is obvious that *application* of the model in *explanation* is convincing, in any given case, only to the extent that certain supplementary hypotheses are believed to hold.

Explanation in terms of *motives* has at times been interpreted as a challenge to the deductive pattern of explanation. Such interpretation has occasionally based itself on G. Ryle's discussion in *The Concept of Mind*.[2] Ryle wishes to construe mental-conduct terms as referring not to alleged mental happenings but rather to alleged dispositions to behave in certain ways under specifiable circumstances. Motives are, in particular, not happenings and so cannot be causes;[3] they are, rather, generalized dispositions of usually complicated sorts. To explain an action by reference to its motive is thus not to connect it with a cause, but rather to classify it under a general disposition. The statement:

He boasted from vanity.

must, according to Ryle, *not* be construed to mean:

He boasted and the cause of his boasting was the occurrence in him of a particular feeling or impulse of vanity.

Rather, Ryle interprets the statement as:

He boasted (on meeting the stranger) and his doing so satisfies the law-like proposition that whenever he finds a

---

[1] Karl R. Popper, *The Poverty of Historicism* (London: Routledge & Kegan Paul, 1957), p. 141. By permission of the publisher and the author.

[2] Gilbert Ryle, *The Concept of Mind* (London: Hutchinson House, 1949). By permission.

[3] *Ibid.,* p. 113.

chance of securing the admiration and envy of others, he does whatever he thinks will produce this admiration and envy.[4]

Now, the thesis that motives are not happenings but dispositions, and hence not causes, clearly does not conflict with the deductive pattern as we have presented it. For the pattern at no point depends on a special construal of motives, on a particular distinction between happenings and dispositions, or on any use of the term 'cause' at all, as we have seen. Nor can it plausibly be argued that dispositions (as typically illustrated in recent philosophical discussions) cannot themselves be connected with properties of any sort by laws, nor be described as initial conditions within given explanatory arguments. Solubility, brittleness, viscosity, weight, color, skill, for example, are all plausibly construed as dispositions of one or another kind, the conditions and effects of which it may be important to determine. Vanity may, accordingly, also be taken as connected through laws with a variety of conditions, concomitants, and consequences.

It may, however, be urged that Ryle is offering a new explanatory pattern. "The explanation," he says, "is not of the type 'the glass broke because a stone hit it', but more nearly of the different type 'the glass broke when the stone hit it, because it was brittle'."[5] It is supposed here, presumably, that we have no independent (dispositional or structural) criteria of brittleness plus some law to the effect that objects satisfying such criteria break when struck. We have already noted, in the previous paragraph, that such criteria and such a law are by no means out of the question in fact. Let us, however, take this example as Ryle intends us to, in such fashion that brittleness is, roughly, the tendency of an object to break when sharply struck.[6] We now explain why a given glass broke at a given moment, knowing that it was struck at that moment, by offering the information that it was brittle, which is expressed as "a law-like general hypo-

[4] *Ibid.*, p. 89.
[5] *Ibid.*, p. 50.
[6] *Ibid.*, p. 89.

thetical proposition." But this explanation *conforms* to the deductive pattern, rather than *diverging* from it. The contrast Ryle points out is between cases where the ordinary expression of an explanation uses the 'because'-clause to refer to a "happening," and cases where it uses the 'because'-clause to refer to a "disposition." But *this* contrast is irrelevant to the deductive pattern; in fact both examples here conform to this pattern.

Ryle, in fact, stresses the incompleteness of motive-descriptions as explanations, in that they require reference to what he calls 'causes', which, when supplied, yield deductive accounts. Thus, he writes:

> The general fact that a person is disposed to act in such and such ways in such and such circumstances does not by itself account for his doing a particular thing at a particular moment; any more than the fact that the glass was brittle accounts for its fracture at 10 p.m. As the impact of the stone at 10 p.m. caused the glass to break, so some antecedent of an action causes or occasions the agent to perform it when and where he does so . . . an action's having a cause does not conflict with its having a motive, but is already prescribed for in the protasis of the hypothetical proposition which states the motive. . . . we already know just what sorts of familiar and usually public happenings are the things which get people to act in particular ways at particular times.[7]

Ryle seems here not to be proposing an alternative to the complete deductive pattern but rather to be pointing out a special sort of incomplete explanation. In contrast to cases in which the explanation sketch omits reference to laws but states the relevant initial conditions, Ryle here focuses on cases where the initial conditions are left unstated, though the explanation formulates the relevant law-like traits of individuals.

Perhaps, however, the challenge to the deductive pattern consists in this: motives, like brittleness in Ryle's example, are expressed by laws of an individual's behavior, and thus are not

[7] *Ibid.*, pp. 113-114.

truly *general,* as required by the deductive pattern. This seems a fair criticism, especially since some writers (notably Popper)[8] have construed general laws as completely unrestricted in scope, as lacking any individual reference. Hempel and Oppenheim also, in Part III of their study,[9] wish to construe laws as containing no essential occurrences of designations for particular objects, though restricting this requirement to fundamental laws.

The latter authors, however, recognize basic difficulties in trying to formulate criteria to accomplish their purpose, and give up the attempt to realize this purpose, in the paper mentioned. Yet they do hope for some such criteria of unrestrictedness of scope, and wish to apply them to laws. It is such a hope that is challenged by motive explanations. The challenge is not to the deductive pattern as we have earlier presented it. For (R2) *assumes* the notion of general law and is thus neutral to alternative analyses. But, insofar as this notion is *independently* analyzed in such a way as purportedly to rule out generalizations referentially restricted to particular individuals, motive-explanation seems to provide a valid counterexample to the analysis.

Such an analysis is, however, extremely difficult on other grounds (as we have already noted) and it is perhaps worth illustrating here what some of the difficulties are. It is, first of all, useless to interpret unrestricted scope in terms of syntactic generality, for the latter can always be achieved. For motive-statements in particular, according to Ryle's account, a statement such as:

Albert is bad-tempered.

receives some such analysis as:

Whenever Albert is provoked, he responds harshly.

which is itself presumably to be taken as:

$(x)(t) (x = \text{Albert} \cdot \text{Provoked } x, t \supset \text{Responds harshly } x, t)$

[8] Popper, *The Logic of Scientific Discovery,* sections 13-15.
[9] Hempel and Oppenheim, "Studies in the Logic of Explanation," p. 155.

The latter statement is clearly general with respect to objects and times. The next suggestion is to eliminate 'Albert', as it is a singular designation. Consider, then, any predicate (or "predicate complex") that, in fact, applies uniquely to Albert, or take as primitive the *predicate* 'is albert', which has (in fact) this unique application,[1] and rewrite as follows:

$$(x)(t) \ (Ax \cdot Px, t \supset RHx, t)$$

Or, in terms of descriptions, rewrite as:

> For all objects x and all times t, if x is identical with the object z which is albert, and is provoked at t, then x responds harshly at t.

In either case, we have eliminated the singular designation, 'Albert'. It may, however, now be objected that, though we have, in effect, gotten rid of all singular designations (Russell's theory of descriptions eliminates the singular *description* in the latter version),[2] the trouble is that we retain the predicate 'is albert' which in fact does apply only to one thing. We might, however, readily single Albert out (as earlier suggested) by means of some set of predicates (exclusive of 'is albert') none of which singly applies to just one thing. Alternatively, we might reconstrue the original motive-statement as a generalization, not about the individual enduring thing Albert, but rather about all its momentary time-slices:

> For all x, if x is an albertian time-slice and if x is provoked, then x responds harshly.

Finally, consider the class of things never provoked, which includes no people but, for example, all tables. Now apply the predicate 'K' to everything which either belongs to this class or is identical with the familiar, enduring Albert. The predicate 'K'

---

[1] See Willard Van Orman Quine, *Methods of Logic* (New York: Henry Holt & Company, 1950), pp. 218-224; and *From a Logical Point of View*, pp. 7-8.

[2] Bertrand Russell, *Introduction to Mathematical Philosophy* (London: George Allen & Unwin, Ltd., 1919; 2d ed., 1920), chap. xvi, pp. 167-180.

applies to many things, clearly. Yet it enables us to supplant our original motive statement with the following:

$$(x)(t) \ (Kx \cdot Px, t \supset RHx, t)$$

This formulation gives us the same effect as the original. For no K but Albert ever satisfies the antecedent, as a whole, since he is the only K who is ever provoked. The generalization thus enables us to conclude that he responds harshly at t, given his actually being provoked at t; on the other hand, there is no warrant for drawing the false conclusion that some table, for example, responds harshly at a given time.

Enough has perhaps been said to indicate that an independent analysis of unrestrictedness of scope faces its own general difficulties. Such an analysis can hardly be relied on at present to yield a clear decision as to whether or not motive-explanation is indeed unrestricted in scope. In fact, it provides no clarification even of the *sense* of such a decision. Moreover (as we have earlier argued), there is, in any event, no clear challenge here to the deductive pattern itself.

8. Teleological Explanation: Beliefs and Desires

In the last section, we criticized the view that an account of a man's goals or reasons in itself affords a complete explanation of his conduct. We suggested the importance of supplementary hypotheses regarding his beliefs, rationality, and abilities, and perhaps other assumptions as well. Our argument thus constituted a defense of the deductive pattern, in that it denied the explanatory self-sufficiency of accounts of reasons or goals, which admittedly do not, by themselves, satisfy the deductive pattern.

Our argument did not, however, establish that the supplementation of such accounts with suggested auxiliary hypotheses *does* fulfill the deductive pattern in a satisfactory manner. In fact, though it is easy to construct simplified models of such supplementation which appear to accord with the deductive pattern, these models also reveal serious problems of interpretation, especially with regard to ontology. Since so much of explanation in psychology and history, not to mention everyday contexts, hinges on reference to goals or reasons, these problems are of crucial importance; they represent perhaps the single greatest obstacle to a deductive account of explanation or some elaboration thereof.

We may approach these problems by considering, quite generally, the question of teleological descriptions, i.e., those apparently referring to the ends of action rather than to its determinants. How, in particular, is reference to the goals of an act to be understood, and how is it to be related to causal accounts? One suggestion is to construe ostensible mention of goals future to a given act as referring rather to ideas of such goals prior to the act, and, hence, capable of figuring in relevant causal explanantia.

The motivation for this suggestion may be seen by reference to the following example:

(1)   John decides (at *t*) to take a pre-medical course, in order to qualify for entrance to medical school.

Of what explanatory value is (1)'s apparent reference to John's future qualification, i.e., his qualification at some time later than *t*? If he does in fact qualify, he will do so following the time of his decision, and the decision cannot, therefore, be causally explained by his qualification. On the other hand, if John never does, in fact, qualify—let us suppose he fails to complete his pre-medical training—we surely cannot take his qualification as causally relevant to his decision, for there is, literally, no such qualification. What sense shall we then make of the fact that, although John's qualification is possibly fictional and, in any event, later than his decision, he does decide on a pre-medical course in order to qualify for medical school? The natural suggestion is to say that John's *desire to qualify* and *his belief that qualification is contingent on choosing a pre-medical course* jointly determine his decision. Even if his desire is in the end thwarted and his belief in fact false, they are both nonetheless real and they both precede the decision in question. *Goal-ideas* (as we may label both desires for goals and beliefs concerning them) thus supplant the goals themselves in interpreting statements similar to (1).

There are limits which it seems reasonable to impose upon the scope of such interpretation. Statements of function and "goal-directedness," for example, are asserted in biology and the social sciences, and they, also, employ the 'in-order-to' operator or some equivalent. Yet we do not wish to attribute desires or beliefs to biological organs or processes, to the lower organisms, or to social institutions or practices. C. J. Ducasse has suggested that:

> the disrepute into which teleological explanations have fallen is doubtless due to their having been so frequently . . . put forth in cases where the existence of the agent appealed to and of his beliefs and desires was not already known, but invented outright and purely *ad hoc* . . . But when antecedent evidence for their existence is present (e.g., when the hypothetical agent is a human being), a teleological explanation is methodologically quite respectable, although, like any other, it may in a given case not happen to be the correct one.[3]

Thus, the goal-idea interpretation is to be restricted to instances where independent support can be found for the postulation of appropriate beliefs and desires. For the case of individual human beings, at any rate, such interpretation seems both possible and plausible.

Ducasse considers the proper scope of such interpretation as embracing genuine cases of *purpose,* and suggests the following features as essential elements in such cases:

    I. *Belief* by the performer of the act in a law . . . e.g., that if X occurs, Y occurs.

    II. *Desire* by the performer that Y shall occur.

---

[3] C. J. Ducasse, "Explanation, Mechanism, and Teleology," *Journal of Philosophy,* XXII (1925), 150-155. By permission. Reprinted in Feigl and Sellars (eds.), *Readings in Philosophical Analysis,* pp. 540-544. The passage referred to appears on pp. 543-544 of Feigl and Sellars.

    III. *Causation by that desire and that belief jointly*, of the performance of X.[4]

The sort of rule governing explanation of the performance of X is suggested by Ducasse to be:

    IV. If an agent believes that Y is contingent upon X and desires Y, then that agent is likely to do X.[5]

We now have, in Ducasse's suggestions, the materials for constructing a very simple model of explanatory arguments which not only appeal to goals but also conform to the deductive pattern. We shall present such a model based on (1), with a view toward illustrating the serious problems of ontological interpretation mentioned earlier.

We ask, "Why does John choose a pre-medical course?" and we receive the following statements in reply, which represent a filling out of (1) to the point where satisfaction of the deductive pattern is presumed:

(2)   John desires John's qualification for entrance to medical school.

(3)   John believes that John's qualification for entrance to medical school is contingent on John's choice of a pre-medical course.

(4)   Whenever someone desires something, believing that it is contingent on something else, he performs this latter thing.

The explanation (2)-(4) is clearly artificial, and simplified even with respect to our previous discussion. Thus, (2) may be taken as giving John's *reason for* choosing a pre-medical course, *his goal in* doing so. (3) provides a supplementary item of information regarding his *belief* as to the conditions upon which his goal is contingent. Finally, (4) provides a generalization connecting goal and belief with performance, and hence enabling deduction of the explanandum:

(5)   John performs John's choice of a pre-medical course.

---

[4] *Ibid.*, p. 543 in Feigl and Sellars. (Italics in original.)
[5] *Ibid.*

No provision is made in (4), however, to ensure that the agent's *abilities* are adequate to perform those acts upon which his goals are believed by him to be contingent. Some such provision is, however, ideally necessary, since limitations upon every agent's power prevent his performing *some* of the acts that are believed by him necessary to the fulfillment of certain of his desires. There is still a further complication in that, even where a given act of this kind lies within an agent's power, he may not be able to perform *both* it *and* another, also believed necessary to the fulfillment of some desire of his, and also within his power. Thus (4) ideally needs some reference to *other,* possibly conflicting, desires of the agent, as well as complexes of them, for analogous reasons. Further refinement, in the form of value-rankings for these desires and their complexes, is perhaps desirable so as to prevent undue weakening of (4), enabling the generalization to hold for any given act except where it conflicts with some act believed necessary for a desire (or complex) with *higher* value-rank. Serious problems attend the provision of all the foregoing qualifications of (4), and they are not to be minimized.

Supposing, nevertheless, that such qualifications have been made satisfactorily, and assuming (2)-(4) to have been appropriately expanded, the resulting argument would still be a *simplified* model in applying the amended generalization to all agents whatever. The generalization may, in fact, be taken as characterizing a minimal form of rationality of conduct, and surely not all agents exemplify it. We might, ideally, wish to propose some independent specification of rationality, and to restrict the use of explanatory generalizations such as (4) to acts of agents satisfying this specification. Even so, it may be that any such generalization holds, at best, of any given agent, only in some weakened, statistical version, so that its explanatory use falls only within a statistically expanded category of explanations rather than within the strictly deductive pattern.

Despite its extreme artificiality, however, the argument (2)-(4) will serve to illustrate the general difficulties earlier mentioned: difficulties plaguing all attempts to supplement accounts of men's goals in such manner as to approximate the deductive pattern. For these difficulties are neutral to the various refinements suggested above. Even if, for example, (4) is restricted to the single agent in question, is, moreover, complicated in such a way as to take ability and conflicting desires into account, and is, furthermore, either statistically weakened or construed as merely an idealization to be approached in specific cases, it will still represent a generalization tying together desire, belief, and performance. Any such generalization will be subject to the difficulties in question.

We may, then, look back unashamedly at (4) as originally given, and see what these difficulties are. In symbols, (4) becomes:

(6) (x) (y) (z) $((\text{Desires } xy \cdot xB \text{ (Conting } yz)) \supset Pxz)$

that is: For all x, y, and z, if x desires y and believes that y is contingent on z, then x performs z. We are to understand 'z's range to be restricted to acts or choices of the agent x in question.

How shall we, however, construe the range of the variable 'y', representing what x desires? We cannot, surely, take it as restricted to actual things, for "objects of desire" cannot generally be inferred to exist. In the argument (2)-(4), for example, it may be presumed that (2) is true, i.e., that:

John desires John's qualification for entrance to medical school.

Yet to suppose that (2) uses 'desires' as a two-place predicate to express a "desire-relation" between two actual things (i.e., John, and John's qualification for entrance to medical school), so that we may infer:

(7) $(\exists y)$ $(\text{John desires } y)$

is to admit a falsehood if, in fact, John fails his pre-medical course and never qualifies at all. For in such an eventuality, there exists no such thing as John's qualification for entrance to medical school. Nonetheless, the presumption, in such a case, is not only that (2) remains true, but that the argument (2)-(4) continues to stand as an explanation of John's choice. This argument, moreover, clearly does take 'desires' as a two-place predicate, as is evident from an inspection of (6). For it depends upon instantiation of the variable 'y' by the singular term 'John's qualification for entrance to medical school'.

One proposal is to interpret 'y' as ranging over *possible* things, and to broaden the operative sense of 'existence' so as to include the existence of such possibles. 'Desires' would thus relate *actual* persons and *possible* entities of certain sorts (let us call them 'states'), and (7) would become legitimized as:

(8)   There exists some state *y* desired by John.

where existence of 'y' is, of course, compatible with there being no *actual* qualification by John for entrance to medical school, i.e., with the *falsehood* of:

(9)   John qualifies for entrance to medical school.

The *state* corresponding to (9), representing the object of John's desire, may be symbolized as:

$$s(QJ)$$

and is reminiscent of the *facts* discussed in Section 6 above, as putative objects of explanation. There are, however, important differences. Facts are normally taken as associated solely with *truths,* i.e., as associated only with true statements—and such a construal accords well with their serving to represent explananda which are true. States, on the other hand, are associated with false statements as well (as in the case of (9))—such a construal being motivated by the realization that "objects of desire" may remain forever unactualized. Whereas the force behind the introduction of *facts* was the need to account for the multiplicity of independent and true descriptions of any given thing, the force behind the introduction of *states* is rather the need to account for falsehoods figuring in the characterization of "objects of desire."

There is a further difference. Facts may readily be interpreted as determined by *logically equivalent* truths. For if a given explanandum follows from some explanans, all its logical equivalents also follow from the same explanans. Thus it can never happen that we are led, absurdly, to take some fact both as explained and not explained by the same explanans. We cannot, however, analogously take states as determined by logically equivalent statements. For the relation between John and a given statement, *S,* representing some desired state does *not* guarantee (unlike the deductive relation between explanans and associated explanandum) that any logical equivalent of such a sentence, S', also stands in the same relation. If John's report is taken as one indication of his desires, in fact, then we must be prepared to acknowledge cases where, by his own testimony, he desires:

$$s(P)$$

but not:

$$s(P*)$$

though 'P' and '$P*$' are logically equivalent. Such a case may arise, for example, through John's failing to *realize* the logical equivalence in question.

We could, of course, decree that, in such an event, one item of his testimony is to be rejected: the logical equivalence of 'P' and '$P*$', for example, may be taken as showing that he really *does* desire that P and that $P*$, though he does not realize this. The use of decree should, however, be minimized as far as possible. Further, we now must face the fact that people occasionally report themselves as desiring that such-and-such, where 'such-and-such' is self-contradictory, e.g., John reports his desire that John square the circle, the child reports his desire that he may find the greatest number. Self-contradictory statements are all logically equivalent, however. The present policy would thus require us to decree that the child just mentioned also desires that he may become President and not become President; we should need to say that all those desiring to square the circle also desire to find the greatest number. Such a course seems to fly in the face of the facts.

It seems preferable to propose that states be more finely individuated than facts, that they be determined by narrower classes of sentences than logically equivalent ones. Such a course would minimize the use of decree through multiplying differentiable states. But how and where to draw the line is not clear. Furthermore, no matter how tightly we circumscribe these classes —short of giving each sentence its own class—John, through obtuseness, may report a positive desire with respect to one member of such a class and not to another. In such an event, we should be compelled to decree what he really desires, despite his protestations. Still, the implausible consequences discussed at the close of the last paragraph would no longer need to arise.

We should, however, still have to allow for the child who desires to square the circle or to witness the collision between an irresistible force and an immovable body. To reject the truth of such descriptions, altogether, seems too heavy-handed a procedure, though conceivable. To accept such descriptions, on the other hand, commits us to postulating impossible states, corresponding to *logically* false statements descriptive of "objects of desire," e.g.:

$$s((\exists x) \ (Fx \ \cdot \ {\sim}Fx))$$

We should need further to broaden the notion of 'existence' to embrace impossible states, in order to be able to say, for example:

(10) There exists some state y, namely, there being something both F and not-F, such that John desires y.

Such a course seems much too extreme an expedient for the purpose at hand. Moreover, assuming we have somehow reconciled ourselves to accepting as intelligible the existence of not only possible but also impossible states, we need still to decide precisely how to individuate states. Generally, the wider our criterion, the clearer and the more economical of entities, but also the more reliant on decree; the narrower our criterion, the less reliant on decree, but also the more extravagant of entities, and the more likely to be obscure in itself. One course stands out: the obscurity and use of decree can *both* be reduced, at the limit, by postulating a different state for each different sentence, thus relying on the relatively clear criterion of sentence identity, and allowing for practically any degree of obtuseness in perceiving sentence relationships.[6] But such a course is also ontologically extravagant in the extreme, freely projecting language out upon the world.

The above considerations are reinforced when we note that the variables 'y' and 'z' of (6) appear within the belief-context:

(11)   *x* believes that *y* is contingent on *z*

Obviously, genuine sentences of the above type are often true even when the state *y* is unrealized and the act *z* not performed. Moreover, reports are indicative of *beliefs* as well as *desires*, while John's obtuseness may lead him to offer conflicting belief reports regarding sentences of any degree of similarity, and even to affirm self-contradictions.[7] Again, we seem driven to postulate states as values of variables, and again we face the knotty problems of possibility and impossibility, economy versus extravagance, criterial obscurity and the arbitrariness of decree.

Is there a radical way out of this predicament? Is it perhaps feasible to apply here some of the ideas of Section 6 above, presented as an alternative to an ontology of *facts*? The motivation here is even stronger, in proportion to the greater difficulty attending an ontology of states.

[6] The qualification "practically" is introduced since, in any event, the case must still be allowed in which the very same sentence elicits both agreement and disagreement from a given subject, in the same breath. Alternative treatments are available: (1) a sequential (or oscillatory) interpretation in which the subject's agreement and disagreement are assigned to different time-slices of "the same breath" in question, so that he is said to believe the sentence S at t_1 but to disbelieve it at t_2, (2) a fixed specification of the maximal temporal extent of "the same breath" can be given, and the subject's agreement and disagreement within such limits taken to indicate that (a) he neither believes nor disbelieves the sentence (within the interval), or (b) that he both believes *and* disbelieves it, i.e., believes its denial. The latter interpretation is not self-contradictory, for disbelief is taken not to imply non-belief, i.e., to believe '*P*' and also '~*P*' does *not* imply belief and non-belief of *P*.

[7] In this connection, see Israel Scheffler, "On Synomymy and Indirect Discourse," *Philosophy of Science*, XXII (1955), 39-44; and Noam Chomsky, "Logical Syntax and Semantics," *Language*, XXXI (1955), 36-45.

Let us begin (similarly to the case of explanation) by focusing on 'desires that', as an *operator*, rather than on 'desires', construed as a two-place *predicate*. 'Desires that' is, then, to be taken as an operator, forming sentences when sandwiched between names and other *sentences*. We thus immediately block all questions as to the status of such an entity as may be purportedly denoted by the abstract singular term 'John's qualification for entrance to medical school'. In place of (2), we have, rather;

(12)   John desires that John qualify for entrance to medical school.

(We may ignore the shift to the subjunctive mood in the subsentence of (12).)

We have thus gone from:

(13) $J \, D \, s(QJ)$

i.e., 'John desires the state of John's qualification for entrance to medical school', to:

(14) $J \, \mathrm{DT} \, (QJ)$

i.e., 'John desires that John qualify for entrance to medical school'. Because 'DT' may clearly be seen to be referentially opaque, we must avoid quantifying into the subsentence of (14) from without, i.e., with respect to arguments within the parentheses. The case is parallel to that of 'EF', earlier considered. Just as in the latter case, we may also try construing 'DT (————)' as a predicate-forming operator, such that insertion of a whole sentence between its parentheses yields a one-place predicate applicable to certain entities—in this case, persons, or more generally, organisms.

Unlike the previous situation with respect to 'EF', however, we cannot rest here with the analysis just proposed. For, unlike the previous situation, we are here concerned to reconstruct whole explanatory arguments of the sort represented by (2)-(4). Such arguments, however, involve "teleological" generalizations, such as (4), which clearly take as values "objects of desire" and "objects of belief," representing them by bound variables. Were (2) to be construed after the manner of (14), taking 'DT (QJ)'

as an indivisible, one-place predicate true of John, a teleological generalization such as (4) or (6) would be utterly irrelevant. In particular, we could not dissect 'DT (QJ)' so as to pull out '(QJ)' as "object of desire" for instantiation of the variable 'y' in (6). Analogous remarks hold obviously, also, for a parallel construal of (3) as consisting of 'John' and a single, indivisible one-place 'belief'-predicate. Thus, if we are to reconstruct teleological *argument,* we must somehow reintroduce analyzable structure into the ostensible predicate of (14), and construe belief-attributions in parallel structured fashion. We are, further, concerned to do so without getting entangled with *states.*

Let us, then, attempt to follow what was earlier done with 'EW', in skipping over intervening *facts* and going directly to their associated sentences. Recall that the latter course involved replacing the name-forming operator '$f($———$)$' by the predicate-forming operator 'W $($———$)$', yielding predicates applicable to sentences. A parallel strategy here would involve supplanting the name-forming operator '$s($———$)$' (purporting to denote states) with a predicate-forming operator yielding predicates applicable to sentences, or (as previously concluded) to sentence-inscriptions. The effect of such analysis would be to construe 'desiring that' as representing a special sort of relation between agents and inscriptions.

To avoid confusing the latter relation with the desiring of some (concrete) object by an agent, e.g., 'John desires the book', we need, however, to single out the proposed notion in some special way. Ultimately, to be sure, 'John desires the book' may itself be reduced to the new terms to be proposed, via the sentence 'John desires that John may have the book'. But we must still take special precautions to *avoid* interpreting the proposed relation between agent and inscription as *desiring to have* the inscription in question. All cases of 'desiring to have' are rather themselves to be explained in terms of the relation to be proposed. We shall, thus, introduce the symbol 'DTr' for the new relation, to be read 'desires-true'.[8] Desiring-true some inscription is *independent* from desiring to have it. (*Desiring to have the*

---

[8] This idea is suggested by Quine's notion 'believes-true', in "Quantifiers and Propositional Attitudes," *Journal of Philosophy,* LII (1956), 177-187.

book may then be interpreted, roughly, as *desiring-true some inscription asserting that one has the book.*)

We now replace (12) by:

(15)   John desires-true that John qualify for entrance to medical school.

Symbolically:

(16) J DTr That (QJ)

Now, we take 'That (————)' as a predicate-forming operator, and accordingly interpret 'That (QJ)' as a predicate, so that (16) becomes:

(17) $(\exists x)$ (That $(QJ)x \cdot$ DTr Jx)

read:

> 'There is some x, such that x is a that-John-qualifies-for-entrance-to-medical-school, and John desires-true x'

The range of the variable 'x' is here restricted to concrete inscriptions (though a broadening of the range to include concrete utterances as well is here, as before, also conceivable).

The promise of an inscriptional construal rests not only on the fact that physical objects are clearer elements for *any* theory than possible and impossible states, but also on the fact that inscriptions are likely already to belong to *any* ontology associated with inquiry into human conduct. To avoid going beyond what we are independently committed to is clearly a saving.

That inscriptions (and utterances), furthermore, are natural candidates for the job of supplanting *states* may be seen if we recall for a moment the motivation behind introduction of the latter in the present context. Briefly, we needed objects which could be relied upon to exist despite the thwarting of desires, the falsity of beliefs, and the omission of acts—and even despite the irrationality frequently attending their formulations. Inscriptions (and utterances) clearly seem well-suited to meet these requirements, on general grounds. For their existence is not jeopardized in the least by their own falsity or even self-contradictoriness. When mentioned in descriptions of desire, belief, and conduct, they can clearly be trusted to exist, no matter how irrational the substance described. (To assert the existence of a *state* of there being something both square and not square is a philosophically serious thing to do; to say some *inscription* exists asserting that something is both square and not square is quite innocuous.) Further, since inscriptions must, *in any event,* be acknowledged to exist, it is no ontological extravagance to take them as objects of the 'DTr' relation.

Nonetheless, general reasons alone will not suffice to show that teleological explanations such as (2)-(4) can be successfully construed in terms of an inscriptional ontology. We must therefore return to the particular argument we have discussed, and test the present proposal against the whole of it.

So far, we have replaced (2) by (12), which represents a more natural form of expression, and have proceeded to construe (12) after the manner of (17). The import of this construal is to take ordinary 'desiring that' statements, such as (12), as tantamount to statements expressing a certain relation between agents and inscriptions. The total effect concerns the *logical form and ontological character* of 'desiring that' statements, rather than their *substantive analysis,* i.e., the specification of those conditions under which they hold true. In fact, (17), for example, is presumed true just under those conditions in which (12) is presumed true. Any further, substantive analysis of 'desire', specifying the operative conditions for the truth of (12), and hence of (17), is theoretically welcome, however, as an independent step. (In similar fashion, the representation of 'explanation' statements as relating sentence pairs, in (40) of Section 6 above, was conceived as replaceable by (41), immediately following, incorporating the deductive model taken as a substantive analysis of 'explanation'.)

Statement (17) thus represents a way of construing the logical form and ontology of 'desiring that' statements. Nor can (17) be charged with obscurity by those favoring an interpretation in terms of *states.* For (17) is itself explicable in terms of the latter approach: one can, generally, explain the desiring-true of a given inscription, to proponents of *states,* as the desiring of that state which is purportedly represented by the inscription in question. Also, as noted, the 'desires-true' formulation is to be taken as true under just those conditions in which its ordinary 'desires that' counterpart is considered true. In particular, for an agent to desire-true some given inscription does *not* imply that he produce, possess, wish to possess, be aware of, or even understand the inscription in question.

We need to say, now, what the indivisible predicate 'That (QJ)', of (17), refers to. The decision here is less obvious than the parallel one in the case of explanation, e.g., with respect to 'W (Bk)' of (40) in Section 6. In the latter case, the predicate could readily be taken as denoting every logical equivalent of the sentence within parentheses, since the objective was to gain the effect of *facts,* determined by classes of logically equivalent truths. Such construal of *facts* was itself motivated by the explanans' implying every logical equivalent of each of its explananda.

We have already seen, however, that *states* are likely to be taken as determined by narrower classes than those constituted out of logically equivalent statements. We have further noted that there is room for varying decision on just what narrower criterion to employ for the individuation of states, there being a need to balance the minimization of decree achieved by increasingly narrow criteria, against their greater ontological extravagance and their greater obscurity. We, finally, remarked that obscurity and decree are both minimal for a criterion based on sentence identity, which is, however, maximally extravagant, postulating a different *state* for each sentence.

It is here that inscriptionalism shows one clear advantage. The notion of sentence identity will, in the *present* context, lack the only defect we found in it earlier: if used to determine the reference of 'That (QJ)' and similar predicates of inscriptions, rather than to individuate *states,* it will be free of ontological extravagance, as well as minimally obscure and arbitrary. We shall, therefore, use this notion as follows: We first take as *rephrasals* of one another sentence-inscriptions ordinarily assumed to represent the *same* sentence. We may explain this notion further, as follows: two sentence-inscriptions represent the same sentence if and only if they are *replicas* of each other (i.e., are spelled exactly alike), have similar language affiliation (i.e., both are French, both Italian, etc.), and lack indicator terms (i.e., term-inscriptions which are replicas, though one appears in one of the sentence-inscriptions with one denotation, and another appears in the other sentence-inscription with differing denotation).[9]

We may now fix the reference of 'That (QJ)', in (17), so as to include all and only those sentence-inscriptions which are rephrasals of the sentence-inscription occurring between its parentheses. Clearly, *the latter sentence-inscription itself* is thus included in the denotation of the predicate as a whole. The existence of an inscription denoted by the predicate is thus guaranteed by the existence of the predicate-inscription itself. In general, we take a 'That (————)' inscription as a predicate-forming operator-inscription such that insertion of a sentence-inscription between its parentheses yields a predicate-inscription applying to rephrasals of the insert. (As previously, in the case of explanation, we limit ourselves here to inscriptions and we suppose a single language affiliation for all, though we may note the conceivability of including utterances, as well as translates with differing language affiliation.) In order to avoid difficulties over the symbolically abbreviated 'That (QJ)' in the following process of reconstruction, we now replace (17) by the following, more explicit hyphenated version:

(20) $(\exists x)$ (That (John - qualifies - for - entrance - to - medical-school) $x \cdot \mathrm{DTr}\ Jx)$

Our assumption is that to desire-true any inscription is to desire-true every one of its rephrasals as well. The motivation for this assumption is clear, our intent being to gain the effect of *states* individuated by sentence identity.

[9] The notions of 'replica' and 'indicator' are given in Nelson Goodman, *The Structure of Appearance* (Cambridge, Mass.: Harvard University Press, 1951), chap. xi, pp. 290 ff. The notion of 'rephrasal' is suggested in Scheffler, "An Inscriptional Approach to Indirect Quotation," *Analysis,* XIV (1954), 83-90.

Turning now to the second premise of our teleological argument, (3), we may first eliminate the relatively unclear notion of contingency in favor of a conditional construction, as suggested by Ducasse's treatment. To say that John's qualification is contingent on John's choosing a pre-medical course is to say that if he fails so to choose, he fails to qualify—in other words, if he qualifies, his choice of a pre-medical course may be inferred. We shall, accordingly, restate (3) so as to embody this idea, our purpose being to simplify the treatment to follow.

(21)   John believes that if John qualifies for entrance to medical school then John chooses a pre-medical course.

Just as with *desire,* we shall construe *belief* as relating agents and inscriptions, and analyze (21) as asserting that John is belief-related to an inscription of some particular sort.

The term we shall employ, in analogy to 'desires-true', is 'believes-true', and the import of the analysis is to be understood much as in the former case. That is, the proposal concerns the logical form and ontological character of 'believes that' statements, rather than a substantive analysis of the conditions under which such statements are true. In fact, the construal to be presented is presumed true just under those conditions in which ordinary 'believes that' statements are considered true, no matter what these conditions may be. It follows that, when the 'believes-true' relation holds, it need not be expected that the agent produce, be aware of, or even understand the inscription believed-true. Nor can the proposal well be criticized as more obscure than one appealing to states (or propositions), for the believing-true of an inscription can be explained, in the latter terms, as the believing of that state (or proposition) associated with it. We shall take the that-clause of (21) as one of our 'That (———)' predicates, as before—denoting rephrasals of the sentence following the word 'that'. We shall again here make explicit the guiding assumption, i.e., to believe-true any inscription is to believe-true every rephrasal of it. (21) accordingly becomes:

(22)   ($\exists$x)   (That   (If-John-qualifies-for-entrance-to-medical-school-then-John-chooses-a-pre-medical-course) x · BTr Jx)

We come, finally, to the teleological generalization, (4), which, in addition to the notions of desire and belief, has a notion of performance. We shall here substitute 'makes-true', applicable to agents and inscriptions, and carrying no implication that an inscription made-true is produced or even understood by the agent in question. Making-true a given inscription is, furthermore, explicable (to those who use the terminology of acts, choices, and performances) as performing the act or choice represented by the inscription involved. Given a particular inscription to the effect that John chooses a yellow tie, for example, John makes-true this inscription if and only if he makes the choice described, i.e., if and only if the inscription is in fact true. Thus, unlike inscriptions desired-true or believed-true, every inscription made-true is, in fact, true. It is the case as before, however, that to make-true any inscription is to make-true also every rephrasal of it.

In place of (4), we now have:

(23) $(x)(v)(z)(w)$ $(Kzvw · DTr\ xv · BTr\ xz \supset MTr\ xw)$

where '$Kzvw$' is to be taken as meaning that z is a conditional formed out of v and w, in that order. As a whole, (23) now says:

> For all x, v, z, and w, if z is a conditional formed of v and w, and x desires-true v, and x believes-true z, then x makes-true w.

The range of 'w' is restricted to sentence-inscriptions of the form 'x chooses . . .'; an additional condition is needed to ensure that the argument-inscription of w denotes x, and possibly another to require x to believe-true the latter statement. Strictly, still other refinements are needed. Our problem is to see if even a crude argument can be carried through.

We thus attempt a reformulation of the teleological argument (2)-(4), on the basis of (20), (22), and (23), and the assumptions made along the way. From (20), we learn that John desires-true *some* inscription which is a That (John-qualifies-for-entrance-to-medical-school), and (by our understanding of the 'That (———)' predicate of (20)), we know that this inscription is a rephrasal of the sentence between parentheses following the 'That'. One of our assumptions tells us that to desire-true any inscription is to desire-true also all its rephrasals, so John must desire-true the very sentence-inscription between the parentheses of (20). Furthermore, since the antecedent of the 'That (———)' predicate of (22) is a replica of the latter sentence-inscription, and shares its language affiliation, and since both are free of indicator terms, this antecedent is one of its rephrasals and is thus also desired-true by John.

According to (22), moreover, some rephrasal of the whole conditional within its parentheses is believed true by John, and, since to believe-true any inscription is to believe-true all its rephrasals, John believes-true the very sentence-inscription between the parentheses of (22). The latter is a conditional, of which we have already seen that John desires-true the antecedent. The conditional may thus be taken as z of (23), and its antecedent as v of (23). Its consequent is thus identifiable with w of (23), the conclusion being that John (the x of (23)) makes-true this consequent. We have seen that to make-true an inscription is to make-true every one of its rephrasals. Thus, if we produce a replica of the above-mentioned consequent with identical language affiliation and no indicator terms, then, being a rephrasal of the consequent, it will also be made-true by John. Furthermore, it will *be* true, since inscriptions made-true *are* true. It will thus serve as the needed conclusion of our argument:

(24)   John chooses a pre-medical course.

A somewhat different way of expounding the argument from (20), (22), and (23) to (24) will now be given, so that the essential points may be seen more clearly. Here, we shall avoid explicit reference to the parenthesized sentence-inscription of (22) as providing instantiations for variables of (23).

(22) says that there is some x believed-true by John, such that x is a That (If-John-qualifies-for-entrance-to-medical-school-

then-John-chooses-a-pre-medical-course). Now, the following assumption is made: For every *x*, if *x* is a That (If-John-quali-fies - for - entrance - to - medical - school - then - John - chooses - a-pre-medical-course), then there exist a *z* and a *w* such that *z* is a That (John-qualifies-for-entrance-to-medical-school) and *w* is a That (John-chooses-a-pre-medical-course), and *x* is a conditional formed out of *z* and *w* (i.e., *Kxzw*).

The conclusion drawn from (22) plus the latter assumption is that there are three inscriptions, *x, z* and *w*, such that *x* is believed-true by John, *z* is a That (John-qualifies-for-entrance-to-medical-school), *w* is a That (John-chooses-a-pre-medical-course), and all three are such that *Kxzw*.

Statement (20) tells us that some inscription exists which is both desired-true by John and a That (John-qualifies-for-entrance-to-medical-school). Since to desire-true any inscription is to desire-true all its rephrasals, John desires-true *every* inscription which is a That (John-qualifies-for-entrance-to-medical-school). Applying this result to the conclusion cited in the previous paragraph, we now have assurance that the *z* there mentioned is desired-true by John. It follows, then, that the antecedent conditions of (23) are all satisfied, i.e., there are three inscriptions *x, z*, and *w*, such that *Kxzw*, and John desires-true *z*, and John believes-true *x* (and we already know that *w* is a That (John-chooses-a-pre-medical-course)). We are now warranted by (23) in concluding that John makes-true *w*. Since *w* is made-true, it *is* true, and we may write as a conclusion any of its rephrasals, e.g., (24):

John chooses a pre-medical course.

The foregoing argument needs to be further investigated, to see if it holds up when it is made more precise, and when refinements are added and extension to other cases made. Our purpose has been to explore the possibilities of an inscriptional approach in a preliminary way; no claim to ultimate success is here intended, and, indeed, we have already noted several of the difficulties attending the attempt to carry through *any* analysis of teleological argument in a fully satisfactory manner. Perhaps enough has been said, however, to indicate the seriousness and complexity of the general problem, and to suggest that an inscriptional approach is at least worth pursuing further.

We must, however, take note of a critical observation of W. V. Quine which challenges even the moderate suggestion just put forward.[1] Quine points out that such a sentence as:

Paul believes something that Elmer does not.

presents difficulties for an analysis in terms of 'BTr'. He observes, "It will not do to say that Paul believes-true some utterance that Elmer does not believe-true, for it may happen that no such utterance exists or ever will; believing does not, like saying, produce utterances. . . . Still, the defect is limited to quantifications. It does not touch the explicit idiom '*w* believes that *p*', construed as '*w* believes-true an utterance that *p*'; for, once '*w* believes that *p*' is itself uttered, there has been created a sample utterance that *p*."

Quine suggests that the quantifications are perhaps expendable altogether. But if they are given up, there will be "no need to recognize 'believes' and similar verbs as relative terms at all . . ." He thus proposes that we dispense with the notion of *objects* of belief completely; instead, he advocates taking 'believes that ————' as an operator which, filled with a sentence, produces a one-place predicate applicable to believers. (He generalizes the workings of this operator in further ways, but these are irrelevant to the point here at issue.)

It must surely be admitted that the problematic sentences noted by Quine, i.e., the one reproduced above and his other example:

Eisenhower and Stevenson agree on something.

present a serious difficulty for analysis in terms of 'BTr'. For such analysis would take each of these sentences as asserting the

[1] Willard Van Orman Quine, *Word and Object* (New York and London: published jointly by The Technology Press of The Massachusetts Institute of Technology and John Wiley & Sons, Inc., 1960), pp. 214-216. By permission.

existence of some particular inscription or utterance, of which no sample is provided within the sentence itself.[2] It is, further, true that such sentences are expendable without serious loss; as Quine puts it, "Such quantifications tend anyway to be pretty trivial in what they affirm, and useful only in heralding more tangible information."[3] Once such information is given, that is, appropriate sample inscriptions or utterances will thereby be created.

But it does *not* follow at all that giving up *such* quantifications as are illustrated by Quine's problematic sentences, i.e., isolated existential quantifications, permits us to give up *all* quantifications over belief objects: it is not the case that, if we give up the problematic quantifications noted, there will be no further need to construe 'believes' as a relative term.

For (as we have already noted in the case of (14), dealing with desire) we cannot rest with a construal which stops short of analysis in relational terms, if our concern is to reconstruct teleological *argument*. Such argument involves generalizations, such as (4), taking objects of desire and belief as values. To treat 'believes that ———' and 'desires that ———' as predicate-forming operators would rule out teleological generalizations of this sort; it would correspondingly render teleological

[2] It might be suggested that this difficulty is (for all practical purposes concerned with the interpretation of actual belief-descriptions) removed if we adopt a somewhat artificial notion of inscriptions, in line with a suggestion of Nelson Goodman and Willard Van Orman Quine in "Steps Toward a Constructive Nominalism," *Journal of Symbolic Logic*, XII (1947), 106. The suggestion is to construe inscriptions as including "all appropriately shaped spatio-temporal regions even though they be indistinguishable from their surroundings in color . . ." Certain idealizations would seem to be required to make the suggestion plausible, e.g., all inscriptions believed-true would perhaps need to be construed as belonging to the same language, and to be governed by deliberate semantic rules (or there might be other devices to the same effect), for the *natural context* of the inscriptions could no longer be counted on to eliminate ambiguities.

In any event, while there seems no conclusive argument against the suggestion, the treatment in the text, which follows, does not at any point rest on it.

[3] Quine, *Word and Object*, p. 215.

explanation unintelligible. Putting the point positively, the need for construing 'believes' as a relative term and for quantifying over belief objects is not limited to problematic existential statements of the sort noted by Quine. In teleological argument, such quantification serves the purpose of linking together an indefinite number of particular explanations of conduct through generalizations similar to (4). (The other premises in such explanations, as we have seen, *will* normally contain sample inscriptions of the appropriate sort.) There is thus ample motivation for analysis in terms of 'BTr', even if isolated existential statements, of the sort noted by Quine, are given up.

9. Teleological Explanation: Self-regulating Behavior

We have, in the last section, seen some of the problems presented by teleological discourse to proponents of the deductive model of explanation. We have, further, explored an inscriptional proposal for interpreting such discourse in terms of *goal-ideas,* that is, desires for, and beliefs concerning, *goals.*

As mentioned earlier, however, there are reasonable limits to such an interpretation, since teleological description seems wider in scope than the class of cases where there is independent support for the postulation of beliefs and desires. If the latter cases are called 'purposive', as suggested by C. J. Ducasse, we need also to acknowledge teleological description of non-purposive behavior in animals and men, as well as in social institutions and perhaps elsewhere too. For such cases primarily, the suggestion has been made to interpret teleological accounts as descriptions of self-regulating processes, which exhibit plasticity as well as directedness—and which seem, moreover, to raise no theoretical difficulties for usual conceptions of causal explanation.

Such an interpretation, like the earlier one, has seemed to have its reasonable limits: whereas the "goal-idea" interpretation needed to beware of ascribing ideas to the lower animals and to unconscious processes, the "self-regulation" interpretation needs to avoid oversimplifying fully purposive action in man and the higher animals. It is to the reasonably restricted use of the

latter interpretation that we shall here primarily address ourselves. Our main interest is to test the adequacy of the interpretation even when it is limited to non-purposive cases.

We shall begin by referring to a recent and widely known
paper by A. Rosenblueth, N. Wiener, and J. Bigelow,[4] in which
the notion of self-regulation is applied to teleological accounts.
Convinced that "purposefulness (is) a concept necessary for the
understanding of certain modes of behavior,"[5] and that its importance has been slighted as a result of the rejection of final
causes as elements of explanation, these authors propose to
interpret purpose itself as behavior "directed to the attainment
of a goal, i.e. to a final condition in which the behaving object
reaches a definite correlation in time or in space with respect
to another object or event."[6]

In order to carry through their interpretation, the authors introduce the terms 'input', 'output', and 'feedback', as follows: 'input' applies to events external to an object that modify the object
in any manner. 'Output', on the other hand, refers to changes
produced in the surroundings by the object. 'Feedback' may be
used in two different ways. It may be applied to objects (such as
electrical amplifiers), some of whose output energy is returned as
input. In such cases, feedback is *positive,* in that the output re-
entering the object "has the same sign as the original input signal,"[7] thus adding to this signal rather than correcting it. On the
other hand, feedback is *negative* when the object's behavior is
"controlled by the margin of error at which the object stands at a
given time with reference to a relatively specific goal."[8] In such
cases, "the signals from the goal are used to restrict outputs
which would otherwise go beyond the goal."[9]

With the notion of 'negative feedback' at hand, the authors

[4] Arturo Rosenblueth, Norbert Wiener, and Julian Bigelow, "Behavior, Purpose and Teleology," *Philosophy of Science,* X (1943), 18-24.
By permission of the publisher.
[5] *Ibid.,* p. 23.
[6] *Ibid.,* p. 18.
[7] *Ibid.,* p. 19.
[8] *Ibid.*
[9] *Ibid.*

propose that teleological behavior be construed as behavior controlled by negative feedback.[1] "All purposive behavior," they say, "may be considered to require negative feedback. If a goal is to be attained, some signals from the goal are necessary at some time to direct the behavior."[2] A machine may, of course, be constructed in such a way as to impinge on a luminous object, although the machine is insensitive to light, as well as to other stimuli emanating from the object. It would, however, be a mistake to consider such impingement behavior *purposive,* inasmuch as "there are no signals from the goal which modify the activity of the object *in the course of the behavior.*"[3]

By contrast, say the authors, some machines are "intrinsically purposeful," for example, "a torpedo with a target-seeking mechanism."[4] The behavior of such objects involves "a continuous feedback from the goal that modifies and guides the behaving object."[5] The path followed by the torpedo, for example, is controlled by the signals it receives from the moving target.

If the authors be understood simply as recommending the extension of certain teleological idioms to selected forms of behavior of independent interest, there can be no quarrel with them based on the ground that their conception of teleology is inadequate. For in such a case, they would not be setting forth an analysis of teleology so much as striving to improve the description of the behavior in question through increased use of teleological language. If, however, as appears to be the case, they intend also to provide an *analysis* of teleological notions, their proposal may properly be judged by seeing how satisfactorily the analysis accounts for acknowledged instances of teleological behavior.

In the light of our earlier remarks about a reasonable restriction of the "self-regulation" idea to non-purposive cases, it will be instructive to test the proposal initially by reference to pur-

[1] *Ibid.,* p. 24.
[2] *Ibid.,* p. 19.
[3] *Ibid.,* pp. 19-20. (Italics in original.)
[4] *Ibid.,* p. 19.
[5] *Ibid.,* p. 20.

posive behavior, since the authors purport to characterize "all purposive behavior" in terms of negative feedback, in the manner outlined above.

Purposive behavior is to be thought of as directed toward "a final condition" in which the object achieves correlation with respect to some other entity. Since the goal of such behavior is described as something which emits signals guiding the behaving object, the goal cannot itself be identified with the final condition of correlation mentioned above. For one thing, this final condition, if it occurs at all, is later in time than the behavior in question, and cannot therefore be assumed to guide it, if the notion of "final causes" acting upon earlier events is rejected. For another, the authors describe cases of "undamped feedback," in which a purposive machine, by increasingly larger oscillations, overshoots the mark and *fails altogether* to attain the final condition toward which its behavior is directed, though such behavior has presumably been modified by signals from the goal. The goal, as described by the authors, cannot, therefore, be identified with the final condition of correlation they speak of, and it must rather be construed as that entity with which correlation is supposed to occur if the behavior is successful, i.e., what may be called 'the goal-object.' This goal-object, even where correlation fails to occur, *may* plausibly be construed as emitting signals that modify the activity of the behaving object.

However, the existence of such an entity as a goal-object cannot be assumed in every case of purposive behavior. As pointed out by R. Taylor,[6] a man's purpose in groping about in the dark may be to find matches that are in fact not there, his purpose in going to the refrigerator may be to get an apple when, in point of fact, there are no apples in the refrigerator. Men have sought the philosopher's stone and the fountain of youth—and the purposiveness of their behavior in these quests cannot be denied despite the non-existence of the appropriate goal-objects. In each such case, the behavior in question must be admitted to be purposive, and yet in none is it guided by signals emitted from a

[6] Richard Taylor, "Purposeful and Non-purposeful Behavior: A Rejoinder," *Philosophy of Science*, XVII (1950), 327-332.

goal-object, correlation with which represents the final condition toward which the behavior is directed. Generally, if a man's purpose is to obtain object O, we cannot infer the existence of something x, identical with O, such that he seeks x. Nor can we infer, from the fact that a man's purpose is to obtain something of kind K, that there is something of kind K for which he strives. In the cases so far discussed, there is at least an *apparent* reference to a goal-object, though to infer the *existence* of a goal-object would be fallacious. Some cases of purpose lack even *apparent* reference to a goal-object. The mystic striving to become more humble through spiritual training cannot readily be described as someone trying to obtain object x, nor as someone whose behavior is directed toward correlation with x, guided by signals emanating from it.

Such criticism as has just been presented argues the inadequacy of the Rosenblueth-Wiener-Bigelow interpretation only with respect to purposive cases. Indeed, R. Taylor supposes that we have here an "irreducible difference" between human beings and machines,[7] suggesting thereby that the difficulty we have discussed (which may be called *the difficulty of the missing goal-object*) does not arise for non-purposive instances, on the Rosenblueth-Wiener-Bigelow account. As against this suggestion, the following considerations appear to indicate that the same difficulty arises also with respect to non-purposive behavior, in non-human as well as human organisms, and conceivably in machines too.

Consider a standing passenger thrusting his foot outward suddenly in order to keep his balance in a moving train, a rat depressing the lever in his experimental box in order to secure a food pellet, an infant crying in order to attract its mother's attention. To describe each of these cases as has just been done is to provide a teleological account relating the behavior in question to some selected end. It is not, however, to attribute purpose to the organism concerned, in the sense of our previous instances, for example. The knight's purpose in traveling far and wide may be to

[7] *Ibid.*, p. 330.

find the Holy Grail—he has chosen to search for it in the hope of finding it. The man's purpose in opening the refrigerator door may be to get an apple within—he then opens it with the intention of getting an apple within. It would normally be thought peculiar, however, to describe the train-rider's sudden kick as a product of choice or as an expression of intention. It seems similarly inappropriate to describe the rat as choosing to depress the lever, or as depressing it with the intention of securing a pellet. Finally, we do not generally say of an infant, even when it cries in order to attract its mother, that it has chosen to cry, or that it cries with the intention of attracting its mother—though it may of course do so at a later stage of development, when its crying will be interpreted quite differently by its elders. These cases are presented here as illustrative of a large group for which we willingly offer teleological accounts but withhold ascriptions of intention, choice, and purpose.

It does not take much reflection to see that the difficulty of the missing goal-object arises even with respect to such cases, if we attempt to analyze them in accord with the Rosenblueth-Wiener-Bigelow proposal. We cannot, for example, plausibly suppose our train-rider to be receiving guiding signals from some region with which his foot is to be correlated. Neither, when the psychologist stops replacing the rat's pellets, can we describe the rat as receiving directive signals from some such pellet. Nor, finally, when the infant's mother, expecting her baby to sleep, steps out for a moment to the corner store, is she available for the issuing of signals guiding the infant's behavior toward final correlation with herself. The proposal we have been considering cannot, therefore, be judged generally adequate even if we restrict it to non-purposive teleological behavior, nor does it seem to suffice even for non-human cases.

For at least some non-purposive cases, an interpretation in terms of learning may throw light on teleological description, where analyses in terms of self-regulation break down. In the case of the infant, for example, it may be suggested that our 'in order to' description of its present crying reflects our belief that this crying has been learned as a result of the consequences of like behavior in the past—more particularly, as a result of having, in the past, received its mother's attention. Having initially cried as a result of internal conditions C, and having thereby succeeded in attaining motherly solace, representing a type of rewarding effect E, the infant now cries in the absence of C, and as a result of several past learning sequences of C followed by E. The infant's crying has thus been divorced from its original conditions through the operation of certain of its past effects.[8] These past effects, though following their respective crying intervals, nonetheless precede the *present* crying interval which they help to explain. The apparent future-reference of a teleological description of this present interval is thus not to be confused with prediction, nor even with mention of particular objects in the current environment, toward which the behavior is directed. Rather, the teleological statement tells us something of the genesis of the present crying and, in particular, of the prominent role played by certain past consequences in this genesis. Such an account is perfectly compatible with usual conceptions of causal explanation, and, though sketchy and hypothetical, it indicates why goal-objects may very well be missing in some cases for which teleological description is nonetheless appropriate. It indicates also that we have in this respect no irreducible difference between human beings and machines, since machines capable of learning through the effects of their own operations are equally subject to such teleological description.

The interpretation of teleology proposed by R. B. Braithwaite,[9] though it resembles the Rosenblueth-Wiener-Bigelow proposal, is considerably different in detail and restricts itself explicitly to what Braithwaite calls "goal-directed behavior" as distinct from "goal-intended behavior,"[1] thus avoiding criticisms such as that of Taylor, based on purposive cases. Braithwaite's

[8] For an illuminating treatment of this and related points, see R. S. Peters, "Symposium: Motives and Causes," *Aristotelian Society Supplementary Volume XXVI* (London: Harrison and Sons, Ltd., 1952), pp. 139-162.

[9] Braithwaite, *Scientific Explanation*, pp. 319 ff.

[1] *Ibid.*, p. 325.

use of the idea of self-regulative behavior is deliberately moderate; he wants to interpret "all teleological explanations which are not reducible to explanations in terms of a conscious intention to attain the goal."[2]

That the notion of *causal chains* is fundamental in the analysis of teleology is, for Braithwaite, shown by the fact that the organism's behavior does not directly produce the goal; it constitutes, rather, part of a causal sequence of events progressing toward the goal. What, however, distinguishes teleological causal chains from all others with which science is concerned? Here Braithwaite follows E. S. Russell in proposing as the main clue "the active persistence of directive activity towards its goal, the use of alternative means towards the same end, the achievement of results in the face of difficulties."[3] Such plasticity of behavior is "not in general a property of one teleological causal chain alone: it is a property of the organism with respect to a certain goal, namely that the organism can attain the same goal under different circumstances by alternative forms of activity making use frequently of different causal chains."[4] To specify this plasticity further, Braithwaite provides a schematic description.

We have, let us suppose, some object *b* which, in the normal case, is to be taken as a physical or organic system. Every event at any time in *b* is assumed determined by the whole preceding state of *b* taken together with the set of actual field or environmental conditions causally relevant to this event. Consider now a causal chain *c*, comprised of events in the system *b* during a particular interval and following immediately upon the initial state *e* of the system. Suppose also that the set of actual field conditions causally relevant to the events comprising the chain is *f*. Then *c* is uniquely determined by the initial state *e* taken together with the set of field conditions *f*.

Causal chains may now be related to a goal gamma as follows.

[2] *Ibid.*

[3] Quoted from E. S. Russell, *The Directiveness of Organic Activities* (Cambridge, England: Cambridge University Press, 1945), p. 144, by Braithwaite, *Scientific Explanation*, p. 329. By permission of the publishers.

[4] Braithwaite, *loc. cit.*

Every chain ending in a gamma-event without containing any other such event is a gamma-goal-attaining chain. Relative to a given initial state e of b, we may consider the class of all (possible) sets of field conditions f uniquely determining chains that are gamma-goal-attaining. This class is the variancy ϕ, with respect to b, e, and gamma, comprising the "range of circumstances under which the system attains the goal."[5]

Plasticity may be attributed to the system when the variancy has more than one member, so that the goal may be attained under alternative environmental circumstances, though not necessarily by means of alternative causal chains. Teleological explanations assert that the behavior in question is plastic, and are intellectually valuable to the extent that this plasticity is not asserted on the basis of known causal laws of the system's mechanism, but rather on the basis of observation of the conditions under which similar behavior has taken place in the past. Further, teleological explanations predict the occurrence of some gamma-goal-attaining chain on the basis of knowledge of the system's plasticity; they predict, in other words, that the set of field conditions that will in fact occur is a member of the appropriate variancy ϕ, on the ground that ϕ includes the class ψ of all sets of field conditions likely to occur.

It is at once apparent that, since Braithwaite does not construe goal-direction in terms of a relation to some *goal-object* but rather in terms of the *variability of appropriate field circumstances,* the difficulty of the missing goal-object does not arise in his scheme. Fido's pawing at the door need not be controlled by signals from outside; it need only lead to his being let out under alternative circumstances, say when his master is at home or when only his master's young son is at home. The rat need not, as he depresses the lever, be receiving any stimuli from the pellet that drops into his cup only after the lever is depressed; it is enough that his depressing of the lever results in his obtaining the pellet under a variety of experimental conditions.

---

[5] *Ibid.,* p. 330. The beginnings of causal chains seem problematic, on this view. Does the definition imply that a cat's capture of its first mouse ends a single mouse-attaining chain that began with the birth of the cat, for example?

Braithwaite's interpretation seems, however, subject to other difficulties. For he appears to hold that particular teleological explanations do not merely ascribe plasticity to the behavior being explained, but also predict *goal-attainment* in the circumstances that will in fact ensue. It is perhaps worth noting as a minor difficulty in this view that its use of the term 'explanation' is peculiar, bearing little relation to causal explanation. Of crucial importance, however, is the fact that teleological descriptions, whether or not they be thought to qualify for the title 'explanation', do *not* generally predict the attainment of the goal indicated. It is interesting that, despite the requirement of Rosenblueth, Wiener, and Bigelow for a *goal-object*, they allow for non-attainment or *goal-failure* in their examples of undamped feedback resulting in an overshooting of the target. But it is easy to multiply other examples of goal-failure. If Fido, trapped in a cave-in, is in fact never reached, is it therefore false that he pawed at the door in order to be let out? If, as in the case previously described, the psychologist stops replacing the consumed pellets with new ones, is it false to say the rat continues to depress the lever in order to obtain a pellet? To suppose, with Braithwaite, that all teleological explanations carry with them an "inference that the set of relevant conditions that will in fact occur in the future will fall within the variancy"[6] is to answer the preceding questions affirmatively and quite unplausibly.

The *difficulty of goal-failure* may, of course, be avoided if the prediction of goal-attainment is eliminated from the content of teleological descriptions. Retaining the rest of Braithwaite's scheme, we should then take such descriptions simply as attributing plasticity to the behavior in question, with respect to the goal indicated. We should be saying of the system b exhibiting the state e that there is more than one possible set of field conditions f, such that, were f conjoined with e, some suitable goal-attaining chain would ensue. We should *not*, however, be predicting that one of these sets will in fact be presently realized, and our statement would therefore be protected from falsification through goal-failure.

[6] *Ibid.*, p. 334.

This proposal is, however, immediately confronted with a new difficulty that we may call *the difficulty of multiple goals;* the proposal becomes too inclusive to differentiate between acceptable and unacceptable teleological descriptions, in an indefinitely large number of cases. These cases may be indicated schematically in Braithwaite's terms. Imagine that for the system b, and relative to the present state e of this system, the class of those sets of field conditions f_1 uniquely determining gamma-goal-attaining chains has more than one member. The system in state e is thus plastic with respect to gamma. Suppose, now, that the class of those sets of field conditions f_2 uniquely determining delta-goal-attaining chains relative to b and e also has more than one member. The same system in state e is thus also plastic with respect to delta. If our teleological description of the system's present behavior embodies neither a prediction of the attainment of gamma nor a prediction of the attainment of delta, but restricts itself merely to an assertion of the plasticity of this behavior, we should be able, with equal warrant, to frame our teleological description either relative to gamma or relative to delta. We should, that is, be able to say either that b exhibits e in order to attain gamma or that b exhibits e in order to attain delta. This is, however, exactly what we cannot generally say.

The cat crouching before the vacant mouse-hole is crouching there in order to catch a mouse. Since no mouse is present, there will in fact be no goal-attainment. Nevertheless, the cat's behavior is plastic, since there are various hypothetical sets of field conditions, each set including one condition positing a mouse within the cat's range, such that, in conjunction with the cat's present behavior, each set determines a mouse-attaining causal chain. On the other hand, there are also various other hypothetical sets of field conditions, each set including one positing a bowl of cream within the cat's range, such that, conjoined to the cat's present behavior, each set determines a cream-attaining causal chain. It should therefore be a matter of complete indifference, so far as the present proposal is concerned, whether we describe the cat as crouching before the mouse-hole in order to catch a mouse or as crouching before the mouse-hole in order to get some cream. The fact that we reject the latter teleological description while accepting the former is a fact that the present proposal cannot explain.

A limiting case of this difficulty occurs when the state e is one for which we should reject *every* positive teleological description. Imagine, for example, that e is the state of physical exhaustion, and that the relevant class of field-condition sets is the one just considered in connection with mouse-attainment, suitably supplemented by conditions stipulating the cat's recuperation and assumption of a crouching position before the mouse-hole. The present proposal would then warrant us in saying, absurdly, that the cat is physically exhausted in order to catch a mouse.

Other examples of the difficulty of multiple goals arise in cases where every gamma-goal-attaining chain is also a delta-goal-attaining chain or contains such a chain as a part, so that if the variancy with respect to gamma has more than one member, so has the variancy with respect to delta. Consider, for example, an infant crying in order to get its mother's cuddling, which is always preceded by the sound of its mother's footsteps. Since every set of field conditions determining a cuddling-chain in this situation also determines a footstep-chain, and since we may assume the class of such sets determining cuddling-chains to have more than one member, we may infer that the class of sets determining footstep-chains also has more than one member. Thus we should again be warranted by the present proposal in saying either that the infant cries in order to receive its mother's cuddling, or that it cries in order to hear its mother's footsteps. The proposal again proves too inclusive to differentiate between teleological descriptions we accept and those we reject.

Can the wanted distinctions be made on the basis of the learning interpretation suggested earlier? The answer seems perhaps to be "yes" with regard to the examples we have considered. Thus, it may be suggested that we do not believe the cat has learned to crouch before the mouse-hole as a result of having been rewarded with a bowl of cream for having done so in the past. Nor do we suppose the infant's crying to have been learned as a result of having heard its mother's footsteps following past crying intervals. Nonetheless, it would be premature to propose the learning interpretation as a generally adequate analysis simply on the basis of the examples above considered. It may, further, be properly objected that the notion of 'learning' is itself too obscure as yet to provide a resting-point for analysis of teleological descriptions.

Perhaps the best that can be done at present is to make some general observations that seem warranted by our analyses of the current and preceding sections, as well as Section 5 above. These analyses seem to indicate that it would be a mistake to expect a single interpretation for all statements considered teleological. It seems more reasonable to develop several lines of approach. Furthermore, it seems likely that not all interpretations will result in assimilating teleological descriptions to the category of explanations, in the spirit of the deductive pattern.

Thus, though "teleology" generally involves some apparent reference to the future as explanatory of the past, several varieties of "teleology" have seemed distinguishable. So-called purposive cases seem naturally interpretable as purporting to explain conduct by reference to *antecedent* goal-ideas concerning the future. We have explored some of the difficulties and possibilities in connection with this plausible interpretation.

Some non-purposive cases seem amenable to interpretation by reference to negative feedback, i.e., a given item of behavior is explained by the action of antecedent signals from a goal-object toward which the behaving system is moving. The flavor of futurity is here gotten through projection of the path of motion in accordance with a knowledge of the system's mechanism. Other non-purposive cases seem amenable rather to an interpretation in terms of learning through effects of *past* trials. All of the above cases seem, at least in principle, assimilable to the category of explanation as conceived in the spirit of the deductive pattern, though difficulties still obstruct such actual assimilation.

By contrast, any interpretation in terms of plasticity of behavior, even if it could somehow be made to surmount the difficulties noted above, would not, it seems, yield explanations in the same sense. It would rather single out certain *descriptions* of behavior, i.e., those relating a given item to some hypothetical later consequence in special ways. Such descriptions might, of course, support certain predictive arguments with the aid of supplementary hypotheses. But these arguments would provide no "causal" explanation of the items described, that is, they would not explain why these items had occurred.

Finally, "functional" accounts (discussed in Section 5) have seemed also to relate given items to selected outcomes, providing *descriptions* incapable of yielding explanations of these items, in the "causal" or "deductive" spirit. Here, however, arguments may be constructed, with the help of supplementary hypotheses, supporting inferences from the selected outcomes to the items in question, providing *substantiations* of these items. And, of course, an *independent* (though confusing) use of the term *'functional explanation'* is possible, by which reference is made to "explanation" *of* an item's function (i.e., an *account of* its contribution to the economy of the organism) rather than to explanation *why* the item has occurred, *by reference to* such function.

The class of teleological statements thus seems to be a loose assortment, the members of which vary considerably in logical weight and explanatory potential. Though all may, in common parlance, be said to explain, and though each may be a candidate for answering some ordinary 'Why?' question, the varieties seem to require separate constructive analyses to reveal their several roles in scientific argument.

PART II

Significance

1. Explanation and Criteria of Significance

We have already indicated in general how the notion of cognitive significance enters into discussions of explanation: Explanation has been said to require formulation in terms that are cognitively significant. Let us here examine the connection in detail, with reference to the Hempel and Oppenheim study.

(R3) of this study, it will be recalled, requires the explanans to have *empirical content*. What is the force of this requirement? Presumably, it is to rule out as explanatory such accounts as the following answer to the question why water has cooled after being placed over a flame for a while and then removed: "The water had initially been deprived of its glubbification through action of the flame (which generally has this effect); removed from the flame, it has become increasingly glubbified again and hence cooler, in accord with the general principle that glubbification varies inversely with warmth."

Such accounts seem clearly defective despite their inclusion of general principles, and their ability to yield the desired explanandum as a consequence. They cannot be accepted, even though there are respectable explanations (e.g., in terms of the behavior of imperceptible particles) which also seem like gibberish to the layman and equally removed from direct observation. It may be said, to be sure, that our glubbification explanans is simply not true, and hence defective in violating (R4). But why are we prepared to say, even in advance of accumulating evidence, that accounts in terms of molecules are *worth* examining for truth, whereas accounts in terms of glubbification are not to be taken seriously, even as possible explanations? The natural idea is that, whereas the molecular account is, at worst, false, the glubbification account is not even eligible for falsehood: it is meaningless in the cognitive sense, that is, neither true nor false. Surely failing to satisfy (R4), it further fails to satisfy even a more primitive requirement, that of *cognitive significance*, which, for statements neither analytically true nor analytically false, reduces to *empirical significance*.

Elaborating this natural idea, we might say that accounts which are cognitively significant may be worth entertaining and worth examining for truth on their merits, for they are, in fact, either true or false. Empirically significant accounts, in particular, fall in the province of empirical science, for they are not only in fact true or false, but their truth or falsehood is not decidable by reference to their forms or meanings alone; observation is required in addition. On the other hand, accounts which are not analytically true or false, and also not empirically significant, are surely not worth entertaining in science. For, being neither true nor false, they are surely not true, and so cannot possibly serve as explanations at all. Thus, applying (R3) before (R4), we ensure that our explanans is not unworthy of the effort of empirical investigation; satisfying (R3), it must not only be cognitively significant but dependent upon observation for settlement of its claims to truth. We avoid not only genuine statements whose truth status is a function of their forms or meanings, but also purported statements lacking meaning altogether, and so neither true nor false.

To accomplish this aim in a general and precise manner, however, we need a criterion for empirical content or significance, which is simply assumed by (R3). Having such a criterion, we could combine it with independent criteria for analyticity to form an overall criterion of cognitive significance. Such a criterion would enable us to circumscribe clearly the class of all truths and falsehoods, separating these decisively from purported statements that are in fact not genuine. We could, further, define the scope of empirical science as embracing just the empirically significant statements, within the larger class.

Several historical strands lead up to the recent efforts to formulate a criterion of empirical significance, notably the British empiricists' attempted reduction of knowledge to sense experience, and Kant's critique of metaphysics. We shall not here review this background nor recount the complicated history of later developments associated with the doctrines of pragmatism, positivism, and operationism. Rather, we shall consider systematically the central problem of formulating a suitable criterion of significance, and its proposed use in defining the scope of empirical science.

2. Conditions of Adequacy for Defining a Criterion

What conditions must be met by any successful definition of a criterion of significance, for the purposes outlined above? To formulate such conditions will enable a clearer specification of the problem and will facilitate the evaluation of proposed solutions to it.

The point of having a criterion of significance, as we have seen, was to be able to rule certain doctrines, *prior to investigating their truth-claims,* as neither true nor false, and hence unworthy of serious examination. A line was to be drawn by the criterion between doctrines which are either true or false, and doctrines which are neither. We may, then, set down as the first condition of adequacy governing any successful definition of significance the requirement that every sentence satisfying such a definition be true or false and, conversely, that every true or false sentence satisfy the definition. This condition of adequacy may be put thus:

> C.A. I: For every sentence *S, S* is true or false if, and only if, *S* is significant.

C.A. I represents a condition of material adequacy. It allows us to criticize any proposed definition of significance if it turns out either that (1) something satisfying the definition is neither true nor false, or that (2) something true or false fails to satisfy the definition.

It is clear, furthermore, that C.A. I could not itself serve as the desired definition, for it tells us only that a doctrine lacks significance (is meaningless) if it is neither true nor false, giving us no way of bypassing issues of truth and falsehood in evaluating controversial doctrines. What was desired, rather, was a criterion *independently applicable*, enabling us to judge, for any doctrine, whether it was *not unworthy* of having its truth-claims investigated. The anti-metaphysical motivation of early proposals had precisely this point: to avoid getting enmeshed in substantive arguments with metaphysicians, and to rule out their doctrines in advance by reference to some independent mark of meaninglessness.

A. J. Ayer's Introduction to his second edition of *Language, Truth, and Logic* appears to set forth something in the nature of C.A. I as a governing condition for his "principle of verification." Thus, he writes,

> I should, however, claim that there was at least one proper use of the word "meaning" in which it would be incorrect to say that a statement was meaningful unless it satisfied the principle of verification; and I have, perhaps tendentiously, used the expression "literal meaning" to distinguish this use from the others, while applying the expression "factual meaning" to the case of statements which satisfy my criterion without being analytic. *Furthermore, I suggest that it is only if it is literally meaningful, in this sense, that a statement can properly be said to be either true or false.* Thus while I wish the principle of verification itself to be regarded, not as an empirical hypothesis, but as a definition, it is not supposed to be entirely arbitrary.[1]

Another condition of adequacy represents the intent to reduce non-analytic significance to *experience or observation*. The idea behind this condition has already been intimated: The truth-status of some statements is a function of their forms or meanings

[1] A. J. Ayer, *Language, Truth, and Logic* (2d ed.; London: Victor Gollancz, Ltd., 1947), pp. 15-16. (My italics.) By permission of the publisher and Dover Publications, Inc.

alone; these are the analytically true and analytically false (briefly, analytic) statements, which may thus be evaluated through inspection of their forms or meanings. Analytic significance is, in this sense, a matter of forms or meanings. Statements neither analytically true nor analytically false are those whose truth-status is not a function of their forms or meanings alone; they cannot be evaluated simply by inspection of their forms or meanings. But what else is there, as a basis of evaluation, if not experience, or the realm of things revealed by empirical observation? Non-analytic significance must, then, be a matter of experience, or observation.

The empiricistic philosophy here expressed set the framework within which early attempts at a definition of significance were made. It had several appealing features. It gave explicit recognition to the role of observation and experiment in science. It, further, provided a neat mapping of the cognitive terrain. Logic and mathematics were held to be analytic, hence not to *need* observation, while 'glubbification' and similarly worthless hypotheses were ruled nonsensical, so not *deserving* of observation. Between these territories lay the domain of empirical science, neither analytic nor nonsensical, and consisting of statements both needing and deserving observation.

Non-analytic significance, accordingly, was to be characterized (without appeal to truth or falsehood) in terms of *observation* or *experience*. To make this idea somewhat more exact, we shall here introduce the notion of an *observation-sentence* as (roughly) recording the result of an observation. The attempt was, then, to construe all non-analytic, significant statements as linked by a specified logical relationship to the class of observation-sentences. Various formulations in terms of verifiability by experience, confirmation through observation, or prediction of observable occurrences may be interpreted as so many attempts to link non-analytic significant assertions to observation-sentences, through some particular logical relationship.

We may perhaps formulate our second condition of adequacy thus:

C.A. II: There is some logical relation R, such that for every sentence S, S is significant if, and only if, S is analytic or related by R to some observation-sentence O.

We may refer to this as a condition of empiricist adequacy.

To illustrate, let us again refer to Ayer, who writes: "Let us call a proposition which records an actual or possible observation an experiential proposition. Then we may say that it is the mark of a genuine factual proposition, not that it should be equivalent to an experiential proposition, or any finite number of experiential propositions but simply that some experiential propositions can be deduced from it in conjunction with certain other premises without being deducible from those other premises alone."[2]

Finally, no matter what definition was adopted, it must not yield the result that all sentences are significant (e.g., by radically expanding the notion of falsehood to embrace such hypotheses as the glubbification theory). Though such a requirement is perhaps not needed as a separate item, it is convenient to list it as such, and we do so here, referring to it as a condition of non-universality:

C.A. III: It is not the case that, for every sentence S, S is significant.

The intended mode of application of a definition meeting the conditions C.A. I-III is indicated by Ayer's statement, "Our charge against the metaphysician is not that he attempts to employ the understanding in a field where it cannot profitably venture, but that he produces sentences which fail to conform to the conditions under which alone a sentence can be literally significant. Nor are we ourselves obliged to talk nonsense in order to show that all sentences of a certain type are necessarily devoid of

[2] *Ibid.*, pp. 38-39. The logical relation specified in this passage is a complex one, but it is clear enough how to define a term 'R', expressing it; the suggestion is, then, that a non-analytic significant sentence S is one for which there is some observation sentence O, such that S stands in relation R to O.

literal significance. We need only formulate the criterion which enables us to test whether a sentence expresses a genuine proposition about a matter of fact, and then point out that the sentences under consideration fail to satisfy it."[3]

To sum up, it was hoped that a definition satisfying C.A. I-III would do two things: (1) characterize every true-or-false doctrine in such a way as to enable us to reject in advance, rather than having to investigate, the truth-claims of every *other* doctrine, and (2) reduce non-analytic significance to experience or observation, i.e., show that every non-analytic truth-question relates, in the last analysis, to matters of observation—that non-analytic doctrines which do not so relate lie outside the boundaries of significance altogether. (Kant and Hume were to be joined, clarified, and vindicated at once: Kant's insistence on the exclusion of some issues as beyond the limits of human reason (C.A. III) was to be fused with Hume's construction of factual knowledge out of experience (C.A. II).)

3. Criteria Based on Complete Verifiability or Falsifiability

Various attempts to construct a definition of significance have been critically reviewed by Hempel.[4] Briefly, definitions requiring what he calls "complete verifiability in principle" or "complete falsifiability in principle" turn out to violate C.A. I.

Empirical significance in the sense of *complete verifiability* is interpreted by Hempel in the following way:

> S is empirically significant if and only if S is not analytic and S is logically implied by some finite and logically consistent class of observation sentences.

[3] *Ibid.*, p. 35.

[4] Carl G. Hempel, "Problems and Changes in the Empiricist Criterion of Meaning," *Revue Internationale de Philosophie*, XI (1950) 41-63. Reprinted in Leonard Linsky (ed.), *Semantics and the Philosophy of Language* (Urbana, Illinois, University of Illinois Press, 1952), pp. 163-185. The "complete verifiability" formulation which follows is a paraphrase of Hempel's statement on p. 167 of Linsky.

Such a definition is not satisfied by non-analytic general statements, since these are not logically derivable from finite sets of observation-sentences. Yet we believe some such statements, e.g., empirical laws in science, to be true. Hence some true statements turn out *not* significant by the definition, that is, C.A. I is violated. Equally, such mixed-quantification statements as:

> For any substance, there exists some solvent.

cannot be logically derived from finite sets of observation-sentences. Since we hold at least some such sentences to be either true or false, C.A. I is again violated.

Furthermore, suppose S to satisfy the definition, i.e., to follow logically from a finite and consistent set of observation-sentences. Now consider any arbitrary formula N to which neither our definition nor our intuition accords any significance, e.g., 'glubbification varies inversely with warmth'. The compound alternation sentence S v N (read: "S or N") must now likewise satisfy the definition for it is itself a logical consequence of S, which is, by hypothesis, a logical consequence of a finite set of observation-sentences; S v N must therefore itself be a consequence of the same set of observation-sentences. It must, therefore, be empirically significant, even though it is, as a whole, neither true nor false but nonsense. We have again a violation of C.A. I, i.e., a statement significant by the definition but neither true nor false.

Another difficulty, pointed out by Hempel, is the following: If C.A. I is to hold, then—since the denial of every true or false sentence is itself true or false—denials of significant sentences must themselves be significant. That is, C.A. I tells us that all significant sentences are either true or false. Take any such significant sentence and form its denial. This denial must, then, again be true or false—false if the original sentence chosen was true, and true if the original sentence chosen was false. Thus, this denial must, again by C.A. I, be significant since all true or false sentences are significant.

Yet the definition we are considering violates this result. Consider, for example, an observation-sentence which tells us that some particular surface is blue. Such a sentence implies that something is blue:

$$(\exists x) \; (\text{Blue } x)$$

and the latter is thus empirically significant by the definition and hence, *a fortiori,* significant. Yet its denial is a statement that everything is not blue:

$$(x) \; (\sim \text{Blue } x)$$

which is not analytic nor, furthermore, is it ruled empirically significant by the definition, being a universally quantified statement. It follows that it is not significant at all by the definition, though it is true or false, being a denial of an admittedly significant sentence. We have here again, therefore, a violation of C.A. I.

Definitions based on *complete falsifiability* are subject to analogous objections. An empirical, completely falsifiable statement is one decisively refutable, that is, refutable by a finite set of observation-sentences; its denial follows from such a set, though not analytic. As Hempel formulates it, this condition yields the following definition:

> S is empirically significant if and only if $\sim S$ is not analytic and $\sim S$ is logically implied by some finite and logically consistent class of observation-sentences.[5]

This definition attributes empirical significance to denials of completely verifiable statements, as the latter were construed by the previous definition. Whereas, however, the previous definition ruled out non-analytic universal statements, admitting at least some existential statements (provided their vocabulary was appropriate, enabling derivation from observation-sentences), the present definition has the opposite effect. It rules out existential statements, since their universal denials are not completely verifiable, but it does grant empirical significance to at least some universal statements—those whose existential denials are formulated in the right vocabulary to enable derivation from observation-sentences.

[5] *Ibid.,* in Linsky, pp. 169-170. The version in the present text is a paraphrase.

But we do believe some purely existential statements to be true and some to be false, hence significant and, further, empirically significant since not analytic. For example, 'There is at least one chair' and 'There are centaurs' are true and false, respectively, hence both significant and, moreover, empirically significant; yet the present definition rules them both as lacking significance since their denials are not completely verifiable. This is again a violation of C.A. I. Another such violation is provided by mixed quantifications which the definition rules as lacking significance because their denials are also mixed quantifications and, as we have seen earlier, not completely verifiable. Nevertheless, for some such sentences and their respective denials, we hold one member of the pair to be true and the other false, e.g., 'For any substance there is at least one solvent' and 'Some substance has no solvent'.

Suppose, now, that S satisfies the complete falsifiability definition. Consider any formula N both intuitively meaningless and unfalsifiable, e.g., 'Something is a glubbifier'. The conjunction $S \cdot N$ (read: "S and N") must now satisfy the definition likewise. For, by hypothesis, $\sim S$ follows from some finite, consistent observation-set O. But $\sim S$ logically implies $\sim S \vee \sim N$. Therefore O logically implies $\sim S \vee \sim N$. The latter statement is, however, just the denial of $S \cdot N$, which thus turns out satisfying the present definition, though as a whole neither true nor false but nonsense. Again, a violation of C.A. I.

Finally, we have a violation of C.A. I hinging on the fact that the definition rules the denials of some significant sentences to be themselves lacking in significance. Thus, for example,

$$(x) \ (\text{Blue } x)$$

is declared significant by the definition, while its denial:

$$(\exists x) \ (\sim \text{Blue } x)$$

is ruled empirically meaningless and, since non-analytic, lacking significance altogether, though it is true or false, being a denial of an admittedly significant sentence.

4. Falsifiability as Criterion of Significance and as Criterion of Demarcation

Hempel mentions in a footnote[6] that the idea of using falsifiability as a criterion to separate empirical science from both the formal sciences, on the one hand, and metaphysics, on the other, is due to K. R. Popper, but says he does not know whether or not Popper would agree to his formulation, which we discussed in the preceding section. Popper in fact does employ falsifiability as a criterion of *demarcation* (as he puts it) between science and metaphysics, but he rejects the use of falsifiability as simultaneously a criterion of *meaning*. For him, falsifiability is a property that may be used to draw a line between two groups of perfectly meaningful non-analytic statements.[7] It seems that both the term 'science' and the contrasting term 'metaphysics', as well as the adjectives 'metaphysical' and 'empirical', are being used ambiguously as between Popper and those philosophers concerned to define a criterion of significance.

For the latter, as we have seen, the realm of empirical science exhausts the class of non-analytic significant statements, and metaphysics is beyond the pale. For Popper, on the other hand, empirical science comprises only a proper subset of the non-analytic significant statements while metaphysics comprises another subset of the same set of statements. Since falsifiability has become the center of a tangled controversy over the scope of science, the present section will digress somewhat, to consider critically the two sorts of criteria with which it has been associated. It will be hard to avoid the conclusion that, when due note is taken of ambiguities in the key notions mentioned above, the appearance of radical disagreement over the scope of empirical science vanishes. In its place we shall find *two* problems with respect to determining this scope, rather than conflicting answers to the same problem.

[6] *Ibid.,* p. 170.

[7] Karl R. Popper, *The Logic of Scientific Discovery* [translation of *Logik der Forschung*] (London: Hutchinson & Co., Publishers Ltd., 1959), p. 40, footnote *3.

The search for a criterion of empirical significance was, as we have seen, an attempt to draw a line around all non-analytic doctrines which were also, as a matter of fact, true or false, hence genuine statements. Every non-analytic doctrine outside the line was to be a non-statement, a bit of nonsense. Among non-analytic doctrines then, the aim was to draw a line between sense and nonsense. Philosophers engaged in the search for a criterion of significance (we shall refer to them here as *positivists*) often spoke of doctrines on the nonsense side of the line as *metaphysical,* partly by way of contrast with the realm of *empirical science,* understood as exhausting the class of non-analytic, significant statements, partly in the conviction that certain doctrines of traditional metaphysics were in fact not genuine statements, but only purported statements masquerading as truths. These philosophers did not, however, wish to deny that the corpus of writings constituting traditional metaphysics also contained genuine statements of a non-analytic sort.

On the other hand, they spoke of non-analytic statements on the sense side of the line as representing the scope of empirical science, in the belief that such statements cannot be evaluated purely by reference to linguistic form or meaning, but require also some appeal to observation in order to be reasonably accepted or rejected. Their point was not to suggest that such a statement as, for example, 'There are blackboards' belongs to one or another of the systems of scientific theory, or is a likely candidate for some such system, but rather to indicate that it makes a claim, in principle, to be evaluated in an empirical-scientific manner, i.e., by reference to observation, subject to the control of objective canons of judgment.

Popper's intent in proposing a criterion of demarcation is quite different. He offers no criteria of significance and does not propose to draw a line between non-analytic sense and nonsense. He assumes from the start a class of genuine non-analytic statements. Within this class, he draws a line between falsifiable and non-falsifiable statements. The former he calls 'scientific', the latter, by contrast, 'metaphysical'. In fact, he stresses his primary interest in theoretical systems rather than in individual statements, and his problem, in contradistinction to that of the positivists, is to characterize generally *systems of scientific theory* rather than *those statements which, in principle, may be scientifically evaluated.*

The distinctive feature of his characterization of scientific *systems* is falsifiability, and, having determined this feature, we may now apply it to the classification of any given *statement*, if we like —provided we bear in mind that for *sets* of statements, it is the falsifiability of the whole which counts. Thus, the statement 'There are blackboards' is judged meaningful but unfalsifiable, hence lacking the distinguishing feature of scientific systems, hence metaphysical, despite the fact that it may be evaluated after the manner of empirical-scientific investigations, through appeal to objectively controlled observation, e.g., it is a consequence of the observation-sentence 'This is a blackboard'.

In short, the positivists strive for a distinction between non-analytic sense and nonsense, whereas Popper strives to distinguish, within the realm of sense alone, between systems that are scientific and those that are not. Thus, when the positivists speak of empirical science, *they* refer to the whole area of non-analytic significance; science represents *for them* the realm of non-formal truths and falsehoods. When Popper speaks of science, *he* refers only to part of this realm, that part which, in his view, has the distinguishing mark of systems of scientific theory. When the positivists deplore metaphysics, they deplore nonsense. When Popper speaks in praise of metaphysics, he praises what the positivists have never deplored. The fact that different distinctions are involved means that the label 'metaphysics' is ambiguous and the two attitudes are compatible.

There are, to be sure, practical *verbal* issues here in the choice of labels. Shall we use the label 'metaphysics' for the nonsense class, and so employ the "emotive force" of the term 'nonsense' to "push" people away from historical writings ordinarily called 'metaphysical', or shall we avoid this "push" by a different use of the label? Shall we, by the positivists' broad use of the term 'science', employ its positive connotations to foster scientific attitudes to all non-formal claims, or shall we restrict the label to likely systems of theory? There are, undeniably, practical, "causal" differences attached to variant choices of so-called emotive labels. Nonetheless, the ambiguities of these notions, as employed by Popper and the positivists, render their opposing pronouncements on science and metaphysics theoretically compatible.

It may, of course, be the case that real differences remain, in the application of their *common* categories to particular statements. For instance, it *may* be that there are individual doctrines which would be judged differently by Popper and the positivists as belonging to the sense or nonsense class. In any event, such differences, if they exist, do not imply that a genuine controversy is represented by opposing general declarations put in terms of the ambiguous label 'metaphysics'. Suppose *A* says that *S* makes sense and *B* denies that *S* makes sense. It still does not follow that they contradict each other simply in *A*'s saying, "Every bit of metaphysics, i.e., *nonsense*, is deplorable" and in *B*'s saying, "Not every bit of metaphysics, i.e., *unfalsifiable sense,* is deplorable."

It seems, thus, rather misleading for Popper to write, "The fact that value judgments influence my proposals does not mean that I am making the mistake of which I have accused the positivists —that of trying to kill metaphysics by calling it names. I do not even go so far as to assert that metaphysics has no value for empirical science. For it cannot be denied that along with metaphysical ideas which have obstructed the advance of science there have been others—such as speculative atomism—which have aided it . . . I am inclined to think that scientific discovery is impossible without faith in ideas which are of a purely speculative kind . . . and, to that extent, metaphysical."[8] If the previous interpretation here given is sound, positivists have opposed nonsense rather than speculation, whereas Popper here defends not nonsense but significant non-analytic doctrines that happen to be unfalsifiable. Which sort of metaphysics, in short, are the positivists accused of wrongly trying to kill? As Popper himself empha-

[8] *Ibid.*, p. 38.

sizes, "Note that I suggest falsifiability as a criterion of demarcation, but not of *meaning*. . . . Falsifiability separates two kinds of perfectly meaningful statements: the falsifiable and the non-falsifiable. It draws a line inside meaningful language, not around it."[9] This seems a clear indication that Popper's intended distinction is wholly different from the positivists' intended distinction.

If there are, as we have argued, two problems to be recognized here rather than one, is there a discernible order of priority between them? Are positivists to be criticized for dealing with the problem of characterizing significance rather than with the problem of characterizing scientific systems? Can it be said that, in identifying non-analytic significance with the realm of the empirical, positivists are to be blamed for failing to distinguish bona fide scientific systems, with the allegedly characteristic feature of falsifiability, from statements which, though true or false and hence significant, do not clash with experience, and are hence metaphysical?

Such a criticism of the positivists is easily met. Every program, after all, addresses itself to certain problems and not to others, and every distinction leaves others yet to be made. One obvious and sufficient reply is to point out that the same clearly holds for Popper's stress on falsifiability as a mark of scientific systems. By restricting the term 'empirical' to just such systems, Popper fails to distinguish non-empirical significant expressions from nonsensical expressions, both types lacking the crucial feature of falsifiability.

If the sense-nonsense distinction is added to falsifiability, Popper can of course remedy this defect. But, by the same token, if falsifiability is added to the positivistic separation between sense and nonsense, positivists can equally remedy the defect charged against them. That is, they can subdivide the empirical realm into the falsifiable empirical statements on the one hand and the unfalsifiable empirical statements on the other, instead of, as with Popper, subdividing the nonempirical realm into the nonempirical significant expressions and the nonempirical non-

[9] *Ibid.*, p. 40, footnote *3.

sensical expressions. All the distinctions in question emerge in either way, and the differences concern only the choice of labels. For example, shall we call the statement:

There exists at least one blackboard.

empirical though unfalsifiable, or nonempirical though significant? Or, alternatively, shall we call it non-metaphysical but unfalsifiable, or non-scientific but not nonsensical? These issues are verbal only (not to say uninteresting in the extreme) and give no ground for the criticism we have been discussing.

There seems, nonetheless, one asymmetry which favors the positivists rather than Popper. No critic has suggested that the line between non-analytic sense and nonsense depends, for its drawing, upon falsifiability. All critics, including Popper, *reject* the use of falsifiability in distinguishing sense from nonsense, and none has argued that falsifiability is *required* by the positivists in the solving of *their own* problem, in the drawing of their own line. The criticism we have just earlier discussed is rather that the positivists need some reference to falsifiability for the making of supplementary distinctions, for the solving of other problems they have ignored.

By contrast, Popper's intended line of demarcation between science and metaphysics depends upon the notion of significance, which is thus presupposed by him for the solution of *his own* problem. As he says, "Falsifiability separates two kinds of perfectly meaningful statements: the falsifiable and the non-falsifiable. It draws a line inside meaningful language, not around it."[1] *Metaphysics,* for him, is to represent not *all* purported statements which lack falsifiability, but only those which are also meaningful. *Science* is to include the falsifiable but also to exclude nonsense, and the latter condition is an extra condition since, as Hempel has pointed out, the conjunction of falsifiable *S* with nonsensical *N* is likewise falsifiable. The demarcation of science from metaphysics (in Popper's approach) thus depends on an independent appeal to the notion of meaningfulness, for its own success.

[1] *Ibid.*

Despite the clear statement that falsifiability "draws a line inside meaningful language," the dependence of Popper's intended demarcation upon the notion of meaningfulness does not seem to be equally clearly acknowledged throughout; the ambiguous term 'metaphysical' proves treacherous in use. We shall see this in looking closely at Popper's defense of falsifiability as a criterion of *demarcation*, against the criticisms of Hempel, directed at falsifiability as a criterion of *meaning*.

Hempel's first criticism, as we have seen, pointed out the unwarranted exclusion of purely existential statements and mixed quantifications from the realm of significance. Popper easily parries this by admitting that such statements fail, indeed, to satisfy the falsifiability criterion, but denying that, as he employs it, the criterion thus excludes these statements from the domain of significance. On the contrary, these statements are allowed significance and they may, further, figure *within* scientific systems. Moreover, application of the criterion to scientific systems *as wholes* never yields the judgment that *they* are unfalsifiable.[2]

Hempel's third criticism is also easily countered. The point here, it will be recalled, was that the criterion fails to yield the result that denials of significant statements must themselves be significant. Popper's answer is that, since he does not use the criterion as a mark of significance, the asymmetry of falsifiability as between universal statements (e.g., 'Everything is blue') and their existential denials (e.g., 'Something is not blue') simply does not bear on the stated result regarding significance. The universal statement and its existential denial may both be allowed significance, though they are unequal with respect to *scientific* in contrast to *metaphysical* status.[3]

It is in the answer to Hempel's second criticism that the dependence of Popper's criterion on appeal to some anterior notion of significance becomes clearly relevant, though it is blurred by a crucial shift of terminology. Popper discusses this criticism, to the effect that, as he puts it, "The conjunction of a meaningful

[2] *Ibid.*, section 4; p. 40, footnote *3; pp. 69-70; p. 70, footnote *1.
[3] *Ibid.*, p. 70, footnote *2; p. 85, footnote *1.

statement and a 'meaningless pseudo-sentence' would become meaningful," a consequence which he admits is "absurd" and fatal to falsifiability as a criterion of meaning or significance. His answer here is, in effect, that scientific systems as *wholes* need to be falsifiable, but that not every statement within such a whole needs also to be falsifiable. Thus, he writes, "Empirical theories (such as Newton's) may contain 'metaphysical' elements. But these cannot be eliminated by a hard and fast rule; though if we succeed in so presenting the theory that it becomes a conjunction of a testable and a non-testable part, we know, of course, that we can now eliminate one of its metaphysical components."[4]

The crucial shift here is from the term 'meaningless pseudo-sentence', which is used to describe Hempel's objection, to the terms 'metaphysical elements' and 'metaphysical components', which are used in giving Popper's reply. The latter terms are, however, crucially ambiguous in the present context. On Popper's view, they denote doctrines or purported statements which are not meaningless but *significant*. His answer, taken literally, thus begs the question as to how to distinguish conjuncts which are significant from those which are not.

The objection was that, if S is falsifiable, then S conjoined with any arbitrary purported statement N is likewise falsifiable. If the criterion of falsifiability functions not as criterion of significance but as a mark of scientific status, the objection still holds that meaningless purported statements are allowed by the criterion as components of scientific systems. As bona fide conjuncts, they are detachable as theorems; scientific systems are thus allowed by the criterion to yield meaningless theorems. To answer that *metaphysical*—and hence significant—conjuncts are to be allowed generally in science is thus beside the point. The objectionable consequence is avoidable only if Popper's criterion, even for his own purposes in defining scientific systems, is supplemented by some device for ruling out nonsensical conjuncts, either a criterion of significance or a primitive notion of significance enabling a distinction between sense and nonsense. In

---

[4] *Ibid.*, p. 85, footnote *1.

either case, the adequacy of falsifiability as a criterion of demarcation, in Popper's own terms, depends on a concept of significance. It is *not* here argued that therefore Popper's program should not be independently undertaken or even preferred. The point is only that any criticism of the positivists for not marking out the distinction sought by Popper is misguided. Further, if there is any asymmetry as between the two *problems* involved, it favors the notion of significance rather than that of falsifiability.

Assuming, now, that falsifiability fails as a criterion of *significance,* we may independently ask how it fares as a criterion of *scientific status,* conceived in the spirit of Popper's problem. To avoid difficulties already discussed, we must beware of begging any questions by controversial use of the terms already shown to be ambiguous. For the same reason, let us assume that we are now dealing only with purported statements that are also, in fact, genuinely significant. (We shall consider the present question briefly, before returning to the main theme of our discussion, i.e., *significance.*)

Popper wants a sharp division between scientific and metaphysical ideas. He writes, "I . . . take it to be the first task of the logic of knowledge to put forward a concept of *empirical science,* in order to make linguistic usage, now somewhat uncertain, as definite as possible, and in order to draw a clear line of demarcation between science and metaphysical ideas—even though these ideas may have furthered the advance of science throughout its history."[5] This passage speaks of *ideas,* and his Section 15, for instance, clearly speaks of certain *statements* (strictly existential ones) as "metaphysical." Nevertheless, as already noted, his primary interest is in systems.[6] The position may perhaps be interpreted as follows: The distinguishing feature of scientific systems is falsifiability, and this feature effects a *general distinction* applicable to all statements, of any degree of composition. As a *requirement,* however, it holds only for scientific systems taken as wholes, and not also for each statement within such systems.

[5] *Ibid.,* pp. 38-39.
[6] *Ibid.,* section 16; p. 85, footnote *1.

Falsifiable, hence scientific, systems may have unfalsifiable, hence unscientific or metaphysical statement-components. Thus, Popper writes, "An *isolated* existential statement is never falsifiable; but if taken *in a context* with other statements, an existential statement *may in some cases* add to the empirical content of the whole context; it may enrich the theory to which it belongs, and may add to its degree of falsifiability or testability. In this case, the theoretical system including the existential statement in question is to be described as scientific rather than metaphysical."[7]

It may be asked what is excluded by a restriction of the falsifiability requirement to whole systems. Any unfalsifiable system S presumably becomes part of some falsifiable system by simply having conjoined to it a trivial (preferably true) falsifiable statement O, e.g., 'All pencils on the desk are yellow'. The expanded system S', consisting of S and O, can always replace S without difficulty. The line of demarcation between S and S' is clearly not an important line, surely not the goal of "the first task of the logic of knowledge."

Nor will more significant exclusiveness result from requiring (for every system not throughout falsifiable) a greater integration among system-components, so that they must, e.g., function jointly to yield some falsifiable consequence. For S may be supplemented with $S \supset O$ to yield O, not yielded by either of these components alone. Again, such a supplementary statement can always be found by choosing some trivial (and preferably true) falsifiable statement as O.

Nor will the requirement of a separate falsifiable component as axiom of the system (yielding some other such component not otherwise derivable) make much difference. We can, for example, replace S by $S \cdot ((S \cdot O_1) \supset O_2)$ and join the whole latter statement to O_1 as an additional falsifiable statement. We now derive the falsifiable consequence O_2, not yielded by any premise singly. Again, such trivial supplementation is always available.

It may be objected, with respect to the latter example, that if such supplementation is to be effective in preserving S, we must

[7] *Ibid.*, p. 70, footnote *1. (Italics in original.)

accept O_1 and O_2, and if so, we can say $O_1 \cdot O_2$ directly, thus eliminating the need for S. This is perhaps what Popper suggests in saying, "If we succeed in so presenting the theory that it becomes a conjunction of a testable and a non-testable part, we know, of course, that we can now eliminate one of its metaphysical components."[8]

But the fact remains that the whole system including S is falsifiable and hence scientific, by the criterion. A may wish to eliminate S, but B may wish to keep it, and so long as not every *statement* is required to be falsifiable but only every *whole system*, B is meeting the requirements in keeping S and, furthermore, in calling his system 'scientific'.

We may now, perhaps, attempt to develop a notion of *degree* of falsifiability and of scientific character for systems, and try to show that B's system stands lower on this scale than A's. Such an idea is surely legitimate and important (and Popper's contribution in this regard is a noteworthy one). But a notion of degree no longer gives a sharp and significant demarcation between science and metaphysics. Rather, we end up with a multiplicity of distinctions in *degree of scientific status* and not a hard and fast barrier separating science from metaphysics.

Such considerations raise other questions as to the interpretation and appropriateness of the metaphysical category as Popper employs it. His use can hardly be said to provide an accurate reflection of our preanalytic application of this notion; we do not preanalytically judge 'Something is a table' to be a metaphysical statement. He is presumably taking the adjective 'metaphysical' as equivalent to '*non-scientific*' (but applicable only to genuine statements). If, however, he takes metaphysical *ideas* or *statements,* to be perfectly admissible components of *scientific systems,* it seems then to be a misleading understatement of the case to say, "It cannot be denied that along with metaphysical ideas which have obstructed the advance of science there have been others—such as speculative atomism—which have aided it."[9] Metaphysical ideas are, for him, not merely heuristic aids, but legitimate building blocks of science. What is then the point of

[8] *Ibid.,* p. 85, footnote *1.
[9] *Ibid.,* p. 38.

labeling certain of these blocks 'metaphysical'? What is the allegedly overriding importance of such labeling for the "logic of knowledge"?

Perhaps the point is to accord, thus, a kind of second-class citizenship to unfalsifiable statement-components of systems, corresponding to our alleged desire to separate them out and eliminate them as soon as we find it possible to do so. This would seem, however, to conflict with the first-class role of such statements when they are considered not only as bona fide ingredients embedded in scientific systems but as elements conflicting with such systems. Each purely existential statement, for instance, serves to negate an indefinite number of falsifiable systems, i.e., all those implying its universal, falsifiable denial. The first importance of a sharp line of demarcation between science and metaphysics seemed dubious in the light of earlier arguments leading to the notion of *degree* of scientific status of *systems*. The question here, with reference to *statements,* is whether the idea of such a line does justice to the logical work performed by unfalsifiable statements.

In response to this question, it might be suggested that in the actual process of falsification, it is not the purely existential statement but the statement ascribing a property to some individual referred to by proper name that is of paramount importance. Thus, for example, to falsify:

(1) $(x) \ (Fx)$

we need only the existential statement:

(2) $(\exists x) \ (\sim Fx)$

which is logically equivalent to:

(3) $\sim (x) \ (Fx)$

the formal contradictory of (1). Yet, in practice, it might be argued, we do not simply find (2) but rather a stronger statement, such as:

(4) $\sim Fa$

from which (2) follows as a logical consequence. Thus (2) is only an intermediary in the process of actual falsification.

In answer to this argument, it might be said, first of all, that even the role of intermediary just specified is still too important to be given a second-class status. But, secondly, it is not quite right to say that (2) is only an intermediary in the manner outlined. For the argument that it is depends on saying that it is a consequence of (4). W. V. Quine has shown, however, that it cannot be considered to be a consequence in the strict sense. The principle of existential generalization, by which (2) is gotten from (4) is, in Quine's words, "a principle only by courtesy. It holds only in the case where a term names and, furthermore, occurs referentially . . . The principle is, for this reason, anomalous as an adjunct to the purely logical theory of quantification. Hence the logical importance of the fact that all singular terms, aside from the variables that serve as pronouns in connection with quantifiers, are dispensable and eliminable by paraphrase."[1]

In short, the crucial inference from (4) to (2) is valid only on the assumption that '*a*' names something in fact, that *a* really exists. But this is itself clearly an existential assumption.

Popper employs, however, a category of *basic statements,* interpreted as "singular existential statements," i.e., 'There is a so-and-so in the region *k*'. Such singular existential statements yield purely existential statements, i.e., 'There is a so-and-so', when reference to particular space-time regions is dropped, and "a purely existential statement may indeed contradict a theory."[2] His conception appears to be, then, that (2) is intermediary in the actual process of falsification of (1), since (2) is gotten from a *basic statement,* e.g.:

(5) $(\exists x)\ (x$ is in region $k \cdot \sim Fx)$

Are basic statements *themselves* falsifiable, however? On the

[1] Willard Van Orman Quine, *From a Logical Point of View* (2d ed.; Cambridge, Mass.: Harvard University Press, 1961), p. 146. Copyright, 1953, 1961, by The President and Fellows of Harvard College. By permission of the publisher and the author.

[2] Popper, *The Logic of Scientific Discovery,* pp. 101-102.

one hand, Popper says, "Here we shall assume that falsifiable basic statements exist."[3] Yet he also says, "A basic statement must have a logical form such that its negation cannot be a basic statement in its turn,"[4] and that basic statements are needed "in order to decide whether a theory is to be called falsifiable, i.e. empirical."[5] In writing of strictly existential statements, he declares them "non-empirical or 'metaphysical' " just on the ground that *no basic statement can contradict them*.[6] But exactly the same seems to follow from the latter passages about basic statements themselves, since they are not contradicted by basic statements in turn. Key falsifying statements though they may be, they would (it seems) turn out to be classified as 'non-empirical' or 'metaphysical' elements by the falsifiability criterion of demarcation.

5. Criteria of Incomplete Verifiability

We return now to the problem of defining significance, having seen the failures of complete verifiability and complete falsifiability as bases for appropriate definitions. It may, incidentally, be noted that an attempt to overcome the deficiencies of both these sorts of basis by combining them, to rule empirically significant *either* completely verifiable *or* completely falsifiable statements would still not be adequate. For though such a definition would indeed have the advantage of admitting both purely universal and purely existential statements, it would continue to rule some mixed quantifications meaningless while continuing to deem significant both certain alternations and certain conjunctions with nonsensical components.

We may now consider definitions which do not require either complete verifiability or complete falsifiability, but only some looser logical tie to observation. We may look, first, at a definition such as A. J. Ayer's original proposal in *Language, Truth,*

---

[3] *Ibid.*, p. 84.
[4] *Ibid.*, p. 101.
[5] *Ibid.*, p. 100.
[6] *Ibid.*, p. 69.

and Logic, which confers empirical significance on *S* if, and only if, in conjunction with additional premises, *S* logically implies some observation statement not implied by these additional premises alone.[7] Such a definition, frequently offered by pragmatists as well as positivists, models itself plausibly on the way theories are employed to yield predictions in science. The theories themselves are neither conclusively proved by the observational evidence at hand nor conclusively disproved. They do, however, make some observational difference in the sense that, added to our knowledge, they yield observational consequences otherwise not yielded.

Nonetheless, the definition fails in that it has the effect of ruling all doctrines whatever to be significant, including, for example, our previously cited glubbification theory, thus violating C.A. III. As Ayer admitted in acknowledging the criticism of I. Berlin,[8] every doctrine satisfies the definition, since, given any such doctrine *N,* it can be conjoined with another, *N* ⊃ *O,* yielding the observation statement *O,* which does not follow from the latter alone.

Other difficulties arise if a revised definition is proposed, which restricts the range of additional premises, so as to block violation of C.A. III in the manner described. For no matter how narrowly we restrict these premises, if *S* yields *O* when conjoined with given permissible premises, *S* strengthened by conjunction of any *N* will continue to yield *O,* given the same permissible premises. Thus *S · N* turns out significant for such a revised definition, provided *S* is. The revised definition, accordingly, violates C.A. I even if it does succeed in satisfying C.A. III.

The attempt to restrict the range of permissible additional premises was, in fact, made by Ayer in the Introduction to the second edition of *Language, Truth, and Logic.* He proposed to require that the additional premises be either analytic, or else independently shown to be empirically significant in accord with

---

[7] Ayer, *Language, Truth, and Logic,* chap. i.

[8] I. Berlin, "Verifiability in Principle," *Proceedings of the Aristotelian Society* (London: Harrison and Sons, Ltd., 1939), pp. 225-248.

the definition itself. Ayer's revised definition is given in two parts, in terms of direct and indirect verifiability:

> (i) *S* is *directly verifiable* if it is either itself an observation-statement, or yields an observation-statement *O* in conjunction with other observation-statements which do not themselves logically imply *O*.
>
> (ii) *S* is *indirectly verifiable* if
>> (a) in conjunction with other premises it yields at least one directly verifiable statement *D* not yielded by these other premises alone, and if (b) these other premises are all either analytic, directly verifiable, or independently shown to be indirectly verifiable.[9]

The whole definition now requires every non-analytic significant *S* to be either *directly* or *indirectly* verifiable.

We have already seen the motivation for, as well as one defect of, this revised definition. The motivation, briefly, is to avoid violating C.A. III, to avoid qualifying every *N* as empirically significant. Does the definition accomplish its purpose? It may be worthwhile to examine one intended application in detail, the way in which *N* ⊃ *O* is presumably ruled out as a general additional premise, in considering arbitrary *N*.

First, *N* ⊃ *O* will *not* be an observation-statement *at least* in those cases where *N* is not; it will therefore not be possible to conjoin it, generally, with *N* to show the latter directly verifiable under clause (i) of the definition. Nor will it be possible to use it generally to show *N* indirectly verifiable under clause (ii) of the definition. For *N* ⊃ *O* is not analytic unless *N* implies *O,* in which case it is directly verifiable independently under clause (i). Where *N* ⊃ *O* is *not* analytic, it cannot be generally supposed directly verifiable since, though it yields *O* when joined with *N, N* is not in every case an observation-statement. Finally, to assume *N* ⊃ *O* indirectly verifiable, generally, would require us to suppose *N* generally analytic or directly verifiable (which we cannot do), or independently shown to be indirectly verifiable, for which we have no *general* demonstration; we surely

---

[9] Ayer, *Language, Truth, and Logic*, p. 13. The version here given is a paraphrase rather than a direct quote.

cannot, at this point, circularly appeal to the indirect verifiability of $N \supset O$ to show that of N. Thus the revised definition has apparently succeeded in avoiding the prior difficulty that $N \supset O$ might be used in every case to show N significant. Apparently we *now* have a definition that satisfies C.A. III.

We can nevertheless *conjoin* N to a verifiable statement, to form another verifiable statement which is, as a whole, nonsense; thus, C.A. I will still be violated. For example, $O_1 \supset O_2$ is directly verifiable by the definition, since it yields O_2 when it is conjoined with O_1, which does not yield O_2 by itself.[1] But now add N to the above conditional statement to form $N \cdot (O_1 \supset O_2)$. The latter conjunction also yields O_2 when conjoined to O_1, which does not itself yield O_2. The conjunction is thus also directly verifiable and hence significant, no matter what N is taken to be, e.g., our glubbification theory. The revised definition, though apparently satisfying C.A. III, thus again violates C.A. I.

A. Church has, moreover, proved that the revised definition *does not really satisfy* C.A. III anyway. In a review of Ayer's second edition, Church shows that the definition rules every statement or its negation empirically significant, provided only that there are three observation-statements such that none implies any other.[2]

Church's argument may be explained as follows: Assume O_1, O_2, and O_3 to be observation-statements none of which implies either of the other two. Now consider the statement:

(4) $((\sim O_1 \cdot O_2) \vee (O_3 \cdot \sim S))$

(4) is directly verifiable by the definition, since it yields O_3 when conjoined with O_1, while (by hypothesis) O_1 itself does not yield O_3.

Now conjoin (4) with S. The conjunction implies O_2, which is an observation-statement, hence also directly verifiable. Thus, S, which is any arbitrary statement-formula, yields a directly

---

[1] The letter 'O', with or without subscripts, is used here and in related passages to represent observation statements; different subscripts signify that the statements are logically independent.

[2] Alonzo Church, "Review of A. J. Ayer, *Language, Truth, and Logic*, Second Edition," *Journal of Symbolic Logic*, XIV (1949), 52-53.

verifiable statement, O_2, when it is conjoined with the directly verifiable premise, (4). *If O_2 is not also implied by (4) alone, then S is thus indirectly verifiable by the definition we are considering.*

Suppose, however, that O_2 *is* implied by (4) alone. (4) has the form of an alternation or disjunction, and is therefore logically implied by each of its disjuncts, taken separately. Thus the disjunct:

(5) $(O_3 \cdot \sim S)$

in particular, implies (4). Since we have supposed (4) to imply O_2, a consequence of this supposition is that (5) implies O_2. But by hypothesis, O_3 does not *itself* imply O_2. Rather, O_2 *is* implied by $\sim S$ conjoined to O_3. *It follows that $\sim S$ is directly verifiable, all on the assumption that (4) alone implies O_2.*

But either (4) does not alone imply O_2, or it does. Thus either S is indirectly verifiable or else $\sim S$ is directly verifiable. Thus, every statement-formula or its negation is empirically significant provided that O_1, O_2, and O_3 are logically independent.[3]

6. Criteria of Translatability

The definitions so far considered have turned out defective. Construing empiricist adequacy after the manner of C.A. II,

[3] P. Nidditch, in "A Defence of Ayer's Verifiability Principle Against Church's Criticism," *Mind, LXX* (1961), 88-89, has proposed an escape from the first horn of Church's dilemma: He bars the conjoining of (4) with S since, although (4) is directly verifiable, not every one of its components (in particular, S) can be assumed analytic, directly verifiable, or independently shown to be indirectly verifiable. He thus extends Ayer's condition (ii)b to sentence-components.

Consider, then, the statement:
(4*) $(S \cdot (O_1 \vee (\sim O_2)))$
which is directly verifiable since it yields O_1 when conjoined with O_2, which does not itself yield O_1. Now S and O_1 jointly yield (4*), while O_1 alone does not, unless it implies S itself. Thus, every statement S whatever, unless it is simply a logical consequence of an observation-statement, is indirectly verifiable, even under the present construal of Ayer's criterion. I am indebted to Joseph Ullian, "A Note on Scheffler on Nidditch," *Journal of Philosophy, LXII* (1965), 274-275, for supplying (4*) and for correcting my original version of the above argument.

they have been unable to avoid violations of C.A. I or C.A. III. Moreover, certain sorts of definitional repair seem doomed to failure, e.g., no further restrictions on additional premises, for definitions of the Ayer type, can reasonably be expected to rule out all conjunctions with nonsensical components.

If C.A. II is retained as the governing standard of empiricist adequacy, if, that is, we try to locate empirical significance in some logical relationship to observation-statements, it seems likely that we shall continue to violate C.A. I or C.A. III, which are more fundamental. C. G. Hempel has, in effect, proposed giving up C.A. II as criterion of empiricist adequacy. His alternative idea suggests the specification of an artificial empiricist language with restricted vocabulary and explicit rules and, then, the characterization of significance as translatability into such language.[4]

Control over the vocabulary of such a particular base language would eliminate nonsensical terms such as 'glubbification', while control over its syntax would eliminate nonsensical combinations of remaining signs. The old problem of nonsensical conjuncts added to significant statements is resolved by simply excluding from the language the nonsense signs they contain. On the other hand, by incorporating into the machinery of the language the standard logical syntax, we allow all sorts and degrees of quantification, and provide for the significance of all denials of statements within the language. Further, since not all statements are translatable into such empiricist language, the difficulty of universality is avoided. The basic idea is, then, to strive for a characterization of significant statements generally, in terms of a relation T (translatability) to a language E, much as logical truths may be described as those bearing a complex relation R to listed logical constants (i.e., such that free reinterpretation of all their components other than these constants fails ever to produce a falsehood).

---

[4] Hempel, "Problems and Changes in the Empiricist Criterion of Meaning," in Linsky, p. 173. Hempel remarks that the translatability idea of significance seems to him to have "its origin in Carnap's essay, *Testability and Meaning* (especially part IV)."

Hempel's alternative to C.A. II may be formulated as:

C.A. IIA: For every sentence *S*, *S* is significant if, and only if, there is some empiricist language *L*, such that *S* is translatable into *L*.

This reorientation is best *not* conceived as tantamount to a new *definition* of significance, but rather as a new way of construing the character of such a definition. Ideally, we still need to specify some *particular* language *E*, translatability into which would constitute significance. The reorientation has a certain immediate appeal, however, in resting significance on a base language subject to our deliberate manufacture. Controlling the base language, we can, presumably, design and redesign it until it has attained a form enabling us to draw just the line we require between sense and nonsense.

Nonetheless, there is a fundamental difficulty involved in the reorientation represented by C.A. IIA, which is independent of problems relating to the detailed specification of *E*. The difficulty relates rather to the notion of translatability. Recall that we do not expect *E* to *contain within itself* all significant statements. The proposal is rather to construe translatability into *E* as a *link between E* and all significant statements falling outside *E*.

What sort of link is this? Presumably, it must be *legitimate* translatability, in accord with "real" rather than merely "nominal" definitions of constituent terms. These definitions, that is, must not be merely arbitrary correlations but must reflect the predefinitional meanings of the terms defined. Were this not so, every purported statement would turn out significant, since every purported term can be arbitrarily correlated (by nominal definition) with some primitive term or complex of terms within *E*. Indeed, every whole purported statement could be arbitrarily correlated with some sentence in *E*, and since thus translatable, would have to be reckoned significant.

Such a consequence is surely not intended. Rather, the definitions enabling translation are conceived as governed by extra-formal requirements relating to the familiar meanings of defined terms. A definition, in the present context, must presumably reflect within E whatever relevant meaning the defined term has predefinitionally. A statement is, then, translatable into E only if legitimate definitions of this sort enable us to transform it into a sentence in E. Our glubbification theory can, it is true, be *arbitrarily* correlated with any sentence in E, say 'The moon is yellow', but this correlation will not here qualify as *translation* inasmuch as it does not even pretend to match the two statement-forms with respect to their meanings; indeed the glubbification theory has no predefinitional meaning to be matched. Thus it is that C.A. IIA does not envisage simply admitting all purported statements, but hopes effectively to rule some of them out.

Translatability involves, then, a matching of "predefinitional" with "postdefinitional" meanings. What is involved in such matching, i.e., what does it mean to judge a definition as giving an accurate account of a term within a system or a language? Various answers have been given to this question. It has been suggested that the matching involved depends on identity of meaning and, alternatively, that it depends on identity of refer-ence only. N. Goodman has argued that both these requirements are too strong, and that not even identity of reference (or exten-sion) can reasonably be required, but only a certain isomorphism of extensions.[5]

We need not enter into the technicalities involved in these various proposals, beyond noting two points: (1) the require-ments are ordered, in that identity of meaning implies exten-sional identity, which itself implies extensional isomorphism. On the other hand, extensional isomorphism does not imply exten-sional identity, nor does the latter imply meaning-identity. Exten-sional isomorphism is, thus, the weakest requirement proposed, and must itself be satisfied if any of the others is satisfied. (2) What extensional isomorphism requires of a legitimate definition is that it should enable truth-value preserving translations of certain statements in which we are particularly interested. Indeed, Goodman considers the latter condition, without specification of statements of particular interest, to be a criterion of adequacy for

[5] Nelson Goodman, *The Structure of Appearance* (Cambridge, Mass. Harvard University Press, 1951), chap. i.

any satisfactory view of the definitional matching in question. Suppose, that is, we are given such a statement of special interest, prior to translation, and that it is true. Legitimate definitions will need to preserve this truth-value for the statement as suitably transformed, i.e., when defined terms are replaced by defining terms throughout.

Thus, for a sentence S to be legitimately translatable into E, it must be transformable into a bona fide sentence S' belonging to E, through the application of legitimate definitions: i.e., when all suitable components of S are replaced by primitive counterparts of E in accord with definitions which, at the very least, meet the demands of extensional isomorphism. And every such definition must be truth-value preserving for at least *some* translated statement in which the defined term in question figures initially. (Note, particularly, that in order, generally, to translate S into E, we need *not* determine the truth-value of S.)

Now it seems clear that, even where legitimate definitions exist for all components of a sentence S, S may still not be translatable into E; it may happen that, when all definitional replacements are made, the resulting string of signs turns out to be a jumble rather than a bona fide sentence of E. Consider the purported sentence,

(1)   Quadruplicity drinks procrastination.

discussed by Russell.[6] This sentence will fail to be translatable into E if E bars such a *combination* of signs in its own terms, i.e., if it contains some rule preventing the E-counterpart of 'drinks' from relating the E-counterparts of the English abstract nouns 'quadruplicity' and 'procrastination'. It may nonetheless be true that legitimate definitions exist for the three terms of (1), with respect to E. That is, a definition may exist for each of these terms which preserves the respective truth-values of certain other statements in which the given term appears, upon translation into E. These other statements must, it is true, be estimated as to truth-value, and hence judged significant independ-

[6] Bertrand Russell, *An Inquiry into Meaning and Truth* (New York: W. W. Norton & Co., 1940), p. 222.

ently. But to do this does not require a prejudgment as to the significance or lack of significance of (1). Thus, to rule (1) not translatable into E does not require a begging of the question at issue.

If (1) turns out not to be translatable into any empiricist language, it will lack significance, under C.A. IIA. The ability of C.A. IIA to exclude, in principle, at least some cases of meaninglessness, hinging on syntactic jumble, seems clear. Indeed, there is a sense in which (1) may be said to be intuitively grammatical (or unjumbled) in form, unlike, for example:

(2)   Seven quickly John street's by if.

Intuitive grammaticalness is, as Chomsky has suggested, a matter of degree.[7] (2) seems obviously excludable by syntactic restrictions, and (1), though less ungrammatical, seems also excludable through syntactic means. If we judge (1) *worthy* of exclusion, we will group it with (2) as jumbled. The notion of "jumble" thus relates not to intuitive grammaticalness but perhaps simply to the possibility of excluding a sentence through syntactic restriction, coupled with the independent obnoxiousness of the sentence. Are all obnoxious sentences construable as jumbled? Can they all be shown not translatable into E, for example, without a begging of the issue?

The answer would seem to be negative if we consider purported statements containing nonsensical would-be predicates, e.g.:

(3)   'Twas brillig and the slithy toves
                   Did gyre and gimble in the wabe.[8]

(4)   Some vessels contain glubbified water.

To rule (4), for instance, untranslatable into E, we must judge it not transformable into a bona fide sentence of E by means of legitimate definitions. To judge the legitimacy of available defi-

[7] Noam Chomsky, *Syntactic Structures* (The Hague: Mouton & Co., 1957), pp. 35-36, footnote 2; p. 42, footnote 7.

[8] Lewis Carroll, "Jabberwocky," *Through the Looking-Glass and What Alice Found There* (1872).

nitions we must, as we have seen, refer to an independent listing of statements in which components of (4) appear and in which such statements are judged true or false (hence significant).

This much causes no trouble. But the peculiarity of the word 'glubbified' is that no statement in which it figures is true or false at all and, hence, that no such statement appears on our independent list. But to say that no such statement is true or false is to say that (4) itself lacks significance, for it is itself one of these statements. We have assumed the meaninglessness of (4) in showing it untranslatable into *E;* such untranslatability thus provides no independent test of the meaninglessness of (4).

We may try to avoid this circle in applying the translatability test, in the following way: We may say that when a word such as 'glubbified' fails to appear on our independent list in some statement with specified truth-value, this signifies not that all its sentential contexts lack significance, but only that we do not *know* of any such context with truth-value and, hence, significance. If we take this course, however, we can no longer say that no legitimate definition of 'glubbified' exists. We therefore cannot say that (4) is not translatable into *E*. In fact, since all determinations of legitimate translatability depend on our list, we can no longer decide either way with respect to the significance of (4). Thus, if we interpret absence of a constituent from our list as sufficient to rule (4) out, we beg the question; if we do not beg the question, we no longer have sufficient grounds for ruling (4) out. For the whole class of purported statements containing nonsensical would-be predicates, the translatability test is thus either insufficient or superfluous as a criterion for exclusion.

7. Inclusion in an Empiricist Language

The basic conception of C.A. IIA is preserved if we take inclusion rather than translatability as the key relation in question, i.e., if we characterize significant statements as those *belonging* to empiricist languages. We should then have, instead of C.A. IIA,

C.A. IIB: For every sentence S, S is significant if, and only
            if, there is some empiricist language L, such that
            S is included in L.

(By inclusion is here intended just the fact that S belongs to L.)

Such a criterion seems to retain the idea of using a base language as a point of reference, and avoids the difficulties attaching
to translatability. Nevertheless, a serious restriction in generality
results. Recall that the attempt to define significance was initially
construed as aiming at a general yardstick applicable to all
statements and purported statements. Recall, in particular, that
the idea behind C.A. IIA was to use E as a base from which to
build such a yardstick for all purported statements whatever.
Translatability into E was to be a necessary and sufficient condition of significance generally.

Once having given up translatability in favor of inclusion,
however, (as in C.A. IIB) we can no longer hope to get such
a general yardstick through building some specific language E.
For, whereas translatability into E holds for certain statements
outside E, inclusion in E holds for no statement outside E. Thus,
in constructing E, we can at best hope (by reference to inclusion)
to get a sufficient condition, but not a necessary condition for
significance generally.

We might wish to retain C.A. IIB as a *definition* of significance
itself, rather than as a *criterion of adequacy* guiding the construction of a specific language E. In this way, we might retain
full generality, but we should not perhaps get very far in the way
of enlightenment, for we should be depending on the predicate
'is an empiricist language', which seems hardly clearer, as a
general idea, than 'is significant', which we are trying to explain.
If there were a general, independent method available for characterizing empiricist languages, we could both retain generality
and achieve illumination. But this possibility does not seem
promising since such a characterization (if we had one) would
presumably rest on a general notion of 'experience' or 'observation-predicate', which seems not much clearer than that of 'empiricist language' itself. It appears preferable, therefore, to con-

struct by a detailed procedure some specific language E, clearly exemplifying empiricist ideals.[9]

If we indeed decide to use C.A. IIB not as a definition itself, but only as a guide to the construction of E, we then arrive at a sufficient but not a necessary condition of significance—namely, inclusion in E. We are then committed to the significance of all sentences within E, but not to the non-significance of any sentence outside E. We may, it is true, be guided in constructing E by the desire to exclude certain sentences independently judged to be without significance, but exclusion from E will not constitute a general criterion of meaninglessness. In fact, the attempt at a general criterion is, in this way, given up in practice.

We arrive at a new problem: to construct some language E, purified of meaninglessness as independently recognized, but commodious enough to include all our acceptable beliefs in a given domain or, indeed, in all the various domains of science. This problem is no longer an attempt at providing a general definition of significance. For, even if E is satisfactorily constructed, we cannot dismiss excluded sentences as meaningless without independent judgment, since E at best furnishes only a sufficient condition of significance. A consideration of the nature of this new problem will lead us into several controversial issues in the theory of science.

8. Disposition Terms, Observational Predicates, and Observable Elements

We shall not here attempt to construct a language E for science. We shall, rather, examine the projected outlines of a scientific

---

[9] A general term such as 'experience' or 'observation-predicate' might well serve a limited function as constituent of a criterion of adequacy guiding the construction of a specific language; nonetheless such construction may be judged necessary to render the theory at issue in precise and unambiguous form. (Cf. the case of the general term 'logical constant', which needs to be supplanted by a finite list before theses concerning logic can take on precision and be discussed with rigor.) M. White has discussed the general issue, and argued the case for "finitizing" philosophical theses, in "A Finitistic Approach to Philosophical Theses," *Philosophical Review*, LX (1951), 299-316.

language *E,* attending to structural elements of such a language which have been widely discussed in recent years.

We may begin by listing those likely features of *E* that seem relatively trouble-free. We may suppose a basic logic providing, in standard fashion, for truth-functional operations on whole sentences, and quantificational analysis of sentences involving individual variables and predicates of any degree. We suppose also that this basic logic is supplemented with a logic of classes or with a logic of wholes and parts.[1] If we imagine only a supplementation of the latter kind, we face special problems relating to the interpretation of mathematics, which is more naturally interpretable as making reference to classes. For the *nominalist,* who refuses to adopt a class logic, such special problems need to be faced as part of the general question, namely, whether *E* can accommodate accepted scientific statements.[2] Here we shall consider not special problems of this sort, arising only for nominalists or others with particular requirements, but rather general problems faced by all concerned with the construction of *E.*

One such problem relates to what have been called 'disposition terms', seemingly required for any suitable *E,* though considered not generally definable by its observational vocabulary. So far, in speaking of *E,* we have presupposed only a "logical" vocabulary, e.g., joint denial, universal quantification, membership, or overlapping. Such logical vocabulary needs, however, to be supplemented with a "descriptive" or "extra-logical" vocabulary, for scientific purposes. We suppose it to be specified by a (finite) list of primitive *observational* predicates (of varying de-

[1] See Goodman, *The Structure of Appearance,* pp. 42-55, for such a logic, i.e., a calculus of individuals. Such a calculus was first presented by Lesniewski, "O Podstawach Matematyki," *Przeglad Filozoficzny,* Vol. XXX-XXXIV (1927-1931), and an independent version developed by Henry S. Leonard and Nelson Goodman, reported in Leonard's dissertation at Harvard: *Singular Terms* (1930). A later account is given in Leonard and Goodman, "The Calculus of Individuals and Its Uses," *Journal of Symbolic Logic,* V (1940), 45-55.

[2] The nominalist's problems are discussed in Nelson Goodman, "A World of Individuals," in I. M. Bochenski, Alonzo Church, and Nelson Goodman, *The Problem of Universals* (Notre Dame, Ind.: University of Notre Dame Press, 1956), pp. 15-31.

gree). Such predicates are assumed applicable with a fair degree of reliability, within a sufficiently large range of (suitable) elements, after only few observations of the elements in question.

The above is by no means intended as a rigorous definition of 'observational vocabulary'; it is only a rough, practical indication of the sorts of extra-logical predicates that may be expected to be maximally clear (with respect to application) within E. The explanation is (roughly) that of R. Carnap.[3] Clearly the phrases 'fair degree of reliability' and 'sufficiently large range of (suitable) elements' are systematically vague, and the number of observations qualifying as "few" is open to variable interpretation. Moreover, the notion of 'an observation', upon which the explanation rests, is fluid. Shall we, for example, construe it as including only *scrutiny with the unaided eye,* or shall we allow it to encompass also *examination of an object with the help of instruments?* Such looseness in the notion of 'an observation' is unavoidable and indicates that, although this notion may provide some practical guidance in the process of constructing E, it needs eventually to be supplanted by reference to a finite listing of predicates taken as *observational for E.*

Whatever decisions are made in setting forth such a list, however, the question of *disposition terms* arises. Thus, this question is neutral as between differing decisions on observationality. In this sense, the characterization of disposition terms relative to a given observational vocabulary, taken as a base, represents a general problem for the theory of science.

We have given a rough account of *observational predicates* by reference to observation of elements. We may, now, give a rough account of elements that may be considered *observable*: An element is observable relative to a given predicate if this predicate is, with sufficient reliability, applicable to it after only

[3] Rudolf Carnap, "Testability and Meaning," *Philosophy of Science,* III (1936), 454-455. By permission of the publisher. "A predicate 'P' of a language L is called *observable* for an organism (e.g. a person) N, if, for suitable arguments, e.g. 'b', N is able under suitable circumstances to come to a decision with the help of few observations about a full sentence, say '$P(b)$', i.e. to a confirmation of either '$P(b)$' or '$\sim P(b)$' of such a high degree that he will either accept or reject '$P(b)$'."

few observations of the element in question. An element is further observable for *E* if some predicate of *E*, primitive or defined,
is reliably applicable to it after only few observations of the element in question.[4]

We now assume *E* to contain a fixed list of observational primitives; its variables will thus clearly have a range which includes
elements observable for *E*. An important point must immediately
be noted. Having decided upon a fixed list of observational
predicates, and thus an ontology including observable elements,
we must *not* suppose that the extra-logical vocabulary of *E* will
now be *throughout* observational nor that *E*'s ontology will be
throughout observable.

Take first the case of the extra-logical vocabulary of *E*. What
we have so far admitted is a list of *primitive* predicates, each one
observational in the sense outlined. It does not follow that every
predicate *definable* by these primitives within *E* will itself be
observational in the same sense, provided the specific interpretation of this sense remains fixed. Consider the following simple
example: Assume as primitive predicates the terms,

'*W*' (is white)
'*O*' (is odorless)
'*S*' (is salty)

each one reliably applicable, after only one observation, within
a sufficiently large range of appropriate elements, say, small
particles. We may now introduce, by definition, a new predicate,
as follows:

$$Kx =_{df} (Wx \cdot Ox \cdot Sx) \vee (\sim Wx \cdot \sim Ox \cdot \sim Sx)$$

'*K*' applies to *x* if *either* *x* is white, odorless, and salty *or,* on the
other hand, *x* is neither white, nor odorless, nor salty.

Assuming the single observations required for applying '*W*',
'*O*', and '*S*', respectively, to be "independent," '*K*' will now be

---

[4] Some generalization for many-place predicates is needed, of course.
E.g., an element *x* might be taken as observable relative to a two-place
predicate if there were some element *y* such that this predicate were
applicable to *x* and *y* with sufficient reliability after sufficiently few
observations of *x* and *y*.

likely to require three observations for a decision that it holds of a given element (and at least two for a decision that it does not) if the initial level of reliability is to be maintained.

Thus, observationality has to be understood as, at best, a requirement placed on the extra-logical *primitive* terms of E. As such, the requirement is enforced only after all eliminations of defined terms have been carried out in accord with the definitions. Any non-observational predicate is, accordingly, permissible if eliminable by definition in terms of the observational primitives. But the definiens in such a definition (e.g., the right side of the definition above given for 'K') remains, as a whole, *not* observational, though formulating "a condition" expressible in a language under tight observational restrictions.

Take now the case of elements. Having imposed a requirement of observationality on the primitive extra-logical vocabulary of E, we have ensured that the ontology of E will include observable elements. But, in adopting our primitives, we indirectly determine the range of elements in the ontology as including everything satisfying at least one place of these primitives.[5] Even for an observational primitive, there will normally be some minimal element we will wish to construe as *satisfying* it, though not *observable* relative to it. (E.g., some very small though visible particle, or large though distant star, may be such that the predicate 'is white' holds of it, though this predicate is not reliably applicable to it without more than the minimum number of observations.) Thus, already in choosing our primitive *observational* vocabulary, we will normally have admitted minimal elements within its range that cannot all be assumed to be *observable* for E. Furthermore, our logical machinery will normally generate, out of minimal observable elements satisfying the primitives, other elements that may well be non-observable. For example, if we have a part-whole logic, we will need to acknowledge that every two elements have a sum.[6] The sum of two (observably) white stars will then be white, but it may not itself be observable relative to 'is white'; reliable application of this predicate to the sum may require more than the minimum number of observations.

---

[5] Goodman, *The Structure of Appearance,* pp. 85-86.
[6] *Ibid.,* pp. 46, 85-86.

We have suggested that observationality be construed as a requirement on primitive extra-logical terms of *E*. Non-observational terms will thus be admissible if definable by means of the observational primitives. *Disposition terms* present the problem of dealing with non-observational terms which appear to be needed for the formulation of important scientific doctrines in *E*, but which do not seem to be thus definable.

9. The Interpretation of Disposition Terms

Disposition terms purport to describe not what given elements *are* or *do* in fact, but rather what they are *able* or *likely* to be or do, what they have the *power* or *tendency* to be or do, whether or not they are or do so in fact. We have seen that lists of observational terms vary, and it may be added that one man's dispositional term is another man's observational term. The problem of dispositionality is, however, independent of such variation. Given *any* list taken as observational and in this sense descriptive of what things manifestly are or do, how shall we deal with terms not on this list which seem required, in order to describe what things have a disposition, tendency, or capacity to do? To say that something is now at 100° C. is not to say it is now registering 100° C. on a thermometer with which it is in contact. To say that a man is irritable is not to say that he is at the moment showing symptoms of irritation. Such characterizations seem necessary to science, yet not observationally definable; they seem clearly to outstrip the reach of pointer-readings and manifest symptoms.

The classical treatment of the problem is that of R. Carnap.[7] He points out that, though we can clearly apply suitable tests in given instances, to determine whether or not a disposition term applies to some element, the observational vocabulary used to describe such tests is generally inadequate to define the disposition term in question.

Suppose, for example, that the relational predicate '. . . weighs

[7] Carnap, *op. cit., Philosophy of Science*, III (1936), 420-471; IV (1937), 2-40.

five pounds at time ———' is not one of our observational primitives, but that among these primitives we have predicates sufficient to describe the procedure of weighing objects on a particular scale S. Now, we offer the following definition (where x's being on scale S is interpreted as its being the maximal thing on S):

> x weighs five pounds at time $t =_{df}$ (x is on scale S at $t \supset S$'s pointer points to "5" at t)

The definition is formulated with the help of the 'if-then' connective, yielding a conditional statement as definiens:

> *If x is on S at t, then S's pointer points to "5" at t.*

This conditional definiens, interpreted in accord with the basic logic of E as so far specified, is equivalent to:

> *x is not on S at t, or S's pointer points to "5" at t.*

But this definiens applies to everything which is not on scale S at t. The definition as a whole thus attributes a weight of five pounds (for every t) to the moon, Mount Vesuvius, and the Eiffel Tower. A three-pound object on S at t_1 would correctly be judged not to weigh five pounds at t_1, but, taken from the scale, its weight would immediately (by the definition) jump to five pounds at t_2. If an analogous definition were offered for four pounds, every object not on S at t would weigh both five pounds and four pounds at t.

We may offer an improved definition with subjunctive form:

> x weighs five pounds at time $t =_{df}$ (If x *were* on scale S at t, then S's pointer *would* point to "5" at t)

Such a definition seems intuitively more accurate, but is of no help to us here if the problem remains as it has initially been described. For this problem is to show:

> x weighs five pounds at time t

to be eliminable from E, which contains, in addition to basic standard logic, a minimal vocabulary descriptive of weighing apparatus and pointer-readings. The definition we are considering, however, employs a subjunctive connective 'if . . . were ————, then - - - would ———— ————'. This connective is included neither in E's basic logic nor its extra-logical vocabulary, nor is it itself known to be definable in E.

The problem of construing this connective is, moreover, no easier than that of explaining disposition terms. Thus, suppose we were simply to add the subjunctive connective to E's primitive apparatus. If the original feeling of uneasiness with disposition terms results from their seeming to express not what x overtly is or does but rather what x is capable or likely to be or do, then a definition such as the above, in subjunctive form, will avail little in removing this uneasiness. For it explains the disposition term in question not by reference to actual pointer-readings but by reference to hypothetical ones under hypothetical conditions —in terms of pointer-readings x has the power to produce, whether it does so in fact or not. But the notion of *power* is just what we wanted to explain. If pointer-readings will help us at all, they will need to be actual, not hypothetical or potential.

10. The Method of Reduction Sentences

Carnap has proposed a general method of "reduction sentences" for introducing disposition terms, which neither defines these terms nor requires a subjunctive construction. In effect, Carnap proposed that his method of reduction be added to the standard method of definition as a way of introducing new terms into a language such as E. The motivation for this proposal was to provide E with greater resources, enabling it to build concepts more freely on the basis of observational primitives. Disposition predicates, it was hoped, might thus be admitted and tied to observation, while restrictions could be maintained excluding other, objectionable predicates. The method of reduction sentences was thus proposed as a small but necessary liberalization of the concept-forming machinery of science.

The method may be illustrated here by reference to the example of the previous section. In place of our initial definition, which proved badly inaccurate, we may write the following "reduction sentence":

$(x)(t)$ (x is on scale S at $t \supset$ (x weighs five pounds at $t \equiv S$'s pointer points to "5" at t))

The difficulties encountered by the first attempt at definition above discussed are here avoided. For though this whole sentence is still true of every object x not on scale S at t, the sentence no longer attributes to every such object x the weight of five pounds at t. Such a weight, at time t, is assigned only to such an object x as is on S at t, and, moreover, is such that S's pointer points to "5" at t. For an object on S at t, the sentence gives a necessary and sufficient condition for its weighing five pounds at t. For an object not on S at t, the sentence leaves the question of its weighing five pounds at t indeterminate.

We now see how it is that a reduction sentence may be said to formulate a test for application of a given disposition term. *Given* certain standard or experimental conditions defining a limited class, a specified test result is to be taken as a sign that the disposition term in question applies to some member of the class. On the other hand, no *definition* is provided, inasmuch as no condition is given which is both necessary and sufficient for application of the predicate generally. Thus, for objects not on scale S at t, we have no means of eliminating references to *their* weighing five pounds at t, in favor of some equivalent condition.

Carnap's method involves, as remarked above, a giving up of definition as the sole mode of introducing non-observational predicates into E. He is willing to admit any of the latter, in effect, as primitives, provided certain postulates in the form of reduction sentences are laid down, connecting these non-observational primitives to the observational ones.[8] The strength of

[8] See Henry S. Leonard, "Review of Rudolf Carnap 'Testability and Meaning,'" *Journal of Symbolic Logic*, II (1937), 50. Leonard remarks: "As a form of postulate, the reduction sentence is certainly unobjectionable, and that it does 'reduce' the predicate in question is undeniable. But that it is appropriate as a device for introducing a new term is certainly dubious."

See also Nelson Goodman, *Fact, Fiction, and Forecast* (Cambridge,

Carnap's idea is that it liberalizes admission qualifications for would-be scientific terms. We do not ask for complete observational determination (through definition) for every applicant for scientific status. If usage is firm enough to allow a partial determination but no more, this will be sufficient for admission. The growth of relevant knowledge consequent upon admission may be expected to allow further specification of observational content.

The question may be raised, however, as to whether any real restriction is effected by requiring reduction sentences at all, or whether the requirement admits virtually all predicates into E. Let 'T' represent a predicate applicable to x when and only when x fulfills certain test conditions, let 'R' represent a predicate describing some test reaction of x, and let 'D' represent some disposition predicate of x, to be introduced. Imagine, now, either of the following sentences to be the sole reduction sentence for 'D':

(RS1) $Tx \supset (Dx \equiv Rx)$
(RS2) $Tx \supset (Rx \supset Dx)$

(We suppose, for (RS1), that 'Tx' is not always false, and, for (RS2), that '$Tx \cdot Rx$' is not always false, for otherwise 'D' would remain indeterminate with respect to every x.)

Now a reduction sentence similar to (RS1) or (RS2) can be found for every predicate or would-be predicate, once small adjustments are made. That is, for every term or would-be term which is *excluded* by the requirement that some reduction sentence must connect it to observational primitives, there is another term, no less objectionable, that is *admitted*.

For example, 'glubbified' is presumably excluded since (1) neither it nor its negate is even partially determined by prior usage to apply to any x, whereas (2) every attempted reduction sentence for 'glubbified' (assuming, recall, non-vacuous 'Tx' for

Mass.: Harvard University Press, 1955), p. 60, footnote 11: "To introduce a term by means of reduction postulates is to introduce it as an ineliminable primitive."

(RS1), and non-vacuous '$Tx \cdot Rx$' for (RS2)), has the effect of assigning 'glubbified' or 'not glubbified' to some x.

Yet, we must nevertheless admit as a predicate:

(Q)   'is a paper clip and is in desk d at t or is not a paper clip and is glubbified'

taking: 'is a paper clip' as 'T'
and: 'is in desk d at t' as 'R'.

For, given any object with the test property T, i.e., any paper clip, then (RS1) formulates a necessary and sufficient condition for its having the so-called property Q, namely, its being in desk d at t, while (RS2) offers the latter as at least a sufficient condition. This may be seen if we consider these two reduction forms as applied to Q:

(RSQ1) If x is a paper clip then (x is a paper clip and in desk d at t or not a paper clip and glubbified $\equiv x$ is in desk d at t)

(RSQ2) If x is a paper clip then (x is in desk d at $t \supset x$ is a paper clip and in desk d at t or not a paper clip and glubbified)

In each of these cases, assuming Q to be the applicant for entry into the vocabulary of E, usage is firm enough to ground the specified reduction sentence. Thus Q is admissible via a reduction sentence, and being ineliminable through definition, may now be as freely used as any of our primitives. Note especially that its admission legitimizes its application to non–paper clips, in which case it is equivalent to 'glubbified' itself. If, for example, we wanted to formulate an inverse "law" for glubbification and warmth with respect to liquids, we can now do so for Q-ness and warmth. If, on the other hand, we found the first law objectionable, we should find the second equally so.

It is no doubt true that neither (RSQ1) nor (RSQ2) *specifies* an observational interpretation for Q in the case of non–paper clips. It remains equally true that Q is connected by a reduction sentence to our observational primitives, and is therefore admissible (by the method of reduction sentences) to our extra-logical vocabulary. In like manner, all applicants would seem to be admissible, through the building in of some trivial partial determination. The net result seems tantamount to abandonment of the requirement of observationality altogether.

It might be suggested that Q is not to be freely used, but applied only within the limits of its determination as so far spelled out in our reduction sentences, i.e., it is to be reserved for describing paper clips only. If so, however, we do not need reduction sentences at all, for we can explicitly define the property of being a paper clip and in desk d at t.[9] On the other hand, if we want to use Q also beyond the limits of determination by given reduction sentences (i.e., in application to non–paper clips), we can no longer claim that introducing Q by reduction sentence is harmless in that Q has had to pass a significant observational test. The reduction sentence clearly provides no control over uses of Q for which it specifies no interpretation, and, as we have seen, it may specify an interpretation only for the most trivial sort of case.

It seems that we have these two alternatives: Either (a) we claim that applying Q to non–paper clips accords with some clear, established usage or observational practice in science which cannot itself be described by means of primitives of E, or (b) we claim that applying Q to non–paper clips accords with no such usage or practice but is nonetheless needed for some scientific purpose.

If (a) is the case, we may follow the easier course of adding Q to our primitives as an observational term on its specific merits, rather than adopting the wholesale method of reduction sentences. (Such a course would require us to determine that Q was indeed applicable with sufficient reliability, over a sufficiently wide range, upon few enough observations of the elements in question.) If (b) is the case, we must give up the requirement of observationality for the language of science. We

---

[9] See Goodman, *ibid.*, p. 50; and Israel Scheffler, "Prospects of a Modest Empiricism," *Review of Metaphysics*, Vol. X, Nos. 3-4 (March, June, 1957), especially section 12.

must then try to specify the ways in which such non-observational terms as Q are needed for scientific purposes, and face the problem of how to interpret them. The latter problem relates to the general question of so-called *theoretical terms,* said to be necessary for science though beyond the reach of observation. We shall discuss this question in later sections.

Here, we shall briefly consider one line of argument in favor of admittedly non-observational primitives whose application is only partially specified, by reduction sentences. The argument is that such primitives serve the purpose of suggesting and incorporating new information gained by continuing research, and allowing the expression of generalizations embodying such new knowledge.[1] To illustrate, consider the following reduction sentences for 'J':

(RSJ1) $Px \supset (Jx \equiv Bx)$
(RSJ2) $Sx \supset (Jx \equiv Rx)$

(RSJ1) specifies the application of 'J' where 'P' holds but leaves open the question of 'J's application where 'P' does not hold. (RSJ2) further specifies 'J's application in the case where 'S' holds.

Suppose now that we have reasonably good grounds for accepting the law:

(1) $(x) (Px \cdot Bx \supset Gx)$.

Since, by (RSJ1), we infer every x that is both P and B to be J as well, we are naturally led to the conjecture that

(2) $(x) (Jx \supset Gx)$

may be true as well, and, if so, that

---

[1] Several variants of the main line of argument are available. Compare the discussion in Carl G. Hempel, *Fundamentals of Concept Formation in Empirical Science* (Chicago: University of Chicago Press, 1952), pp. 23-29, especially pp. 28-29, as well as in the (earlier) papers of Carnap: "Testability and Meaning," *op. cit.,* III, 449, and A. Kaplan, "Definition and Specification of Meaning," *Journal of Philosophy,* XLIII (1946), 281-288. See also Nelson Goodman's review of the latter paper in *Journal of Symbolic Logic,* XI (1946), 80.

(3) $(x) (Sx \cdot Rx \supset Gx)$

may also hold as a law since, by (RSJ2), '*S*' and '*R*' together determine '*J*'. This, in fact, is a hypothesis we may now test, a hypothesis independent of (1), but suggested to us by virtue of the link with (1) that '*J*' provides, through our two reduction sentences.

Imagine, now, that instead of introducing '*J*' through partial specification by (RSJ1), we had explicitly defined '*J*' as follows:

(D1) $Jx =_{df} Px \cdot Bx$

and in place of (RSJ2), we had explicitly defined the new term '*K*' as follows:

(D2) $Kx =_{df} Sx \cdot Rx$

(in view of the fact that '*P* · *B*' and '*S* · *R*' are known to represent independent conditions).

Then, having (1), we should be able to deduce and not merely conjecture that (2) holds, using as a premise (D1). But we have no longer any reason for moving from (2) to (3), lacking (RSJ2).

Furthermore, if (3) is independently conjectured and holds up, we can no longer construe it and (1) as falling under (2) as "specializations." Instead, corresponding to (3), we should get:

(4) $(x) (Kx \supset Gx)$

as (2) corresponds to (1). So, in two respects, we have fared worse with definition: we have lost the basis for conjecturing (3), and we cannot represent (3) and (1) under a unified, larger generalization.

The force of the foregoing argument seems, upon reflection, to be wholly illusory. The reduction sentence treatment ("RST," for short) indeed enables us to move from (1) to (3), and to tie them together under the generalization (2), because it specifies '*J*' as a common necessary condition of '*P* · *B*' and of '*S* · *R*'. However, the definitional treatment ("DT," for short) enables the specification of such a common factor as well. Consider:

(D3) $\qquad\qquad Mx =_{df} Jx \vee Kx$

Now, everything that is both P and B is, by (D1), shown to be J and, by (D3), shown to be M as well. Thus, given (1), as before, we have exactly the same basis for conjecturing

(5) $\qquad\qquad (x)\ (Mx \supset Gx)$

as we earlier had for conjecturing (2).

Furthermore, by (D2) and (D3), S and R together determine M, and we may therefore infer from (5) our earlier hypothesis:

(3) $\qquad\qquad (x)\ (Sx \cdot Rx \supset Gx)$

In sum, given (1), it is an equally natural conjecture under DT that (5) is true as it is under RST that (2) is true; furthermore, from each of the latter, under each treatment respectively, (3) follows as a deductive step. Finally, just as RST allows us to represent (1) and (3) as specializations of (2), so DT allows us to represent them as specializations of (5). Any question as to why 'M' should have been singled out as a common necessary condition of '$P \cdot B$' and '$S \cdot R$' would be out of order if directed polemically against DT. For the same question could be asked of 'J', under RST. Conversely, any analogy between the properties $P \cdot B$ and $S \cdot R$, supporting their linking through 'J' (introduced by reduction sentences) equally supports their linking through 'M' (introduced by definition).

We have just considered one argument in favor of non-observational primitives partially determined by reduction sentences. This argument, which claims for them a distinctive function in suggesting and expressing new hypotheses, we have found wanting. (We shall consider other arguments relating to the general issue of theoretical terms later on.) For the present, let us briefly consider the alternative suggestion that selected disposition terms might be added to our stock of observational primitives, on their individual merits.

This might, at first, be thought a strange suggestion, since dispositions are "hypothetical" rather than "manifest" entities. But disposition predicates are, typically, applicable to those entities already admitted in determining our observational vocabulary. To say that a man is irritable may seem to refer to some *tendency* to be provoked easily, but the statement does not affirm the *existence of irritability* as a tendency, property, or dispositional trait. Rather, it affirms *irritability* of a man, which is just to say that the man is irritable, i.e., it is to apply the term 'is irritable' to a man, an entity we may suppose within the original range of things acknowledged in *E*.

Furthermore, if observationality of predicates relative to this range is, in any event, a variable matter, partly determined by decision, there seems no compelling theoretical reason for denying, in advance, to every term customarily labeled 'dispositional' the status of observational predicate. That a man is exhibiting aggressiveness under provocation may, on any account, be taken as an observational matter, since such a description is typically applicable after a few observations of the man in question. But is this case so far removed from the case of a man judged to be irritable upon observation of his muscular tension, facial expression, posture, or speech, as well as selected environmental clues?

We may, to be sure, *normally explain* our 'irritability'-ascriptions by appealing to *hypothetical* aggression under provocation, but this is surely no general reason against taking 'is irritable' as observational. It may even be the case that such a predicate turns out *fully definable* by observational terms within our *initially specified* vocabulary. That a particular term (e.g., 'is irritable') is dispositional *with respect to given terms* within *E* (e.g., 'exhibits aggression') cannot thus be taken as an adequate argument that it is not definable within *E*.

Consider, for example, phonograph records. We may classify some of these as 'played' and others as 'playable'. The latter term applies, e.g., to played records as well as to unplayed records accidentally shattered before ever reaching the turntable. We should, perhaps, normally attempt to explain the latter term by appealing to the notion of 'played' records, supplemented by the notion of possibility, or potentiality, or the use of subjunctive locutions. We cannot, nevertheless, assume that 'playable' is inherently, or even within our assumed language, hypothetical in reference. For every playable record is also describable in terms of its form, minute contours, material, and history, and 'playable' is thus likely to be definable in terms which may be taken as observational, without recourse to possibility or the use of the subjunctive.

To sum up, the mere fact that a given term is labeled 'dispositional,' or that it is clearly dispositional *with respect to given terms* within E, does not imply that the term is problematic in a serious way. It may be that the term is definable by E's current observational vocabulary, or by an acceptable extension of this vocabulary. The term *may* even be readily construable as observational itself. Adding such terms, piecemeal, to E may increase E's powers while avoiding the general difficulties of the method of reduction sentences.

11. The Problem of Theoretical Terms

We have suggested the possibility of reconstruing at least some disposition terms as observational. However, while there may be no *general* reason against doing this (as we have argued), we may in given cases find such a course repugnant. Suppose this happens in the case of a particular disposition term D, i.e., we are *not* willing to construe it as observational, *nor* can we define it by means of our primitives, even when these are suitably supplemented by additional observational terms. Suppose, finally, that D is needed for some purpose to which E is to be put. If we admit D, we give up the observationality requirement. We, furthermore, face the double problem of (1) specifying the peculiar function of D and (2) providing a way to interpret statements containing D. This double problem may be identified with what is generally called "the problem of theoretical terms." We may designate its two components, 'the problem of function' and 'the problem of interpretation'.

The problem of theoretical terms has just been explained by reference to a certain *disposition* term D. Sometimes a special class of *transcendental* terms is singled out for separate treatment in connection with this problem. We have above noted that disposition terms typically apply within the range of E's ontology as already determined by choice of its observational vocabulary. Transcendental terms, e.g., 'is an electron', do not appear to be interpretable in this manner; they seem rather to appeal to a new range of elements. The predicate 'is an electron' not only seems itself non-observational and resistant to definition by our observational primitives; it furthermore purports to denote things outside the range of our hitherto determined ontology.

Now, it is true that, as argued in the previous section, reduction sentences can be found for *every* would-be predicate, given the possibility of trivial adjustments. Thus, granted that no suitable test or reaction conditions are available for reduction sentences introducing 'is an electron', we can, nevertheless, find such conditions for 'is a kelectron', which applies to everything that is either a paper clip in desk d at t or not a paper clip and an electron. The possibility of introduction by means of reduction sentences thus fails to draw a significant line between dispositional and transcendental terms. Nonetheless, there does appear to be a real difference with respect to whether a term is wholly satisfied within the initially determined ontology or not.

We shall, however, not treat transcendental terms separately. For the expansion of a hitherto determined ontology does not in itself appear objectionable; addition of a new observational term may have the same effect, for example. It is rather the fact that transcendental terms are not considered observational nor observationally definable that is crucial. But in this respect they resemble troublesome disposition terms. Thus we shall here treat them both under the rubric of *theoretical terms*.

12. The Problem of Function and the Problem of Interpretation

The method of reduction sentences was earlier criticized for admitting virtually all terms or would-be terms into E. This would have had the effect of obliterating the distinction between bona fide theoretical terms of science and, say, nonsense words such as 'glubbified'. Since inclusion in E was to have served as a sufficient condition of significance, this effect would have been disastrous. If we were now to react to the problem of theoretical terms by simply dropping the observationality restriction and providing nothing else, the result would (it seems) be equally undesirable, for we should again obliterate the distinction between bona fide constituents of scientific theory and nonsense. We cannot maintain the strict requirement of observationality if we admit the need of science for theoretical terms; we cannot simply drop the requirement and leave it at that, for in so doing we should be pooling together legitimate, functional, theoretical terms and nonsensical would-be predicates. It would seem that we need some way of admitting the former and excluding the latter.

It would be well to be flexible in our approach. Rather than trying to propose some rule for *admission* of theoretical terms, for the sake of fulfilling some function specified in advance, and then testing the proposed rule, a different strategy might be entertained. One might start with given scientific systems, embodying theoretical terms assumed to be doing some work and hence "legitimate," and one might then study the effects of *eliminating* these terms. (Some results of this sort are available in connection with work of W. Craig, to be dealt with in Section 20.) Suffice it to say here that (irrespective of preferred strategy) to specify precisely the *function* of "legitimate" theoretical terms in science would be to answer one part of the main problem. To answer the other part would be to provide an *interpretation* for these theoretical terms, in a sense that will be made clearer in the following section. Here, we shall merely try to indicate, in a general way, why the problem of interpretation needs to be considered independently of the problem of function.

Recall that we initially asked about E whether it could be constructed so as to be (1) significant throughout *and* (2) resourceful enough to embrace all of science. What has so far been *suggested* is that science outstrips observational restrictions, so that *if* E is to meet condition (2) above, it must presumably give up the observationality requirement. Further, unless it excludes some non-observational notions it will surely violate condition (1) above. Suppose, now, that we could distinguish "legitimate" theoretical notions from other non-observational notions by some criterion of function in science. We might, then, propose to use this criterion in building *E*, so as to exclude some non-observational terms. It would not, however, follow that condition (1) would thereby be satisfied. That there be *some* exclusion is required in order that the condition be satisfied; it does not follow that every exclusion guarantees that the condition *is* satisfied. In particular, it is possible that, among the theoretical terms admitted by our criterion of function, there might be some which rendered non-significant every statement-formula in which they appeared. To have answered the problem of function would thus be (at most) to have helped delineate the *contents* of scientific language; it would remain to provide an interpretation of these contents with respect to the issue of significance.

The philosophical interest in this matter is deep-rooted. The notion of significance is related both to the idea of intuitive clarity, and to the idea of an effective systematic account of the world. Where these diverge, philosophical conflict ensues. The rise of modern science has been judged by many writers to have aggravated such conflict because of its increasing abandonment of familiar qualitative terms in favor of abstract theoretical ones, lending themselves to comprehensive systematization.[2] This judgment needs the support of an objective and precise characterization of the functioning of theoretical terms in science.

Such characterization does not itself, however, dictate a particular resolution of the philosophical conflict. To provide an *interpretation of science as characterized,* with particular reference to the issue of significance, is thus another and an independent problem. Divergent approaches to this problem of interpretation exist, which are compatible with the same solutions

[2] For philosophical discussions of related questions, see, for example, Alfred North Whitehead, *Science and the Modern World* (New York: Macmillan Co., 1948), and John Dewey, *Experience and Nature* (Chicago: Open Court Publishing Co., 1925). A discussion of science and "intelligible principles" is found in Philipp Frank, *Philosophy of Science* (Englewood Cliffs, N.J.: Prentice-Hall, 1957), chaps. i, ii.

to the problem of function. We turn now to a description of some of these divergent approaches.

13. Approaches to the Problem of Interpretation: Pragmatism and Fictionalism

The question before us is whether E can be so constructed as to be (1) significant throughout and (2) capable of expressing all of science. We noted also that the notion of significance is related both to (A) intuitive clarity and to (B) provision of an effective systematic account. Let us now assume that an answer to the problem of function provides some workable distinction between "legitimate," or bona fide theoretical terms, and other non-observational terms or would-be terms, explaining why the former are needed in science. This answer tells us, in effect, that such terms are important ingredients of the systematic accounts provided by science. Unfortunately, however, these terms include some which are not intuitively clear.

In the face of this conflict, two alternative attitudes may be distinguished: the pragmatic and the fictionalistic. The *pragmatic attitude* consists in deliberately giving up the connection between significance and (A) (intuitive clarity), while holding fast to the connection between significance and (B) (provision of an effective systematic account). It turns out that all bona fide theoretical terms, being important ingredients of scientific systems, are constituents of significant statements in the sense of (B). If E is now designed to admit all such terms but not other non-observational ones, the reply to the main question above seems, to the pragmatist, quite possibly affirmative. That is to say, the inclusion of needed theoretical terms of science will *not* dictate a *negative* reply. For the pragmatist's interpretation the problem of theoretical terms thus "reduces to" the problem of determining their function in scientific systems. The price paid is the divorce of significance from the notion of intuitive clarity. The pragmatist tries, however, to motivate his course by offering considerations with which we shall deal in the following section.

The *fictionalistic* attitude, by contrast, maintains the associa-

tion of significance with (A) (intuitive clarity), but is prepared
to abandon the connection with (B) (provision of an effective
systematic account). Thus, although we assume a criterion
singling out bona fide theoretical terms, these terms are not
established, for the fictionalist, as elements of significant statements. Rather, those judged by him to be intuitively obscure will
be taken as rendering their containing statement-forms non-
significant. It follows that, if E is designed so as to permit among
its non-observational terms all and only those qualifying as
"legitimate" by our functional criterion, we may imagine E as
satisfying condition (2), but *not* also condition (1). Alternatively, if we ensure that E satisfies (1), we will thereby be likely
to exclude at least some "legitimate" scientific theory, and will,
as a consequence, violate (2).

To the main question above, the fictionalist thus replies in the
negative. He has retained the connection between significance
and intuitive clarity. The price he pays, however, is that the
problem of theoretical terms does not, for his interpretation,
"reduce itself to" the problem of function. In choosing to design
E so as to satisfy (1), and so to provide a vehicle for uniformly
significant discourse, he finds that a functional portion of science
falls outside E, resisting construal as literally significant. He must,
then, if he is not simply to reject science out of hand, provide
some special treatment of this surplus portion. Several such fictionalistic treatments will be distinguished in the discussion to
follow, but we must first turn to a closer examination of pragmatism and its consequences.

14. Pragmatism

Pragmatism, as noted above, is willing to cut the tie between
significance and intuitive clarity in order to be able to incorporate all of science into a uniformly significant language E. Theoretical terms, supposed isolable by their functions in effective
systems, are to be considered genuine constituents of significant
discourse, that is, discourse true or false of the world. Pragmatism thus emphasizes function, utility, and system in science,

and sees significance in these terms rather than as independently specifiable.

The pragmatist is willing to admit that at least some theoretical terms are, from an intuitive standpoint, obscure. But he claims that such obscurity is a poor index of lack of cognitive significance, however relevant it may be in other respects. The standard of significance, argues the pragmatist, ought not to hinge on intuitive judgment, but should rather reflect the actual practice of scientific system-building, which provides the most comprehensive, useful, and well-tested accounts of the world that we have. Functional utility within such systematic accounts should, accordingly, be taken as a feature to be *built into* our standard of significance, rather than as creating some special problem of interpretation through conflict with a pre-scientific, intuitive standard. The effect of the pragmatist's approach is to relate *significance* to the environing system of the term or statement in question. But he finds this wholly congruent with the systematic import of empirical *tests,* with the fact that testing in science applies, not to single statements, but to the systems in which they are embedded.

The pragmatist's decision, which amounts, in effect, to accepting the whole of science as significant without further, special interpretation, has, clearly, a certain advantage in point of economizing intellectual effort. But, by the same token, it might be said to surrender the critical standpoint afforded by an independent demand for intuitive clarity, a demand which might be defended (at least in part) as important for science itself. There are times when intellectual effort should not be saved but rather expended, when conflicts between the "system" and "understanding" should not be smoothed over, but rather taken seriously. Such considerations might perhaps be urged against the pragmatist's readiness to construe the notion of significance in such a way as to bring it into line with what is acceptable in science. These considerations seem rather to favor the fictionalistic attitude.

The pragmatist's course has, on the other hand, the virtue of continuity with a dominant motivation of the initial quest for a criterion of significance. The aim was, it will be recalled, to apply such a criterion to any given doctrine before investing the energy needed to decide the validity of its truth-claims. A doctrine qualifying by the criterion would be shown not unworthy of investigation, since true or false in fact. A doctrine not qualifying would be shown clearly not worth investigating, since neither true nor false. Now, for the pragmatist, every theoretical term passing the test of functional utility, and thus of interest to the scientist, is indeed capable of serving as a constituent in significant statements. By contrast, the fictionalist holds that some theoretical terms passing the test of functional utility are nonetheless obscure, rendering all containing statement-forms non-significant, and therefore surely not true. The fictionalist will not, however, wish to legislate to the scientist by declaring these statement-forms *not worthy of investigation* as elements of systems. The fictionalist, unlike the pragmatist, will thus need to give up the idea that only those doctrines that are significant are potentially worthy of scientific investigation. He will need to say that, in addition, non-significant statement-forms with "legitimate" theoretical components may also be worthy of scientific interest, though not as possible truths.

15. Fictionalism and Its Varieties

The fictionalist is willing to reject the assumption that science is throughout significant, in order to continue construing significance as associated with intuitive clarity. He is thus prepared to live in a divided and, to that extent, uneasy world. His decision makes it possible for him to sustain the critical potential of an independent demand for intuitive understandability, but commits him to a divided attitude to *de facto* science. Part of science is to be taken as significant and expressible within *E,* and the rest as non-significant and falling outside *E.* The *E*-portion is subject to attributions of truth, falsehood, belief, and evidence, whereas the non-*E* portion is not. Yet, the fictionalist cannot spurn the latter wholly, since he is prepared to admit its functional "legitimacy" and, hence, its interest for the scientist. At most, he can deny it to be either true or false.

Depending on the fictionalist's positive attempts to deal with this non-E portion, we may distinguish different forms of fictionalism. In the following sections, we shall discuss (1) "instrumentalistic" and (2) "eliminative" varieties as the two main forms, and we shall, further, distinguish several sorts of eliminative fictionalism. The division between (1) and (2) consists in this: for (1), the non-E portion of science is simply to be construed as useful machinery, whereas for (2), it is to be eliminated in favor of something which falls within E.

16. Instrumentalistic Fictionalism

The instrumentalistic fictionalist (or "instrumentalist," as we shall henceforth call him) does not propose to eliminate the non-E portion of science, but simply to treat it differently from the E-portion. Unlike the latter, which he holds significant and therefore true or false, confirmable or disconfirmable, and possibly expressive of belief, he treats the non-E portion as mere machinery, not to be qualified in any of these ways, though useful in the scientist's work. Corresponding to the above attributions, he may in fact propose alternative expressions to be applied to non-E theories. He may, for example, ask whether such theories are of *scientific interest,* whether they *hold or fail,* whether they are *supported or violated, useful or not, adopted, held, employed* or *abandoned, rejected, revised.* In short, the instrumentalist's answer to the problem of interpretation is to reserve the language of truth, evidence, and belief for just the E-portion of science, and to describe the non-E portion in other terms. Though, like all fictionalists, the instrumentalist holds that a uniformly significant E is not capable of absorbing all of science as a *de facto* body of doctrine, he is able to make a weaker affirmation, i.e., he can say that E as he construes it *is* capable of expressing all *genuine assertions or beliefs* contained in the body of science. This affirmation is, however, a direct consequence of his decision to allow scientific doctrines to be qualified as genuinely assertive and expressive of belief only if they fit within E as he construes it.

17. Empiricism, Pragmatism, and Instrumentalism

If empiricism is taken as the thesis that a uniformly observational language is capable of expressing all of our scientific system of beliefs, then pragmatism may be taken as denying this thesis. For pragmatism holds scientific doctrines involving theoretical terms to be significant, hence expressive of our scientific beliefs, though not formulable in thoroughly observational language. Instrumentalism, on the other hand, may be readily put in such a way as to uphold the thesis of empiricism above mentioned since, *if* intuitive clarity is taken to require observationality, instrumentalism simply denies to all non-observational doctrines the status of belief-vehicles. Since the instrumentalist course is a consistent one, pragmatism cannot claim to have shown that the thesis of empiricism is false. Yet, since nobody doubts for a moment that the terminology of belief, truth, and evidence can be deliberately *stipulated* to apply only to certain portions of science and not to others, instrumentalism thus upholds the thesis of empiricism only in a most trivial sense.

The opposition between pragmatism and instrumentalism thus seems to lack important substance, and it is perhaps not surprising that the two positions are frequently confused, and that writers occasionally vacillate between them. For the issue appears to involve nothing more than alternative decisions as to the application of epistemological labels. Beyond the limits of intuitive clarity, the instrumentalist is glad to admit the functional utility of theoretical machinery, though withholding the attribution of 'significance' and associated terms. Within the limits of what *he* considers significant, the pragmatist, in his turn, is perfectly willing to admit that many theoretical statements lack the intuitive transparency of observational statements, though he applies to both sorts the language of truth, evidence, and belief. Both pragmatism and instrumentalism are committed to searching for an answer to the problem of function; but beyond that, there is no difference in program, but only an alternative set of terminological decisions. The instrumentalistic terminology does, of course, represent a standard of significance independent of accepted scientific systems. But this maintenance of an independent standard of significance (which, in contrast to pragmatism, appeared to us a fictionalistic virtue) is not turned to much critical use by instrumentalism. That is, it does not issue in any proposal for alteration or reformulation of non-significant portions of *de facto* science, but only in a resolve to talk about them differently. Pragmatists and instrumentalists might be judged, therefore, to be similar in spirit despite verbal differences; they are happy with science as it is.

18. Eliminative Fictionalism

The eliminative fictionalist (or "eliminatist," as we shall henceforth refer to him), like the instrumentalist, finds part of science falling outside E and not qualifiable as literally significant. But he finds it impossible to let matters rest with an appropriate adjustment of his terminology of significance, truth, evidence, and belief. Recognizing the scientific utility of the non-E portion, he nonetheless seeks to eliminate this portion in favor of an E-substitute (i.e., a substitute expressible in E) of no less utility. He is thus committed to finding such a substitute, or a method for constructing one. Ideally, he wants to achieve this goal for all of the non-E portion, but he is, of course, glad to see it realized piecemeal, for particular segments.

It is this commitment of the eliminatist which differentiates him from the instrumentalist no less than from the pragmatist. It represents a resolve not merely to talk in non-pragmatic ways about science, but to strive for a reformulation of science itself which will not be worse than the original in point of utility and will, moreover, be superior in point of intuitive clarity. The fact that such a reformulation is sought indicates that, unlike both the pragmatist and the instrumentalist, the eliminatist is not happy with science as it is. But it need not be taken to imply either a rejection of science in the everyday sense of the term, nor a denial of the scientific worthwhileness of non-E theories. It represents rather an intellectual dissatisfaction with the divorce between intuitive clarity and comprehensive systematization, which we noted earlier, and an attempt to heal the rift so as to make significance whole again.

As to the empiricist thesis discussed in the previous section, fulfillment of the (typical) eliminatist program would clearly uphold the thesis. Fulfillment is, however, by no means automatic. In order that the eliminatist's goal be realized, all non-observational doctrines of science need to be shown replaceable by observational ones of at least equal utility. And such replaceability, in accord with suitable criteria of utility, is not at all obvious in advance. We shall discuss briefly three forms of the eliminatist approach.

19. Eliminative Fictionalism: Syntactical Form

The point here is to construct a syntactical metalanguage as an *E*-substitute for the non-*E* portion of science. The non-*E* portion itself is taken as an *uninterpreted* object language ("OL" for short) with fixed vocabulary of symbols, a specifiable set of symbol strings constituting formulae, a subset of these constituting primitive formulae, and certain sequences of formulae constituting valid transformations. The syntactical metalanguage ("SL" for short) governing this object language *is* however, interpreted, its apparatus including extra-logical terms referring to elements of the object language. Within SL, the vocabulary of OL is described, and definitions may be stated for terms applying to formulae of OL, to primitive formulae of OL, to valid transformations of OL, proofs in OL, and so forth. Some truths about OL may be chosen as axioms of SL, and other truths may then be obtained as SL-theorems. In short, the syntactical interconnections of OL are described within SL, but no imputation of significance is made with respect to any element of OL.

Such a metalanguage as SL may, perhaps, be construed as replacing the non-*E* portion for scientific purposes, in the following way. A theory *T*, belonging to this portion, is normally presumed to be a premise such that together with other non-*E* doctrines *D* and *E*-statements *S*, other *E*-statements *R* may be derived. The role of *T* + *D* (both non-*E*), here, is to effect a transition from the *E*-statements *S* to the *E*-statements *R*. *T* + *D* may thus be taken as part of a "machine" (i.e., OL) such that, plugging S into it, R somehow emerges. The metalanguage SL may be supposed to describe the operation of the machine.

Suppose, for example, that we take S to be true. We need a method of plugging it into our machine. This may be supposed to involve, first, a rule for *correlating* it with some symbolic formula of OL, the rule itself statable as a metalinguistic *adjunct* to SL. (Perhaps the easiest rule to imagine is one by which S is made to correspond to an identically spelled, though uninterpreted, formula of OL.) The second part of the plugging-in method may be construed as presenting the machine-correlate of S, linked with T and D (and possibly other primitive or proven formulae of OL), in some fixed order, concluding with a presentation of the machine-correlate of R. The machine does the rest, yielding (in the positive case we are considering) the signal 'valid transformation'. Less metaphorically, the sequence of presented OL formulae may be shown, in SL, to be a valid transformation in OL. We next unplug the machine-correlate of R appearing at the end, i.e., we get its E-correlate, namely, R itself, which *is* a significant statement, and we may now decide to accept it as true or to subject it to test.

It would seem to be the case that any work the theory $T + D$ does in connecting S and R, when this theory is construed to be significant, can be done equally well when it is taken as a mechanical device in the manner just described. Further, the latter construal seems possible no matter what S and R are imagined, assuming they belong to E. Adopting the theory $T + D$ can, however, for the latter construal, no longer be said to consist in accepting *it* as true, or even in accepting *it* as worthy of test for truth. Such adoption may, however, consist in a resolution to accept as true or testworthy all statements gotten out of the OL machine as R was gotten. Furthermore, since we now have an explicit description of the mechanism of OL, we may attempt to sum up the import of our resolution in some such statement as:

(M) All statements gotten out of OL in the proper way are true.

The latter statement is itself metalinguistic, but it would appear to be beyond the resources of SL. For one thing, it talks of statements, i.e., elements of *E,* rather than just formulae of OL. For another, it uses the semantic (not syntactic) notion 'true'. Finally, the reference to "the proper way" requires explanation not only in terms of OL's syntax, but also in terms of correlation-rules by which true *E*-statements may be fed into, and drawn from, the machine. So, to describe the present approach as aimed at the construction of a syntax of OL is not (it would seem) a complete account; in fact SL needs syntactic and semantic expansion to back up such a statement as (M). Unlike instrumentalism, however, the present approach does not merely refrain from treating the non-*E* theory as significant, while continuing to treat as significant each original *E*-statement. Rather, it may provide us with a new statement such as (M) which, representing the effective content of our original commitment to the non-*E* theory, is yet itself within the scope of *E,* and hence literally significant. We are thus not simply removing the theory from significance-status to instrument-status; we are construing it as abbreviatory of a new statement making a claim to truth.

Furthermore, the success of such a construal is not an automatic or routine matter, but depends on whether the original theory is clear enough, simply as a mechanism, for its structure to be formulated in a metalanguage and, moreover, a metalanguage which itself falls inside *E.* The issue depends, in part, on the particular theory in question and, in part, on the specifications adopted for *E.*

An instructive example is afforded by the work of Goodman and Quine on the interpretation of mathematics, in their study, "Steps Toward a Constructive Nominalism."[3] They are here concerned, not with the problem of theoretical terms in natural science, in the spirit of our prior discussions, but rather with the possibility of a nominalistic interpretation of mathematics. Yet there are strict parallels: if intuitive clarity is construed as re-

[3] Nelson Goodman and Willard Van Orman Quine, "Steps Toward a Constructive Nominalism," *Journal of Symbolic Logic,* XII (1947), 105-122.

quiring nominalism, how is classical mathematics to be treated, in view of its apparent immunity to exhaustive nominalistic translation, and its consequently ineradicable posit of abstract entities such as classes? Mathematics is undeniably useful and therefore, for the pragmatic spirit, worth taking as significant and moreover, true. The instrumentalist would here incline rather to withholding epithets of 'truth' and 'significance' from mathematics and applying instead such notions as 'convenience' and 'effectiveness'. Goodman and Quine take still another tack—they construct a syntax for mathematics.

More precisely, finding themselves unable to translate all of mathematics into nominalistic language, they construct a nominalistic syntax language enabling them to talk *about* the untranslated residue rather than assert it. As they describe their idea:

> Our position is that the formulas of platonistic mathematics are, like the beads of an abacus, convenient computational aids which need involve no question of truth. What is meaningful and true in the case of platonistic mathematics as in the case of the abacus is not the apparatus itself, but only the description of it: the rules by which it is constructed and run. These rules we do understand, in the strict sense that we can express them in purely nominalistic language. The idea that classical mathematics can be regarded as mere apparatus is not a novel one among nominalistically minded thinkers; but it can be maintained only if one can produce, as we have attempted to above, a syntax which is itself free from platonistic commitments. At the same time, every advance we can make in finding direct translations for familiar strings of marks will increase the range of the meaningful language at our command.[4]

The success of such a program was not at all obvious in advance. For though the structure of mathematical theory might have seemed, *prima facie*, clear enough to be captured by a metalinguistic description, an essential requirement was that this

[4] *Ibid.*, p. 122. By permission.

description be, itself, free of platonistic features. This requirement was built into the standard of intuitive clarity defining the
program of the authors, thus setting a general condition for its
success. The success actually achieved in this case, as well as the
program itself, were thus of considerable interest.

Returning to the problem of interpreting theoretical terms in
science, it seems clear that no general guarantee can be given of
the success of the syntactical approach we have been considering. As suggested earlier, theories themselves vary in the degree
to which they are clearly articulated, and dovetailed into surrounding statements. Further, standards of intuitive clarity and
associated specifications for E may differ, both in the interpretation of the requirement of observationality, and in the possible
addition of other requirements. For example, the non-nominalist
has, in platonistic syntax, initially greater resources than the
nominalist with which to attack his problem.

A more critical point, furthermore, arises. The syntactical features of mathematics are deductive. They require of a metalanguage the notion of a theorem and a proof, for example, but not
such notions as those of evidence, credibility, or confirmation. If
the work of theories in science needs to be described by means
of the latter as well as the former notions, the wanted metalanguage will need to refer to non-deductive features of theoretical
object languages, and these may well turn out to be not purely
syntactic. In this event, the basic idea of syntactic fictionalism
would require expansion to allow for a metalanguage that might
well be pragmatic (and semantic) as well as syntactic.

20. Eliminative Fictionalism: Craigian Form

Whereas the fictionalism just considered strives to replace the
non-E portion of a domain of science with a metalinguistic substitute *referring to* the "workings" of this portion in relating E-
statements to one another, the idea we shall now consider strives
for an object-language substitute expressing these same relationships (and falling wholly within E). Recent discussion of this
idea has been stimulated by a result of W. Craig, to the effect
that, for every system with both observational and theoretical

terms, another system exists, containing only observational terms, but nevertheless yielding every theorem of the initial system which is throughout observational. In Craig's words,

> If *K* is any recursive set of non-logical (individual, function, predicate) constants, containing at least one predicate constant, then there exists a system whose theorems are exactly those theorems of [the system] *T* in which no constants other than those of *K* occur. In particular, suppose that *T* expresses a portion of a natural science, that the constants of *K* refer to things or events regarded as 'observable', and that the other constants do not refer to 'observables' and hence may be regarded as 'theoretical' or 'auxiliary'. Then there exists a system which does not employ 'theoretical' or 'auxiliary' constants and whose theorems are the theorems of *T* concerning 'observables'.[5]

Craig provides a method for specifying, on the basis of *T*, the substitute system *T**, containing as theorems just those theorems of *T* whose constants are wholly drawn from *K*. (In rough outline, the method is as follows: Each sequence of signs in *T* is given a Gödel number; thus each proof, in particular, has such a number. For any conjunction $A \cdot A \cdot \ldots \cdot A$, we count the number *n* of repetitions of *A*, and determine (in a finite number of steps) whether *n* is the Gödel number of a proof in *T*, whether, in particular, it is the Gödel number of a proof of *A*, and whether the constants of *A* are wholly drawn from *K*. If all these conditions are satisfied, we choose the original conjunction as an axiom of *T** (and derive *A* as a theorem of *T** by applying the rule 'If $A \cdot A \cdot \ldots \cdot A$, then *A*').)[6] The system *T** is shown by Craig to contain just the observational theorems of *T*.[7]

[5] William Craig, "On Axiomatizability Within a System," *Journal of Symbolic Logic*, XVIII (1953), p. 31, text and footnote 9. By permission.

[6] For a general account, see William Craig, "Replacement of Auxiliary Expressions," *Philosophical Review*, LXV (1956), 38-55. By permission.

[7] A pertinent illustration may be given, harking back to the picture outlined in the second paragraph of Section 19 of the present Part. We

In a concise critical account of Craig's result,[8] C. G. Hempel indicates the ways in which Craig's replacing system might substitute for its original. Hempel writes, "Craig's result shows that no matter how we select from the total vocabulary V_T' of an interpreted theory T' a subset V_B of experiential or observational terms, the balance of V_T', constituting the 'theoretical terms', can always be avoided [in a particular sense]." This sense, which Hempel distinguishes from definability and translatability, he calls "functional replaceability" and describes as follows: "The terms of T might be said to be avoidable if there exists another theory T_B, couched in terms of V_B, which is 'functionally equivalent' to T in the sense of establishing exactly the same deductive connections between V_B sentences as T."

Hempel offers, however, two objections to Craig's method for constructing a "functionally equivalent" substitute system. The first objection is that the system gotten by this method "always has an infinite set of postulates, irrespective of whether the postulate set of the original theory is finite or infinite, and that his result cannot be essentially improved in this respect . . . This means that the scientist would be able to avoid theoretical terms only at the price of forsaking the comparative simplicity of a theoretical system with a finite postulational basis, and of giving up a system of theoretical concepts and hypotheses which are

---

there construed a theory as a premise allowing a transition from E-statement S to E-statement R. Now if the original theory T provides premises (e.g., $S \supset H$ and $H \supset R$) effecting a transition (by means of the theoretical constant, 'H') from observational S to observational R, it contains also an observational theorem: $S \supset R$. Thus, in retaining the latter and all similar observational theorems, T^* preserves the transitions of T from observational to observational statements. In general, if the theory T yields R, given S, then it yields also the observational conditional, $S \supset R$. (See Carl G. Hempel, "The Theoretician's Dilemma," in Herbert Feigl, Michael Scriven, and Grover Maxwell (eds.), *Minnesota Studies in the Philosophy of Science* [Minneapolis: University of Minnesota Press, 1958], II, 75-76.)

[8] Carl G. Hempel, "Implications of Carnap's Work for the Philosophy of Science," to appear in the forthcoming Rudolf Carnap volume of the *Library of Living Philosophers,* ed. P. Schilpp. (The manuscript copy of this article which was made available to me by Professor Hempel may diverge, in minor respects, from the version to be published.) By permission of the publisher and the author.

heuristically fruitful and suggestive—in return for a practically unmanageable system based upon an infinite, though effectively specified, set of postulates in observational terms."[9] Analogous comments have been made by Craig himself.[1]

This objection indicates how the problem of function impinges on the problem of interpretation. Were it established that Craig's substitute system retains the functional utility of the original, the problem of interpretation would be solved by his result, since this substitute system is throughout observational (i.e., within the scope of E). The original might then, in effect, be construed as a kind of shorthand for the substitute. The present objection, however, challenges the assumption that the substitute indeed retains the functional utility of the original.

Now such a challenge could always be trivially sustained if it needed only to point to *some* difference between original and substitute. For any two systems are in some way different. Even to require the challenger to point to some difference *in utility* would seem to be insufficient, for certain differences in utility appear to be clearly irrelevant to the problem at hand. In particular, suppose it granted that the substitute system is indeed less suggestive, less manageable, and less heuristically fruitful than the original. It might nonetheless be argued to represent an intellectual gain if it did in fact do the same deductive and inductive work. For we should then be able to interpret the original as a kind of shorthand for the substitute and should, by the same token, *legitimize* its use where convenient in practice, rather than calling for its thorough eradication from practice. The situation seems parallel to that of definition.

If equivalence in suggestiveness and manageability were to be required in the case of ordinary definition, we should hardly be able to define at all. In defining, we try, rather, to find equivalents fulfilling extensional requirements only. We try to minimize the complexity of our apparatus of primitive terms at the cost of replacing conveniently short definienda by complicated definien-

---

[9] *Ibid.*
[1] Craig, "Replacement of Auxiliary Expressions."

tia couched in terms of few primitives. No one intends such definientia to be used in practice in place of their definienda; the latter are in fact *legitimized* through their definitions. Neither does anyone maintain that the formulation of such definitions therefore represents no intellectual gain.[2]

However, Hempel's present objection indicates also that there is a difference in deductive structure between the original system and its Craigian substitute, a difference with regard to whether the postulates are finite or infinite in number. Goodman has stressed this difference as showing that the substitute in fact does not do the same deductive work as the original. It does, to be sure, incorporate the whole class of observational assertions (postulates-or-theorems) of the original, but it does not systematize them economically, as the original does, through specifying some finite number of them from which all the rest flow.

Goodman writes, "Evidently preservation of all theorems in non-suspect language is far from enough. What more, then, is required? For one thing, that the replacing system have an appreciable degree of deductive coherence or economy. The chief purpose of proof in a philosophical system is less to convince of truth than to integrate. If every theorem has its own postulate, no integration is achieved."[3] If such integration is counted as one feature of the functional utility of theories, then the Craigian substitute fails to retain the functional utility of the original. It is, of course, possible to make this *particular judgment* with regard to Craig's substitute without solving the general problem of function, i.e., defining the nature of the integration that is here relevant, as a feature of functional utility.

We turn now to a consideration of Hempel's second objection,[4] which presents a new challenge to the assumption that the Craigian substitute retains the functional utility of the original.

[2] See Quine, *From a Logical Point of View*, pp. 26-27, and Goodman, *The Structure of Appearance*, chap. i.

[3] Nelson Goodman, "Review of W. Craig, 'Replacement of Auxiliary Expressions,' " *Journal of Symbolic Logic*, XXII (1957), 318.

[4] Hempel, "Implications of Carnap's Work for the Philosophy of Science."

The present challenge consists in pointing out that the non-*E* portion of science establishes *inductive* as well as *deductive* relationships among *E*-statements, and that the Craigian substitute fails generally to preserve all these inductive relationships. Hempel's illustration exhibits the general point clearly; we therefore reproduce it here. The term 'magnet' is to be taken as the sole *theoretical* term in the following illustrative sentences:

(1)   The parts obtained by breaking a rod-shaped magnet in two are again magnets.

(2)   If *x* is a magnet, then whenever a small piece *y* of iron filing is brought into contact with *x,* then *y* clings to *x*. In symbols:

$$(x) \ (Mx \supset (y) \ (Fxy \supset Cxy))$$

(3)   Objects *b* and *c* were obtained by breaking object *a* in two, and *a* was a magnet and rod-shaped.

(4)   If *d* is a piece of iron filing that is brought into contact with *b*, then *d* will cling to *b*.

Now, argues Hempel, given the singular statement (3), then with the aid of the general statements (1) and (2), we are able to deduce the singular statement (4). That is, (3) tells us that *a* was a rod-shaped magnet from which *b* and *c* were gotten by breaking *a* in two. The general statement (1) states that all parts gotten by breaking rod-shaped magnets in two are themselves magnets, from which it follows that *b* and *c,* in particular, are magnets. But, as (2) informs us, if something is a magnet, then if any piece of iron filing is brought into contact with it, this piece of iron filing will cling to it. It thus follows that, since *b* is a magnet, if *d* is a piece of iron filing brought into contact with *b,* *d* will cling to *b,* as stated by (4).

But note that the singular premise (3) contains the theoretical term 'magnet' in application to *a*, e.g., the subsentence:

(5)   *Ma* ('*a* was a magnet')

Note, further, that (5) is not itself *deducible* from purely observational sentences via (2), since the latter states that *if* something is a magnet, *then* a certain observationally expressible condition holds, and it does not also state the converse; it gives a necessary though not a sufficient observational condition for being a magnet. Thus, if (4), which *is* a purely observational singular sentence, is to be gotten, by means of the general theory (1)-(2), from other such sentences, we need somewhere to introduce an *inductive* step in the argument. For example, if (5) were itself to be gotten inductively from purely observational singular sentences, then, since the rest of (3) is purely observational and singular, (3) would, as a whole, be traced back to a purely observational singular base, and, by the argument already given above, so would (4). The general theory (1)-(2) would have served thus to link (4) with a set of (non-theoretical) premises not capable of yielding it deductively.

Looking again at (2), we can, moreover, conceive how (5) might indeed be gotten inductively from purely observational singular sentences. For though the consequent of (2) states a general observational condition which is not sufficient to support a deductive inference back to its antecedent, a finite series of substitution instances of the consequent, with '*a*' in place of '*x*', might in suitable circumstances constitute a reasonable inductive basis for asserting (5). Assume, for example, that we have a large number of instances of '*Fay* $\supset$ *Cay*' and no instance of '*Fay* $\cdot$ ~*Cay*'. We further take all "instances" to have non-vacuous antecedents and so to be stronger than simple substitution instances, e.g.:

(6) $(Fae \cdot Cae) \cdot (Faf \cdot Caf) \cdot \ldots \cdot (Fam \cdot Cam)$

Then, (6) supports '(y) $(Fay \supset Cay)$', which is the consequent of (2) as instantiated with respect to *a* taken as *x*, i.e.:

(7) $Ma \supset (y)$ $(Fay \supset Cay)$

The consequent of (7) in turn may be taken as providing inductive grounds for its antecedent, under suitable conditions— for example, when likely alternatives have been eliminated, or when no likely alternatives are available. But the antecedent in question is '*Ma*', namely, (5). Thus (6) is a purely observational, singular premise lending inductive support to (5), by virtue of the general theoretical statement (2).

Recall, now, that (5) is the sole theoretical subsentence of (3), the rest consisting of purely observational singular sentences, i.e.:

(8) b and c were obtained by breaking a in two, and a was rod-shaped.

Thus, (3) consists of the conjunction of (5) and (8), (5) being *inductively* based on (6), and (8) being an immediate *deductive* consequence of itself, with the result that (3) as a whole is now gotten from the conjunction of (6) and (8), consisting purely of observational, singular sentences. Given (3), we have already seen that (4) follows deductively from it, taken together with the general theory (1)-(2).

In sum, the general theory (1)-(2) effects a connection which is *not* purely deductive between certain observational statements, i.e., (6) + (8), and others, namely, (4). If this theory is construed as belonging to the non-E portion of science and the observational statements as belonging to the E portion, the non-E portion is here shown to function in establishing non-deductive (or, briefly, inductive) relationships among E-statements. If the Craigian substitute fails to preserve these relationships, it will be reasonable to charge that it fails to retain the functional utility of the original, especially in view of the general inductive import of science. In fact, as Hempel argues, the Craigian substitute does not generally preserve the inductive connections among E-sentences, established by the original, though it does succeed in retaining all the deductive connections. Let us see how this happens with respect to our present example.

We need first to decide what the original system consists in. Let us suppose it contains (1), (2), (6), and (8) as axioms. Then neither (5) nor (3) is a theorem, since (5) is not deducible from these axioms, as we have seen. Thus (4) is no theorem either, since, lacking (3) as a premise, it is not deductively derivable from the other axiomatic statements of the system. The Craigian substitute preserves all and only the observational theorems of the original. It thus retains (6) and (8), and it excludes (1) and (2), as well as (5), (3), and (4). Furthermore, unlike the original system described above, which provides inductive grounds for the statement (4), the Craigian substitute gives no inductive grounds for (4) at all. This will be seen by recalling that the original chain leading to (4) consists of two parts; the first, going from (6) + (8) to (3), depends on (2), and the second, going from (3) to (4), depends on both (1) and (2), which are lacking in the Craigian substitute.

Suppose we specify the original system differently—for example, we take its axioms to be (1), (2), and (3). In this case, as we have seen, (4) will be a theorem, as will (7) and (8). The Craigian substitute here will retain (4) as well as (8), and will exclude (1), (2), (3), and (7). But whereas the original system, containing (1) and (2), thereby enables inductive support to accrue to (4) from (6) + (8), the substitute system will not, lacking (1) and (2) as intermediaries. If, to the above three axioms of the original, (6) is added, then it too will be retained as a theorem of the Craigian substitute along with (4) and (8). But though (4), (6), and (8) will thus figure as theorems in both original and substitute systems, only the original will contain the crucial (1) and (2) by means of which (4) is inductively traced back to (6) + (8). In any event, if one aspect of the scientific function of theories such as (1)-(2) is their establishing certain inductive connections among *E*-statements inside or outside the theories themselves, it seems clear that their respective Craigian substitutes do not generally fulfill the same function.

Nor is this result surprising, upon reflection. For since these substitutes are not logically equivalent to their respective originals, but rather weaker consequences of them, they need not, on *any* likely view of induction, sustain the same inductive relations as these originals, even among purely observational sentences. One plausible suggestion is that the functional utility of the originals depends in part on their greater strength, on their going out on more inductive limbs. The relative weakness of the substitutes would seem to ensure that they have proportionately less utility.

This conclusion might, perhaps, be forestalled if the relative weakness of the substitutes were balanced by a relative increase of simplicity or systematic integration, but, as we have seen, they are in fact deficient precisely with respect to systematic integration, by comparison with their originals.

Various ways of strengthening the Craigian substitutes might be proposed, in order to remedy their relative weakness in isolation. If, for example, we could independently specify, generally, which sentences confirm which, relative to any theoretical system, we might supplement the given Craigian substitute by a specification of the confirmation-pairs relative to its original system. Such an attempt would, however, obviously hinge on a prior and independent solution of the problems of inductive logic.

Short of this, an attempt might be made, in each specific case, to strengthen the Craigian substitute with hypotheses designed to yield those inductive relations, established by the original system, in which we are particularly interested. With reference to the above example, for instance, the crucial inductive relation is that which obtains between (6) (giving instances of '$Fay \supset Cay$') *plus* (8) ('b and c were obtained by breaking a in two, and a was rod-shaped'), and (4) ('If d is a piece of iron filing brought into contact with b, then d will cling to b'). Let us symbolize 'x is rod-shaped' by:

$$'Rx'$$

and 'x and y were obtained by breaking z in two' by:

$$'Bxyz'$$

Then the inductive relation in question is established by the following statement, which contains no theoretical term:

(I) $(x) \{[(y) (Fxy \supset Cxy) \cdot Rx] \supset (z) [(\exists w) (Bzwx) \supset (u) (Fzu \supset Czu)]\}$[5]

Given (6), we have inductive support for:

[5] This formula was suggested to me by C. G. Hempel, as an improvement over my initial version.

(II) $(y) (Fay \supset Cay)$

Sentence (8) tells us that:

(III) Ra

We thus accept the main antecedent of (I) as holding of a, taken as x. Sentence (8) also tells us that b and c were gotten by breaking a in two. Taking b as z in the main consequent of (I), we know that *its* antecedent is true, namely, there is in fact some object w, i.e., c, such that b and c were obtained by breaking a in two. It therefore follows that for *any* object u, if it is a piece of iron filing brought into contact with b, it will cling to b. Thus it follows that this condition holds in particular for d. But the latter conclusion is identical with (4).

To attempt such a specific supplementation of the Craigian substitute in each case means, however, that Craig's method is no longer being advanced as a general solution to the problem of eliminating theoretical terms. In fact, (I), (8), and (6) alone might be proposed, independently, as an alternative to the systems discussed above containing (1) and (2), irrespective of the Craigian substitute altogether. Such a proposal is, moreover, geared to *this specific* example, and has not emerged from a general method.

21. Eliminative Fictionalism: Ramseyan Form

We shall consider, as our final example of eliminative fictionalism, an idea due to F. Ramsey and considerably discussed recently.[6] Like the Craigian version just treated, the Ramseyan strategy is one which replaces a scientific system with a non-E portion by an object-language substitute yielding the very same E-theorems, and itself falling wholly within E. We shall discuss this strategy in some detail in the present section; the main idea may here be suggested, in a preliminary way, as follows: The procedure is (roughly) to conjoin all axiomatic statements of the

[6] Frank Plumpton Ramsey, *The Foundations of Mathematics*, ed. R. B. Braithwaite (New York: Humanities Press, Inc., 1931), chap. ix, "Theories." By permission of the publisher and Routledge & Kegan Paul, Ltd.

system in question, then to replace all non-*E* (or theoretical) predicate constants by distinctive variables throughout (having first eliminated by paraphrase all *singular* theoretical terms), and, finally, to prefix the whole resulting expression by existential quantifiers governing the newly introduced variables.

The statement gotten in this way is the Ramseyan substitute, purified of all theoretical (non-*E*) constants, yet (as we shall see in detail presently) yielding the same observational consequences as the original, and retaining, moreover, a comparably integrated structure. The latter feature is due to the fact that, unlike the operation of the Craigian strategy, statements containing theoretical terms are here not wholly expunged; on the contrary, they are slightly altered and thus preserved. The alteration, moreover, consists simply in replacing certain predicate constants by predicate variables governed by initial quantifiers. Aside from these added quantifiers, which are tacked on to the front of the substitute, the internal *form* of the latter is identical with that of the original (taken as the conjunction of all axiomatic statements of the original).

Yet, in switching from constants to variables, we weaken and thus hope to clarify our total assertion: rather than purporting to make some *definite*, though obscure, attribution to an object, we now say merely that there is *some* attribution to be made, qualifiable in whatever further detail we are able to supply. The shift is comparable to the change from *individual* constants to *individual* variables, i.e., from

(1)   George Washington was a U.S. President and George Washington slept here.

to

(2) $(\exists x)$ (x was a U.S. President · x slept here).

In the transition from (1) to (2), the individual proper name 'George Washington' is supplanted by the individual variable 'x', governed by an initial existential quantifier, '$(\exists x)$', to be read, 'There is some individual object x, such that . . .'. Suppose, now, that we take 'was a U.S. President' as a theoretical term to be eliminated. This term is a *predicate* rather than *individual constant*. Statement (2) appears to be making some definite attribution to an object by means of this predicate. We can, however, eliminate this definiteness by forming (2)'s Ramseyan substitute, which does, for the above predicate constant of (2), what (2) did for the proper name of (1):

(3) $(\exists\phi)(\exists x)$ $(\phi x \cdot x$ slept here$)$

This Ramseyan substitute no longer contains the theoretical term 'was a U.S. President'. It says rather that there is *something* which is characteristic of some x, and that this same x slept here. In both (2) and (3), the non-theoretical consequence 'Some x slept here' is preserved, but (3) has the extra advantage of avoiding the objectionable predicate in question.

Note, however, that this advantage is bought at a price. First of all, there is a certain ambiguity in saying, as we suggested above, that (3) is a *weaker* assertion than (2). It is more *indefinite*, to be sure, in the sense that, where (2) employs a specific predicate of individuals, (3) speaks instead of something, ϕ, characteristic of individuals. But (2), on the other hand, though it *uses* a specific predicate of individuals, says nothing about there *being something* which is characteristic of individuals, whereas (3) does in fact say that there is some such thing, ϕ. The indefiniteness of (3) thus requires the positing of a realm of entities characteristic of the individuals which are alone posited by (2).

Whereas the existential quantifier of (2) may therefore be read straightforwardly 'There is some individual object x, such that . . .', we cannot thus read the first existential quantifier of (3). We need, in fact, to determine some reading for the latter which will make clear what sort of entity is here said to exist. Further, we need to specify a way of construing 'ϕx'. Two possibilities suggest themselves: We may read the quantifier, 'There is some property ϕ, etc.' and construe 'ϕx' as 'x has the property ϕ'. Alternatively, we may read the quantifier, 'There is some class ϕ, etc.' construing 'ϕx' as 'x is a member of the class ϕ'. In either case, (3) makes (despite its indefiniteness) a stronger ontological claim than (2), asserting not only the existence of some individual but also the existence of some non-individual—property or class.

The latter consequence is clearly objectionable to nominalists, but even those who are generally prepared to admit the existence of properties or classes may wish to minimize the scope of their non-nominalistic commitments. Waiving such considerations for the moment, however, the adoption of (3) seems to involve payment of another price. To say simply that there is *some* property or class characteristic of x is, for the non-nominalist, to say something wholly trivial. For if x exists, as (3) claims, it surely has the property of being self-identical, for example, and belongs to the class of self-identical individuals.

This consequence may, however, be attributed to the paucity of (2). It might be argued that any real theory may be expected to supply many more interrelationships among its theoretical terms, and across the boundary between its theoretical and observational terms, so that its Ramseyan substitute is not likely to have quite the same triviality. Suppose, for example, that (3) were supplemented by a clause stipulating that all members of ϕ are Americans. It would follow that x is American. Moreover, it would no longer be the case that (3), as supplemented, is a trivial consequence merely of there being some x such that x slept here.

Another way of putting this point is as follows: In view of the fact (for the non-nominalist) that everything has at least one property (or belongs to at least one class), the assertion that some x slept here yields the original unsupplemented (3) by itself, and the theory (2) is thus not required as a basis from which to construct (3) as its Ramseyan substitute. But, first of all, if this Ramseyan substitute in fact succeeds in preserving all non-theoretical consequences of (2), any charge of triviality directed against the substitute might be plausibly redirected against the theory itself. Secondly, not every theory for which a Ramseyan substitute can be gotten is in fact subject to an analogous charge of triviality. For were (2) to contain an extra condition to the effect that all U.S. Presidents are American, its Ramseyan substitute would say of some *x* which slept here not simply that *some* φ is characteristic of it, but also that this φ is such that everything of which it is characteristic is American. And surely there is no principle of non-nominalistic .logic that everything whatever is characterized by something which entails being American.

So far, we have dwelt on simple examples. We shall now turn to the general grounds for the claim that Ramseyan substitutes preserve the same *E* (or observational) consequences of their respective originals. Afterward, we shall consider the broader question whether these substitutes retain the functional utility of their originals.

The claim that Ramseyan substitutes yield the same observational consequences as their originals may be divided into two parts: (a) Every observational consequence of a given Ramseyan substitute is a consequence also of its original, and (b) Every observational consequence of a given original is a consequence also of its Ramseyan substitute. Part (a) may be justified by recalling that the Ramseyan substitute results from existential generalization of its original, with respect to certain of its predicate constants; if we take such constants as denoting entities and allow generalization governing predicate variables to take place at all, we shall regard the existentially generalized statement as implied by its original. If the original implies its Ramseyan substitute, it implies also every one of the latter's consequences, including, surely, the observational ones.

We shall outline the justification of part (b) as given in a proof of H. G. Bohnert,[7] whose argument may be sketched as follows: Assume *T* to be the theoretical subset of the descriptive vocabulary *V* belonging to some language *L*. Let '$E_T(S)$' represent the result of existentially generalizing the sentence *S* of *L*, with respect to each member of *T* contained in *S*. (If, e.g., our previous illustrative sentence (2) be taken as *S*, than $E_T((2))$ is (3).) If *no* member of *T* occurs in *S*, *S* is equivalent to $E_T(S)$. Analog-

[7] Herbert Gaylord Bohnert, *The Interpretation of Theory* (Doctoral dissertation, University of Pennsylvania, 1961). By permission of the author.

ously, let '$U_T(S)$' represent the result of universally generalizing S with respect to every member of T in S. (This means replacing such members by appropriate variables and prefixing to the resulting formula universal quantifiers governing these variables.) S is an O-sentence if and only if it contains no member of T, and otherwise a T-sentence.

What needs now to be shown is that every O-sentence, S', implied by any given S, is implied also by $E_T(S)$. Now, by hypothesis, S implies S', i.e., the conditional they form, which may be represented by '$S \supset S'$', is logically true. By a general logical rule of inference, $U_T(S \supset S')$ may then be asserted. But the latter is the antecedent of a logically true conditional which may be represented as:

$$U_T(S \supset S') \supset (E_T(S) \supset E_T(S'))$$

construed as a "metatheorem" reflecting
    '$(x) (Fx \supset Gx) \supset ((\exists x) (Fx) \supset (\exists x) (Gx))$'.
Having earlier asserted $U_T(S \supset S')$, we may, therefore, now assert:

$$E_T(S) \supset E_T(S')$$

Since the latter represents a conditional (implied by a logical truth) the antecedent, $E_T(S)$, implies the consequent, $E_T(S')$. Since S' has been assumed an O-sentence from the start, however, it contains no member of T and is hence equivalent to $E_T(S')$. It follows that the above antecedent, $E_T(S)$, therefore implies S' as well, and this is the desired conclusion.

We turn now to the question whether Ramseyan substitutes retain the functional utility of their respective originals. The retention, by these substitutes, of the observational consequences of their originals does not decide the present question. For it will be recalled that Craigian substitutes also retain just the observational theorems of their respective originals and yet have been plausibly argued to be deficient in functional utility by comparison with these originals.

Nonetheless, we have already noted, toward the beginning of the present section, that one specific argument to this effect fails for the Ramseyan substitute though not for the Craigian. That is, the Ramseyan substitute does, in fact, retain a degree of deductive integration comparable to its original, in marked contrast with the Craigian substitute. Whereas the latter simply collects all the observational theorems of the original, so to speak, and takes as postulate some logically equivalent variant of each, the Ramseyan substitute retains the postulational form of the original, merely changing the status of theoretical predicates from constants to variables; within the scope of its new existential quantifiers, the structure of the substitute is unchanged.

The switch to variables governed by existential quantifiers does, as we have intimated, impose a special need to construe the original initially as a conjunction, so that recurrent theoretical constants may be replaced by variables reflecting such recurrence, through falling within the same quantificational scopes. Looking back, for example, at (1), we note that its existential generalization, (2), with respect to the constant 'George Washington', says that some x was *both* a U.S. President and a thing which slept here. If, in place of (1), we had had:

(1A)   George Washington was a U.S. President

and

(1B)   George Washington slept here

and had accordingly generalized these sentences separately as:

(2A)   ($\exists x$) (x was a U.S. President)

and

(2B)   ($\exists x$) (x slept here)

we should have failed to incorporate in our generalizations the fact that the recurrence of 'George Washington' in (1A) and (1B) signifies that some one object satisfies both predicates employed. For though the same letter 'x' appears as a variable in (2A) and (2B), the scope is different in each case. (2A) thus says 'Something was a U.S. President', and (2B) says 'Something slept here', but both together clearly fail to imply that some one thing both slept here and was a U.S. President. Generalizations (2A) and (2B) together are thus weaker than (2), implied by it but failing to imply it in turn. Generalization (2) itself is, of course, weaker than (1) or ((1A), (1B)) to begin with, and there is a special point in not weakening it further.

An analogous argument holds for the switch from predicate constants to predicate variables, as well: we are interested in the existential generalization of the whole statement rather than in the conjunction of such generalizations of its individual conjuncts. Since, moreover, a set of statements is equivalent to the conjunction of all, then, given such a set as our original, we are concerned to get the existential generalization of the conjunction of all members of the set. The upshot is that the set needs to be conjoined throughout prior to generalizing, with the result that the Ramseyan substitute is itself a single sentence, where the original may have been a set of individual sentences.

This consequence, however, does not appear to affect the Ramseyan substitute adversely in point of functional utility. The overall objective of eliminative fictionalism is to provide, in some way, an E-substitute for the original contaminated by non-E elements. The original needs, of course, to be clearly specified, and fixed throughout the process by which the substitute is gotten. The feature we have just considered means that we cannot derive the Ramseyan substitute by operating on component postulates of our original sequentially; we need to have them all before us as initially given. But, in the first place (it might be argued), any program for interpreting theoretical components of science needs to start from a clearly formulated body of statements to which the program is to be applied. In the second place, the derivation of the Ramseyan substitute from the conjunction of original statements characterizes the *manner* by which the substitute is gotten rather than the functioning of the substitute itself. Unless some deficiency can be shown in the way the substitute functions, by comparison with the original, the mere fact that it is the result of generalizing the conjunction of original postulates will constitute no objection.

Bohnert has, however, suggested a functional deficiency in the

Ramseyan substitute, which stems from its being a single, existentially quantified statement: it precludes the making of single theoretical assertions with independent meaning. To illustrate, we may refer to the example of the previous section in which the term 'magnet' was taken as theoretical. There is no difficulty in supposing that the general theory of magnets is replaced by a Ramseyan substitute, in which the predicate 'is a magnet' disappears in favor of the predicate variable 'ϕ' and its existential quantifier, in context, e.g.:

(4) $(\exists \phi) \ (\ldots \phi \ldots)$

But now imagine that we have examined a given metal rod, a, and wish to say of it that it is a magnet, perhaps with the idea of applying the general theory in the present instance. Such application to instances is indispensable to the functioning of scientific theories, but how are we to represent it according to the Ramseyan strategy? We cannot, surely, operate on:

(5) a is a magnet

to get another Ramseyan substitute:

(6) $(\exists \phi) \ (\phi a)$

For the 'ϕ' of (6) is wholly independent of the 'ϕ' of (4); (6) says merely that a has *some* property (or belongs to some class) —a trivial consequence of non-nominalistic logic, as we have above seen. Our intent was to relate a to the general theory, (4), but we have in fact failed to do this. Rather, we have treated (5) as an isolated and new theory, bare of all those detailed connections built into the context of 'ϕ', within (4). It is then no wonder that the Ramseyan substitute of (5) turns out trivial.

The problem arises from the fact that the predicate constant, 'is a magnet', free of scope restrictions, enables independent statements such as (5) to link up with the general theory of magnets, formulated separately. On the other hand, the scope restrictions attending variables operate so as to sever the connections between (4) and (6). The critical consequence is that the original theory allows for (5), whereas the substitute does not allow for a comparable singular theoretical attribution: the substitute seems thus to be clearly deficient in scientific utility.

There are, however, arguments that mitigate the negative conclusion just stated. Consider, first, that (6) is inadequate because it takes (5) as an isolated theory. But we have seen that every observational consequence of (5) is preserved by (6), just as every observational consequence of the general theory of magnets is preserved by (4). What more can be required? The point to note is that, even though this is the case, it does *not* follow that every observational consequence of the general theory *plus* (5) is preserved by (4) *plus* (6). The point may be seen clearly in reference to the following pair of statements, where '*M*' is a theoretical component and '*O*' an observational one, and where *neither* yields *any* observational consequence by itself, though they both yield '*O*', in combination.

(7) $M \supset O$
(8) M

The trouble is thus attributable to the fact that, in asserting (5) as a premise to be employed in combination with the general theory, we may be generating additional observational content not captured by (4) + (6). But this addition represents a strengthening of our original theory: we in fact have a *new* original, consisting of the general theory plus (5). It is then no cause for surprise that, in reference to this *new* original, (4) + (6) should appear deficient in utility; indeed, the latter conjunction is not the relevant Ramseyan substitute, and does not generally preserve the original's observational content. Once recognizing, however, that adoption of (5) amounts to conjoining another premise to the theory, we no longer take (4) + (6) as our Ramseyan substitute, but rather a new, single, comprehensive statement based on the conjunction of the theory and (5). This *new* substitute is again guaranteed to preserve all the observational content of the latter conjunction. The variable 'ϕ' which is now associated with *a* links up directly with its recurrences in the new substitute, since all such recurrences fall within the same scope of the initial quantifier '$(\exists \phi)$'.

The problem of linkage between theory and singular theoretical attribution seems thus to be solved once we keep clearly in mind *what* original is being considered, and avoid adding separate Ramseyan substitutes for separate components of this original. The point may be put differently: For any strengthening of a given original theory by addition of singular theoretical premises, there is a Ramseyan substitute which preserves all the observational consequences of the strengthened theory. There is thus no degree of power to generate observational content, which is possessed by original theories through singular attributions, and which is not also possessed by their bona fide Ramseyan substitutes.

It is, nonetheless, of interest to note that when the new Ramseyan substitute is constructed for the theory of magnets plus (5), what corresponds to (5) will be not the *sentence* (6), but the *clause*[8] 'ϕa', within the scope of the initial quantifier '$(\exists\phi)$'. Put otherwise, the transition from (4) to the new substitute, which is motivated by addition of (5) to the original theory, consists in the conjoining of 'ϕa' to the other clauses of (4) governed by '$(\exists\phi)$'. Generally, given a particular Ramseyan statement, we are able to expand it to absorb singular theoretical attributions, in the sense that we may supplement it with intrascope clauses, similar to 'ϕa'. Thus, the criticism that Ramseyan substitutes are deficient in scientific utility through inability to cover singular theoretical attributions may be countered. For though such attributions are here embodied in clauses rather than isolable statements, the net result in observational content, as well as for practical purposes, appears to be the same.

The general idea of handling clauses as units of scientific inference and communication has been treated in Bohnert's study, and its consequences for semantics and pragmatics suggestively explored. The inspiration is provided by Ramsey himself, who says:

> Any additions to the theory, whether in the form of new axioms or particular assertions . . . are to be made within

---

[8] The term is Bohnert's (*ibid.*).

the scope [of the initial quantifiers]. They are not, therefore, strictly propositions by themselves just as the different sentences in a story beginning 'Once upon a time' have not complete meanings and so are not propositions by themselves. . . .

So far, however, as *reasoning* is concerned, that [we have no] complete propositions makes no difference, provided we interpret all logical combination as taking place within the scope of a single prefix . . . For we can reason about the characters in a story just as well as if they were really identified, provided we don't take part of what we say as about one story, part about another.[9]

We ignore here the technical issues involved in setting up a general theory of inference and communication using clauses as units. One point of interpretation should, however, be noted. It is, in a sense, misleading to say what was said earlier, i.e., that the clause 'ϕa' corresponds to the singular assertion (5), 'a is a magnet'. For the clause itself asserts nothing and attributes nothing. *In context,* it attributes to a the very same property which the whole sentence asserts to exist *and* to satisfy those conditions represented by other clauses. This means that the clause itself is as much theoretical as singular. Similarly, it represents one of the conditions the sentence claims is satisfied by the theoretical property asserted to exist. Thus, the other clauses are not "isolable," either, all the clauses representing so many conditions on the property ϕ, asserted by the whole sentence to exist. It might thus be said that the line between *general theoretical* and *singular theoretical* components of science is erased by the Ramseyan construction, in any significant sense. But there is here no argument, so far, to show this construction therefore deficient in scientific utility.

We need, now, however, to consider the question of inductive arguments, which provided an obstacle to the Craigian strategy considered in the previous section. There, the difficulty was that the Craigian substitute failed to preserve the inductive connec-

---

[9] Ramsey, *The Foundations of Mathematics,* pp. 231-232.

tions among *E*-statements sustained by its original. The failure resulted, as we saw, from the substitute's lack of theoretical premises upon which certain inductive links depended.

To explore the matter in relation to Ramseyan substitutes, we shall revert to the illustration of the previous section. (To avoid conflict with the numbering of sentences in the present section, we shall refer to sentences of this illustration by corresponding Roman numerals.) The initial four sentences were as follows:

(I)   The parts obtained by breaking a rod-shaped magnet in two are again magnets. In symbols:

$$(x)(y)(z) \ ((Bxyz \cdot Mz \cdot Rz) \supset Mx \cdot My)$$

(II)   If *x* is a magnet, then whenever a small piece y of iron filing is brought into contact with *x*, then y clings to *x*. Symbolically:

$$(x) \ (Mx \supset (y) (Fxy \supset Cxy))$$

(III)   Objects *b* and *c* were obtained by breaking object *a* in two, and *a* was a magnet and rod-shaped. In symbols:

$$Bbca \cdot Ma \cdot Ra$$

(IV)   If *d* is a piece of iron filing that is brought into contact with *b*, then *d* will cling to *b*. Symbolically:

$$Fbd \supset Cbd$$

Additional sentences referred to were:

(V)   *a* was a magnet. Symbolically:

$$Ma$$

(VI)   *e* is a piece of iron filing brought into contact with *a* and *e* clings to *a*, and so for *f* and *m*, etc. Symbolically:

$$(Fae \cdot Cae) \cdot (Faf \cdot Caf) \cdot \ldots \cdot (Fam \cdot Cam)$$

(VIII)   *b* and *c* were obtained by breaking *a* in two and *a* was rod-shaped. Symbolically:

$$Bbca \cdot Ra$$

The argument, it will be recalled, was that the singular and observational conclusion (IV) follows deductively from (III), (I), and (II), but that (III) contains the theoretical subsentence (V), as well as the observational and singular (VIII). Subsentence (V) is, however, inductively supported by (VI), in virtue of (II). Thus (III) as a whole is (inductively) supported by the observational and singular base consisting of (VI) and (VIII). The critical chain of reasoning thus consists of two parts: (1) the first from (VI) + (VIII) to (III), depending on (II), and (2) the second from (III) to (IV), depending on both (I) and (II). In the case of the Craigian substitute, this chain was broken through lack of (I) and (II) as theorems.

To simplify our discussion, we shall not consider the variety of original systems discussed in the last section. We take as our original here simply (I) and (II). The Ramseyan substitute will then be equivalent to:

(IX) $(\exists \phi) (z) \; \{[\phi z \supset (x) (y) \; (Bxyz \cdot Rz \supset$
         $\phi x \cdot \phi y)] \cdot [\phi z \supset (v) \; (Fzv \supset Czv)]\}$

The question now is whether (IX) enables inductive support to accrue to (IV) from (VI) and (VIII). In particular, let us ask whether we can here go from (VI) to 'ϕa', as we went from (VI) to (V) with the original theory.

Note how the present question differs from that of *singular theoretical attribution,* earlier discussed. There, the problem was to reflect in Ramseyan manner the fact that *theoretical* terms are applied to instances in such a way as to generate new observational content from the linkage of general theory and its applications to cases. The problem was met by joining singular and general clauses within the same quantifier scopes, and avoiding the conjunction of separate Ramseyan substitutes for separate components of the original in which given theoretical terms recur, whether these components be general or singular.

Here, (VI) is *not theoretical* but *observational* (and moreover generates no *new* observational consequences by being conjoined to (I)-(II)). Whether we represent the original, (I)-(II), plus (VI), by (IX) plus (VI), or by an expanded (IX), including (VI) as an intra-scope component, is a matter of complete indifference, since (VI) contains no variable governed by the initial quantifier of (IX), being unaltered by Ramseyan processing. (The same clearly holds for (VI) plus (VIII), which are both needed to support (III), but we may focus here on (VI) alone.)

Whereas the earlier problem was one of ensuring that Ramseyan-substitute variables were linked through scope, the present problem is to link a putative intra-scope clause containing a variable (i.e., 'ϕa') with an observational sentence containing no variable, (i.e., (VI)). Now, this problem appears literally senseless, for 'ϕa' is not a statement at all, and so can receive no confirming support whatever; what would it mean to say that 'ϕa' was in fact true? Were this view of the matter decisive, (IX) might well be said to be deficient in utility by comparison with (I)-(II). As in the case of the Craigian substitute, it might now be said that the greater strength of the original ensures its greater utility by forcing it out on more inductive limbs.

We may, however, try to interpret the process of confirmation in such a way as to allow for the wanted inductive linkage. Instead of thinking of 'ϕa' as the unit to be confirmed, we may suppose rather that we are confirming 'ϕa'-as-governed-by-the-quantifier-prefix-of-(IX). (IX) says that some ϕ fulfills certain conditions, and we take (VI) to indicate that exemplification by a is another condition on ϕ. We, in effect, take (VI) as supporting the *inclusion* of 'ϕa' within the main scope of (IX). Since, as we saw above, the line between general and singular theoretical assertions is blurred in Ramseyan form, we might, perhaps, wish to construe (VI) as supporting the whole expanded (IX) (though the intuitive basis for asserting such specific support in this case is obscure).

An analogous case dealing with individual variables may perhaps be illuminating. Investigating a problematic death, a detective reasons thus:

(D)   Someone x deliberately brought about this death and anyone doing so would have been in the vicinity at the appropriate time, and would have been in a hurry to get away shortly thereafter. Now someone hurrying from the scene shortly after the time of death was seen to have been wearing a blue raincoat. Probably x wore a blue raincoat.

The conclusion 'x wore a blue raincoat' is not a deductive consequence of the detective's premises but, at best, inductively supported by them. However, in itself, it is not a sentence at all. Nor is its purport to say merely '$(\exists x)$ (x wore a blue raincoat)'. Rather, it claims that the x in question is also responsible for the crime, i.e., 'x wore a blue raincoat' is construed as falling, along with 'x deliberately caused this death', within the scope of the prefix 'Someone'.

We now need, however, to face an important difficulty. Consider the theory:

(9) $(x) \, ((Mx \supset Px) \cdot (Mx \supset Rx))$

where only 'M' is theoretical, and consider its Ramseyan substitute:

(10) $(\exists \phi)(x) \, ((\phi x \supset Px) \cdot (\phi x \supset Rx))$.

The theory (9) is not "analytic" nor a "logical truth," though it has no ("non-analytic") observational consequences. (10) also has no observational consequences, but it is, furthermore, "analytic" or logically true (in higher, non-nominalistic logic) in that some interpretation can be found for 'ϕ' which will make (10) true no matter how its constants 'P' and 'R' are interpreted.

The Ramseyan substitute (10) says that *some* ϕ is such that, for every x, if x is ϕ then it is P, and if it is ϕ, then it is R. But this is true no matter how 'P' and 'R' are interpreted. For let x be ϕ if and only if x is both P and R. Then, everything x will be such that it is not ϕ or it is P and also R. In other words, (10) is true in any case. (Furthermore, 'ϕ' is here interpreted in such a way as not to *require* it to be null.)

Suppose, now, that we examine a given object a, and find:

(11)   *Ra.*

Using (9), we may take (11) as an inductive sign that:

(12)   *Ma*

is true, and, combining (12) with (9), we may now deduce:

(13)   *Pa.*

Theory (9), in other words, employs the theoretical '*M*' to tie '*P*' and '*R*' together.

But, using (10) rather than (9), can we take (11) to indicate 'ϕa' inductively, and again proceed to (13)?

According to the interpretation suggested above, we should be able to interpret the process as one by which (11) confirms:

(14) $(\exists \phi)(x) \ ((\phi x \supset Px) \cdot (\phi x \supset Rx) \cdot (\phi a))$,

a statement which yields (13) deductively, and which is no longer "analytic" itself. But the trouble is that (10) is "analytic," i.e., true irrespective of all reinterpretations of '*P*' and '*R*'. It is thus equally true that:

(15) $(\exists \phi)(x) \ ((\phi x \supset \sim Px) \cdot (\phi x \supset Rx))$

If (11) is an inductive sign that '*Pa*' is true (i.e., (13)), using (10) as a premise, then (11) ought by the same token to be an inductive sign that:

(16) $\sim Pa$

is true, using (15) as a premise. We have thus no ground for supposing that (11) provides any selective confirmatory support for (13) whatsoever.

The case of the original theory (9) is vastly different. For though it has no observational consequences, it is not logically true or "analytic," and, if true, cannot be presumed to remain true when altered to yield:

(17) $(x) \ ((Mx \supset \sim Px) \cdot (Mx \supset Rx))$

Accepting (9) therefore, we need not also accept (17), and so can take '*Ra*' as providing selective support for '*Pa*'. The inductive superiority of (9) over (10) seems thus to be patent.

Nor will it do to expand our conception of the substitute (10), as we expanded the substitute earlier to meet the problem of singular *theoretical* attributions. For the additional premise '*Ra*', here, is observational and is not governed by the quantifier '$(\exists \phi)$' of (10). Thus, if

(18) $(\exists \phi)(x) \, ((\phi x \supset Px) \cdot (\phi x \supset Rx) \cdot (Ra))$

is true, so is:

(19) $(\exists \phi)(x) \, ((\phi x \supset \sim Px) \cdot (\phi x \supset Rx) \cdot (Ra))$

and if (18) gives inductive support to (14) and thereafter to '*Pa*', (19) gives equal support to:

(20) $(\exists \phi)(x) \, ((\phi x \supset \sim Px) \cdot (\phi x \supset Rx) \cdot (\phi a))$

and thereafter to '$\sim Pa$'.

We seem forced to conclude that the greater strength of the original (9) gives it greater inductive utility. Nor is the example we have just considered unique in this respect, nor too simple to be taken seriously. In fact, if we look back again at an example discussed in another connection in Section 3 of Part I above, we shall find an analogous result.[1]

We take for consideration a theory *Th* consisting of the following statements:

(i)	$(x) \, (Px \supset Gx)$
(ii)	$(x) \, (Px \supset Tx)$
(iii)	$(x) \, (Px \supset Vx)$
(iv)	$(x) \, (Px \supset Ex)$
(v)	$(x) \, (Px \supset Sx)$
(vi)	$(x) \, (Ix \supset Fx)$
(vii)	$(x) \, (Px \supset Ix)$

Statements (i)-(v) jointly tell us that every specimen of white phosphorus has a garlic-like odor, is soluble in turpentine, in vegetable oils, and in ether, and produces skin burns. Statement (vi) tells us that anything with an ignition temperature of 30° C. bursts into flame when surrounded by air in which a thermome-

---

[1] Our earlier treatment introduced some special refinements of this example but, for present purposes, we may employ it in its original form, as given by Hempel, "The Theoretician's Dilemma," pp. 78-79.

ter shows a reading above 30° C. Statement (vii), finally, informs us that white phosphorus has an ignition temperature of 30° C.

In this example, just '*P*' and '*I*' are considered theoretical terms, all the others being observational. Now, *Th* is, as a whole, not "analytic," though it has no observational consequences (that are also "non-analytic"). Nonetheless, it allows a plausible inductive step of the following sort. Given an object *b* satisfying the consequents of (i)-(v), i.e., given the truth of:

(viii) $Gb \cdot Tb \cdot Vb \cdot Eb \cdot Sb$

we assume, as an inductive guess, the truth of:

(ix) $Pb.$

Once having the latter, we combine it with (vii), to yield (deductively):

(x) Ib

and we combine (x), in turn, with (vi), to yield:

(xi) Fb

as a deductive consequence, of an observational sort.

Now the Ramseyan version of *Th* is equivalent to:

R(th) $(\exists\phi)(\exists\psi)(x) \ \{(\phi x \supset \psi x) \cdot [\phi x \supset$
         $(Gx \cdot Tx \cdot Vx \cdot Ex \cdot Sx)] \cdot (\psi x \supset Fx)\}$

where 'ϕ' replaces '*P*', and 'ψ' replaces '*I*'. R(th), also, yields no observational (and "non-analytic") consequences, but, unlike *Th,* it is itself "analytic," i.e., true irrespective of specific interpretation of its constants, on some mode of interpretation of 'ϕ' and 'ψ'.

For let ϕ be taken as the intersection of *F* and *G* and *T* and *V* and *E* and *S* (no matter how the latter are interpreted), and let ψ be identified with *F*. (That is to say, let *x* be ϕ if and only if *x* is *F* and *G* and *T* and *V* and *E* and *S*, and let *x* be ψ if and only if *x* is *F*.) Then the first clause of R(th) will hold of everything, for whatever is *F* and *G* and *T* and *V* and *E* and *S* is surely *F*. The second clause will also hold true of everything, since whatever is

F and *G* and *T* and *V* and *E* and *S* is *G* and *T* and *V* and *E* and *S*. Finally, the third clause will hold of everything, since whatever is *F* is *F*. R(th) is, then, true in any event (and '*φ*' and '*ψ*' are not required to be null by the interpretations fixed for them here).

Can we now proceed, as before, from (viii) to (xi)? Can we go from (viii) to '*φb*', and thence to '*ψb*', and lastly, to '*Fb*', where '*F*' is now interpreted *specifically* as applying to things bursting into flame in air above 30° C.? To sanction such a step, appealing to the truth of R(th), would be arbitrary unless we sanctioned every analogous step involving some other specific interpretation of '*F*'. In particular, the statement:

R(th)* $(\exists\phi)(\exists\psi)(x)\ \{(\phi x \supset \psi x) \cdot [\phi x \supset$
                $(Gx \cdot Tx \cdot Vx \cdot Ex \cdot Sx)] \cdot (\psi x \supset \sim Fx)\}$

is also true, though the original '*F*' has been reinterpreted here as applying to all things non-*F*, i.e., all things *not* bursting into flame in air above 30° C. Here, however, (viii) leads inductively to '*φb*', thence to '*ψb*', and, finally, to:

(xii) $\sim Fb$

which is the negation of (xi). R(th) thus gives us no selective, i.e., genuine, inductive support for (xi) as against (xii). Again, we seem compelled to acknowledge the inductive superiority of *Th* over its Ramseyan substitute R(th).

We have already seen that simply expanding the Ramseyan substitute does not solve the problem as it seemed to do for the case of singular *theoretical* attributions. Nor does there seem any obvious and uniform way of otherwise strengthening the substitute in such a way as to meet the problem. It thus seems hard to avoid the conclusion that Ramseyan substitutes are not always inductively equal to their originals. Certainly, also (and unlike their Craigian counterparts), they require a stronger ontological base than their originals, as earlier pointed out. In sum, though by comparison with Craigian substitutes they retain an integration comparable to their respective originals, they appear beset by their own problems of ontological strength and inductive weakness.

PART III

Confirmation

1. Explanation, Significance, and Confirmation

Explanation has been construed as a matter of subsuming particulars under laws, and has been taken widely as requiring formulation in cognitively significant terms. The notions of law and of significance seem both, it has been suggested, interpretable by means of the idea of confirmation: laws may be described as (true) generalizations capable of receiving confirmatory support from their positive instances, in this respect unlike (true) "accidental" generalizations (e.g., 'All the people in this house are between 5'7" and 5'10½ " in height'), which do not gain in credibility with each known positive instance. Significant sentences, in their turn, may be described as those confirmable or disconfirmable through observation, i.e., sensitive to observational test.

Both interpretations have, however, encountered serious obstacles. We have seen, in the last Part, the difficulties involved in criteria of significance resting upon the idea of a link with observation sentences. We have further noted the willingness of fictionalistic philosophies to grant that certain portions of science are useful and, moreover, sensitive to observational test, though not literally significant. Significance would thus seem to be not merely a function of sensitivity to observational test, construed as an independent criterion of confirmability. Confirmability itself, it would seem, is not simply a matter of sensitivity to observational test, but is rather to be *understood* as restricted to *significant* sentences; it cannot, then, *explain* significance.

As to the interpretation of laws noted above, the seemingly clear concept of confirmability through positive instances has turned out to be difficult to analyze, and, indeed, the very notion of a positive instance has yielded unsuspected puzzles approaching paradox. The difficulties besetting the two interpretations mentioned seem, however, perhaps different in effect. To explain significance in terms of some independent criterion of confirmability or disconfirmability without ultimate circularity seems unlikely, in view of the considerations noted in the last paragraph. On the other hand, no such circularity seems similarly to threaten the interpretation of law: were we to succeed in giving a satisfactory account of the conditions under which instances confirm their generalizations, we should then be able plausibly to interpret laws as those true generalizations satisfying such conditions, and, hence, as those whose instances confirm them.

Since explanation involves *laws* (and not simply generalizations), analyzing confirmation promises, further, to illuminate the idea of explanation. Further, since a lawlike generalization is confirmed by its known instances and itself applies to further instances, these known instances simultaneously support the generalization and an indefinite number of posits besides. Such a generalization may, in fact, be interpreted as a policy, adopted on the basis of available evidence, for dealing with actual cases that lie beyond the evidence. Accidental generalizations, by contrast, do not appear to gather support from their known instances, nor do these instances support corresponding posits: granted, for example, that the residents of this house *so far examined* fall between 5'7" and 5'8" in height or else have been to Pisa, we should not wish to posit that Smith, a new resident, must have been to Pisa since he is six feet tall.

Lawlike generalizations serve, further, to guide our judgment of hypothetical cases: 'If that pencil *had been* a magnet, it *would have* attracted the iron filings lying near it'; this assertion is supported by a generalization about magnets, which we take to be not only true but lawlike as well. By contrast, even if we have examined all residents of a given house, from the time it was built until the time it was torn down, and determined that all were between 5'7" and 5'10½" in height, we should not say, for example, that had Centerville's seven-foot-tall basketball hero been a resident of this house, he too would have been between 5'7" and 5'10½" in height. An analysis of confirmation thus seems likely to illuminate explanations (or, more broadly, substantiations) as well as posits and judgments of hypothetical cases, for all these seem to involve lawlike generalizations.[1]

We have suggested that such generalizations might be construed as policies for judging actual as well as hypothetical cases. We must not, however, confuse the generalizations themselves with their uses in the construction of particular judgments. Though they may be represented as policies for dealing with cases, they may, *in themselves,* also be represented as satisfying the scientist's search for a network of true principles providing a comprehensive account of the world. Nonetheless, it is not enough for these principles to be *true;* they must be *lawlike* as well. Though the scientist need not be pictured as a man primarily concerned with the judgment of particular cases, the network of principles he takes as an account of the world is one he considers capable of guiding such judgment.

The principles adopted at any given time may thus be regarded as, in an important sense, intermediary, resting upon available data as to particulars, and serving to channel our judgments regarding further particulars. Such a conception is widespread, and we have, in Part I, noted its background in Hume's analyses. There, however, our concern was explanation; we shall review the matter briefly from the perspective of our present interest in confirmation.

2. Hume's Challenge and the Generalization Formula

The starting point for modern discussions of confirmation, and inductive reasoning generally, is Hume's denial of necessary

---

[1] On these points, see Nelson Goodman, "The Problem of Counterfactual Conditionals," *Journal of Philosophy*, XLIV (1947), 113-128; reprinted in *Fact, Fiction, and Forecast* (Cambridge, Mass.: Harvard University Press, 1955), chap. i, pp. 13-34.

connections of matters of fact: between data recorded in our evidence and particular judgments regarding cases not yet examined there is a breach which deductive inference is powerless to overcome. Effects cannot be simply deduced from their causes, nor can predictions be logically demonstrated on the basis of available evidence garnered from past experience. If, however, the truth of our predictions is not guaranteed by deduction from accumulated evidence, what can be their rational justification? This challenge to justify induction (or non-demonstrative inference), arising out of Hume's analysis, has evoked a variety of replies from philosophers.

Leaving aside the response of skeptics, who are willing to make the verbal admission that all induction is indeed without rational foundation, and that of unregenerate deductivists, who strive vainly to show Hume's analysis wrong, we find several types of philosophic reaction. One approach is to postulate some overarching principle of uniformity, attributed either to nature or to the mind, which may be added to special inductive premises to fill out deductively the argument from data to prediction. This approach has been subjected to severe criticism on a number of counts. If the original problem was to justify inductive conclusions since these are not logically deducible from the body of available data, the principle of uniformity itself stands in need of the same justification, for it, too, is not deducible from the data.

To treat it as a fundamental presupposition of all inductive inference does not, moreover, provide a relevant answer to the problem, for presuppositions may or may not themselves be justified, irrespective of what *they* serve to justify *if* they are taken for granted. The question thus remains as to how the principle of uniformity is *itself* justified, granting, for the sake of argument, its status as a presupposition of induction. If it is not itself justified, we have no reason for accepting it and so cannot use it to justify particular inductions. If it be said that it does not *require* justification, the same might more easily be said of the more modest particular inductions from which the problem arose; the problem is here, in effect, postponed only to be rejected rather than solved. On the other hand, if the principle *is* itself to be justified, *independent* considerations must be introduced for this purpose, considerations which might be naturally assumed to justify the particular inductions directly. In any event, the justifying argument will now rest not on the principle, but on these considerations themselves.

There is still a further basic difficulty in supposing a principle of uniformity to underlie induction. Not all characteristics of cases described in our available data are expected to hold true of the unknown cases in which we are interested. (In the example of the last section, we did not expect Smith to have the property of being between 5'7" and 5'8" tall or having visited Pisa; we surely could not have supposed him to share the space-time locations of examined residents, or to have the property of being identical with one of them.) To be relevant at all, the principle would thus need to be carefully circumscribed, on pain of justifying too much.

Further, supposing this requirement met, the proposed justification would still be too strong, for it would, if successful, turn proper inductive arguments into deductions. Given true statements as data, the predictions yielded with the help of the principle would, in every case, be true; conversely, a false prediction would indicate false data to begin with. In fact, however, we do not suppose our (proper) inductive conclusions to be true or else derived from false data. Rather, we consider it not only possible, but frequent, that a reasonable inductive conclusion from accurate data turns out to be false. Such an eventuality *may,* for example, be taken to show that some (reasonable) theoretical hypothesis needs to be withdrawn, not necessarily that the evidential data must have been false, or else that the reasoning itself was improper. To suppose otherwise is to suppose that inductive propriety requires us to anticipate nature in such a way as always to come out right; such propriety could never be judged before the fact, at least with complete confidence that the judgment was itself proper, in the same sense, in its prediction of success. On the other hand, if such judgment be said to be warrantable as proper, even though complete confidence in success is lacking before the event, some weaker standard of propriety here is being used, of the sort normally associated with inductive reasoning. Such a weaker standard is what requires justification. For such a standard is theoretically applicable, *before* the event, to our anticipations of nature, which may or may not turn out successful. But what justifies such a standard?

A second approach offers the forthright answer: past experience. Consider all those specific procedures by which we decide among alternative predictions, before the event, in all scientific domains. This set is, as a whole, justified by its past successes: having employed it in making previous predictions which have, on the whole, come out true, we are now rationally justified in using it to formulate our current predictions, since they too will, on the whole, come out true.

This approach has seemed to most critics to beg the question. The problem, after all, arose from the fact that our predictions are not logically demonstrable on the basis of past experience, and so cannot be guaranteed true by reference to such experience. If it is felt that such a situation is unsatisfactory unless some further, special justification is provided, the present proposal hardly improves the situation. For the proposal simply assumes that the past successes of our predictive procedures, as recorded in our current evidence, warrant us in predicting that these procedures will be successful in the future as well. But the latter prediction is itself not logically demonstrable on the basis of current evidence, any more than the particular predictions giving rise to the problem in the first place. We have, it turns out, justified the making of these particular predictions by assuming precisely the doubtful point at issue.

Another approach takes the view that we make predictions purporting to be *probable,* rather than *true,* in the light of the available evidence. Thus, proper induction indeed does *not* require that the prediction be satisfied by the actual outcome, in any given case. Rather, we attach a certain, sufficiently high, probability to the predicted event if a sufficiently large proportion of comparable events has already been determined, within a suitable wider class of alternative events. We are justified in making our individual prediction, then, since analogous predictions will be right in a high proportion of cases, as against their alternatives.

Here again, however, we have assumed the principle at issue in formulating the argument of justification. For this argument supposes that the relative proportions of alternative events under consideration may be predicted to be, in the future, what they have been recorded as being, in the past. But such a prediction is surely not logically deducible from the recorded evidence. This approach is actually quite similar to the previous one we have considered, in that a general predictive policy is first projected into the future on the basis of past experience, and particular predictions are then justified by reference to the policy in question. No more than the previous approach, however, does the present one avoid a begging of the question.

In the light of the serious troubles affecting the above answers to Hume's challenge, radical measures have more and more been favored in recent years. For the previous replies have, in fact, been extravagantly rationalistic in their assumptions: they have accepted too much as known, and have put too much store in deduction as a paradigm of justification. We have detailed this double extravagance in the proposal of a uniformity principle, which would have the effect of turning proper inductive arguments into deductions, and the further consequence that predictions concerning unexamined cases might be guaranteed true on the basis of true recorded data.

The other two approaches, appealing to the previous successes of our predictive procedures, or to the previous relative frequency of events comparable to the predicted event, also display the same sort of extravagance, even though they allow that any *particular* prediction may be false although based on true data. For each of these approaches assumes that the past efficacy of a predictive *policy* (either specified independently or by reference to past relative frequencies) guarantees its future efficacy. Thus, each approach rules out the possibility that true data affirming the past efficacy *of this policy* may properly yield a false prediction of its future efficacy.

But, as Hume's original analysis shows, we do not, in fact,

know how to guarantee the truth of any judgment of an unexamined case on the basis of recorded cases. It is no wonder, then, that a purportedly guaranteeing principle of uniformity itself lacks guarantees, nor is it surprising that particular predictions cannot be justified, even in a weaker sense than demonstrability, by appeal to a *policy* allegedly guaranteed to continue efficacious for unexamined intervals under consideration.

However inductive judgments are to be justified, then, they must all be acknowledged to lack airtight guarantees based on available data. No matter how justified, they may turn out false in fact, despite being based on true statements of the evidence. This feature is, indeed, what distinguishes them from deductive conclusions. But, and here is one radical proposal, the assumption that ideal rational justification *requires* some kind of deductive guarantee must be totally rejected, whether the guarantee be applied to particular predictions or to the policies that guide them. On the contrary, the normal and proper use of such expressions as 'rational', 'reasonable', 'justified', 'based on good reasons', etc., sanctions their application to statements referring to unexamined cases and, hence, to statements *not* deducible from accumulated data.

As interpreted by the previous approaches discussed, Hume's challenge to justify inductive conclusions is a demand for some sort of deductive rationale underlying such conclusions. This, however, is an extravagant, because impossible, demand. The proper response is therefore a rejection of it rather than an attempt to satisfy it. Once it is rejected, we are no longer tempted to think of induction as a kind of defective deduction. We recognize that the concept of justification is *genuinely* applicable in the first instance not only to arguments which satisfy deductive criteria, but also to arguments which do *not* satisfy deductive criteria—carrying us beyond what is deducible from their premises.

The idea just outlined has been characterized as radical, and indeed it is radical relative to the approaches earlier considered, in rejecting not only their assumptions, but also the very problem presented by Hume's challenge, *as they conceived it*. There is an important sense, however, in which the present idea is not radical: it may be plausibly interpreted as a return to Hume's own conceptions. For, as we have already seen, Hume was perfectly clear about the lack of advance guarantees of the truth of our predictions. He was equally clear that no manner of justifying our inductive conclusions could preclude their turning out false after all. He was thus not demanding a deductive rationale underlying induction, and, in fact, he offers his analysis as a proof that reasoning from cause to effect is not purely deductive but requires experience. To recall a passage already quoted (in Section 1 of Part I), "Having found, in many instances, that any two kinds of objects—flame and heat, snow and cold—have always been conjoined together; if flame or snow be presented anew to the senses, the mind is carried by custom to expect heat or cold, and to *believe* that such a quality does exist, and will discover itself upon a nearer approach."

Inductive reasoning is conceived as reflecting the mind's development of a habit, connecting the expectation of one quality with the occurrence of another, following frequent conjunction of the two qualities in past experience. Any attempt to ground the expectation mentioned, by means of deduction from the occurrence of the quality previously conjoined with it, must surely fail. But, calling upon past experience, we can determine whether a given inductive conclusion accords with the typical manner of the mind's operation, that is, whether it accords with a habit based on past conjunctions, or not.

This Humean conception of the matter is very much the same as the radical proposal of recent years, though the latter shifts from psychological to linguistic terminology. Instead of speaking of the mind's forming of habits, this recent proposal refers rather to the normal uses of the terms 'justified', 'based on good reasons', and so forth. The upshot is, however, quite similar: inductive arguments carry us to conclusions which outstrip available evidence, and they are not grounded in any deductive rationale. Rather, they belong to a more inclusive class of arguments to which we find ourselves impelled to assent, and whose characterization requires appeal to some factor beyond deduction, either the typical habit-forming propensity of the mind, or the typical uses of justificatory terms.[2]

Indeed, Hume's characterization goes considerably beyond the recent linguistic approach we have been considering. The latter simply points out that the normal use of justificatory terms applies these terms to statements beyond the deductive reach of the evidence. This observation, though true, is woefully inadequate. For not every statement beyond the deductive reach of the evidence is justified, though some are. Outstripping the evidence is, to be sure, no bar to justification, but neither does it guarantee justification. The question thus remains as to the basis, i.e., the conditions, of justification of inductive arguments. If we are to answer this question, we must go on to formulate the specific criteria by which some inductions are justified as reasonable, while others are rejected as unreasonable, though both groups outstrip the available evidence. It is this task which Hume indeed undertakes, in his theory of habit formation; he says, in effect, that the uniform, past conjunction of events constitutes a criterion which marks some inductions off from all the rest as those we find compelling, in virtue of their forming a habit.

This idea is also represented by a modern version, which has found wide favor not only among philosophers, but among scientists as well. According to this modern version, predictions are made in conformity with general theories that have worked in the past. There is here no implication that past success *guarantees* future success, but only the suggestion that the past success of theories provides a *criterion* for singling out those predictions regarded as justified at any given time. What leads us to make one particular prediction rather than its opposite is not its deducibility from evidence, but rather its congruence with a generalization thoroughly in accord with all such evidence, and (hence) the correlative disconfirmation of the contrary generalization by the same evidence. This idea will be referred to here

[2] The contribution of the recent approach may, nevertheless, be its insistence that inductive support of particular conclusions constitutes justification in the only appropriate sense.

as "the generalization formula," and will be examined in our following discussions.

Of course, if no relevant evidence is available to decide between a given generalization and its contrary, or if the available evidence is mixed, neither generalization will support a particular inductive conclusion. But it is only to be expected that every limited body of evidence will fail to decide between *some* generalization and its contrary, and, hence, that we will generally not be able to choose between *every* particular prediction and its opposite. It is sufficient, therefore, for a formulation of the criteria of induction to show how *certain* bodies of evidence enable us to decide between *certain* conflicting inductions. This the generalization formula seems to accomplish. For, if the evidence consistently supports a given generalization, then the contrary generalization would seem to be *ipso facto* disqualified, and our particular inductive conclusions selected for us. There are, of course, details to be taken care of, relating to such matters as the calculation of degrees of support which generalizations may derive from available evidence, but, in principle, we seem to have our answer to the challenge of induction.

This estimate has, however, been thoroughly upset by recent investigations. We shall outline some of the critical developments in the following sections. The leading question underlying these developments should, however, be noted here, by reference to the generalization formula. According to the latter, inductive justification rests on appeal to *generalizations that are consistently, hence selectively, supported by the evidence* at hand. Such generalizations are analogous to the *habits* of which Hume spoke as based upon regular conjunctions in past experience, and selective of expectations for the future. They are, moreover, conceived as identifiable with the lawlike, general principles of the scientist, which guide not only his expectations, but his judgments of unknown and hypothetical cases generally, his explanations and substantiations of particular events, and his representations of the world.

These principles, not deducible from available evidence, have nonetheless worked in the past, and so may be said to *rest on* experience, to be borne out or confirmed by the evidence. But what, exactly, *is* this relationship between generalization and evidence, which is indicated by the expressions 'rests on', 'is supported by', and their numerous variants? This is the basic question motivating recent critical studies of *confirmation,* which have revealed obscurities in the very notion of a generalization's positive instances, and have, moreover, radically upset the idea that uniformly positive instances constitute the base upon which scientific generalizations rest.

We shall, indeed, organize the account to follow by considering the latter two points in relatively independent fashion. First, we shall ask what it means to say that a bit of evidence accords with, or represents a positive instance of, a given generalization. For the generalization formula maintains that those generalizations are selected which are thoroughly in accord with all available evidence, i.e., for which such evidence consistently contains positive instances in every relevant case.

Secondly, we shall ask whether the notion of positive support by instances, in the manner outlined, is indeed sufficient to characterize the selection of generalizations through experience. We have already noted, for example (in the previous section), the *prima facie* difference between lawlike and accidental generalizations, only the former apparently confirmable by instances. Should such a difference itself prove resistant to explanation in terms of the generalization formula, it would clearly show the formula to be too inclusive. It would, further, indicate the need for an independent analysis of the conditions of confirmability, so as to rule out the selection of accidental generalizations. But this phase of the problem will concern us only after we have dealt with the question of instances which may properly be said to accord with a given generalization.

3. Hempel's Study of Qualitative Confirmation

The task before us now is to state the conditions under which a statement represents a positive instance of a generalization, i.e., accords with it. We begin by reviewing C. G. Hempel's important study of the problem.[3] In conformity with his usage, we shall formulate this problem as one of defining '*e* confirms *h*'. This latter phrase is natural from the standpoint of the generalization formula, which views the confirmation of a generalization in terms of instances that accord with it. We have above indicated, however, that this view is itself to be critically examined in the sequel. Thus, it is important to avoid begging the question here, as to whether or not every instance that *accords with* a hypothesis *h* in fact *confirms* it. We shall, therefore, need to exercise care in using Hempel's terminology to discuss his study; we shall understand by '*e* confirms *h*' simply '*e* accords with *h*', or '*e* represents a positive instance of *h*'. The further question whether the *selection* of general hypotheses, i.e., their *confirmation,* may be adequately accounted for in the latter terms, is to be left entirely open for later discussion.

Hempel's concern in the study under consideration is *qualitative* rather than comparative or metrical. He is not here attempting to define a notion of more-or-less accord, enabling us to judge *h* as having *more* (or less or equal) *accord with e,* as compared to the accord of *h'* with *e'.* Nor is his purpose to define a measure of the degree to which *e* accords with *h.* He wants, rather, to define the conditions under which *e* accords with *h,* or represents a positive instance of *h.* Furthermore, his aim is decidedly not to propose rules for *generating h* out of *e;* in fact he holds this task to be an impossible one. What he wants is a definition which may be applied to a *given pair* of statements *e* and *h,* in such a way as to enable us to decide whether or not *e* accords with *h,* or, as he puts it, *e* confirms *h.* As a related aim, he wants analogous definitions for '*e* disconfirms *h*' (i.e., violates, is in contradiction with, or represents a negative instance of *h*), and '*e* is neutral with respect to *h*'.

Hempel presents a critique of two standard conceptions of confirmation, in the course of which he develops adequacy con-

[3] Carl G. Hempel, "A Purely Syntactical Definition of Confirmation," *Journal of Symbolic Logic,* VIII (1943), 122-143; and "Studies in the Logic of Confirmation," *Mind,* N.S., LIV (1945), (I) pp. 1-26; (II) pp. 97-121. By permission.

ditions he then tries to satisfy in framing his own definitions. The critique is, however, of considerable independent interest. The first conception he deals with is a very widespread one indeed; he takes for analysis, however, a particularly clear statement of it by Jean Nicod, labeling it 'Nicod's criterion'. This statement reads:

> Consider the formula or the law: *A entails B*. How can a particular proposition, or more briefly, a fact, affect its probability? If this fact consists of the presence of *B* in a case of *A,* it is favorable to the law '*A entails B*'; on the contrary, if it consists of the absence of *B* in a case of *A,* it is unfavourable to this law. It is conceivable that we have here the only two direct modes in which a fact can influence the probability of a law . . . Thus, the entire influence of particular truths or facts on the probability of universal propositions or laws would operate by means of these two elementary relations which we shall call *confirmation* and *invalidation*.[4]

It is worth noting, incidentally, how this passage exemplifies the generalization formula. The last sentence seems to assimilate laws to universal statements generally, and to suppose them uniformly *confirmed by* instances construed as positive. We must here again bear in mind the need to avoid begging the question whether or not additional factors (of confirmability) are required in order for *positive* instances to become *confirming* instances. Again, we shall therefore understand the first part of Nicod's criterion minimally, that is, as a rule for deciding when the evidence *accords with,* or *represents a positive instance of,* a general hypothesis.

Hempel points out that Nicod's statement limits his criterion to cases where the hypothesis has the form '*A entails B*'.[5] Symbolically, this form is rendered by Hempel as:

---

[4] Jean Nicod, *Foundations of Geometry and Induction,* trans. P. P. Wiener (London: Kegan Paul, Trench, Trubner & Co. Ltd., 1930), p. 219. By permission of the publisher.

[5] Hempel, "Studies in the Logic of Confirmation," (I) pp. 9-10.

(1) $(x) (Px \supset Qx)$ [Both not required by Nicod's statement]

and he interprets Nicod's criterion as holding, of any particular object, *a,* that it confirms (1) if and only if it satisfies both its antecedent and its consequent, disconfirms (1) if and only if it satisfies the antecedent but not the consequent, and is neutral with respect to (1) if and only if it does not satisfy the antecedent at all.

In other words,

(2) $Pa \cdot Qa$

represents confirming evidence for (1),

(3) $Pa \cdot \sim Qa$

represents a disconfirmation of (1), and both

(4) $\sim Pa \cdot Qa$

and

(5) $\sim Pa \cdot \sim Qa$

represent evidence neutral to (1) (thus making it unnecessary to determine *a*'s status with respect to the question whether or not it is *Q,* if *a* has already been determined to be not-*P*).

Hempel further suggests the extension of this idea to universal conditionals with more than one quantifier, e.g., 'Twins always resemble each other'—symbolically:

(6) $(x)(y) (Txy \supset Rxy)$

for in the latter case, the confirming instance need only be held to consist of an ordered pair of objects rather than a single object: such a pair is confirming if and only if it satisfies both the antecedent and consequent of (6), is disconfirming if and only if it satisfies only the antecedent of (6), and is neutral in every other case. (Analogous adjustments are indicated where the quantifiers exceed two in number.)

Hempel then proposes the following points in criticism of Nicod's criterion, as interpreted above. First, he suggests that any adequate criterion should be applicable to statements of any form, and not restricted to universal conditionals alone; in particular, it should apply also to existential statements and to statements with mixed quantifiers.

Secondly, with reference to the two statements:

(7) (x) (Raven x $\supset$ Black x)

and

(8) (x) ($\sim$ Black x $\supset$ $\sim$ Raven x)

Nicod's criterion rules that a black raven confirms (7) but not (8), to which it is neutral, since failing to satisfy its antecedent; similarly, a non-black non-raven is ruled to confirm (8) but not (7), to which it is neutral, in virtue of failing to satisfy *its* antecedent. But (7) and (8) are logically equivalent, and should thus bear exactly the same relationships to all instances. Nicod's criterion, on the contrary, makes confirmation dependent not only on the invariant "content" of a hypothesis, but also on its variable form. Further, every universal conditional has some equivalent for which *no* instance can be a confirming instance by Nicod's criterion. Thus, for example,

(9) (x) ((Raven x $\cdot$ $\sim$ Black x) $\supset$ (Raven x $\cdot$ $\sim$ Raven x))

is logically equivalent to (7) and (8), yet no object can confirm it, since none satisfies the self-contradictory condition expressed by its consequent. But surely, since logically equivalent to (7) and (8), (9) should not only *have* confirming instances, but it should have the *same* confirming instances as belong to (7) and (8). To summarize Hempel's second criticism, Nicod's criterion violates a requirement which may be taken as a general adequacy condition for definitions of confirmation: *the equivalence condition.* This condition demands that everything confirming any sentence confirm also every logically equivalent sentence.

On the basis of the two criticisms above described, Hempel rejects Nicod's criterion. However, such rejection does *not* mean that, for conditionals such as (7), for example, Nicod's criterion does not formulate a *sufficient* condition of confirmation. Indeed, it seems reasonable to hold that, for *such* conditionals (excluding those of more than one variable, for which Hempel produces a striking counterexample),[6] Nicod's rule does give a sufficient condition of confirmation. That is to say, if something does in fact meet the rule's specifications, satisfying both antecedent and consequent of some *h*, it is a confirming instance of *h*.

But here Hempel notes a surprising set of consequences, which he labels "paradoxes of confirmation," resulting from the joint adoption of the equivalence condition and of Nicod's rule as a sufficient condition. Consider, for example, an object *b*, satisfying both antecedent and consequent of (8). By Nicod's sufficient condition, *b* confirms (8). But (7) is logically equivalent to (8). Therefore, by the equivalence condition, *b* confirms (7) as well. However, *b* is a non-black non-raven; thus any such object, e.g., a gray chair, a red book, a green scarf, confirms the general hypothesis that all ravens are black. Moreover, consider another equivalent of (7), namely:

(10) (x) ((Raven x v ~Raven x) $\supset$ (~Raven x v Black x)).

By Nicod's sufficient condition, any object *c* confirms (10) if it is or is not a raven, and, in addition, is not a raven or black. In other words, any non-raven whatever, as well as any black object, confirms the hypothesis (7), that all ravens are black.

These so-called paradoxes of confirmation, emerging from the joint operation of perfectly plausible conditions, call into question our most natural conceptions of what it is that constitutes an *instance* of a generalization. It is no wonder that they have occa-

---

[6] *Ibid.*, p. 13, footnote 1. The counterexample is this: Consider:

(S1) (x) (y) $(\sim(Rxy \cdot Ryx) \supset (Rxy \cdot \sim Ryx))$

Then (S1) is equivalent to:

(S2) $(x)(y)$ (Rxy)

Now, given that *a* and *b* are such that *Rab* and ~*Rba,* the couple (a, b) satisfies both antecedent and consequent of (S1), and, by Nicod's criterion, thus is favorable to (S1). But since, by hypothesis, we have ~*Rba,* which flatly contradicts (S2), and hence (S1), the couple (a, b) clearly disconfirms (S1).

sioned a good deal of discussion, and have given rise to several alternative proposals for dealing with the situation. We shall discuss some of these proposals, and the problem in general, in later sections. Meanwhile, it is here sufficient to note that the equivalence condition is violated by Nicod's original statement, and the latter is therefore rejected by Hempel. He takes the equivalence condition as necessary for any adequate conception of confirmation, his reasons being that logically equivalent statements have the same content (i.e., imply the same consequences and follow from the same premises), and are freely interchanged, as merely formal variants, in scientific argument.

The second conception of confirmation criticized by Hempel is one that is based on the notion of prediction; he therefore refers to it as the prediction-criterion of confirmation. According to this conception, general hypotheses are confirmed by successful predictions based upon them. Thus, as Hempel explains, the hypothesis:

(11) (x) $((\text{Metal } x \cdot \text{Heated } x) \supset \text{Expands } x)$

yields the prediction:

(12)   Expands a

when supplemented by the premise:

(13)   Metal a · Heated a

Now, if the prediction (12) is in fact successful, as determined by observation, and added to the initially accepted observational premise (13), the total statement (13) + (12) will lend support to (11). Putting the matter another way, since (12) is logically derivable from (13) + (11), but not from (13) alone, the conjunction (13) + (12) confirms (11). If the conjunction (13) + (12) is accepted on independent observational grounds, there will be a reasonable strengthening of our confidence in (11). For a prediction based on (11) has in fact been borne out by experience.

Consider now the sentences:

(14)   Metal b · Heated b

and

(15) $\sim$ Expands b

The conjunction (14) + (15) disconfirms (11), since (14) and (11) together yield as a consequence:

(16)   Expands b

which contradicts (15), or, since (15) and (11) together yield as a consequence:

(17) $\sim$Metal b v $\sim$Heated b

which contradicts (14). The conjunction (14) + (15) is, in fact, incompatible with (11); it disconfirms (11), representing the failure of a prediction based upon it.

The conception just illustrated is then explicitly formulated, as "the prediction-criterion," by Hempel:

> Let H be a hypothesis, B an observation report, i.e., a class of observation sentences. Then
> (a) B is said to confirm H if B can be divided into two mutually exclusive subclasses B_1 and B_2 such that B_2 is not empty, and every sentence of B_2 can be logically deduced from B_1 in conjunction with H, but not from B_1 alone.
> (b) B is said to disconfirm H if H logically contradicts B.
> (c) B is said to be neutral with respect to H if it neither confirms nor disconfirms H.[7]

With reference to this criterion, Hempel proposes the following criticisms. First, as in the case of Nicod's criterion, there is here a restriction to hypotheses of special sorts; in the present case, to those involving universal conditionals in which the predicates are observational. For hypotheses asserting regular associations of non-observational, or theoretical, properties, the criterion does not apply. The predictive use of such hypotheses involves

[7] *Ibid.* (II), p. 98.

warranted non-deductive steps linking observational and theoretical properties; to revise the prediction-criterion so as explicitly to allow for such linkage would render it pointless as a
definition of confirmation, for such a definition seeks, itself, to
explain warranted non-deductive reasoning. Furthermore, even
where all predicates *are* observational, the prediction-criterion is
not always applicable; it does not, for example, apply to purely
existential hypotheses or generally to statements with mixed
quantifiers. Consider, moreover, an example of Hempel's:

(18) $(x) ((y) (Rxy) \supset (\exists z)(Sxz))$.

In order to say that a given object a satisfies the antecedent of
(18), we should need to know that a stands in the relation R to
every thing y; normally, we assert such a statement as '(y)
(Ray)' rather on the basis of a *non-deductive* step from observation-statements relating a to several things not presumed to exhaust the range of the variable 'y'. Furthermore, suppose the
antecedent is presumed to hold of a, the consequence derivable
by means of (18) would still not be a prediction, in the sense of
an observation-sentence. It would rather state '$(\exists z) (Saz)$', i.e.,
'Something stands in the relation S to a', a statement which does
not itself yield an observation-statement, but is derivable from
(and hence presumably confirmed by) the observation-statement
'Sab'.

Secondly, while the prediction-criterion does satisfy the equiv-
alence-condition (since, roughly, it does not differentiate confirming statements in terms of the *form* of the hypothesis used to
derive the prediction), it fails to satisfy another condition which
appears to be a general requirement for any adequate definition
of confirmation. This is what Hempel calls the "special consequence condition," which demands of every statement confirming h that it also confirm every consequence of h (since every
such consequence formulates just the content of h, or some part
thereof). The prediction-criterion violates this condition, since it
takes the confirming statement to consist of two parts, one derivable from the other conjoined with h. But such a derivation
does not generally persist when h is replaced by a consequence
of h.

Thirdly, the prediction-criterion does satisfy what Hempel calls a "converse consequence condition," that is, it qualifies a given statement e as confirming every statement implying h, if e confirms h. For, if e confirms h, then, according to the criterion, part of e follows from the other part conjoined with h, and, clearly, will continue to follow when h is replaced by any statement implying h. The converse consequence condition, however, leads to a clearly undesirable result when taken jointly with the special consequence condition—the result *that every observation-sentence confirms every hypothesis.* For, assuming that every statement confirms (because it implies) itself, e confirms e; by the converse consequence condition, e thus confirms the conjunction $e + k$, *no matter what k asserts,* since the conjunction implies e. Finally, since e confirms $e + k$, the special consequence condition implies that e also confirms k, which follows from $e + k$. Thus the prediction-criterion not only fails to satisfy the independently desirable special consequence condition, but it satisfies the converse consequence condition, which is in conflict with it. Hence, any modification of the criterion incorporating the special consequence condition would lead immediately to trouble.

Even independently of its conflict with the latter condition, moreover, the converse consequence condition seems undesirable. For, as we have seen, it yields (assuming e confirms e) the conclusion that e confirms $e + k$. This may not appear as shocking as the disastrous result mentioned in the last paragraph, perhaps because of the familiar view that induction moves in a direction opposite to deduction, from a statement of the evidence to any statement logically implying it. However, if we reflect that k is totally unrestricted as to form and material content, and that k's truth is required for the truth of $e + k$, it becomes quite unintuitive to take the latter whole conjunction as confirmed by e. Similarly, it is intuitively unsatisfactory to suppose $h + k$ confirmed by e if e represents a successful prediction based on h. Accordingly, the prediction-criterion is not even a satisfactory *sufficient* condition of confirmation, unless the hypotheses it declares to be confirmed are somehow restricted to such as are similar to (11) in relevant respects.

Having criticized and rejected the conceptions of confirmation embodied in Nicod's criterion and the prediction-criterion, Hempel draws together the adequacy conditions emerging from his critique and supplements them with others, so that the following list results:

I. A condition we may refer to as one of *general applicability,* requiring adequate definitions to apply to the confirmation of statements of any logical form.

II. *Entailment* condition, requiring that any statement entailed (i.e., logically implied) by an observation report be confirmed by it.

III. *Consequence* condition, requiring that, if an observation report confirms every member of a given class of statements, it confirm also every logical consequence of this class.

  III a. *Special Consequence* condition, requiring that any observation report confirming any given statement confirm also every one of its logical consequences. (IIIa is satisfied if III is.)

  III b. *Equivalence* condition, requiring that any observation report confirming any given statement confirm also every one of its logical equivalents. (IIIb is satisfied if IIIa is, and, hence, if III is.)

IV. *Consistency* condition, requiring that every logically consistent observation report be logically compatible with the class of all the statements it confirms. (This condition implies

  IV a. that no consistent observation report confirms any statement with which it is logically incompatible, and

  IV b. that no consistent observation report confirms any statements which contradict one another.)

V. A condition we may refer to as the *inverse equivalence* condition, requiring a statement to be confirmed by every logical equivalent of any observation report confirming it.[8]

These conditions set the stage for Hempel's own proposal, which he calls "the satisfaction criterion of confirmation." They represent specifications his construction is designed to meet. They are not held to be *absolute,* or in some special sense *demonstrable;* rather, each is held to be a reasonable requirement for the construction of a confirmation theory, and they seem, moreover, to fit well together, apparently yielding no conflicts of the sort generated by the special and converse consequence conditions. It is thus clear that variant formulations of adequacy requirements are feasible, and Hempel discusses, in particular, a "more liberal" version in which IV is omitted, though its corollary IVa retained. For his own construction, he adopts the "rigorous" version embodied in the list given above—such adoption, however, is in no way intended to deny the interest of alternative formulations. In fact, Hempel claims his construction to be generalizable in such a way as to satisfy only some "more liberal" alternative of the sort above described.

Although his adopted set of conditions is a "rigorous" one, its fulfillment cannot be taken as a *sufficient* requirement for the adequacy of any definition or criterion of confirmation. To define 'confirms' as 'logically implies' would, as Hempel notes, satisfy the adopted set although it would not be materially satisfactory. Thus, adoption of the set amounts to taking its fulfillment as a *necessary* requirement for the adequacy of any proposed definition. Beyond satisfying this set, every such definition must meet further, material requirements—it must "mirror" the notion of confirmation, as applicable in ordinary and scientific contexts.

The satisfaction criterion proposed by Hempel fulfills the conditions I-V, and is, furthermore, judged by him to be materially adequate. However, there is one important limitation he points out: his definitions apply only to languages of relatively simple logical structure—to quantificational languages without identity,

---

[8] This is a rearranged list, with new numbering but, with the exception of I and V, the names of the conditions listed are Hempel's.

and barring quantifiers for predicate variables. These languages are presumed to have individual constants, and predicate constants of any degree. They allow only the formation of sentences composed exclusively of such constants, individual variables and quantifiers, logical symbols for denial, conjunction, alternation, and the conditional, and signs of punctuation. The primitive predicate constants are, furthermore, all assumed to be observational. Hempel thus does not present his construction as a generally adequate theory of confirmation. To have such a generally adequate theory, he believes it necessary to take account of more complex languages, and he acknowledges that the task is likely to increase in difficulty proportionately to the increase in logical richness of the languages under consideration. Thus, he views his satisfaction criterion as a partial answer to the problem—for simple cases only, leaving the more complex cases to further research.

With this limitation in mind, we turn now to the details of Hempel's construction. He takes an observation report to be any sentence containing no quantifiers. Thus, observation reports will consist of sentences applying observational predicates (of any degree) to individuals (represented by individual constants), and of negations, alternations, conjunctions, and conditionals composed of such sentences. The basic idea behind the construction is this: If a hypothesis can be shown to hold true within the finite class of those individuals mentioned by the observation report in question, this report will be said to confirm the hypothesis, and otherwise it will not be said to confirm the hypothesis. The report is thus construed as confirming a hypothesis if and only if the report shows that the hypothesis would be true were the universe to be restricted to the domain of individuals mentioned by the report. More precisely, a confirming report (relative to a given hypothesis) logically implies just what the hypothesis asserts when its range is restricted to the class of objects mentioned by the report.

To represent the latter idea of restricted assertion, the notion is introduced of the C-development of a hypothesis h, i.e., the development of h relative to the class C. This notion has been characterized, in the last sentence of the previous paragraph, by appeal to "semantic" ideas, i.e., that of a class of mentioned objects, and that of assertion relative to some such class. In his *Journal of Symbolic Logic* paper on the subject,[9] Hempel provides a "purely syntactic" characterization, i.e., one which refers exclusively to logical features of hypothesis and report, and to their constituent signs. For our present purposes, the details are unimportant. It will be sufficient to achieve an intuitive grasp of the idea in "semantic" form, and to see its applications in the following examples. For

(19) (x) (Raven $x \supset$ Black x)

and the class C of individuals a, b, and c, the C-development is:

(20)   ($\sim$ Raven a v Black a) · ($\sim$ Raven b v Black b) · ($\sim$ Raven c v Black c)

since (19) is equivalent to:

(21) (x) ($\sim$ Raven x v Black x)

which literally says that no matter what individual x is chosen, x is not a raven or black. Given just the class C above, (20) represents the assertion of (21) applied to each and every member of C.

For the existential hypothesis:

(22) $(\exists x)$ (Unicorn x)

and the same class C as above, the C-development is:

(23)   Unicorn a v Unicorn b v Unicorn c

since (22) literally says that some individual is a unicorn, and (23) spells out the import of this assertion for C, that is, it states a condition which is true if and only if (22) holds true of C, or is *satisfied* within C.

For the same class C and the hypothesis:

(24) $(x)(\exists y)$ (Likes xy)

[9] Hempel, "A Purely Syntactical Definition of Confirmation."

initially understood as applicable to people, and asserting that everyone likes someone, the *C*-development is:

(25)   (Likes *aa* ∨ Likes *ab* ∨ Likes *ac*) · (Likes *ba* ∨ Likes *bb* ∨ Likes *bc*) · (Likes *ca* ∨ Likes *cb* ∨ Likes *cc*)

since if and only if (25) is true does (24) hold true for the class *C*.

For *C* and the hypothesis:

(26)   (∃*x*) (*y*) (Likes *xy*)

the *C*-development is:

(27)   (Likes *aa* · Likes *ab* · Likes *ac*) ∨ (Likes *ba* · Likes *bb* · Likes *bc*) ∨ (Likes *ca* · Likes *cb* · Likes *cc*)

since if and only if at least one of the individuals, *a*, *b*, and *c*, likes all three is (26) satisfied within *C*.

For any class *C*, and any hypothesis which contains *no* quantifiers, we stipulate that the *C*-development of the hypothesis is to be taken as the hypothesis itself.

Having the notion of the development of a hypothesis relative to a class, Hempel next defines 'directly confirms' and, more generally, 'confirms', as follows:

(D1)   An observation report *B* *directly confirms* a hypothesis *H* if *B* entails (logically implies) the development of *H* for the class of those objects which are mentioned essentially in *B*.

(D2)   An observation report *B* *confirms* a hypothesis *H* if *H* is entailed (logically implied) by a class of sentences each of which is directly confirmed by *B*.

Disconfirmation and neutrality are then defined thus:

(D3)   An observation report *B* *disconfirms* a hypothesis *H* if it confirms the denial of *H*.

(D4)   An observation report is *neutral with respect to* a hypothesis *H* if *B* neither confirms nor disconfirms *H*.

Before we illustrate how these definitions apply to some of our above examples, it will be well to note the reference to '*essential mention*', which appears in (D1). This reference is motivated by the wish to satisfy the inverse equivalence condition (V).[1] For *if* '*essential mention*' *were eliminated in favor of mere* '*mention*', see what would happen. Consider the hypothesis:

(28) $(x)(Px)$

which is directly confirmed and therefore confirmed by:

(29) Pa

since 'Pa' implies the development of (28) for the class of objects mentioned by (29), namely, the class consisting of a alone. (For this development is itself 'Pa', and is thus implied by (29).)

Now consider the fact that

(30) $Pa \cdot (Qb \vee \sim Qb)$

is logically equivalent to (29). By the inverse equivalence condition, (30) ought also to confirm (28), but it does *not*, under the present supposition. For the development of (28) relative to (30) is:

(31) $Pa \cdot Pb$

since both a and b are mentioned in (30). Clearly, (30) does not imply (31), and so does not *directly confirm* (28). Nor does (30) directly confirm each of several sentences which together imply (28), and so (30) does not *confirm* (28) either. The trouble is, however, avoided if we can eliminate 'b' from the development (31), and we can do this if we can somehow isolate the mention of b in (30), as "inessential." In fact, 'b' occurs twice in (30) as part of an "atomic" component 'Qb', which is itself wholly eliminable from (30): this component figures only within the logically true conjunct '$Qb \vee \sim Qb$', and is hence elim-

[1] See Hempel, "Studies in the Logic of Confirmation," pp. 110-111, footnote 1. He refers to a discussion with Dr. Olaf Helmer in connection with the clarification of this point. (The point is important if observation reports are not restricted to classes or conjunctions of observation sentences, but include all compounds of observation sentences, without quantifiers, e.g., also alternations and conditionals.)

inable, along with the whole conjunct, from (30); (30) is logically equivalent to (29), which lacks the component '*Qb*' altogether. Thus '*Qb*' can be said to occur inessentially (twice) in (30), and we may now characterize *b*'s mention in (30) as *inessential* also, since *b* is mentioned only in components of (30) occurring inessentially therein. Finally, we require, for direct confirmation, that the observation report imply the development of the hypothesis for the class of just those things mentioned *essentially* (i.e., mentioned but not only inessentially) in the report. The difficulty is thus taken care of, since we now take the relevant development of (28) with respect to (30) to be (29); surely (29) *is* implied by (30), which therefore directly confirms (and so confirms) the hypothesis (28).

Let us now illustrate the application of Hempel's definitions to our sample sentences, introduced above. For (19), a report with essential mention of *a*, *b*, and *c* is directly confirming if and only if it implies (20), and is disconfirming if and only if it confirms the denial of (19). The latter denial is:

(32) $(\exists x)$ (Raven x · ~ Black x)

and its development for the class C, consisting of *a*, *b*, and *c*, is:

(33)   (Raven a · ~ Black a) v (Raven b · ~ Black b)
        v (Raven c · ~ Black c)

To disconfirm (19), a report (with essential mention of *a*, *b*, and *c*) would need either to imply (33) and so directly to confirm (32) or to confirm directly such sentences as together imply (32). A report neither confirming nor disconfirming (19) would be irrelevant, or neutral, to it.

Direct confirmation of (22) by a report with essential mention of the members of C would involve its implication of (23). Analogous direct confirmation of (24) hinges on the implying of (25). Finally, similar confirmation of (26) would depend on implication of (27).

4. Critical Discussion of the Satisfaction Criterion

There have been several lines of critical response to Hempel's study. One line is represented by those who seek a *quantitative* analysis of confirmation, that is, a notion admitting of *degrees*, and who are thus not satisfied by a study of qualitative confirmation.[2] Another line is represented by those who find fault with one or another of Hempel's adequacy conditions I-V, and so reject the effort to satisfy the set. Finally, there is still another line, represented by those who are unhappy with the whole effort to define confirmation, feeling, as they do, that confirmation is too tenuous, variable, and subjective a notion to admit of fruitful analysis.

We shall not here explore the foregoing lines of criticism, for they are not relevant to our main concerns. It may, however, be worthwhile to comment briefly on each, at this point. First, it is surely desirable to strive for a quantitative notion of confirmation, but the fact that a given study does not yield such a notion indicates only that it is limited, not that it is defective.

Secondly, while criticisms of Hempel's adequacy criteria are serious considerations deserving detailed analysis, it does not follow, from the fact that given criteria may be faulty, that there is no interest in a construction satisfying them. For the very effort to develop *some* consistent set of criteria, and the process of construction itself, may reveal points of general relevance for any alternative. In particular, Hempel's critique of Nicod's criterion and of the prediction-criterion, his discovery and treatment of the paradoxes of confirmation, and his discussion of conflicts among certain criteria are of general importance. In view of such conflicts, furthermore, it seems unlikely that *any* consistent alternative choice of criteria will wholly avoid violating *some* criterion which appears, in itself, to be perfectly plausible. There is thus some degree of theoretic license legitimately claimed by anyone seeking a systematic account.[3] Finally, in view of the relatively

[2] See, for example, Carl G. Hempel and Paul Oppenheim, "A Definition of 'Degree of Confirmation,'" *Philosophy of Science*, XII (1945), 98-115. The text here refers, however, primarily to negative critics of the study of qualitative confirmation.

[3] Goodman has remarked, for example, in *Fact, Fiction, and Forecast*, p. 85, footnote 5, that "since our commonsense assumptions taken in combination quickly lead us to absurd conclusions, some of these assumptions have to be dropped; and different theorists may make different decisions about which to drop and which to preserve."

early stage in which the analysis of confirmation finds itself, and in view of the complexity and variety of the contexts in which the term 'confirmation' figures, it seems likely that a multiplicity of analyses will be required to render the term adequately.

The third line of criticism noted above points out the variability and subjectivity of the term 'confirmation'. While there is no *decisive* answer to criticism of a philosophical program, short of its actual fulfillment, neither can a program be shown to be misguided simply by reference to the variability or subjectivity of the term which it proposes to clarify. Variability may be overcome by a systematic interpretation which fastens on a determinate set of contexts of the term in question, reconstruing or ignoring its functions elsewhere. Subjectivity (within such a determinate set) is fatal only if it is general, that is, only if there is no substantial body of cases in which the term is clearly applied or withheld in practice. For every term (under any interpretation) has some areas of subjectivity, or indeterminacy of application. Were the mere existence of a range of subjectivity, coupled with contextual variability, to preclude systematic definition, no such definition could have been produced for any physical term, nor indeed, for any other. In the case of 'confirmation', though there is surely, on any likely interpretation, a range of cases within which judgment is subjective or indeterminate, there is also, surely, a substantial body of cases where it is clear that the term applies, and another where it is clear that it fails to apply.

We here thus assume the reasonableness of an attempt, such as Hempel's, to define systematically a notion of qualitative confirmation, and we further consider it worthwhile to attend to his construction, which is guided by conditions I-V. For our special purposes, his study is important, because it indicates very clearly some of the main difficulties in analyzing the idea of *an instance according with a hypothesis*. It thus reveals one surprisingly problematic aspect of the generalization formula, for which hypotheses are selected that accord with instances in past experience.

In the remainder of the present section, we shall comment on a specific feature of Hempel's construction, which further underlines the problematic aspect just mentioned. In the following section, we shall address ourselves to the paradoxes of confirmation, which have aroused widespread interest as a challenge to confirmation theories generally.

The feature of Hempel's construction to which we now turn is its limitation to languages in which all predicate constants are observational. We have noted this explicit limitation earlier, but a reason for it may now be seen by reference to definitions (D1)-(D4). For all these definitions hinge on the notion of *the development of a hypothesis* for a class of objects mentioned in some observation report—which report itself *implies the development* in question. The development of a hypothesis, moreover, always applies its constituent predicate constants to elements of which the report asserts something *observational.*

Now, if the hypothesis h contains only "non-observational," theoretical, predicate constants (and is not logically true, as may be generally presumed), its development will apply such constants in a non-trivial way to individual elements mentioned by the observation report in question. The latter report will *not,* being throughout observational, imply this development (assuming it is consistent), and so will not directly confirm h.

Nor will it confirm $h,$ for to do so, it would need to confirm directly each member of a class K of statements implying h. But suppose h (with theoretical constant 'T') is, for example:

(1) $(x)\ (Tx),$

which is implied by the class K of sentences:

(2) $(x)\ (Ox)$

and:

(3) $(x)\ (Ox \supset Tx)$

Then the report 'Oa' will indeed directly confirm (2) but not (3), for it will not imply the appropriate development '$\sim Oa\ \mathbf{v}$ Ta'. Thus it will fail to confirm the purely theoretical (1). On the other hand, the report '$\sim Oa$' will directly confirm (3) but not

(2), and thus will also fail to confirm (1). Or, suppose we have the purely theoretical h:

(4) $(x)(T_1x \supset T_2x)$

implied by the class K of sentences

(5) $(x)\ (T_1x \supset Ox)$

and:

(6) $(x)\ (Ox \supset T_2x)$

Then the observation report '$\sim Oa$' will directly confirm (6) but not (5), while the report 'Oa' will directly confirm (5) but not (6). Suppose, finally, that h is:

(7) $Ob \supset Tb$

which is implied (given 'b' as an individual name) by:

(8) $(x)\ (Ox \supset Tx)$

Here, the report '$\sim Oa$' confirms (though it does not directly confirm) (7), but (7) is not purely theoretical, and, furthermore, '$\sim Oa$' also confirms '$Ob \supset \sim Tb$', as it directly confirms also the contrary of (8), i.e., '$(x)\ (Ox \supset \sim Tx)$'. Given the purely theoretical

(9) Tb

it is no longer implied solely by (8), but *is* implied by (8) and:

(10) Ob

The report 'Ob', however, confirms only (10) but not (8), while '$\sim Oa$' does the exact opposite. The compound report '$Ob \cdot \sim Oa$', finally, confirms (10) but not (8) (it fails to imply '$(\sim Oa \lor Ta) \cdot (\sim Ob \lor Tb)$'). In no case is the purely theoretical (9) confirmed at all. The possibility of confirming purely theoretical hypotheses or regular associations of observational and theoretical properties (without also confirming their contraries) seems thus ruled out by the satisfaction criterion.

We have earlier noted Hempel's criticism of the prediction-

criterion on the ground that it fails to apply to hypotheses asserting regular associations of theoretical properties, as well as his
criticism that it does not apply to the confirmation of hypotheses
of all logical forms. Yet only the latter criticism is transformed
into a condition of adequacy, i.e., what we have called *general
applicability*. Conceivably, one might hope that all theoretical
predicates could be defined by observational ones, and that theoretical assertions might then be replaceable by (complex)
observational assertions. Thus, to allow the confirmation of hypotheses of any logical form would be to assure, in principle, the
confirmability of theoretical assertions.

But it would seem hazardous to rest confirmation theory
on such a hope. Hempel, for example, in criticizing the prediction-criterion, remarks that "a hypothesis to the effect that a
given ray of light is plane-polarized has to be considered as a
general hypothesis which entails an unlimited number of observation sentences; thus it cannot be logically inferred from, but
at best be confirmed by, a suitable set of observational findings."[4]
This passage suggests (if it does not imply) a possibility that
needs to be taken seriously in confirmation theory. The theoretical attribution of plane-polarization might entail but not be
equivalent to even an unlimited number of observation sentences,
i.e., '*x* is plane-polarized' might not be replaceable by any definiens consisting solely of observational constants, and variables
under any degree and type of quantification. In short, it might
not be observationally eliminable.

To satisfy the condition of general applicability cannot, therefore, in general be assumed to imply that the confirmability
of purely theoretical hypotheses has been assured. It follows that
Hempel's satisfaction criterion is subject to criticism on the latter count, no less than the prediction-criterion. It follows, further, that its general adequacy requires extension not only to
logically more complex languages, but also to languages with
theoretical vocabularies. Such extension clearly requires consideration of the problem of theoretical terms, discussed in the last

---

[4] Hempel, "Studies in the Logic of Confirmation," p. 99. (My italics.)

Part; it is, moreover, by no means obvious how to proceed in making this extension, for theoretical terms are just those which cannot figure in forming observation reports. Even if the notion of an *instance according with a hypothesis* is satisfactorily explained for purely observational languages, then, it seems likely that theoretical languages present problems of a different order, requiring solutions of quite different sorts. Nor, short of the actual presentation of such solutions, does there seem to be even intuitive clarity as to what might be involved in the notion of an instance of a purely theoretical hypothesis.

5. The Paradoxes of Confirmation: Hempel's Treatment

In Section 3 above, we noted certain surprising consequences of joining the equivalence condition with Nicod's rule, taken as a sufficient condition of confirmation. Let us review the matter by recalling the following sentences:

(1) (x) (Raven $x \supset$ Black x)
(2) (x) ($\sim$ Black $x \supset \sim$ Raven x)
(3) (x) ((Raven $x \vee \sim$ Raven x) $\supset$ ($\sim$ Raven $x \vee$ Black x))

An object b, satisfying both antecedent and consequent of (2) is, by Nicod's (sufficient) condition, a confirming instance of (2). Sentence (2) is, however, logically equivalent to (1). Therefore, by the equivalence condition, b is a confirming instance of (1), though it seems paradoxical to suppose a non-black non-raven to confirm the hypothesis that all ravens are black. (The above argument can, of course, be put with equal force in terms of the *report* '$\sim$ Black $b \cdot \sim$ Raven b', rather than the *object b.*)

Furthermore, (1) is also logically equivalent to (3), and should thus, by the equivalence condition, be confirmed by any object, c, that confirms (3). By Nicod's condition, however, c confirms (3) if it is a black raven, or else a non-raven, black or otherwise. Thus any non-raven confirms the hypothesis that all ravens are black, and any black object confirms the same hypothesis. By analogous argument, we get the surprising result that any non-raven or black thing confirms the hypothesis that all non-black things are non-ravens. Now these "paradoxical" results flow from conditions which seem, in isolation, perfectly reasonable, even obvious. That an object satisfying both antecedent and consequent of a universal conditional such as (1) *confirms* it seems the most elementary truth about confirmation. That logically equivalent statements have exactly the same weight, as elements of scientific argument, and, in particular, are identically related to instances, seems equally plain. The obviousness of these conditions accounts for the widespread interest accorded the paradoxes of confirmation. For, quite irrespective of concurrence with Hempel's own "satisfaction criterion," there is broad consensus as to these conditions themselves. Consequently, there has been general concern over their engendering problematic results.

Of interest to our main theme is the way in which the apparently innocent idea of *a generalization's positive instances* turns out to have unforeseen complexities; the generalization formula, using this idea, is thus not as straightforward as it seems. In the present and the following sections, we shall, however, isolate the question of the paradoxes themselves and consider some of the discussions to which they gave rise, attending first to Hempel's treatment and then to further proposals. Following these considerations, we shall pick up the main thread once more.

It will be recalled that Hempel rejects Nicod's criterion (i.e., as being both a necessary and sufficient condition of confirmation) in part because it violates the equivalence condition. He, further, proposes an alternative criterion which does satisfy this condition. Since his criterion, moreover, gives the same results as Nicod's rule, taken *as a sufficient condition* only, it is clear that the paradoxes of confirmation arise within Hempel's construction. We may illustrate this fact by referring again to (1), (2), and (3) above. The developments of these sentences, for the object *b,* are, respectively (using '*R*' for 'Raven', and '*B*' for 'Black'):

(4) $\sim Rb \lor Bb$

(5) $Bb \lor \sim Rb$

(6) $(\sim Rb \cdot Rb) \lor (\sim Rb \lor Bb)$

Clearly, the report:

(7) $\sim Bb \cdot \sim Rb$

implies each of the above developments (4), (5), and (6), thus directly confirming, and therefore confirming, each of (1), (2), and (3).

Clearly, too, the report:

(8) $\sim Rb$

alone, also confirms (1), and (2) and (3) as well, as does the report 'Bb' (which we shall not further discuss, for brevity). Finally, the report:

(9) $Rb \cdot Bb$

confirms not only (1) and (3), but (2) also.

It is apparent that Hempel himself needs to give some account of the paradoxes in order to make his construction plausible though, as we have suggested above, these paradoxes are by no means peculiar to his construction. Now these "paradoxes" are not formal contradictions; they do not render their containing theories inconsistent. Rather, they represent a violation of our initial sense of the range of positive instances. A construction containing them thus collides with our intuitions in the matter. Intuitively, for example, we take reports (7) and (9) to be quite unequal in their force relative to (1), the latter report clearly positive, the former not. Conversely for (2), we take (7) intuitively as representing a positive case, unlike (9). Intuitively also, we judge (8) as a positive case of neither (1) nor (2). Yet, a construction yielding the paradoxes equalizes the force of (7), (8), and (9) with respect to (1) and (2). What is needed, then, is an explicit treatment of the conflict between construction and intuition: we may modify the construction so as to bring it into line with our intuition, or we may maintain our construction, offering an explanation of the intuitive divergence which shows why this divergence may be disregarded for theoretical purposes. Hempel takes the latter course. Before presenting his own explanation of the intuitive divergence, however, he criticizes two alternative proposals, based on the idea that scientific hypotheses should not be represented as universal conditionals, after the manner of (1). The first proposal suggests that the hypothesis 'All ravens are black' should rather be represented as:

(10) $$(x) \ (Rx \supset Bx) \cdot (\exists x) \ (Rx)$$

while the hypothesis that no non-black thing is a raven should be represented as:

(11) $$(x) \ (\sim Bx \supset \sim Rx) \cdot (\exists x) \ (\sim Bx)$$

each case with an attached premise asserting the existence of an object satisfying the antecedent-predicate. The effect of this proposal is to break the equivalence between 'All ravens are black' and 'No non-black thing is a raven', for, clearly, (10) is not logically equivalent to (11).

Now, for the object b, the development of (10) is:

(12) $$(\sim Rb \lor Bb) \cdot (Rb)$$

while the analogous development of (11) is:

(13) $$(Bb \lor \sim Rb) \cdot (\sim Bb)$$

The report (9), i.e., '$Rb \cdot Bb$', clearly implies (12) but not (13), which it contradicts. On the other hand, the report (7), i.e., '$\sim Bb \cdot \sim Rb$', does just the reverse, implying (13) but contradicting (12). The report (8), i.e., '$\sim Rb$', implies neither, though it contradicts only (12). Thus (9) but not (7) confirms (10) (which replaces (1)), while (7) but not (9) confirms (11) (which replaces (2)), and (8) confirms neither. We have, it seems, explained the intuitive inequalities between (7), (8), and (9) while maintaining our construction intact. For the construction itself yields these inequalities with respect to (10) and (11), and while it is perhaps natural to err in using (1) and (2) rather than the former pair to represent scientific hypotheses, our intuition is satisfied as soon as this error is noted and duly corrected.

The foregoing proposal is, however, rejected by Hempel for the following reasons: First, the suggested representation of general hypotheses conflicts with accepted scientific practice, which construes as equivalent such paired statements as 'All sodium salts burn yellow' and 'Whatever does not burn yellow is no sodium salt'. To represent them, in the usual way, as universal conditionals preserves their equivalence, while to represent them, according to the proposal, as conjunctions of such conditionals with disparate existential sentences destroys their equivalence.

Secondly, the proposal is ambiguous as respects alternative conditional formulations. Hempel's example is: 'If a person after receiving an injection of a certain test substance has a positive skin reaction, he has diphtheria'. Using obvious abbreviations, we have at least the following symbolic alternatives:

(14) $\qquad (x)\,((Px \cdot Ix \cdot Rx) \supset Dx)$

(15) $\qquad (x)\,((Px \cdot Ix) \supset (Rx \supset Dx))$

(16) $\qquad (x)\,(Px \supset ((Ix \cdot Rx) \supset Dx))$

The proposal gives us no way of telling which alternative to pick, and hence no way of deciding which existential statement to construe as implied by the original hypothesis, whether '$(\exists x)\,(Px \cdot Ix \cdot Rx)$', or '$(\exists x)(Px \cdot Ix)$', or '$(\exists x)(Px)$'.

Finally, many scientific hypotheses clearly do not make an existential claim at all. We may here include, perhaps, cases where the denial of such a claim is implicit in the context, as well as cases where the attribution of such a claim appears highly implausible, the theory having rather an "ideal," "hypothetical," or "contrary-to-fact" interpretation. Hempel writes,

> . . . it may happen that from a certain astrophysical theory a universal hypothesis is deduced concerning the character of the phenomena which would take place under certain specified extreme conditions. A hypothesis of this kind need not (and, as a rule, does not) imply that such extreme conditions ever were or will be realized; it has no existential

import. Or consider a biological hypothesis to the effect
that whenever man and ape are crossed, the offspring will
have such and such characteristics. This is a general hypothesis; it might be contemplated as a mere conjecture, or
as a consequence of a broader genetic theory, other implications of which may already have been tested with positive
results; but unquestionably the hypothesis does not imply
an existential clause asserting that the contemplated kind
of cross-breeding referred to will, at some time, actually
take place.[5]

The second proposal rejected by Hempel is the following:
The representation of a scientific hypothesis should include,
along with the universal conditional, a specification of some
class, taken as the *field of application* of the hypothesis in question. The paradoxes of confirmation arise only when such specification is omitted, the specification serving to limit confirming
instances to the field indicated. Thus (1) and (2) would be
supplanted, respectively, by:

(17) $(x)\ (Rx \supset Bx)$ [Class: Ravens]

and

(18) $(x)\ (\sim Bx \supset \sim Rx)$ [Class: Non-black things]

The report (9), i.e., '$Rb \cdot Bb$', would then confirm the sentence
(17) but not (18), since b falls within the class of ravens but
not non-black things. On the other hand, the report (7), i.e.,
'$\sim Bb \cdot \sim Rb$', would confirm the sentence (18) but not (17),
since b here falls within the class of non-black things but not
ravens. The report (8), i.e., '$\sim Rb$', would confirm neither, since
b here does not fall within the class of ravens, and is not described by the report or any of its consequences as belonging to
the class of non-black things.

Or, on another variant of the same general idea, the class of
ravens might be specified as field of application for (1), '(x)
$(Rx \supset Bx)$', *and* its logical equivalents, thus allowing the report

[5] *Ibid.*, (I), p. 16.

(9) to confirm (1) and all its equivalents, but disallowing both (7) and (8). The latter variant, unlike the first, preserves the equivalence condition. For while, on the first variant, for example, (9) confirms (1) but not (2), the latter variant has (9) confirming both (1) and (2). However, the latter variant (unlike the first) violates Nicod's sufficient condition, since, though (7) satisfies both antecedent and consequent predicates of (2), it is not considered a confirming instance.

Both variants of this second proposal thus deal with the paradoxes by modifying the construction so as to bring it into line with intuition. They yield intuitive inequalities between (7), (8), and (9) only by giving up either the equivalence condition or Nicod's sufficient condition. Indeed, the latter variant, in giving up Nicod's condition, also is at odds with our intuitive judgment of (7) as representing a positive case of (2), unlike (9). The second proposal, as a whole, seems inadequate for it provides no special arguments against those considerations supporting the equivalence condition and Nicod's sufficient condition. What recommends it is the fact that specification of some *field of application* is a weaker device than the conjoining of an existential sentence to a hypothesis, and so it escapes some of the criticism leveled against the proposal previously considered; in particular, it avoids the dubious attribution of existential import to scientific hypotheses.

Nonetheless, as Hempel points out, this second proposal is still subject to other objections made against the first one. The field of application to be specified is not clearly determined. Further, the proposal has "no counterpart in the theoretical procedure of science, where hypotheses are subjected to various kinds of logical transformation and inference without any consideration that might be regarded as referring to changes in the fields of application."[6]

Having rejected the two proposals just considered, involving a change in our representation of scientific hypotheses, Hempel proceeds to his own treatment of the paradoxes of confirmation. As indicated earlier, his course is to maintain the construction

[6] *Ibid.*, p. 18.

incorporating the equivalence condition and Nicod's sufficient condition, *and* to offer an explanation of the intuitive divergence which shows why it may be disregarded theoretically. As he puts it, "The impression of a paradoxical situation is not objectively founded; it is a psychological illusion."[7]

To support the latter judgment, he offers the following considerations: First, there is a prevalent, though mistaken, view that hypotheses of the form 'All A's are B's' are about A's only; perhaps the idea is that such hypotheses assert *something* (i.e., being B) about every element of the indicated *subject class* (i.e., the class of A's). But though the sentence form may, in fact, reflect some special interest in A's, this is a practical or psychological point which does not bear on the logical issue. From a logical point of view, such hypotheses have to be taken as imposing restrictions upon, and thus saying something about, all objects whatever within the logical type of the quantifier expression 'all'. Such hypotheses may be rendered:

(19) $(x) \ (Ax \supset Bx)$

and the latter expression says explicitly that, *no matter what object x is chosen, if x is A, then x is B*—that is to say, *no x is both A and not B, every x whatsoever* is not A, or is B. (19) thus says about *everything* (within the logical type of the variable 'x') that it conforms to the prescription 'not-A or B'. There is, in short, no reason to separate black ravens, non-black non-ravens, and black non-ravens, as instances of 'All ravens are black'.

Secondly, underlying the intuitive inequalities among positive instances of a hypothesis, there is frequently the illegitimate introduction of extra information. Clearly, in judging the relevance of given instances to a hypothesis h according to any construction, we must assume, for each instance, that we have no other information bearing on h; otherwise we may, in actuality, be judging the relevance of *instance + extra information* rather than that of *instance* alone. If we are not careful to exclude disguised references to extra information, we may suppose real inequali-

[7] *Ibid.*

ties to obtain among instances when in fact there are only apparent inequalities, due to extra information we have attached to these instances.

Hempel suggests, as an illustration, the sentence: 'All sodium salts burn yellow',

(20) $(x) (Sx \supset Yx).$

One might feel that yellow-burning sodium constitutes a positive instance of (20), but that neither yellow-burning nor non-yellow-burning non-sodium constitutes such a positive instance. One might attempt to support this feeling, moreover, by arguing as follows: Surely, we should not be adding strength to the hypothesis (20) if we held a bit of pure ice in a colorless flame and found that it did not turn this flame yellow, even though, admittedly, such ice is non-yellow-burning non-sodium, and thus satisfies the equivalent of (20), i.e.:

(21) $(x) (\sim Yx \supset \sim Sx).$

Hempel admits that the latter experiment would indeed fail to produce additional strength for (20), but denies that a general inequality has thereby been shown between instances that are both S and Y and those that are neither. For compare this ice experiment with another, in which an *unspecified* object a is held in a flame and determined to lack Y, and then analyzed as containing no sodium salt. In the latter case, it is no longer paradoxical to hold that the experiment *has* brought forth an instance, a, constituting strengthening evidence for (21), and therefore (20) as well. But the only significant difference between the two experiments is that, whereas a was initially unspecified, the *first* test substance was initially specified as pure ice, which we *independently* know to be free of sodium salt. As a result, we *independently* knew *this* test substance to constitute a positive instance of (20), and the experiment therefore could produce no *new* positive instance. Let us call this first test substance 'b'. Then, the development of (20) for b is:

(22) $\sim Sb \vee Yb$

(since (20) literally says, of everything x, that x is not S or Y). Now, if we already have the information:

(23) $\sim Sb$

we have a premise, concerning *b,* that implies (22), and thus confirms (20); we know *b* to constitute a positive instance, in short. We shall thus not be strengthening (20) by finding experimentally either 'Yb' or '$\sim Yb$', for to conjoin either finding to (23) will still, at most, give us a report on *b* implying (22); it will not give us a *new* positive instance of, i.e., a new object satisfying, (20). No wonder, then, that we felt our first experiment to add no support to (20). The trouble was not, however, that *b* lacked both *S* and *Y,* but rather that *b* was an *old* instance, in virtue of independent information. By contrast, if we are given the object *a,* which we do *not* initially know to be a positive instance of (20), and if we find subsequent reason to accept the report '$\sim Ya \cdot \sim Sa$' on the basis of experiment (such a report implying the relevant development '$\sim Sa \vee Ya$'), we have indeed added support to (20), though *a,* like *b,* lacks both *S* and *Y.*

Analogously, an unspecified item *d,* found to be both *S* and *Y,* strengthens (20); on the other hand, an experimental finding of 'S' for object *e,* initially known to be yellow-burning, adds no strength to (20), since *e* is already known to represent a positive instance of this hypothesis, which asserts that everything is not *S* or *Y.* Thus, whether a given finding will be judged to add strength to a hypothesis does not depend on its producing a special *sort* of instance, among all those considered to be positive by Hempel's (or an analogous) construction. It does, however, depend upon the extra information assumed prior to the finding in question. To preclude all such extra information in judging the relevance of an instance to a hypothesis is thus to remove certain felt inequalities among instances construed as positive by the construction; it helps, accordingly, to dissolve the paradoxes themselves. The exclusion of extra assumptions requires that the question be put properly from the start. As Hempel suggests, in reference to our recent discussion, ". . . we have to ask: Given some object *a* (it happens to be a piece of ice, but this fact is not included in the evidence), and given the fact that *a* does not turn the flame yellow and is no sodium salt—does *a* then constitute confirming evidence for the hypothesis? And now

—no matter whether *a* is ice or some other substance—it is clear that the answer has to be in the affirmative; and the paradoxes vanish."[8]

As we discussed the case of (20), trouble arose because of an initial extra assumption that the test item *i* was not-*S*, or was *Y*, and therefore already known as a positive instance of (20). But is there not, already at this point, sufficient paradox in supposing *i* to be a positive instance simply because not sodium, or yellow-burning? Yet this supposition is required for the earlier explanation to be at all convincing, for it is this supposition which renders further experimental inspection of *i* superfluous. Here again, argues Hempel, intrusion of extra information is at the root of our feeling of strangeness in taking *i* as positive evidence for (20). As a matter of fact, (20) says that everything is not-*S* or *Y*, and if *i* is not-*S*, or if *i* is *Y*, it conforms to the condition laid down as universal by (20). Suppose we rigorously observe what Hempel calls "the methodological fiction" that we have no other evidence under consideration but the single report:

(24) $\sim Si$

Then (24) supports the hypothesis:

(25) $(x)\ (\sim Sx)$

and therefore, surely, the weaker:

(20) $(x)\ (Sx \supset Yx)$.

Or, suppose our sole report to be:

(26) Yi.

Then (26) supports also:

(27) $(x)\ (Yx)$

and surely, *a fortiori*, the weaker (20). Now, we do not normally think of (24) or of (26) as confirming, respectively, the strong hypotheses (25) and (27) (nor of these hypotheses as con-

[8] *Ibid.*, p. 20.

firmed relative to available evidence), because we have independent information that the latter are false, i.e., that there *is* some sodium salt and that there *is* something not yellow-burning. Once recognizing the need to exclude such extra information, however, we no longer find it strange to take our sole report (24) or (26) as providing positive evidence for (20). The conclusion drawn by Hempel is that the paradoxes "are due to a misguided intuition in the matter rather than to a logical flaw in the two stipulations from which the 'paradoxes' were derived."[9]

6. Further Discussions of the Paradoxes of Confirmation

Despite Hempel's attempt to explain the paradoxes as illusions stemming from (i) a faulty view concerning the reference of universal conditionals, and (ii) the improper intrusion of extra information, there has been considerable further discussion of the paradoxes, and several other proposals have been put forward for dealing with them. We will make no attempt, in this section, to give an exhaustive review of this discussion, nor to evaluate every alternative proposal. Rather, we shall attempt to provide some notion of the range of diverse approaches, and to indicate relevant points of general interest for the theory of confirmation.

We turn first to a claim, put forward by J. W. N. Watkins, that the paradoxes are wholly avoidable in a "Popperian theory of confirmation," i.e., a theory construing confirmation not in terms of conforming instances simply, but rather in terms of those instances determined by unsuccessful attempts at falsification.[1] With respect to the hypothesis:

(1)   All ravens are black,

[9] *Ibid.*, pp. 20-21.
[1] J. W. N. Watkins, "Between Analytic and Empirical," *Philosophy*, XXXII (1957), 112-131; and "A Rejoinder to Professor Hempel's Reply," *Philosophy*, XXXIII (1958), 349-355. By permission of the author. The latter was a response to Carl G. Hempel's article in the same volume, "Empirical Statements and Falsifiability," pp. 342-348.

Watkins writes, "On a Popperian theory of confirmation, this hypothesis is confirmed by an observation-report of a black raven, not because this reports an instance of the hypothesis—a white swan is also an instance of it—but because it reports a satisfactory test of the hypothesis: a raven has been examined unsuccessfully for non-blackness. On this view, statements about non-ravens which do not report tests of our hypothesis cannot confirm it."[2]

Presumably the intuitive inequality as between:

(2) $$Ra \cdot Ba$$

and

(3) $$\sim Ba \cdot \sim Ra$$

is explainable by reference to an inequality with respect to *testing*: (2) represents a satisfactory test, whereas (3) does not. Such differences with respect to testing yield just the intuitive inequalities which diverge from Hempel's construction, producing the paradoxes of confirmation. The solution is, then, to alter the construction by suitably incorporating some relevant notion of testing, in order to bring confirmation theory into line with our intuitions in the matter.

Watkins grants, however, that (1) is equivalent to:

(4) All non-black things are non-ravens

and agrees, moreover, that "if observations confirm one formulation of a hypothesis they confirm any logically equivalent formulation."[3] If the idea is, then, to consider (2) as confirming (1) because it reports a satisfactory test of the hypothesis in that a raven has been examined unsuccessfully for non-blackness, we must similarly, it would seem, consider (3) as confirming (4) in that a non-black thing has been examined unsuccessfully for ravenness. But then, since Watkins accepts the equivalence of (4) and (1), as well as the equivalence condition, he must agree that (3) also confirms (1), on his "Popperian theory." Thus,

[2] Watkins, "A Rejoinder to Professor Hempel's Reply," p. 351.
[3] Watkins, "Between Analytic and Empirical," p. 116.

the intuitive inequality as between (2) and (3) is not explainable by reference to an inequality with respect to testing. For no inequality with respect to testing has been produced. If it is a defect of any construction such as Hempel's to accord equal confirmatory weight to (2) and (3) relative to (1), the same defect arises for Watkins' "Popperian theory." If Hempel needs to account for this "paradoxical" divergence of his construction from intuition, then so does the proponent of Watkins' "Popperian theory," for mere adoption of the latter does not avoid the paradoxes.[4]

Responding to arguments of the sort just outlined, Watkins has granted that, in allowing what he calls "flatly conflicting observation reports" (e.g., (2) and (3)) to confirm the same hypothesis, his "Popperian theory" is exactly similar to Hempel's. But he has argued, further, that his "Popperian theory" is less paradoxical than Hempel's, in that it refuses to consider *any* instance as confirming unless it represents a *test* of the hypothesis in question.[5]

This idea is elaborated by Watkins as follows: *First,* as he writes,

> Whether or not a certain experimental situation would provide a test for a theory depends on whether or not existing

---

[4] This paragraph draws on my "A Note on Confirmation," *Philosophical Studies*, XI (1960), 21-23. A similar criticism had earlier been offered by H. G. Alexander, "The Paradoxes of Confirmation," *British Journal for the Philosophy of Science*, IX (1958), 227-233, in a paper that came to my notice only after my note had been written in the spring of 1959.

[5] J. W. N. Watkins, "Professor Scheffler's Note," *Philosophical Studies*, XII (1961), 16-19. By permission of *Philosophical Studies* and University of Minnesota Press. On the points at issue, there was, aside from published papers, a correspondence between Watkins and myself, in response to my "A Note on Confirmation." My published reply to "Professor Scheffler's Note" is "A Rejoinder on Confirmation," *Philosophical Studies*, XII (1961), 19-20. Watkins has set forth an extended presentation of his recent views on these matters, in "Confirmation, Paradox, and Positivism," included in the forthcoming book: *The Critical Approach: Essays in Honor of Karl Popper*, ed. M. Bunge.

knowledge of that situation indicates that further investigation of it might lead to the falsification of the theory. If we already know that object *a* is a black raven, that *b* is black, and that *c* is non-raven, we *know* that further investigation of *a, b,* and *c* will *not* falsify 'All ravens are black' . . . . If, on the other hand, we know that *d* is a grey object, nature not yet ascertained, that *e* is a raven, color not yet ascertained, that *f* is a grey bird, species not yet ascertained, that *g* is a bird in the Hamburg Zoo reputed to be a green raven, then we know that further investigation of *d, e, f,* and *g might* falsify our theory.[6]

Secondly, assuming that we have in every case the requisite conditions for testing the theory, distinctions as to *degree* of confirmation, varying with the severity of the test, still apply. In Watkins' words:

> If various experiments are performed all of whose outcomes turn out to be favorable to the hypothesis, the experiment which best confirms the hypothesis is the one whose outcome, given existing knowledge *minus* the hypothesis in question, was most likely to be unfavorable to the hypothesis. Thus if further investigation of *g,* the alleged green raven in Hamburg, revealed that *g* is not, after all, a non-black raven, that would confirm 'All ravens are black' better than would a further investigation of the grey object *d* which revealed it to be no raven.[7]

Watkins' new argument is thus that Hempel's construction is paradoxical in failing to acknowledge *testing* as a general condition of confirmation.

The way in which Watkins introduces his new argument is worth noting. He writes, "Hempel argued that the 'paradoxes', though counter-intuitive, are harmless and do not constitute an objection to his theory of confirmation. I claimed that they are not harmless. I still consider that claim correct; but . . . my main

---

[6] Watkins, "Professor Scheffler's Note," p. 18.
[7] *Ibid.*

argument in support of it is incorrect . . . Hempel's criterion allows flatly conflicting observation-reports to confirm the same hypothesis only if they are over-specified . . . but on a Popperian criterion two flatly conflicting observation-reports may also confirm the same hypothesis if they are over-specified."[8] (Over-specification is here meant to rule out their being contradictory.) He then goes on to present his new argument that Hempel's theory is paradoxical in failing to acknowledge the notion of testing in appropriate fashion.

Now Hempel's argument for the harmlessness of the paradoxes clearly involved just the *paradoxes of confirmation* as we have earlier discussed them, for example, the construing of reports (2) and (3) as both confirming (1). Watkins' initial argument, that Popperian theory avoids allowing such "flatly conflicting" reports to confirm the same hypothesis, having now been withdrawn, Popperian theory is presumably also faced with the *paradoxes of confirmation*. Now the question is whether or not *these* paradoxes are harmless. Watkins (in the passage just noted) continues to say they are *not* harmless. But he offers no proposal for dealing with them; we have earlier seen, indeed, that the concept of *testing* provides no explanation of the intuitive inequality between (2) and (3). Furthermore, Watkins apparently supposes that his *new* argument supports the superiority of "Popperian theory" with respect to the paradoxes we have all along been discussing. For it is apparently the substitution of the new for the withdrawn argument which supports the continuing claim that these paradoxes are peculiarly harmful to Hempel's confirmation theory. The new argument, however, does *not* address itself to the *paradoxes of confirmation;* it purports rather to reveal a new "paradoxical" consequence of Hempel's theory, which Popperian theory lacks: the consequence that instances satisfying a hypothesis are confirming irrespective of whether they represent tests of the hypothesis in question.

There seems to be a serious confusion here, based on the word 'paradox.' If Watkins holds the original *paradoxes of confirma-*

---

[8] *Ibid.*, p. 17.

tion to be harmful, then they constitute a defect in the Popperian theory as well as Hempel's theory, and he offers no proposal for explaining or eliminating them in "Popperian" terms. If, on the other hand, Watkins is rather concerned to show his new *paradoxical consequence* to be harmful to the one but not the other theory, his argument is simply irrelevant to *the paradoxes of confirmation,* even though it purports to point out a paradox which concerns confirmation. In either event, the claim that the *paradoxes of confirmation* constitute an objection to Hempel's theory, though they are avoidable in a "Popperian theory of confirmation," has not been sustained.

What Watkins' *new* argument does, in effect, is to introduce another independent factor, that of *testing,* into the situation, but this factor is perfectly impartial as between those *intuitively unequal* instances or reports (e.g., (2) and (3)) whose *theoretical equalization* gives rise to the paradoxes of confirmation. That the testing factor is indeed impartial in the manner indicated is explicitly stated by Watkins, in his comparison of Hempel's and Popper's theories:

> Hempel's "instantiation" or "satisfaction" theory of confirmation has the consequence that 'All ravens are black', being instantiated or satisfied by all black ravens, all black things and all non-ravens, is *automatically* confirmed by *any* observation-report that an object is a black raven, or black, or no raven. Popper's testability theory has the very different consequence that 'All ravens are black' is confirmed by an observation-report that an object is a black raven, or black, or no raven *only* if this reports a *test* of the hypothesis. . . . If I want to confirm the hypothesis I can do so, on Hempel's theory, by sitting in my study and listing its familiar contents. Popper's theory prescribes a more arduous course—I must go out searching for, or devising, test situations and then investigate them more closely to see if I cannot falsify the hypothesis.[9]

9 *Ibid.,* p. 18.

The idea is apparently that, provided the evidence represents a test of the hypothesis, it confirms 'All ravens are black' whether it reports a black raven, a non-raven, or a black object, and, no matter which of these it reports, it will *not* confirm the above hypothesis unless it represents a test of the latter. The testing factor thus represents an extra, impartial condition placed on instances in order for them to be confirming.

Watkins might suggest that the *paradoxes of confirmation* have been at least *limited* in scope, in that pairs such as (2) and (3) now confirm (1) only if they are possible outcomes of test situations. But *such* limitation is hardly to the point: the *paradoxes* are here limited only in the sense that the *scope of confirmation* as such has been narrowed. Furthermore, even were there some *interesting* limitation on the paradoxes, such limitation would not constitute an *explanation* of them, i.e., an account of the gap between intuition and construction, with respect to the confirmatory force of instances.

We shall conclude our consideration of Watkins' view with some remarks concerning the new paradoxical consequence he attributes to Hempel's theory: the consequence that instances satisfying a hypothesis are confirming irrespective of whether or not they represent tests of the hypothesis in question. Although this consequence is, as we have argued, independent of the *paradoxes of confirmation,* it will be of interest to consider it on its own account. What is it that is paradoxical about this consequence? Watkins apparently interprets it to mean that we may confirm, i.e., strengthen the support of, a hypothesis at a given time by experimental determinations which are superfluous in the light of knowledge available at that time. Such interpretation is, however, mistaken. It confuses the notion of evidence which is *positive,* with the notion of evidence which *strengthens the support of a hypothesis at a given time.* Watkins, in stressing the latter notion, indicates his concern with a conception of confirmation quite different from that to which Hempel addresses himself. This may be seen if we consider again Watkins' two elaborations of the testing factor. One is clearly irrelevant to Hempel's objectives in that it involves a distinction of *degrees:*

"If various experiments are performed all of whose outcomes turn out to be favorable to the hypothesis, the experiment which *best* confirms the hypothesis is the one whose outcome, given existing knowledge *minus* the hypothesis in question, was most likely to be unfavorable to the hypothesis."[1] As we saw at the very outset, Hempel aims at a *qualitative* characterization of confirming instances. Distinctions of degree among such instances are irrelevant to, but compatible with, this aim.

The other elaboration of the testing factor is not as obviously irrelevant, but equally so in fact. "Whether or not a certain experimental situation would provide a test for a theory depends on whether or not existing knowledge of that situation indicates that further investigation of it might lead to the falsification of the theory. If we already know that object *a* is a black raven . . . we *know* that further investigation of *a* . . . will *not* falsify 'All ravens are black' . . . . If, on the other hand, we know that *d* is a grey object, nature not yet ascertained . . . then we know that further investigation of *d* . . . *might* falsify our theory."[2]

The first point to notice here is the intrusion of the time factor, as indicated by the phrases "existing knowledge," "further investigation," "already know," "not yet ascertained," as well as reference to "experimental situations." Accordingly, an instance does not simply confirm or fail to confirm a hypothesis; it does so at a given *time* (taken as determining a particular state of knowledge, presumably variable also with persons). The gray object *d* is at time *t* not known to be a non-raven (by someone *J*). It is therefore, at *t*, for *J*, capable of being further investigated with negative results. At t_1, *J* determines *d* to be a non-raven; *d* therefore confirms 'All ravens are black' for *J* at t_1. But *d* is thereafter known by *J* to be a non-raven and is thus no longer capable of being further investigated with negative results. Thus, at t_2, *d* does not, for *J*, confirm 'All ravens are black'.

Clearly, the notion involved here does not lend itself to many of the typical uses to which talk of confirmation is put. *J* may,

[1] *Ibid.*
[2] *Ibid.*

for example, insist, at t_2, that d is one item of confirming, i.e., positive, evidence for his hypothesis; he may be bewildered to be told that no sooner does an instance test positively, than it ceases to confirm that for which it provided a positive test. He may be equally bewildered to learn that, as a result, his "best established" beliefs are, *at the moment* (since he is performing no experiments) without confirmation, and hence no better confirmed than his worst. He may, further, maintain that d confirms the hypothesis quite independently of whether anyone else is, at the moment, determining that it is no raven.

Nonetheless, there *is some* notion which seems to operate in the indicated fashion. This is the notion of a given report's *strengthening a hypothesis at a given time (for a given person).* The experimental report, 'd is a non-black non-raven' may, in fact, at t_1, serve to strengthen the hypothesis, 'All ravens are black', for *J*. Further, at t_2, it will not, typically, *again* strengthen the above hypothesis for *J*. This is *not* to say, however, that *J* will no longer regard it as relevant and favorable, nor that he will fail to regard it as constituting positive evidence irrespective of anyone else's state of knowledge. In sum, an instance which *strengthens* must not only be positive but *new;* whether an instance or experiment confirms a hypothesis is ambiguous as between its being merely *positive or favorable,* and its being *strengthening at the time in question.*

We have encountered the notion of *strengthening a hypothesis at a given time,* in the last section, in Hempel's discussion of the ice experiment: if we know initially that a is pure ice, and hence contains no sodium salt, we already know a to be a positive instance of 'All sodium salts burn yellow'. Thus to put a in the flame and find it does not turn the flame yellow is indeed to fail to strengthen the hypothesis, for it can provide no *new* instance of it. It does *not* follow that a is not a favorable instance at all.

Hempel, however, is not concerned to explicate the *strengthening of a hypothesis at a time.* Nor does he offer methodological prescriptions as to how to go about strengthening hypotheses. Thus, he excludes reference to extra information, time, and persons, asking, "Given some object a (it happens to be a piece of ice, but this fact is not included in the evidence), and given the fact that *a* does not turn the flame yellow and is no sodium salt— does *a* then constitute confirming evidence for the hypothesis?"[3] Obviously, even if a given item *does* constitute confirming evidence, in this sense, it will not necessarily *confirm,* in the sense of *adding strength* to the hypothesis at a specified time for a given person. (Clearly, Watkins, in the passage last cited, operates in a context different from that of Hempel.)

If we have indeed two distinguishable notions, then we need independent analyses and an account of their relationships. But it will hardly be possible to charge Hempel's theory with a paradoxical consequence on the assumption that he aims to explain *the strengthening of hypotheses.* For, given his objective of accounting for the non-temporal non-personal notion of a *confirming instance* of a hypothesis, it is not at all paradoxical that such instances turn out independent of the assumed knowledge of persons at given times. Analogously, given the objective of accounting for the *strengthening of hypotheses,* it is not paradoxical that a given item strengthens a specified hypothesis for J at t_1 but not at t_2.

It is thus misleading to say, as Watkins does, "If I want to confirm the hypothesis I can do so, on Hempel's theory, by sitting in my study and listing its familiar contents."[4] (For such contents, though positive, *confirming* instances are, normally, old and do not (for Hempel) strengthen the hypothesis under such circumstances.) As well say that Watkins counsels us, if we are asked for the evidence in support of our views, to disclaim all the accumulated support gathered from tests until five minutes ago, and to devise methods of testing these views in fresh situations. The constructive task, in sum, is to analyze and relate the several ideas associated with 'confirmation', as found in scientific practice, rather than to pit them against one another.

We return again to the paradoxes of confirmation, and address ourselves to the proposal to explain them by reference to the *size of classes* related in certain ways to the hypothesis in ques-

[3] Hempel, "Studies in the Logic of Confirmation," p. 20.
[4] Watkins, "Professor Scheffler's Note," p. 18.

tion. The proposal is due to J. Hosiasson-Lindenbaum,[5] but it has figured in a variety of treatments by other writers. The general approach of Hosiasson-Lindenbaum involves a theory of *degrees* of confirmation, but some of her ideas have relevance for the paradoxes, as we have encountered them, involving *qualitative* confirmation. These ideas are discussed, in the latter connection, by Hempel, in the course of his study.

Of the proposal emerging from these ideas, Hempel writes:

> Stated in reference to the raven-hypothesis, it consists in the suggestion that the finding of one non-black object which is no raven, while constituting confirming evidence for the hypothesis, would increase the degree of confirmation of the hypothesis by a smaller amount than the finding of one raven which is black. This is said to be so because the class of all ravens is much less numerous than that of all non-black objects, so that—to put the idea in suggestive though somewhat misleading terms—the finding of one black raven confirms a larger portion of the total content of the hypothesis than the finding of one non-black non-raven. In fact, from the basic assumptions of her theory, Miss Hosiasson is able to derive a theorem according to which the above statement about the relative increase in degree of confirmation will hold provided that actually the number of all ravens is small compared with the number of all non-black objects.[6]

Essentially the same proposal, though interpreted in terms of the risk of falsification, is presented in a paper by D. Pears.[7] "People," he writes, "are too myopic to verify general hypotheticals, and so want to make the fullest use of the limited evidence which they do get. They therefore consider that a general

[5] Janina Hosiasson-Lindenbaum, "On Confirmation," *Journal of Symbolic Logic*, V (1940), 133-148.

[6] Hempel, "Studies in the Logic of Confirmation," pp. 21-22, footnote 2.

[7] David Pears, "Hypotheticals," *Analysis*, X (1950), 49-63. The passage cited in the text is from p. 50. By permission of the publisher.

hypothetical does not merely escape falsification; but is confirmed to the extent that it ran the risk of being falsified." But, he argues, the raven-hypothesis runs less risk of being falsified when the search for counterexamples (i.e., non-black ravens) is conducted among non-black things than when it is conducted among ravens. If there is, in fact, a counterexample, it is more likely to turn up in the latter case, "since the class of things which are ravens is smaller than the class of things which are not black."[8] This statement about the relative size of the classes mentioned represents an assumption which people make, and their making it explains why black ravens are thought to provide more confirmation than non-black non-ravens. For a black raven is a member of a class, i.e., *ravens,* in which counterexamples have a greater relative frequency than they have in the class of *non-black* things, to which non-black non-ravens belong—*if* there *are* counterexamples at all. Thus, to have eliminated a given member of the raven class as a counterexample is to have done more to show there *are* no counterexamples than is shown when a member of the non-black class is eliminated as a counterexample. To show there are no counterexamples is, of course, just to show that the raven-hypothesis is true, for this hypothesis *is* the denial that there exists anything which is both a raven and non-black.

Finally (paraphrasing Pears' further argument), to determine an object as being no raven or black is to determine simply that it fails of being a counterexample, without also locating it more narrowly within some class (smaller than the universe) where counterexamples must be found if they exist at all. It is, in effect, to have eliminated an object at large as a counterexample to the hypothesis. But, on the assumption that neither the raven class (surely) nor even the non-black class exhausts the universe of objects, the relative frequency of counterexamples, if any, among objects at large in the universe will be smaller than their frequency among either ravens or non-black things. The raven-hypothesis thus runs least risk of being falsified when the search for counterexamples is conducted among objects at large. Hence to show that such an object is eliminated as a counterexample is to do least in showing that there are in fact no counterexamples, i.e., that the raven-hypothesis is true. We now can explain why the determination of something as *non-raven or black* is thought to provide less confirmation for our hypothesis than its determination as *black raven* or *non-black non-raven*.

A hasty reading of the foregoing proposal for explaining the paradoxes might suggest that it is simply irrelevant, since it concerns itself with *degrees* of confirmation. Such a suggestion would be wrong. The proposal does not simply *introduce* distinctions of degree, but purports to show how such distinctions, coupled with natural assumptions about the relative size of classes, *explain* the intuitive inequality among reports, all of which represent *qualitatively* positive instances. The proposal, in effect, maintains as legitimate the equalization of the reports in question, from the standpoint of a qualitative confirmation theory, but explains the resultant divergence from intuition by appeal to assumptions as to class size, allegedly affecting our judgment of degree in just the manner required by intuition.

After presenting an account of Hosiasson-Lindenbaum's version, Hempel criticizes the proposal on the following counts: First, the requisite assumption as to relative class size is not warranted in every case in which the paradoxes arise. It is not simply that ravens happen to be fewer than non-black things whereas, for some other hypothesis than the raven-hypothesis, the antecedent class might not be smaller than the complement of the consequent class. Rather, argues Hempel, even for the raven-hypothesis itself, the required numerical assumption depends in part upon the choice of language within which hypotheses are to be expressed.

If we choose a "thing-language," with physical things of finite size as our individual elements, then we are probably justified in assuming ravens to be fewer than non-black things. On the other hand, if we choose a "co-ordinate-language," in which finite space-time regions are individuals, the raven-hypothesis needs to be expressed in some such manner as, 'Every space-time region which contains a raven, contains something black'. Now, "even if the total number of ravens ever to exist is finite, the class of space-time regions containing a raven has the power of the continuum and so does the class of space-time regions containing something non-black; thus, for a co-ordinate language of the type under consideration, the above numerical assumption is not warranted. Now the use of a co-ordinate language may appear quite artificial in this particular illustration; but it will seem very appropriate in many other contexts, such as, e.g., that of physical field theories."[9]

Secondly, even choosing a thing-language, we must recall that there is no *logical* guarantee that the required numerical assumption is true. If ravens are fewer than non-black things, this is a fact of nature, and "it remains an empirical question, for every hypothesis of the form 'All P's are Q's', whether actually the class of non-Q's is much more numerous than the class of P's; and in many cases this question will be very difficult to decide."[1]

Now Hempel's first criticism, regarding relativity of the numerical assumption to language choice, might be countered as follows: At most what this criticism shows is that the assumption (in the case of the raven-hypothesis, for example) is *unwarranted* for some choice of language. But warrant is not at all to the point. What is needed is an explanation of the source of our intuitive inequalities among evidential reports. For this purpose, it is sufficient to show that the numerical assumption is actually held; it is not further required that it be shown to have warrant. Conversely, to rebut the proposed explanation, it is not sufficient to show the assumption to lack warrant; it must further be shown that it is not actually held. In fact, Pears puts his version of the proposal in just this way: the numerical assumption is one that is generally held, and the fact that it is generally held explains why it is also generally thought that black ravens provide more confirmation than non-black non-ravens. Furthermore, Hempel's own explanation of the paradoxes traces the intuitive inequalities to a prevalent view concerning the reference of universal

---

[9] Hempel, "Studies in the Logic of Confirmation," p. 21, footnote 2.
[1] *Ibid.*

conditionals, which is nonetheless *mistaken,* and to the intrusion of extra information, which is *improper.* Surely, it is no rebuttal of his explanation merely to point out the mistake and the impropriety in question. The foregoing argument is not, however, as sound as it may seem. For consider Hempel's own explanation of the paradoxes. It is true that he traces the intuitive inequalities to a certain view which is held in fact, though mistaken, and to a prevalent intrusion of extra information, which is nonetheless improper. But his *explanatory claim* rests on the assertion that, when the mistaken view is recognized as such and given up, and when the intrusion in question is acknowledged as illegitimate and abandoned, the paradoxes no longer arise, for the intuitive inequalities vanish.

In the present case, however, the situation seems to be quite different. The intuitive inequalities are traced to a numerical assumption which is in fact held; so far the analogy holds. But if the explanatory efficacy of this proposal is to be upheld, it must further be the case that the intuitive inequalities vanish in those cases where the numerical assumption is recognized as unwarranted and accordingly given up. This, however, does not appear to be claimed nor does it appear to happen. Non-black non-ravens still appear intuitively unequal to black ravens with respect to 'All ravens are black' when translation from a thing-language to a coordinate language has been effected (or when the relativity to choice of language has been made clear). The report 'This is a space-time region neither containing anything black nor containing a raven' retains its "paradoxical" character when construed as representing a positive instance of 'Every space-time region which contains a raven, contains something black'. In general, it may be remarked that the direction of this proposal differs from that of Hempel's own answer. Hempel suggested that the paradoxes are *psychological illusions* resting, in every case, on mistaken conceptions which need to be given up. The present proposal suggests that, at least in typical cases, the "paradoxical" inequalities *arise from a real factor in the situation* (i.e., the described class-size relationships), and are thus *not* illusory. This real factor is, however, as we have seen, not pervasive enough to do the job demanded of it.

Thus, the numerical assumption in question cannot be supposed to explain the paradoxes of confirmation. Even though there are cases where the assumption does in fact have warrant, and even granted that our concept of confirmatory *degree* may reflect such warrant in the manner suggested by the proposal, the paradoxes require explanation in other terms.

Hempel's second criticism reinforces this view, by pointing out that the paradoxes are invariant though the numerical assumption cannot be supposed invariably to hold. Where the assumption is doubtful, or clearly false, paradoxicality nonetheless persists. We may illustrate by suggesting the hypotheses 'All molecules are inanimate' and 'All invertebrates lack kidneys'. Whether we take as doubtful or false the required numerical assumptions (i.e., that molecules are fewer than animate things, and that invertebrates are fewer than things not lacking kidneys) it remains paradoxical to take the family cat as a positive instance of either hypothesis.

There is, however, a further criticism, beyond the two presented by Hempel, that may here be offered against the proposal under consideration: it does not fully address itself to the paradoxes of confirmation. These paradoxes involve intuitive inequalities (among reports) *which themselves vary* with respect to logically equivalent versions of "the same hypothesis." The present proposal abstracts from the question of equivalent versions altogether by speaking only of *the raven-hypothesis*. It thus *cannot* explain the paradoxes of confirmation fully.

Consider, for example, the equivalent variants of *the* raven-hypothesis:

(1) $\qquad\qquad$ $(x) \ (Rx \supset Bx)$
(4) $\qquad\qquad$ $(x) \ (\sim Bx \supset \sim Rx)$

and the reports:

(2) $\qquad\qquad$ $Ra \cdot Ba$
(3) $\qquad\qquad$ $\sim Ba \cdot \sim Ra$
(5) $\qquad\qquad$ $\sim Ra \lor Ba$

Paradoxes arise from the fact that the equivalence condition and Nicod's sufficient condition, together, equalize the reports (2), (3), and (5), with respect to (1), and with respect to (4). Such equalization is contrary to intuition, which treats these reports differently. But the intuitive differences *vary* with the formulation of the hypothesis chosen. With respect to (1), (2) appears positive, but (3) and (5) do not. With respect to (4), on the other hand, (3) appears positive, but (2) and (5) do not. Those answers to the paradoxes earlier considered, resting on the attachment of different existential statements to (1) and (4), or the specification of different fields of application for them, or indication of the prevalent but mistaken construal of (1) and (4) as referentially different—all attempt to account for the *variation* of intuitive inequalities among reports, with choice of (1) or (4) to represent *the* (abstract) raven-hypothesis.

The present proposal makes no mention of such variation at all, yielding simply inequalities among (2), (3), and (5). Relative to (1), the main inequality yielded is indeed the one wanted, i.e., (2) comes out better than (3). (The further inequality yielded by Pears' version, that (3) is better than (5), is also welcome, since intuitively (5) appears positive for neither (1) nor (4), whereas (3) appears positive for at least (4).)

But the main inequality yielded is the *reverse* of what is wanted relative to (4). For here, intuition asks that (3) come out better than (2), and the proposal persists in saying that (2) is better than (3). To put it differently, the proposal simply ranks (2), (3), and (5) in degree of confirmation, granting a positive weight to each relative to the raven-hypothesis, *no matter how formulated*. It follows that (2) equally confirms (1) and (4), though intuition denies it confirms (4). It follows also that (3) equally confirms (1) and (4), though intuition denies it confirms (1). (It follows, finally, that (5) equally confirms (1) and (4), though intuition denies it confirms either.)

Though, relative to (1), the qualitative difference between (2) and (3) *is* appropriately correlated with a difference in degree, this latter difference does *not* properly reflect, but runs counter to, the qualitative difference relative to (4). Thus, given the single report (2), there is no explanation of the qualitative difference when we shift from (1) to (4), and, analogously, given the report (3), there is no explanation of the qualitative difference when we shift from (4) to (1).

At best, then, we have in the present proposal only a partial answer to the paradoxes, and one which violates our troublesome intuition as much as it tends to support it. Coupled with the objections discussed above, the last criticism indicates the weakness of the appeal to class size as an explanation of the paradoxes of confirmation. We may, of course, independently wish to acknowledge class size as a relevant factor in determining *degrees* of confirmation, but that is another story.

We turn now to another idea for explaining the paradoxes, suggested by N. Goodman.[2] This idea rests on the observation that logically equivalent statements do not generally have the same or logically equivalent contraries, so that reports equally satisfying logically equivalent statements may yet differ in the way they eliminate alternative hypotheses.

Hempel's answer to the paradoxes, it will be recalled, suggested that the intuitive inequalities are due to (i) faulty views concerning the reference of universal conditionals, and (ii) improper intrusion of extra information (the basic idea of the latter point attributed by him to Goodman). Since the paradoxes are, on this account, due to *faulty and improper* conceptions, Hempel argued that "the impression of a paradoxical situation is not objectively founded; it is a psychological illusion."[3] We have seen how alternative attempts to ground the paradoxes on objective features of the situation (e.g., the testing factor, and class size relationships) failed to yield the desired inequalities in every case, thus reinforcing Hempel's view of the paradoxes as illusory.

Goodman now suggests that even when faulty and improper conceptions are removed, there remains an objective, logical feature of the situation that yields just the inequalities required by intuition. Discussing the confirmation of (1) by (3), he writes:

[2] I am indebted to Goodman for discussion of his idea, which amplified his published treatment in *Fact, Fiction, and Forecast*.

[3] Hempel, "Studies in the Logic of Confirmation," (I) p. 18.

We arrive at the unexpected conclusion that the statement that a given object is neither black nor a raven confirms the hypothesis that all ravens are black. The prospect of being able to investigate ornithological theories without going out in the rain is so attractive that we know there must be a catch in it. The trouble this time, however, lies not in faulty definition, but in tacit and illicit reference to evidence not stated in our example. Taken by itself, the statement that the given object is neither black nor a raven confirms the hypothesis that everything that is not a raven is not black as well as the hypothesis that everything that is not black is not a raven. We tend to ignore the former hypothesis because we know it to be false from abundant other evidence—from all the familiar things that are not ravens but are black. But we are required to assume that no such evidence is available. Under this circumstance, even a much stronger hypothesis is also obviously confirmed: that nothing is either black or a raven. In the light of this confirmation of the hypothesis that there are no ravens, it is no longer surprising that under the articifial restrictions of the example, the hypothesis that all ravens are black is also confirmed. And the prospects for indoor ornithology vanish when we notice that under these same conditions, the contrary hypothesis that no ravens are black is equally well confirmed.[4]

Everything in this passage until the last sentence is familiar, suggesting that the paradoxicality of supposing (3) to confirm (1) is wholly due to improper reference to extra information, and that removal of such reference leaves (2) and (3) on a par with respect to their confirmation of (1). But the last sentence introduces the idea that (3) is still, in a special sense, worse than (2). For whereas (3) confirms (in the "satisfaction" sense) both (1) *and* its contrary:

(6) $$(x) \ (Rx \supset \sim Bx)$$

(2) confirms (1) but disconfirms (6). Report (2) is therefore not, like (3), merely a bit of indoor ornithology.

The situation is, moreover, fittingly reversed when we consider (4). For the contrary of (4) is *not* (6), but rather:

(7) $(x) \, (\sim\!Bx \supset Rx)$

and here we find that, although (2) and (3) both confirm (4), only (3) disconfirms (7), while (2) confirms it. Finally, (5) confirms (1) and (4), but fails to disconfirm either (6) or (7). The report:

(8) $\sim\!Ra \cdot Ba$

is even worse, confirming each of (1), (4), (6), and (7). We thus find the required inequalities in their requisite variation with choice of (1) or (4) to represent *the* raven-hypothesis.

The basic datum upon which the present idea rests is the fact that logically equivalent statements may have contraries which are not logically equivalent to one another. Thus, although (1) and (4) are logically equivalent and thus "have the same content," or "impose the same restrictions upon objects," their contraries, respectively (6) and (7), are not themselves logically equivalent. The suggestion is, then, that reports which alike represent positive instances of the same (abstract) hypothesis may yet differ in their confirming-or-disconfirming relationships to different statements which are contraries of equivalent formulations of the hypothesis in question.

The construction which takes both (2) and (3) as positive instances of (1) is thus correct; the intuitive inequality between (2) and (3) does not require revision of their equal status *with respect to* (1). Rather, the construction itself may show this inequality by yielding differential status respecting (6), for (2) disconfirms (6) while (3) confirms it. An analogous argument gives the desired reverse conclusion where (4) is taken rather than (1).

The upshot of this idea is thus that the paradoxes are not wholly illusory but arise out of intuitions marking objective distinctions of a logical sort. We have, furthermore, a new compli-

cation to cope with, respecting the notion of confirming instances. For to say that a report represents a confirming instance
of a given (abstract) hypothesis is not in itself sufficiently informative with regard to statements that may be taken as contraries. Where a given contrast is intended, say between (1)
and (6), the fact that (3) confirms (1) will not be of much
interest, for it also confirms (6). (It is worth noting here that
the generalization formula wrongly assumes that a hypothesis
has but one contrary, for it speaks of *the* contrary of a hypothesis
being ruled out by positive instances of the latter.)

In ordinary parlance, the intent to make a particular contrast
is indicated by choice of a particular *formulation* of the hypothesis, e.g., (1) rather than (4). The air of paradox results from
(i) such a choice, with its attendant expectation that a confirming report will be one that *selectively* confirms (1), relative to
its contrary, (6); and (ii) the construal of confirming reports
as satisfying the equivalence condition, and therefore *not* guaranteed to fulfill the above expectation. (For we have seen that,
though (3) confirms (4) and *selectively* confirms it relative to
its contrary (7), it does *not* selectively confirm (1) relative to
its contrary, (6).)

Thus, we have some such notion as *selective confirmation*
which does *not* fulfill the equivalence condition—*not* because a
report may satisfy some statement but fail to satisfy its equivalent, but rather because it may satisfy also the contrary of one
but fail to satisfy, and indeed violate, the contrary of the other.
Thus some apology is due to Nicod, for aside from other criticisms leveled against his original criterion, that resting on the
equivalence condition seems to have been too strong. In fact,
the notion of *selective* confirmation *does* go beyond the invariant
content of a hypothesis and does *not* carry across equivalent
formulations. Logically equivalent statements do bear the same
satisfaction relations to all instances but not the same *"confirmation"* relationships generally, unless these are initially reduced
to satisfaction relationships. We thus need to reconsider the
status of the equivalence condition.

Hempel argues that the equivalence condition is necessary

because it would be absurd to suppose that it was "sound scientific procedure to base a prediction on a given hypothesis if formulated in a sentence S_1, because a good deal of confirming evidence had been found for S_1; but that it was altogether inadmissible to base the prediction . . . on an equivalent formulation S_2, because no confirming evidence for S_2 was available."[5]
But take (4) as our case of S_1, and imagine all the evidence to consist of statements such as (3). True, (3) satisfies (4) and also (1). But it also satisfies the contrary of (1), i.e., (6).

Do we have any reason, so far, for predicting that a new-found raven will be black rather than not? Since (1) and (6) together imply that there are no ravens, our new-found raven forces us to give up at least one of these statements. If we give up (6) and predict 'Black', we can retain (4). If we give up (1) and predict 'Not black', we have to give up (4) as well, for (4) and (6) are incompatible, given the existence of our raven. We might suppose we have here a reason for retaining (1) and predicting 'Black'. But, on the contrary, if we predict 'Black', thus saving (4), we shall need to give up another hypothesis hitherto confirmed, i.e., that nothing is black, whereas if we yield (4) and predict 'Not black', we can save the latter hypothesis. Here, it seems, is a case where basing a prediction directly on (4) (i.e., predicting 'Non-raven' for a new instance of 'Nonblack') is beyond suspicion, while basing a prediction directly on its equivalent, (1), is a matter of balanced decision. The reason, furthermore, is *not* that "no confirming evidence" (in the sense of satisfaction) is available for (1), but that whatever is available also supports its contrary, (6).

The foregoing discussion is no argument *for* Nicod's original criterion, which suffers from other defects mentioned earlier. Nor is it an argument *against* constructions such as Hempel's, which satisfy the equivalence condition. For in terms of Hempel's definitions of confirmation, disconfirmation, and neutrality, requisite notions of *selective confirmation,* of various sorts, can be further explained, in (roughly) the manner in which they were introduced in our discussion above. What *has* been sug-

[5] Hempel, "Studies in the Logic of Confirmation," pp. 12-13.

gested is the *importance* of such notions of selective confirmation. We need to *distinguish*, in any event, between *evidence which simply accords with a statement,* and evidence which *accords with it but not also with its contrary* (in the extreme case violating its contrary). It may be further suggested that the *confirming* of a hypothesis perhaps typically involves the *favoring* of it in this way as against a contrary one. Thus, if the concept of a *positive instance* is construed simply in terms of *according with* a given statement, we shall have to provide also for the stronger notion (or notions) of a *positive instance which also favors* the statement in question.[6]

7. Positive Instances and the Generalization Formula

We have been concerned with the question of qualitative confirmation, i.e., the nature of positive instances, because of its bearing on the generalization formula. This formula, it will be recalled, represents a modern reply to Hume's challenge to justify induction. According to the generalization formula, particular judgments regarding cases outside the available evidence are legitimized by their conformity with generalizations that have hitherto worked. Such generalizations are those in thorough accord with available data—whose contraries are thus in conflict with these same data; these generalizations are thus *confirmed by* past experience, and serve in turn, to ground our inductions, which *go beyond* past experience.

The question under what conditions a generalization is in accord with given data has turned out to be surprisingly subtle and complex. We have seen the difficulties Hempel had to overcome in formulating a general account of the conditions under which a given statement represents an instance which accords with a generalization, or is positive with respect to it. Along the

---

[6] These notions must, furthermore, be distinguished from that of *strengthening instances,* i.e., those which are novel at *t,* and accord with, or selectively favor, the hypothesis at stake.

For another sort of development of the general notion of favoring instances, see S. Morgenbesser, "Goodman on the Ravens," *Journal of Philosophy,* LIX (1962), 493-495.

way, we have noted how natural assumptions as to these conditions, seemingly obvious in isolation, have yielded problematic results in combination, forcing the theorist to exercise discretionary judgment in choosing the bases for a consistent view. We have considered the limitations of such popular conceptions as those embodied in Nicod's criterion and the prediction-criterion, and we have, further, remarked the limitations of Hempel's satisfaction criterion: not only is it restricted to logically simple languages, but it confines itself to languages which are purely observational. If the inductions we need to justify in order to meet Hume's challenge include those we base on theoretical systems of science, we clearly need to go beyond the satisfaction criterion, and perhaps beyond the notion of *positive instance* itself and thus beyond the reach of the generalization formula altogether.

Aside from the surprising theoretical complexities of the notion of *positive instance,* and the limitations it may harbor with respect to languages of certain sorts, we have, in addition, noted certain important distinctions, underlying ambiguities in its use with reference to confirmation. At the beginning of our discussion of Hempel's study, we cautioned against prematurely assuming that the natural view of the generalization formula is correct, i.e., that instances which *accord with* a generalization in fact *confirm* it, in the sense of *selecting* it as a basis for particular inductions. We thus used Hempel's 'confirmation' terminology in a minimal sense, taking confirming instances of a hypothesis to be positive instances of it, or those in accord with it. The question whether such instances in fact *select* hypotheses upon which we base particular inductions is a question we left open, and to this question we shall soon turn.

Another distinction of importance is that which emerged in discussion of Watkins' suggested answer to the paradoxes of confirmation: the distinction between instances which are confirming, i.e., *positive,* with respect to h, and those which *strengthen* h at time t, for person J, i.e. (roughly), those representing *new* positive instances of h at t, for J. It is worth noting that the distinction just mentioned is independent of the one previously indicated. For clearly, even if a given instance not only accords with but also selects a particular hypothesis rather than its contrary, it still does not strengthen this hypothesis for every t and J.

In discussing the class-size explanation of the paradoxes, another distinction came to the fore, that between "abstract" and "concrete" senses of such terms as 'hypothesis', 'generalization', and 'theory'. For, as we argued, the class-size answer is inadequate, since it fails to distinguish between statements which are logically equivalent to one another, and refers only to *the* "abstract" raven-hypothesis, rather than to the several "concrete" hypothesis-statements which, by virtue of their logical equivalence, are often said to embody the same "abstract content." As we saw in connection with Goodman's proposed solution, logically equivalent statements may yet have contraries which are not logically equivalent, so that it is false to speak of *the* contrary of an *abstract* hypothesis.

Further, we saw that an instance which is positive with respect to a given statement, in the sense of according with it, may also be positive with respect to its contrary, and thus it may favor neither the original nor its contrary. Thus a distinction needs to be made between saying that an instance i *accords with* hypothesis-statement h, and saying that it *favors* it—between saying that i is a *positive* (or confirming) instance, and saying that it is a *selectively positive* (or confirming) instance of h.

It follows immediately that our caution regarding the use of Hempel's 'confirmation' terminology was well-advised. For not every instance i, satisfying h by his construction, and so constituting a positive (or confirming) instance of h, in fact *confirms h, in the sense of selecting h* rather than its contrary. It further follows that, if the generalization formula is put in such a way as to claim that positive evidence for h automatically selects h by disqualifying its contrary, the formula is wrong. Such an interpretation of the generalization formula was indeed suggested earlier, and must now be given up.

However, a weaker interpretation is possible, which does *not* claim that positive evidence *automatically* selects the hypothesis-statement in question. According to this weaker interpretation a hypothesis-statement is selected by positive evidence only if, as a matter of fact, such evidence is also *selectively positive,* i.e., negative with respect to (satisfying the denial of) its contrary. Accordingly, those hypothesis-statements are selected, at any given time, for which the total available evidence is at least in part selectively positive, while failing to be at all negative.

To say that the hypothesis-statement *h* is selected because *consistently supported* by the evidence is (on the present, weaker interpretation) *not* to say that *h* is selected simply because the evidence is at least partly positive with respect to *h,* and never negative. For we have seen that this condition is fulfilled by the evidence '$\sim Ra \cdot \sim Ba$' with respect to both '(x) $(Rx \supset Bx)$' and '(x) $(Rx \supset \sim Bx)$', and that the evidence thus selects neither. Rather, we now interpret consistent evidential support to require also selectively positive evidence.

Clearly, the notion of *consistent support* of *h* will vary radically, depending on which interpretation it is given. The strong version of the generalization formula claims that *h* is selected by evidence that is partly positive and never negative with respect to *h.* We have seen that this claim must be rejected. But the weaker version of the generalization formula claims only that *h* is selected by evidence that is in part selectively positive and never negative with respect to *h.* This weaker version we have as yet seen no decisive reason to reject. For, if '$\sim Ra \cdot \sim Ba$' fails to select *either* '(x) $(Rx \supset Bx)$' *or* its contrary, '(x) $(Rx \supset \sim Bx)$', the weaker version makes no claim that such selection in fact takes place. We shall hereafter intend the *weaker* version in referring to the generalization formula, and we shall speak of consistent support in the corresponding sense.

Surely, in any event, we cannot hope for some formula that will yield a decision as between every generalization and its contrary. It is sufficient if we have a way of deciding reasonably in certain cases. The weaker version does appear to enable us to decide in certain cases, at least, and to do so reasonably. For example, '$Ra \cdot Ba$' does meet the specification of the weaker version in such a way as to select '(x) $(Rx \supset Bx)$'.

The generalization formula thus, after all, does appear to provide an answer to Hume's challenge, at least within the language-limitations discussed earlier in the present section. For, in terms of the notion of a positive instance (yielding that of a selectively positive, and that of a negative, instance), it provides a rule for *selecting* hypothesis-statements on the basis of past experience, which statements serve to guide our particular judgments regarding new cases.

Nonetheless, the issue needs to be examined further. Just because the weaker version of the generalization formula is superior to the stronger version, it does not follow that the weaker version is not subject to independent difficulties.

We have already noted the *prima facie* difference between lawlike and accidental generalizations, which needs to be taken into account if the generalization formula is not to run into immediate trouble, legitimizing the selection of accidental statements as well as lawlike ones. But more extreme difficulties than this one have in fact been found to confront the generalization formula in recent investigations. We turn therefore, to a direct examination of its adequacy as an account of our particular inductive judgments.

8. Induction and Projectibility

We may profitably begin by considering a passage from J. S. Mill's *System of Logic*. Although it does seem true that, for every particular induction we make, there is some generalization related to it in the manner prescribed by the generalization formula, Mill argues that generalizations which are equally well supported by available evidence vary in the sanction they provide for their respective particular inductions. In other words, the hypotheses designated by the generalization formula do not uniformly sanction the particular judgments based upon them. Mill writes:

> Again, there are cases in which we reckon with the most unfailing confidence upon uniformity, and other cases in which we do not count upon it at all. In some we feel com-

plete assurance that the future will resemble the past, the unknown be precisely similar to the known. In others, however invariable may be the result obtained from the instances which have been observed, we draw from them no more than a very feeble presumption that the like result will hold in all other cases. . . . When a chemist announces the existence and properties of a newly discovered substance, if we confide in his accuracy, we feel assured that the conclusions he has arrived at will hold universally, though the induction be founded but on a single instance . . . Now mark another case, and contrast it with this. Not all the instances which have been observed since the beginning of the world in support of the general proposition that all crows are black would be deemed a sufficient presumption of the truth of the proposition, to outweigh the testimony of one unexceptionable witness who should affirm that in some region of the earth not fully explored he had caught and examined a crow, and had found it to be grey. Why is a single instance, in some cases, sufficient for a complete induction, while in others myriads of concurring instances, without a single exception known or presumed, go such a very little way towards establishing an universal proposition?[7]

Mill may be interpreted as pointing out, in effect, that appeal to the consistent support of past instances, in the spirit of the generalization formula, is too inclusive to represent our normal inductive judgments accurately. For it picks out not only such judgments as are confidently grounded in the chemist's generalizations but also such judgments as are made with very little assurance, if at all, though based on generalizations equally or better supported by past experience than the chemist's. In short, Mill is suggesting the need for further effort to distinguish between what we earlier called "lawlike" and "accidental" generalizations.

[7] John Stuart Mill, *A System of Logic, Ratiocinative and Inductive* (1843) (8th ed.; New York: Harper & Brothers, 1887), Book III, chap. iii, section 3, p. 228.

Mill's own theory of induction holds that "the proposition that the course of nature is uniform is the fundamental principle, or general axiom, of Induction," and that "every induction may be thrown into the form of a syllogism by supplying a major premise," the uniformity of nature appearing as "the ultimate major premise of all inductions." Nonetheless, he holds the principle of the uniformity of nature "to be itself an instance of induction. . . . itself founded on prior generalizations."[8] He believes, further, that the distinctions among generalizations, with respect to the varying degrees of sanction they provide for particular inductions, may be accounted for by reference to larger generalizations, themselves supported by experience, about the reliability of generalizations of different types.[9]

The appeal to a principle of the uniformity of nature to justify induction has already been criticized, in Section 2 of the present Part. The appeal to larger generalizations to distinguish "lawlike" from "accidental" hypotheses may be considered independently, however, and the idea has been found attractive by several theorists who have rejected the notion of the uniformity of nature. We shall therefore discuss this idea in due course, but we need first to note the investigations of N. Goodman, which have aggravated the problem of accidental hypotheses covered by a too inclusive generalization formula.

We consider first an example offered by Goodman, which presents the problem in roughly the same way it appears in the passage from Mill initially cited:

> That a given piece of copper conducts electricity increases the credibility of statements asserting that other pieces of copper conduct electricity, and thus confirms the hypothesis that all copper conducts electricity. But the fact that a given man now in this room is a third son does not increase the credibility of statements asserting that other men now in this room are third sons, and so does not confirm the hypothesis that all men now in this room are third sons. Yet

[8] *Ibid.,* section 1, p. 224.
[9] *Ibid.,* chap. iv, section 2, pp. 231-234.

in both cases our hypothesis is a generalization of the evidence statement. The difference is that in the former case the hypothesis is a *lawlike* statement; while in the latter case, the hypothesis is a merely contingent or accidental generality. Only a statement that is *lawlike*—regardless of its truth or falsity or its scientific importance—is capable of receiving confirmation from an instance of it; accidental statements are not.[1]

But it is Goodman's further formulation of the problem that is crucial, generalizing it to the extreme limit. For what has so far been shown is that, in addition to all credible or sanctioned particular inductions, the generalization formula also selects certain incredible ones. Now Goodman shows that among these incredible ones lie the very negations of our credible inductions. To apply his previous example, it is not merely that by the generalization formula we selectively "establish," in addition to the credible prediction that the next specimen of copper will conduct electricity, also the incredible one that the next occupant of this room to be examined will turn out to be a third son. Rather, we do not even "establish" that the next specimen of copper will conduct electricity, for we can produce a generalization equally supported by the evidence and yielding the prediction that it will not.

We shall put the point specifically in terms of the latter example. While the available evidence (reporting cases of copper uniformly conducting electricity) consistently supports:

(1)   All specimens of copper conduct electricity,

clearly disconfirming (containing negative instances or counter-examples of) its contrary:

(2)   All specimens of copper do not conduct electricity,

this is not sufficient to yield the particular induction concerning a new copper specimen, *c*, to be examined:

(3)   *c* conducts electricity.

[1] Goodman, *Fact, Fiction, and Forecast*, pp. 73-74.

For, though (2) is clearly rejected by the available evidence, according to the generalization formula, and (1) clearly selected by this formula, there is, unfortunately, *another* hypothesis which the formula equally selects on the basis of the same evidence, and which blocks the induction (3).

Clearly, the same evidence must be taken, by the generalization formula, to provide consistent support for:

(4) All specimens of copper are either such that they have been examined prior to time *t* and conduct electricity or have not been examined prior to time *t* and do not conduct electricity,

while clearly disconfirming *its* contrary:

(5) All specimens of copper are either such that they have been examined prior to time *t* and do not conduct electricity or have not been examined prior to time *t* and do conduct electricity,

thus providing sanction for the negate of (3):

(6)   *c* does not conduct electricity

if it be assumed true that

(7)   *c* has not been examined prior to time *t*.

The consequence for the generalization formula is severe. For even if it succeeds in *selecting* (1) rather than (2), it equally *selects* (4) rather than (5), thus providing no basis for differentiating between (3) and (6), and, *a fortiori,* no basis for preferring (3).

We saw earlier the need to distinguish between saying that evidence *accords with* a hypothesis, and saying that it *favors* it as against its contrary. We further suggested that the notion of evidence *confirming* a hypothesis typically involves its favoring it, as against its contrary. Now we see the need for an even stronger notion of favoring or selecting a hypothesis. For a generalization which is merely favored as against its contrary, e.g., (1) relative to (2), may still fail to enable selection between rival particular inductions. We thus require a notion of evidence selecting a hypothesis, not merely as against its contrary, but also as against other rival hypotheses. A formula which does not provide for this more stringent selection fails to explain adequately the manner in which hypotheses are *confirmed* by evidence; correspondingly, it gives us no way to *apply* confirmation to the judgment of new cases.

The argument represented by the illustration (1)-(7) is quite general. It shows that the situation is much worse than we had imagined it earlier. For it is not that the generalization formula yields the desired inductive judgments, together with certain undesired ones based on accidental generalizations, which might somehow be weeded out independently. We find, rather, that the generalization formula does not yield any desired induction whatever.

Merely to be told to choose our inductions by reference to generalizations consistently supported by available evidence is, therefore, to be given worthless advice. Nor does the situation improve with the increase of relevant data over time. For, even if we later find that *c does* conduct electricity, and we accordingly eliminate (6) as false, and add (3) to our evidence, leading to a rejection of (4), we do not thereby eliminate other hypotheses which are exactly like (4) but which specify times later than *t*. Accordingly, no matter how much empirical data we have accumulated, and no matter how many hypotheses like (4) we have disconfirmed up to a given point in time, we still have (by the generalization formula) contradictory predictions or inductions for every case not yet included in our data. No matter how fast and how long we run, we find we are standing still at the starting line.

This predicament holds, to be sure, only for cases assumed to be new. Using our previous example, if neither (7) nor its negate is assumed, then (4) yields neither (3) nor (6), while if (7) is assumed false, then (4) converges with (1), implying (3) rather than (6). This is not surprising, however, since, *if* (7) *is false*, *c* is identical with one of our original evidence cases, all of which are described by the evidence itself as conducting electricity; (3) is thus implied deductively by the evidence at hand together with the assumption of (7)'s falsity, given the general understanding that no cases have been omitted.

As soon as we leave the safe territory of examined cases, however, and try to deal with one we take to be new, the generalization formula yields contradictory inductions, deciding for neither. Furthermore, since the adoption of a generalization constitutes wholesale endorsement of appropriate particular inductions yet to be made, then even if we do not know about some specific case that it is a new one, our unrestricted adoption of generalizations gets us into trouble if we make the assumption of novelty for at least some cases within the relevant range.

Since, moreover, we patently do sometimes choose between contradictory inductions covering new cases, as well as between competing generalizations, the generalization formula must be wrong as an account of our inductive choices. In our previous example, we obviously would *not* in practice hold (4) equally confirmed by the evidence confirming (1), nor would we have any hesitation in rejecting (6) rather than (3). We see here the inadequacy of the generalization formula as a characterization of our inductive choices, and its consequent failure to supply an answer to Hume's challenge.

The failure of the generalization formula consists in its inability to differentiate between such pairs of hypotheses as (1) and (4), with respect to their confirmability by the evidence. The generalization formula, as we have seen, is based on the idea of an instance according with a hypothesis, and such accord is unrestricted with respect to the predicates entering into the hypotheses in question, except for the general requirement that they be observationally definable. We have seen, indeed, Hempel's "purely syntactic" explication of his satisfaction criterion. Whether a syntactic or semantic account is given, however, it will be allowed that instances *accord with* hypotheses irrespective of the descriptive terminology employed (provided it is throughout observationally definable).

It now suggests itself that there are additional restrictions on such terminology, of a non-syntactic and non-semantic sort, which (1) obeys and (4) violates. These restrictions govern what Goodman calls "the projection" of characteristics of our evidence-cases to other cases in induction. They differentiate between (1), as a "projectible" hypothesis, and (4), as a "nonprojectible" hypothesis, the former representing a *proper* mode of projection of evidence-features, the latter not, despite their syntactic and semantic similarity.

Criteria of what Goodman calls "projectibility" pick out just those generalizations which are *confirmable,* i.e., *capable* of receiving selective support from their positive instances as against rival hypotheses and, therefore, of sanctioning particular inductions in turn. Projectible hypotheses may, in individual cases, fail to sanction any particular induction (for example, in cases where two such hypotheses *themselves* happen to conflict), but no non-projectible hypothesis sanctions any induction, no matter how much positive (and even selective) accord there is between it and the available evidence.

In Goodman's view the problem is thus to define projectibility (confirmability, or lawlikeness), which is in turn needed to define induction. As he puts it, "The problem of justifying induction has been displaced by the problem of defining confirmation, and our work upon this has left us with the residual problem of distinguishing between confirmable and non-confirmable hypotheses. One might say roughly that the first question was 'Why does a positive instance of a hypothesis give any grounds for predicting further instances?'; that the newer question was 'What is a positive instance of a hypothesis?'; and that the crucial remaining question is 'What hypotheses are confirmed by their positive instances?' "[2]

A characterization of projectibility would, moreover, have further uses beyond helping to explain induction. Since counterfactual judgments (for example, 'If this salt, which has not in fact been put in water, had been put in water, it would have dissolved') are construable as resting upon just such generalizations as are lawlike or projectible ('Every sample of salt, when put

[2] *Ibid.,* pp. 80-81.

into water, dissolves'), and may, furthermore, themselves be used in explaining dispositional terms, such as 'soluble', a definition of projectibility would seem likely to illuminate the latter areas as well.

It might be thought that projectibility could be easily characterized, simply by ruling out generalizations making reference to time. Recall that, in our above example, the trouble arose because the available evidence was thought to give equal support to (1) and (4). But if the problem is to differentiate between these two hypotheses, and to eliminate the latter, a method seems ready at hand. For whereas the consequent predicate used in (1) (i.e., 'conducts electricity') makes no reference to time, the consequent predicate used in (4) (i.e., 'has been examined prior to time t and conducts electricity or has not been examined prior to time t and does not conduct electricity') makes reference to time of examination; moreover, the latter predicate is derivative since, given such reference, it is wholly explainable in terms of the former predicate. It may further be pointed out that, without assumption (7), making reference to time of examination, no contradiction arises between our inductive judgments (3) and (6). It is only when we add (7) to (4) that (6), which contradicts (3), is derived. Why not use these clues then, as the basis of a rule for eliminating the troublemaking hypothesis (4)—namely, its referring to time, through its temporal and derivative consequent predicate, and, therefore, its requiring an additional assumption about time, to yield one of our contradictory inductions?

The answer is that the situation is easily and wholly reversed. Symbolize the predicate 'conducts electricity' by 'C', and the other, more complicated one, of (4), by 'K'; symbolize 'has been examined before t' by 'E'. Now it is true that, as the present suggestion points out, 'K' is definable as follows:

(8) $Kx =_{df} ((Ex \cdot Cx) \vee (\sim Ex \cdot \sim Cx))$

taking 'E' and 'C' as primitive ideas. However, it is also true that, taking 'E' and 'K' as primitive ideas, 'C' is definable thus:

(9) $Cx =_{df} ((Ex \cdot Kx) \vee (\sim Ex \cdot \sim Kx))$.

Furthermore, in the latter mode of (primitive) description, (1) would become:

(1') All specimens of copper are either such that they have been examined prior to t and are K, or have not been examined prior to t and are not K

while (4) would become simply:

(4')   All specimens of copper are K.

To derive a parallel to (3), we now need to show that the *new* case c is *not K,* and therefore conducts electricity. This we can do if we supplement (1') with our old assumption (7), getting:

(3') c is not K.

And we derive our contradictory particular induction, parallel to (6), from (4') alone, without using (7):

(6') c is K.

Thus, neither the employment by a hypothesis of a predicate referring to time, nor its need of supplementation by a temporal assumption such as (7) in order to produce contradiction, is a reliable clue with which to try to repair the generalization formula. Neither is, strictly speaking, any clue at all.

But perhaps the generalization formula is being applied too narrowly. We have, after all, been considering isolated statements in abstraction from other, relevant and well-established hypotheses. Perhaps if we take into account larger generalizations about the sorts of uniformities found in experience, we shall be able to differentiate among hypotheses in the requisite manner, and without going beyond the generalization formula. This idea was earlier mentioned in our discussion of Mill, as one which has been favored by other writers as well, independently of Mill's general theory of induction. As Mill states the point,

> . . . we need experience to inform us in what degree, and in what cases, or sorts of cases, experience is to be relied on. Experience must be consulted in order to learn from it under what circumstances arguments from it will be valid.

We have no ulterior test to which we subject experience in general; but we make experience its own test. Experience testifies that among the uniformities which it exhibits or seems to exhibit, some are more to be relied on than others; and uniformity, therefore, may be presumed, from any given number of instances, with a greater degree of assurance, in proportion as the case belongs to a class in which the uniformities have hitherto been found more uniform.[3]

In reference to our above illustration, we have, for example, so far ignored the fact that the available evidence also supports (by the generalization formula) a number of hypotheses of the following kind:

(10)   All specimens of iron conduct electricity
(11)   All specimens of wood fail to conduct electricity

and, what is more important, that these in turn lend credence to the following larger generalization:

(12)   All classes of specimens of the same material are uniform with respect to electrical conductivity.

This larger generalization, having independent warrant, and conflicting with (4), serves thereby to discredit it, thus eliminating the troublesome induction (6). In this way, it may be argued, the generalization formula can be rendered viable, simply by taking account of a wider context of relevant hypotheses.

It takes little reflection, however, to see the weakness of such an argument. By reasoning analogous to that initially employed in introducing (4), it will be seen that the very same evidence which supports (10), (11), and (12) also and equally (by the generalization formula) supports:

(10')   All specimens of iron are K
(11')   All specimens of wood are not K
(12')   All classes of specimens of the same material are uniform with respect to being K.

---

[3] Mill, *A System of Logic*, Book III, chap. iv, section 2, p. 232.

This latter large generalization, it will be noted, produces just the opposite effect from that of (12). It conflicts with (1), thereby discrediting *it* and eliminating the induction (3) rather than (6). Which of these conflicting larger generalizations shall we now choose to take account of, (12) or (12′)?

It is evident that we are again face to face with the very problem with which we started, and that the proposal to repair the generalization formula by referring to other, larger hypotheses selected by it serves merely to postpone our perplexity. For these other hypotheses, in conflict themselves, are of no help unless we have some way of deciding which of *them* are projectible. In the face of difficulties such as these, it appears impossible to explain our choice of predictions or inductions by reference to *whether or not they are sanctioned by generalizations consistently supported by past experience,* no matter how widely the scope of this principle is construed. For we shall find such generalizations sanctioning every induction and its contradictory; what we need is some independent method of sorting out the lawlike, or projectible, generalizations from the rest.

We have noted that the time reference of non-projectible hypothesis (4) is no real clue to its non-lawlike character. The complex consequent predicate making explicit reference to time may be replaced by a simple predicate-symbol, e.g., 'K', with the same extension, without effecting any improvement. To say that 'K' is still *implicitly* temporal, because definable by 'C' and the temporal 'E', helps not at all, for by this reasoning 'C' is also implicitly temporal, since definable by 'K' and the temporal 'E'. The distinction *between* 'C' and 'K' has again eluded us.

Now some have, in effect, argued that 'K' is still peculiarly temporal in another sense: if we imagine all the examined elements (past, present, and future) to which 'K' applies, and imagine them further as ordered in the temporal sequence of their examination, we find a radical shift in reference at t: Those elements prior to t in the order conduct electricity, whereas those not prior to t do not conduct electricity. By contrast, 'C' does not radically shift in its reference at any given point in time. We might illustrate this argument by mention of Goodman's example:

(13)   All emeralds are green
(14)   All emeralds are grue

Grue things are those either examined before *t* and green, or not examined before *t* and blue. Clearly, (13) and (14) yield conflicting predictions prior to *t*, respecting emeralds not yet examined. But, the present argument runs, 'grue's reference radically shifts with respect to color, at *t*, whereas 'green's does not. 'Grue' is thus peculiarly temporal.

The trouble with this argument is its failure to acknowledge the *relativity* of the notion of a "shift in reference." '*K*' indeed "shifts" at *t* from elements conducting electricity to those not conducting electricity. But, equally, '*C*' "shifts" at *t* from elements which are *K* to those which are not. 'Grue' "shifts" at *t* from green elements and applies to certain others not green. Equally, however, 'green' "shifts" at *t* from grue elements and applies to others not grue. Just as the appeal to larger generalizations fails to make the wanted distinctions on the basis of uniformities, so the present suggestion fails to make the wanted distinctions on the basis of non-uniformities, or *shifts in reference*. As uniformities may be found everywhere, so non-uniformities or shifts may be found everywhere, by reference to *some* class of elements (or associated predicates) taken as standard. To escape the relativity of such notions, we appear, again, driven beyond the purely syntactic and semantic realms, in order to find restrictions distinguishing certain predicates from others, and, accordingly, projectible hypotheses from the rest. Some have apparently felt that the problem we have been dealing with *must* have some solution based on temporal distinctions; indeed our examples *have* appealed to *time of examination* in introducing the troublesome predicates in each case. Time reference is certainly useful in *explaining* the problem, but is *not* an essential feature of it. What *is* essential is the membership of all actual evidence cases in classes that diverge beyond the evidence. All emeralds in the class of evidence cases, for example, *belong both* to the class of green and to the class of grue things, which, unfortunately, *diverge* for emeralds outside the evidence class. The predicate 'grue' has, to be sure, been explained by reference to time of examination, and '*K*' has also been explained thus; we have, however, already seen that such explanation yields no solution to the problem since these predicates may themselves be taken as primitive, and 'green' and '*C*' introduced by time reference. We have, furthermore, implied, in our discussion of "referential shifting," that *any* predicate whatever can be explained by a time reference, given the freedom to choose the auxiliary primitives required.

Nonetheless, it may be worth showing how the predicate 'grue' might be *explained,* even for the sake of illustration, without time reference at all, so that the last suspicion of temporality may be dispelled. All that is needed is some non-temporal feature characterizing all the accumulated evidence cases and presumed not to characterize the cases beyond. Whatever particular feature may be held to be of this sort, say it is *H,* 'grue' may be explained as applying to everything which has *H* and is green, or lacks *H* and is blue; *H* might be, for example, a feature of geographical location, known to us through special information. But, theoretically, a non-temporal feature is always at hand, should special information fail. For every one of the available evidence cases shares the property of being identical with one or another of them, and this property is, moreover, not possessed by any case beyond the evidence. Suppose that all our available evidence cases consist of the objects *a, b, . . . k.* Then construe 'grue' as applying to everything which is either (i) identical with *a* or with *b* or with . . . or with *k, and* green, or (ii) not identical with *a* nor with *b* nor with . . . nor with *k, and* blue. Clearly, the problem of distinguishing the lawlike "green emerald" hypothesis from the non-lawlike "grue emerald" hypothesis can be explained perfectly well in these terms.

It is worth noting here that, if the problem of distinguishing between (1) and (4) seems beyond the capacity of the generalization formula to resolve, a translation of the formula into terms of *falsification* accomplishes nothing. For (1) and (4) are each unfalsified by the evidence to date, unlike their respective contraries. Yet they conflict for new cases. Perhaps, it will be said, (1) is preferable because it is "structurally" simpler, and it surely is less complicated than (4); it is, for example, shorter. Yet any comparison of hypotheses in terms of structural simplicity alone will clearly yield no solution, for equivalent hypotheses with extensionally equivalent, though different, predicates are always available, which are as complex or simple as you like, by standards of internal structural simplicity. We have above seen, for example, the reversal effected when (1) and (4) are transformed into (1') and (4').

Some have tended to construe simplicity as *weakness,* and others have construed it as *strength.* Goodman has discussed both proposals critically: with respect to the first, he argues that "the principle of maximum safety quickly reduces to absurdity; for it always dictates the choice of a hypothesis that does not go beyond the evidence at all."[4]

"The very opposite proposal," he writes:

> has been advanced by Popper: that the strongest hypothesis not falsified by the evidence should be chosen. But for every hypothesis strong enough to go beyond the evidence, there is an equally strong conflicting hypothesis based upon the same evidence. This is easily shown. Suppose our evidence tells us just that every examined A is a $B,$ and suppose hypothesis H_1 affirms in addition that every (or even some one) other A is a $B.$ Then hypothesis $H_2,$ affirming that every examined A is a B and that every (or the particular one) other A is *not* a $B,$ likewise conforms to the stated evidence. Hence strength is indifferent as between any projection and its opposite. And to exclude every hypothesis that conflicts with another equally strong one unviolated by the evidence would be, once more, to exclude every hypothesis that goes beyond the evidence at all.[5]

We have indeed seen the difficulty of differentiating between (1) and (4) despite their equal strength. Goodman offers the

---

[4] Nelson Goodman, "Safety, Strength, Simplicity," *Philosophy of Science,* XXVIII (1961), 150. By permission of the publisher.
[5] *Ibid.*

following example to show that simplicity, however it be explained, is distinct from both weakness, or safety, and strength:

(i) All maples, except perhaps those in Eagleville, are deciduous.
(ii) All maples are deciduous.
(iii) All maples whatsoever, and all sassafras trees in Eagleville, are deciduous.

He supposes that "we have examined many and widely distributed specimens of maple trees and found them all to be deciduous, and . . . this constitutes our entire evidence." Each of (i), (ii), and (iii) is unfalsified by the available evidence. Then, though (ii) is both stronger and simpler than (i), as well as most preferable, it is clearly, also, weaker, though simpler, than (iii). Goodman concludes:

> The expansion made in (iii) is as unwelcome as the exception made in (i). Hypothesis (ii), although it lies between (i) and (iii) in safety and strength, is simpler than, and preferable to either. This shows that neither safety nor strength is the measure of simplicity, and that simplicity takes precedence over both as a factor in the choice of hypotheses. The delicate problem of balancing safety and strength against each other is significant only as between hypotheses of equal simplicity . . . I am inclined to think that the standards of simplicity for hypotheses derive from our classificatory habits as disclosed in our language, and that the relative entrenchment of predicates underlies our judgment of relative simplicity . . .[6]

9. Goodman's Proposal on Induction

The last sentence of the passage just cited contains the key notion of Goodman's positive proposal on the problem we have been concerned with: how to distinguish lawlike or projectible hypotheses from the rest, in the wake of the failure of the gen-

[6] *Ibid.*, p. 151.

eralization formula. In the above passage, he is concerned to suggest that habitual entrenchment of predicates provides a standard of *simplicity* that outranks considerations of safety or strength in the choice of hypotheses. But we need to consider the general proposal directly.

Goodman's suggestion is to make use of *pragmatic or historical* information that may fairly be assumed available at the time of induction, and to define projectibility in terms of such extra-syntactic, extra-semantic information. The generalization formula, it will be recalled, rests on the notion of *accord* between a hypothesis and given evidence, and makes no use of "material" or historical information concerning the descriptive terminology involved. Goodman now suggests that, in order to specify the generalizations chosen on given evidence, we need not restrict ourselves exclusively to the non-pragmatic features of the statements before us. Rather, he proposes that we use also the historical record of past predictions, or (more generally) projections, and, in particular, the *biographies* of the predicates previously employed projectively. Our hypotheses, he suggests, are chosen not merely by virtue of the way they encompass the evidence, but also by virtue of the way the language in which they are couched conforms with past linguistic practice.

His basic term is 'entrenchment', applicable to predicates in the degree to which they (or their extensional equivalents, that is, words picking out the same class of elements, e.g., 'triangle' and 'trilateral') have actually been previously employed in projection: in formulating particular inductive judgments. To illustrate by reference to our previous example, the predicate 'has been examined prior to time *t* and conducts electricity, or has not been examined prior to time *t* and does not conduct electricity' is less well entrenched than the predicate 'conducts electricity', because *the class it singles out has been less often designated in formulating inductions.* "The entrenchment of a predicate," writes Goodman, "results from the actual projection not merely of that predicate alone but also of all predicates coextensive with it. In a sense, not the word itself but the class it selects is what becomes entrenched, and to speak of the entrenchment of a predicate is to speak elliptically of the entrenchment of the extension of that predicate. On the other hand, the class becomes entrenched only through the projection of predicates selecting it; entrenchment derives from the use of language. But differences of tongue, use of coined abbreviations, and other variations in vocabulary do not prevent accrual of merited entrenchment."[7] Thus, the consequent predicate of (4') is less well entrenched than that of (1'), even though their verbal formulation differs strikingly from that of their respective counterparts of (4) and (1).

The factor of actual historical employment of constituent predicates or their equivalents can thus be used to distinguish between hypotheses such as (1) and (4), which are equal in point of available (and selective) positive instances. Goodman appeals, then, to "recurrences in the explicit use of terms as well as to recurrent features of what is observed," suggesting that the features we fasten on in induction are those "for which we have adopted predicates that we have habitually projected."[8]

With this idea as a guide, Goodman first defines *presumptively projectible hypotheses* (at a time). These are hypotheses which, at the time in question, (i) are supported and not violated by the evidence, and possess as yet undetermined instances (i.e., instances not as yet determined to be positive or negative), and, moreover, (ii) are not eliminated by three special rules (which Goodman sets forth). We shall (for illustrative purposes) mention only the first, which calls for elimination of hypothesis H if it conflicts with K, which has a no-less-well entrenched antecedent-predicate and a better entrenched consequent-predicate, and is, besides, supported and unviolated by the evidence. Such a rule seems clearly to apply to the conflict between (1) and (4), for example.

Next, an *initial projectibility index* is defined for presumptively projectible hypotheses, on the basis of the comparative entrenchment of their predicates. Finally, a notion of *degree of projectibility* is defined by means of the initial projectibility index as modified by indirect information embodied in what Good-

[7] Goodman, *Fact, Fiction, and Forecast,* pp. 95-96.
[8] *Ibid.,* pp. 96-97.

man calls 'overhypotheses', roughly comparable to the "larger generalizations" discussed in the last section; however, he requires these overhypotheses to be themselves presumptively projectible, thus meeting the problem of conflict previously noted.

Goodman's theory, though worked out with considerable subtlety, is nonetheless not offered as a final and comprehensive solution. Moreover, it is explicitly limited to simple universal hypotheses of a presumably observational sort, and addresses itself only to the question of projectibility at a time. He tries "to illustrate some of the resources that a new approach offers us for dealing with a difficult problem."[9]

Nonetheless, *degree of projectibility* is an approximation to the notion of lawlikeness. Further, Goodman suggests that, to the extent that lawlikeness is explained, the general problem associated with disposition terms is solved. For he construes this general problem to call for definition of the *relationship* between "manifest" or observable predicates (e.g., 'dissolves') and their dispositional counterparts (e.g., 'is soluble'); manifest predicates may now be construed (on his view) as related by true lawlike hypotheses to their dispositional mates. Other problems such as the nature of "empirical possibility" are also illuminated by this approach, and some light is shed on the question of counterfactual judgments which, however, still resists complete solution.

The most natural objection to Goodman's proposal is that it provides no explanation of entrenchment itself. In using this notion to explain induction, however, further explanation is not ruled out. Goodman's purpose is to formulate clear criteria, in terms of available information, that will single out those hypotheses guiding our inductive judgments. The strong point of his treatment is that his criteria do indeed seem effective in dealing with the numerous cases he considers.

A possible misconception concerning the use of 'entrenchment' as a basic idea is that it may lead to the ruling out of unfamiliar predicates, thus stultifying the growth of scientific language. Unfamiliar predicates may, however, be well en-

[9] *Ibid.*, p. 117.

trenched if some of their extensionally equivalent mates have been often projected, and they may acquire entrenchment indirectly through "inheritance" from "parent predicates"—that is, other predicates related to them in a special way outlined in Goodman's treatment of overhypotheses. Furthermore, his criteria provide methods for evaluating *hypotheses,* not predicates, so that wholesale elimination of new terms is not sanctioned in his treatment.

10. Reflections on the Justification of Induction

We have seen the inadequacy of the generalization formula as an account of our inductive choices, and we have indicated the main outlines of Goodman's proposal for improving the situation. We shall not, however, pursue the technical development of this proposal further in the present section. Rather, we shall address ourselves again to general features of the theory of induction, in the light of several issues that have occupied us: in particular, we shall consider once again the justification of induction.

Omitting such questions as relate to the scope of Goodman's actual proposal (i.e., its ostensible limitation to projectibility, at a time, of simple universal hypotheses of observational sort), where do matters stand? The generalization formula, resting on the notion of support by positive instances, has been found inadequate to characterize our normal selection of hypotheses through experience. But such inadequacy as a characterization does not mean that consistent evidential support is irrelevant to the confirmation of hypotheses. It shows only that such support is not in itself sufficient to characterize confirmation, leaving open the possibility that supplementation by additional criteria may yield an adequate account. We have seen, in this connection, the proposal of a criterion of projectibility, which is clearly not intended as a characterization of confirmation, but only of *confirmability* by instances. Assuming, for the present, that we have suitable criteria of confirmability, together with the generalization formula as restricted by such criteria, do we now have a sufficient basis for explaining the *confirmation* of hypotheses?

It does not follow that this must be so, from the arguments we have reviewed. For the generalization formula, in itself, was seen to be radically defective, in providing *no* selection at all among hypotheses, of the sort that would differentiate between contradictory inductions. Supplementation by criteria of confirmability does indeed overcome *this* difficulty; it enables at least *some* selection among hypotheses, stringent enough to provide legitimate differentiations among contradictory inductions. But it may well be that there are *further* selections to be accounted for, that some conflicts among equally projectible hypotheses are in fact normally decided by further criteria, in advance of a direct decision on the basis of additional evidence. For example, it may be that some such further criterion, based on a consideration of the relative strengths of competing hypotheses, enters into certain of our inductive choices. *If* this is indeed the case, then there are some selections we normally make among hypotheses, which are *not* explained by a simple fusion of generalization formula and projectibility criteria. The question of further criteria is complex, and surely not yet settled.

Irrespective of the existence of such further criteria, however, it seems clear that the factors so far discussed, namely, consistent evidential support and projectibility via entrenchment, are genuine considerations in induction, in that they account for a wide range of inductive choices. Leaving aside the prospects of extension and refinement which await further studies, and attending simply to the range so far explained, let us now ask if induction has, at least here, been justified.

We have seen the difficulties attending philosophical efforts to answer Hume's challenge. Induction cannot, we saw, be justified through appeal to its alleged presuppositions. Nor can it be justified by reference to the past successes of inductive procedures or predictive policies. Deductive rationales for induction are illegitimate, since inductive judgments are just those whose truth is not demonstrable on the basis of true evidential data.

We noted, further, the recent view that the solution lies in a firm rejection of all demands for a deductive rationale, coupled with an insistence that the concept of justification normally applies to non-deductive inferences. In considering this view, we remarked its failure to specify criteria which differentiate between proper and improper non-deductive inferences, and thus its failure to say under what conditions particular inductions are in fact justified. In the latter respect, we noted that, though it is similar to Hume's own approach, this recent view undertakes less than he did in formulating his theory of habit formation.

We considered, accordingly, the generalization formula as a modern version of Hume's theory, concluding with a review of the theory of projectibility developed by Goodman. At best, we now have a specification that in fact differentiates between proper and improper inductive choices within a significant range. We have thus, in one clear sense, shown certain normal inductive choices to be justified, for we have indicated the rules by which they are singled out from the rest. We have, however, rejected the idea that these rules are immutable features of nature or human nature, and have, in effect, admitted their possible variability.

But in so doing, have we not raised, in an urgent form, the question how the rules themselves are justified? If variety is open to us, what makes our accepted rules preferable? To answer that they are *ours* seems no more satisfying for the theory of induction than for the theory of practice or morals. But, unlike the justification of practical or moral rules, we cannot without circularity justify inductive rules by reference to the consequences they are found to have in experience. Appeal to convention fails to satisfy; appeal to consequences runs in a circle. What is left?

To this problem, Goodman addresses himself in the following words:

> The validity of a deduction depends not upon conformity to any purely arbitrary rules we may contrive, but upon conformity to valid rules . . . But how is the validity of rules to be determined? Here again we encounter philosophers who insist that these rules follow from some self-evident axiom, and others who try to show that the rules are grounded in the very nature of the human mind. I think the answer lies much nearer the surface. Principles of deductive inference are justified by their conformity with

accepted deductive practice. Their validity depends upon accordance with the particular deductive inferences we actually make and sanction. If a rule yields inacceptable inferences, we drop it as invalid. Justification of general rules thus derives from judgments rejecting or accepting particular deductive inferences.

This looks flagrantly circular . . . But this circle is a virtuous one. The point is that rules and particular inferences alike are justified by being brought into agreement with each other . . . The process of justification is the delicate one of making mutual adjustments between rules and accepted inferences; and in the agreement achieved lies the only justification needed for either.

All this applies equally well to induction. An inductive inference, too, is justified by conformity to general rules, and a general rule by conformity to accepted inductive inferences. Predictions are justified if they conform to valid canons of induction; and the canons are valid if they accurately codify accepted inductive practice.[1]

Goodman thus offers a model of rule-justification that escapes the defects of both conventionalism and utilitarianism (i.e., the appeal to consequences in experience). It may be argued that this model is, moreover, of interest for rules of practice as well as rules of induction. For to justify a practical rule by appeal to the nature of its consequences raises the issue of justification once again, with respect to the principle by which these consequences are selected. And to justify the practical rule by showing it to be derived from another, or stipulated by some convention (actual or hypothetical), analogously raises the question of justification with respect to the governing rule or convention presumed. To construe rule-justification as at some point tying rules back to cases seems thus to provide a way of putting a limit on the upward process by which justified rule leads to more general rule or principle, and the latter leads to a further principle, rule, or convention, etc.

Nonetheless, it is important to see that the advantages offered

---

[1] *Ibid.*, pp. 66-67.

by Goodman's model of rule-justification do not require that the other modes of justification be surrendered: it is enough if *at some point* justifying principles are tied back to cases; particular rules may then be justified by *connecting* them with the principles in question. It would, indeed, be an oversimplification to suppose that each and every rule is itself adjusted with cases, independently. Rules may, alternatively, be justified through systematic connectedness with other rules or principles, which are themselves adjusted to cases. In some circumstances, indeed, a "systematic" justification of this sort seems clearly preferable to a direct justification by case-adjustment, for the relevant governing principle is much more basic than the rule being judged, and would dislodge it in case of conflict, even if the rule were supported by direct case-adjustment. It is the case-adjustment of the whole set of principles which is in point, rather than that of any given rule that may be in question.

If these considerations are correct, then another way is conceivable in which rules of induction may be justified. They may be shown to fall under or exemplify more general principles, which are themselves supported by overall case-adjustment. There must, of course, be no appeal to experiential consequences in the process, for such appeal would involve the old trouble of circularity through implicit reference to inductive principles. But appeal to consequences is not the only way in which inductive rules may be connected with larger principles. An alternative is to exhibit these rules as exemplifying more comprehensive principles, themselves ultimately supported by case-adjustment. Such a justification does not, of course, preclude direct case-adjustment of the rules themselves, and may rather reinforce it. However, even where direct case-adjustment exists, such justification would be far from trivial, for it would remove the impression of *uniqueness* from the inductive rules in question, showing them to be akin to others, all alike exemplifying certain accepted comprehensive principles.

If such a course is possible, then the challenge to justify induction may be given an additional interpretation: the challenge is *not* to provide a deductive guarantee of inductive success, nor an elaboration of inductive presuppositions, nor an inductive argument for the reliability of inductive policies. Rather, the challenge is *to show that inductive rules exemplify more comprehensive accepted principles, and are thus not idiosyncratic.*

If we look at a basic feature of Goodman's projectibility rules in this light, we may indicate (in a relatively speculative fashion) some directions in which the answer to such a challenge might be sought. This basic feature is (roughly) the preferability of entrenched over non-entrenched predicates, in the formulation of hypotheses which cover the available evidence and go beyond it.

We have here a kind of conceptual inertia or conservatism which has been remarked also in other contexts, under a variety of labels. Quine writes, for example, of "familiarity of principle," noting that it is such familiarity "we are after when we contrive to 'explain' new matters by old laws; e.g., when we devise a molecular hypothesis in order to bring the phenomena of heat, capillary attraction, and surface tension under the familiar old laws of mechanics. Familiarity of principle also figures when 'unexpected observations' . . . prompt us to revise an old theory; the way in which familiarity of principle then figures is in favoring minimum revision."[2] He thinks of familiarity of principle as a kind of "conservatism, a favoring of the inherited or invented conceptual scheme of one's own previous work."[3]

In another place, he speaks of "the totality of our so-called knowledge or beliefs, from the most casual matters of geography and history to the profoundest laws of atomic physics or even of pure mathematics and logic" as "a man-made fabric which impinges on experience only along the edges." In this fabric, certain statements are more central than others in that they are relatively less likely to be revised in the face of "recalcitrant experience."[4]

---

[2] Willard Van Orman Quine, *Word and Object* (New York and London: published jointly by The Technology Press of The Massachusetts Institute of Technology and John Wiley & Sons, Inc., 1960), p. 20.

[3] *Ibid.*

[4] Willard Van Orman Quine, *From a Logical Point of View* (2d ed.; Cambridge, Mass.: Harvard University Press, 1961), chap. ii, section 6, pp. 42, 43.

For example, we can imagine recalcitrant experiences to which we would surely be inclined to accommodate our system by reëvaluating just the statement that there are brick houses on Elm Street, together with related statements on the same topic. We can imagine other recalcitrant experiences to which we would be inclined to accommodate our system by reëvaluating just the statement that there are no centaurs, along with kindred statements. A recalcitrant experience can, I have urged, be accommodated by any of various alternative reëvaluations in various alternative quarters of the total system; but, in the cases which we are now imagining, our natural tendency to disturb the total system as little as possible would lead us to focus our revisions upon these specific statements concerning brick houses or centaurs. These statements are felt, therefore, to have a sharper empirical reference than highly theoretical statements of physics or logic or ontology. The latter statements may be thought of as relatively centrally located within the total network, meaning merely that little preferential connection with any particular sense data obtrudes itself.[5]

Several points concerning Quine's views are worth notice. Whereas projectibility involves a certain principle of conservation with respect to predicates (or their extensions), Quine refers, in effect, to a principle of conservation applicable to whole systems of statements. It is clear, too, that he takes the latter principle to be relevant not merely to the so-called empirical sciences, but also to logic and mathematics. By "familiarity of principle" he intends a favoring of the whole "conceptual scheme" of statements rather than a favoring of those single *statements* which are most familiar. For the point is to revise the whole system as little as possible, and to do this may require saving relatively unfamiliar but central *statements* and discarding relatively familiar ones with which they conflict, where the opposite choice would give us a more unfamiliar *system*, as a structured whole. Finally, there are two components in Quine's "familiarity of principle,"

[5] *Ibid.,* pp. 43-44.

one counseling minimum revision when the scheme collides with observation or is otherwise found unsatisfactory, the other counseling maximum extension of the scheme to cover new areas that may be brought to light.

Neither of these components of "familiarity of principle" operates alone, on Quine's view. In particular, considerations relating to the "simplicity" of the total scheme enter in, and may, in fact, conflict with the demands of "familiarity of principle." In Quine's opinion, "Whenever simplicity and conservatism are known to counsel opposite courses, the verdict of conscious methodology is on the side of simplicity."[6] Thus, minimum revision under observational challenge is indicated only if no loss in systematic simplicity is anticipated; and maximum extension to new areas is indicated only if it is not accomplished through a sacrifice of simplicity, when compared with alternative ways of incorporating the new material.

We have, then, a suggested principle of conservation of *schemes* as well as a principle of conservation of *predicates* (or extensions)—a principle which is, moreover, not restricted in its application to the empirical sciences. Scheme-conservation, as one principle of scientific strategy, has been frequently noted (under different names), and its justification has not generally been put in terms of demonstrated or probable success. It has more often been held reasonable as effort-saving, or as maximizing intelligibility, where its justification has at all been considered. In the latter form of justification, it has in effect been assimilated to ordinary and philosophical explanations in which the unfamiliar is reduced to the familiar.

The latter idea, moreover, has also been applied to the use of so-called models and analogies in theorizing. A new theoretical scheme seems, in general, to be preferred, in point of intelligibility, to the degree that a familiar model can be provided for it, or an explicit analogy of restricted sort exhibited between it and the inherited scheme. As E. Nagel has written,

[6] Quine, *Word and Object*, pp. 20-21.

. . . an analogy between an old and a new theory is not simply an aid in exploiting the latter but is a desideratum many scientists tacitly seek to achieve in the construction of explanatory systems. Indeed, some scientists have made the existence of such an analogy an explicit and indispensable requirement for a satisfactory theoretical explanation of experimental laws. And conversely, even when a new theory does organize systematically a vast array of experimental fact, the lack of marked analogies between the theory and some familiar model is sometimes given as the reason why the new theory is said not to offer a 'really satisfactory' explanation of those facts. Lord Kelvin's inordinate fondness for mechanical models is a notorious example of such an attitude; he never felt entirely at ease with Maxwell's electromagnetic theory of light because he was unable to design a satisfactory mechanical model for it. More recently, a distinguished physicist has argued that a theory for which no visualizable models can be given is just as good as one for which such models are available, provided that both theories enable us to handle experimental problems equally well; and he has made clear that in this latter respect the mathematical formalism of current quantum theory, for which no satisfactory model of this kind is known, is unusually successful. Nevertheless, he has also registered the uncomfortable sense of loss, shared by many physicists, because quantum theory offers no 'explanation' of the experimental facts—a feeling he attributes to the circumstances that we can construct for the theory no physical model in which the 'interplay of elements [is] already so familiar to us that we accept them as not needing explanation.' (P. W. Bridgman, *The Nature of Physical Theory,* Princeton, 1936, p. 63.) It is a matter of historical record that there are fashions in the preferences scientists exhibit for various kinds of models, whether substantive or purely formal ones. Theories based on unfamiliar models frequently encounter strong resistance until the novel ideas have lost their strangeness, so that a new generation will often accept as a matter of course a type of model which to a preceding generation was unsatisfactory because it was unfamiliar. What is nevertheless beyond doubt is that models of some sort, whether substantive or formal, have played and continue to play a capital role in the development of scientific theory.[7]

It would seem that we have here another principle, of *model*-conservation, which operates where scheme-conservation is overridden, perhaps by the demands of systematic simplicity, in meeting an observational challenge or incorporating new data. In such a case, the more "simple," newly preferred schemes are also more deviant, as a whole, relative to the hitherto accepted schemes, than their rejected alternatives. Now the new principle of conservation would seem to come into play, counseling the relative preferability of such of the "simple" schemes as can be provided with familiar models or analogies, of sorts that may be specified or understood from the context. The contribution of model-conservation to intelligibility might be said to consist in its allowing us to continue seeing the old in the new—if not directly by extension of our old scheme, then by extension of certain features of it, as embodied in explanatory models or analogies with roots in our past thinking. (Parallels might be cited with the field of perception, in which antecedent schemas, categories or sets tend to mold our manner of seeing what is new, thus rendering it "intelligible"; the issues here have been illuminatingly treated by E. Gombrich[8] and N. R. Hanson.[9])

We have sought to indicate, in speculative vein, some directions in which an answer to Hume's challenge might be sought—assuming the challenge is to show that inductive rules are not

[7] Ernest Nagel, *The Structure of Science* (New York: Harcourt, Brace & World, Inc., 1961), pp. 114-115. By permission of the publisher and the author.

[8] E. H. Gombrich, *Art and Illusion* (Bollingen Series XXXV · 5 [New York: Published for Bollingen Foundation by Pantheon Books, Inc., 1960]).

[9] Norwood Russell Hanson, *Patterns of Discovery* (Cambridge, England: Cambridge University Press, 1958).

idiosyncratic. We have, in fact, focused particularly on Goodman's projectibility theory, which contains a qualified principle of conservation of predicates or extensions. We have suggested as relevant parallels the principles we referred to as "scheme-conservation" and "model-conservation," which have to do with cases where the inherited theoretical scheme is under threat of forced revision or requires accommodation to new (though compatible) realms of knowledge. The latter principles, we remarked, are neither isolated nor coordinate. Presumably, there is, aside from the demand to avoid violation by the evidence, also a demand for overall, systematic simplicity, which ranks higher than either principle. Furthermore, model-conservation comes into play, it was suggested, only after scheme-conservation has been applied.

There are, to be sure, numerous questions that have been ignored in our speculations. Our above-mentioned principles have themselves been characterized only very sketchily. The notion of systematic simplicity has, furthermore, hardly been characterized at all. (It is perhaps worth noting, in passing, that systematic simplicity must in some way tie in with restrictions on systematic predicates, for, otherwise, any scheme would be transformable into one that is as simple as you like.) But the main purpose of the present discussion, it should be recalled, is *not* to characterize the operative principles of inquiry, nor even to supply a justification of certain inductive rules. Rather, it is to suggest *a manner of conceiving such justification,* and to illustrate this conception by pointing out some plausible directions for the justification of projectibility principles.

We have proposed that one might justify the projectibility principles by pointing out that they are in fact not idiosyncratic. For, like the other two principles discussed, they exemplify a comprehensive principle of conceptual conservation, which counsels the preservation of as much of our intellectual equipment as possible, provided the weightier demands of fact and systematization are satisfied. The latter principle might, in turn, be further justified as effort-saving, and thus tied to principles of practice, or it might be taken to exemplify a principle of intelligibility and thus tied to common as well as philosophical explanations, and to the realm of perception. Either of the latter courses might be preferred to the other, and they might, of course, be combined; alternatively, they might both be thought superfluous. Wherever the appeal to a more comprehensive justifying principle ends, however, the last such principle in the chain is to be justified through case-adjustment. Though the latter mode of justification is, thus, ultimately required, still the fact that it is postponed for one or two steps may enable us to view the framework of induction as something which is not unique, as something which has a general point, or serves a broader purpose.

We return now to the question of scope. We noted, toward the beginning of the present section, that Goodman's proposal (following the main tradition of discussions of induction) is ostensibly limited to simple universal hypotheses of observational sort: the extra-logical predicates are presumed to denote, and elements are presupposed which may be determined to satisfy these predicates, and so to support or violate the hypotheses under consideration. Perhaps some proposal for extending projectibility theory beyond this scope will be forthcoming. Nonetheless, it is well to note the actual limitation of this scope by reference to *de facto* scientific theories. We have seen, in the last Part, the important place of theoretical constructions which are non-observational, and we have noted several of the issues of interpretation to which they give rise.

More recently, we have noted the principles of scheme-conservation and model-conservation, which are not limited to systems of an observational sort. If it be granted that theoretical notions play an important role in science (e.g., in integrating observational hypotheses into compact systems with inductive import and suggestive value for further inquiry), it will probably also be granted that the principles of scheme-conservation and model-conservation in fact enter into our choices among alternative theoretical constructions. We may, more generally, wish to construe such choices as reasonable in principle, though different in detail from the selection of observational hypotheses on the basis of instances recorded in the evidence.

The question may be raised as to whether we should construe such choices of theoretical scheme as belonging to the domain of confirmation theory or not. The question is surely terminological, but it represents also an issue of *program* for the theory of science: Shall we concentrate on traditional questions of induction, i.e., selection of observational hypotheses more general than the evidence, or rather on investigating those principles which appear to be involved in deliberations over theoretical alternatives? In view of the present meager state of our knowledge concerning both areas, it seems obvious that both alternatives are worthwhile. It seems, furthermore, obvious that investigation should also be directed to the *relationships* among these areas.

What is fundamentally important is to avoid confusing a choice of *program* with the general structure of science. A program may be justified even if it is limited. Alternative programs may be applauded even if one does not embrace them all. To applaud several, however, is not in itself to advance any. Like workers in science itself, students of the theory of science need a sense of balance: a capacity for commitment to limited programs of exploration, and a willingness to welcome alternative commitments by others. If, as in science, the terrain appears to be continuously changing and the ultimate destination not decided in advance, perhaps the theory of science can also learn to travel with uncertainty and to enjoy the journey's excitement.

Bibliography

This bibliography is not intended as an exhaustive guide to the philosophy of science. Rather, it lists some recent writings that may help to provide a general context for the present book, or stimulate the advanced student to search further into special topics. (The Bibliography is not designed to summarize the references in the Notes, nor does it wholly avoid duplicating such references.)

I. General

This group includes general treatises, textbooks, and anthologies.

Braithwaite, R. B. *Scientific Explanation*. Cambridge, England: Cambridge University Press, 1953.

Carnap, R. *Logical Foundations of Probability*. Chicago: University of Chicago Press, 1950.

Cohen, M. R., and E. Nagel. *An Introduction to Logic and Scientific Method*. New York: Harcourt, Brace, 1934.

Danto, A., and S. Morgenbesser (eds.). *Philosophy of Science*. New York: Meridian Books, 1960.

Feigl, H., and M. Brodbeck (eds.). *Readings in the Philosophy of Science*. New York: Appleton-Century-Crofts, 1953.

Feigl, H., and W. Sellars (eds.). *Readings in Philosophical Analysis*. New York: Appleton-Century-Crofts, 1949.

Frank, P. *Philosophy of Science*. Englewood Cliffs, N.J.: Prentice-Hall, 1957.

Goodman, N. *Fact, Fiction, and Forecast*. Indianapolis: Hackett Publishing Company, 1973.

Hanson, N. R. *Patterns of Discovery*. Cambridge, England: Cambridge University Press, 1958.

Hempel, C. G. *Fundamentals of Concept Formation in Empirical Science*. Chicago: University of Chicago Press, 1952.

Körner, S. (ed.). *Observation and Interpretation*. London: Butterworth, 1957.

Madden, E. H. (ed.). *The Structure of Scientific Thought: An Introduction to Philosophy of Science*. Boston: Houghton Mifflin, 1960.

Nagel, E. *The Structure of Science*. Indianapolis: Hackett Publishing Company, 1979.

Pap, A. *An Introduction to the Philosophy of Science*. New York: Free Press of Glencoe, 1962.

———. *Elements of Analytic Philosophy*. New York: Macmillan, 1949.

Popper, K. R. *The Logic of Scientific Discovery*. London: Hutchinson, 1959.

Quine, W. V. *From a Logical Point of View*. 2d ed.; Cambridge, Mass.: Harvard University Press, 1961.

————. *Word and Object*. New York and London: Technology Press of the Massachusetts Institute of Technology and John Wiley & Sons, 1960.

Reichenbach, H. *Experience and Prediction*. Chicago: University of Chicago Press, 1938.

Russell, B. *Human Knowledge*. New York: Simon and Schuster, 1948.

Ryle, G. *Dilemmas*. Cambridge, England: Cambridge University Press, 1954.

Stebbing, L. S. *Philosophy and the Physicists*. London: Methuen, 1937.

Toulmin, S. *The Philosophy of Science*. London: Hutchinson House, 1953.

Wiener, P. *Readings in Philosophy of Science*. New York: Scribner's, 1953.

II. Explanation

Some references in this group deal with (1) interpretation of the deductive pattern, others with (2) application to history or psychology.

1. The Deductive Pattern

Brodbeck, M. "Explanation, Prediction, and 'Imperfect' Knowledge," in H. Feigl and G. Maxwell (eds.), *Minnesota Studies in the Philosophy of Science*, Vol. III. Minneapolis: University of Minnesota Press, 1962.

Eberle, R., D. Kaplan, and R. Montague. "Hempel and Oppenheim on Explanation," *Philosophy of Science*, XXVIII (1961), 418-428.

Grünbaum, A. "Temporally Asymmetric Principles, Parity Between Explanation and Prediction, and Mechanism Versus Teleology," *Philosophy of Science*, XXIX (1962), 146-170.

Hanson, N. R. "On the Symmetry Between Explanation and Prediction," *Philosophical Review*, LXVIII (1959), 349-358.

Hempel, C. G. "Deductive-Nomological vs. Statistical Explanation," in H. Feigl and G. Maxwell (eds.), *Minnesota Studies in the Philosophy of Science*, Vol. III. Minneapolis: University of Minnesota Press, 1962.

Kaplan, D. "Explanation Revisited," *Philosophy of Science*, XXVIII (1961), 429-436.

Nagel, E. "Review of *The Philosophy of Science*, by S. Toulmin," *Mind*, LXIII (1954), 403-412.

Rescher, N. "On Prediction and Explanation," *British Journal for the Philosophy of Science*, VIII (1958), 281-290.

Scriven, M. "Explanations, Predictions, and Laws," in H. Feigl and G. Maxwell (eds.), *Minnesota Studies in the Philosophy of Science,* Vol. III. Minneapolis: University of Minnesota Press, 1962.

Toulmin, S. *The Philosophy of Science.* London: Hutchinson House, 1953.

2. Application to History or Psychology

Dray, W. *Laws and Explanation in History.* London: Oxford University Press, 1957.

Gardiner, P. *The Nature of Historical Explanation.* New York: Oxford University Press, 1952.

———— (ed.). *Theories of History.* Glencoe, Ill.: Free Press, 1959.

Gibson, Q. *The Logic of Social Enquiry.* London: Routledge and Kegan Paul, 1960.

Hempel, C. G. "The Logic of Functional Analysis," in L. Gross (ed.), *Symposium on Sociological Theory.* Evanston, Ill.: Row, Peterson, 1959.

Hook, S. (ed.). *Psychoanalysis, Scientific Method, and Philosophy.* New York: Grove Press, 1959.

Mandelbaum, M. "Professor Ryle and Psychology," *Philosophical Review,* LXVII (1958), 522-530.

Mandler, G., and W. Kessen. *The Language of Psychology.* New York: John Wiley, 1959.

Nagel, E. *The Structure of Science.* Indianapolis: Hackett Publishing Company, 1979.

Popper, K. R. *The Poverty of Historicism.* London: Routledge and Kegan Paul, 1957.

Ryle, G. *The Concept of Mind.* London: Hutchinson University Library, 1949.

III. Significance

This group includes supplementary references dealing with criteria of significance, as well as references concerned, more broadly, with the cognitive status of science, and with ontology.

Carnap, R. "Empiricism, Semantics, and Ontology," *Revue Internationale de Philosophie,* XI (1950), 20-40. Reprinted in L. Linsky (ed.), *Semantics and the Philosophy of Language.* Urbana: University of Illinois Press, 1952.

————. "The Methodological Character of Theoretical Concepts," in H. Feigl and M. Scriven (eds.), *Minnesota Studies in the Philosophy of Science,* Vol. I. Minneapolis: University of Minnesota Press, 1956.

Feigl, H. "Existential Hypotheses: Realistic vs. Phenomenalistic Interpretations," *Philosophy of Science,* XVII (1950), 35-62.

Føllesdal, D. K. *Referential Opacity and Modal Logic*. Doctoral dissertation in Philosophy, Harvard University, 1961.

Hempel, C. G. "The Concept of Cognitive Significance: A Reconsideration," *Proceedings of the American Academy of Arts and Sciences*, LXXX (1951), 61-77.

———. "A Logical Appraisal of Operationism," *Scientific Monthly*, LXXIX (1954), 215-220.

Kaplan, D. "Significance and Analyticity: A Comment on Some Recent Proposals of Carnap." Mimeographed. Paper delivered at the annual meeting of the American Philosophical Association, Pacific Division, Santa Barbara, Calif., December, 1959.

Nagel, E. *The Structure of Science*. New York: Harcourt, Brace & World, 1961. Chapter VI, "The Cognitive Status of Theories."

Popper, K. R. "Three Views Concerning Human Knowledge," in H. D. Lewis (ed.), *Contemporary British Philosophy*, 3d Series. London: Allen & Unwin, 1956.

The Problem of Universals. A symposium with A. Church, "Propositions and Sentences"; N. Goodman, "A World of Individuals"; and I. M. Bochenski, "The Problem of Universals." Notre Dame, Indiana: University of Notre Dame Press, 1956.

Quine, W. V. *From a Logical Point of View*. 2d ed.; Cambridge, Mass.: Harvard University Press, 1961.

———. *Word and Object*. New York and London: Technology Press of the Massachusetts Institute of Technology and John Wiley & Sons, 1960.

Rozeboom, W. W. "A Note on Carnap's Meaning Criterion," *Philosophical Studies*, XI (1960), 33-38.

Scheffler, I., and N. Chomsky. "What Is Said to Be," *Proceedings of the Aristotelian Society*, Volume LXIX. London: Harrison & Sons, 1959.

White, M. *Toward Reunion in Philosophy*. Cambridge, Mass.: Harvard University Press, 1956.

IV. Confirmation

This group includes (1) some general books, and articles dealing with (2) the nature of induction or confirmation, (3) the justification of induction, (4) the paradoxes of confirmation and Goodman's "new riddle of induction."

1. General

Barker, S. F. *Induction and Hypothesis, A Study of the Logic of Confirmation*. Ithaca, N.Y.: Cornell University Press, 1957.

Braithwaite, R. B. *Scientific Explanation.* Cambridge, England: Cambridge University Press, 1953.
Jeffreys, H. *Scientific Inference.* Cambridge, England: Cambridge University Press, 1931.
———. *Theory of Probability.* Oxford: Clarendon Press, 1939.
Kneale, W. *Probability and Induction.* Oxford: Clarendon Press, 1949.
Lewis, C. I. *An Analysis of Knowledge and Valuation.* La Salle, Ill.: Open Court, 1946.
Nagel, E. *Principles of the Theory of Probability.* Chicago: University of Chicago Press, 1939.
Popper, K. R. *The Logic of Scientific Discovery.* London: Hutchinson, 1959.
von Wright, G. H. *A Treatise on Induction and Probability.* London: Routledge and Kegan Paul, 1951.

2. The Nature of Induction or Confirmation

Ackermann, R. "Inductive Simplicity," *Philosophy of Science,* XXVIII (1961), 152-161.
Alexander, H. G. "Symposium: Convention, Falsification and Induction," *Aristotelian Society, Supplementary Volume XXXIV* (1960), 131-144. (See G. Buchdahl, below.)
Buchdahl, G. "Symposium: Convention, Falsification and Induction," *Aristotelian Society, Supplementary Volume XXXIV* (1960), 113-130.
Goodman, N. "The Test of Simplicity," *Science,* CXXVIII (1958), 1064-1069.
Harsanyi, J. C. "Popper's Improbability Criterion for the Choice of Scientific Hypotheses," *Philosophy,* XXXV (1960), 1-9.
Hempel, C. G. "Inductive Inconsistencies," *Synthese,* XII (1960), 439-469.
Kemeny, J. G. "The Use of Simplicity in Induction," *Philosophical Review,* LVII (1953), 391-408.

3. The Justification of Induction

Achinstein, P. "The Circularity of a Self-Supporting Inductive Argument," *Analysis,* XXII (1962), 138-141. (See M. Black [1958], below.)
Black, M. "The Justification of Induction," in M. Black, *Language and Philosophy.* Ithaca, N.Y.: Cornell University Press, 1949.
———. "Self-support and Circularity: A reply to Mr. Achinstein," *Analysis,* XXIII (1962), 43-44. (Reply to Achinstein, above.)
———. "Self-Supporting Inductive Arguments," *Journal of Philosophy,* LV (1958), 718-725.

Burks, A. W. "The Presupposition Theory of Induction," *Philosophy of Science*, XX (1953), 177-197.

Feigl, H. "De Principiis Non Disputandum?" in M. Black (ed.), *Philosophical Analysis*. Ithaca, N.Y.: Cornell University Press, 1950.

Katz, J. J. *The Problem of Induction and Its Solution*. Chicago: University of Chicago Press, 1962.

Madden, E. H. "The Riddle of Induction," *Journal of Philosophy*, LV (1958), 705-718.

Salmon, W. C. "Should We Attempt to Justify Induction?" *Philosophical Studies*, VIII (1957), 33-48.

———. "Vindication of Induction" (with comments by S. Barker and R. Rudner), in H. Feigl and G. Maxwell (eds.), *Current Issues in Philosophy of Science*. New York: Holt, Rinehart and Winston, 1961.

Will, F. L. "Justification and Induction," *Philosophical Review*, LXVIII (1959), 359-372. (Review of G. H. von Wright, *The Logical Problem of Induction* [2d rev. ed.; New York: Macmillan, 1957].)

Williams, D. *The Ground of Induction*. Cambridge, Mass.: Harvard University Press, 1947.

4. The Paradoxes of Confirmation and Goodman's "New Riddle of Induction"

Barker, S. F., and P. Achinstein. "On the New Riddle of Induction," *Philosophical Review*, LXIX (1960), 511-522.

Carnap, R. "On the Application of Inductive Logic," *Philosophy and Phenomenological Research*, VIII (1947), 133-147. (Reply to Goodman [1946], below.)

———. "Reply to Nelson Goodman," *Philosophy and Phenomenological Research*, VIII (1947), 461-462. (Reply to Goodman [1947], below.)

Good, I. J. "The Paradox of Confirmation," Parts I and II, *British Journal for the Philosophy of Science*, XI (1960), 145-148; XII (1961), 63-64.

Goodman, N. "On Infirmities of Confirmation Theory," *Philosophy and Phenomenological Research*, VIII (1947), 149-151. (Reply to Carnap [1947, 133-147] above.)

———. "Positionality and Pictures," *Philosophical Review*, LXIX (1960), 523-525. (Reply to Barker and Achinstein, above.)

———. "A Query on Confirmation," *Journal of Philosophy*, XLIII (1946), 383-385.

Morgenbesser, S. "Goodman on the Ravens," *Journal of Philosophy*, LIX (1962), 493-495.

Ullian, J. S. "More on 'grue' and grue," *Philosophical Review*, LXX (1961), 386-389. (Reply to Barker and Achinstein, above.)

Watanabe, M. S. Discussion of the paradoxes and of Goodman's "riddle in M. S. Watanabe, *Inference and Information* (forthcoming).

Index

A NOTE ABOUT THE AUTHOR

ISRAEL SCHEFFLER is Professor of Education and Philosophy at Harvard University, where he has taught since receiving his Ph.D. from the University of Pennsylvania in 1952. He is the editor of *Philosophy and Education*, the author of *The Language of Education*, and has contributed articles to *The Journal of Philosophy, Philosophy of Science, Analysis, Review of Metaphysics*, and other philosophical and scientific journals.